EAST INDIA
Publishing Company

CONFEDERATE WIZARDS of the SADDLE
Bennett Henderson Young

Published by the
EAST INDIA PUBLISHING COMPANY
Ottawa, Canada

© 2023 East India Publishing Company

Cover Design by EIPC © 2023
9781774268223

www.eastindiapublishing.com

CONTENTS

FOREWORD

Forty-eight years and a half have passed, since the last drum-beat of the Confederate States was heard and the furling of their flag forever closed the most wondrous military tragedy of the ages. Numbers and character considered, the tribute the South paid to War has no equal in human records.

Fifteen hundred years ago on the Catalaunian Plain, where Attila, King of the Huns, styled "The Scourge of God," joined battle with the Romans under Oetius, and the Visigoths led by Thorismund, tradition has it that hundreds of thousands of dead were left on the field. The men who followed the cruel and remorseless Attila were a vast horde, organized for war, with plunder as the highest aim of a soldier's life, and the Romans and Visigoths were men who followed war solely for the opportunity it afforded to enslave, rob and despoil those they conquered. On both sides the men who filled the ranks had neither intelligence nor patriotism, and with each, war was a profession or pastime, devoid in most cases of any exalted purpose, even the dream of a conviction, or the faintest gleam of a principle.

If the dead on that fatal field were numbered by the hundreds of thousands, their demise was a mere incident in the conflicts which were carried on for no truth, and in their loss the world suffered but little more than if as many beasts of burden had been sacrificed on some heathen altar to appease the God of War.

The American war, in the middle of the nineteenth century, dealt on both sides with far different materials. Christianity, liberty, education, culture and refinement had reached a very high limit on the human scale. When the North and South faced each other, moved by patriotism and principle, the legions drawn from the very best materials that the race could offer, with inherited courage, quickened by personal and social pride, and with memories and traditions of great military achievements, and ennobled by ancestral escutcheons of exceeding splendor, there met for battle such men as the world had never before seen, aligned for conflict.

Half a century gives time to gather data, to measure losses, to calculate

1

sacrifices, to weigh difficulties, to figure results, and to look calmly and justly at the history and the conduct of what must ever be classed as one of the great wars of the ages.

The very fact that the South lost lends pathos and sentiment to the story of what her sons accomplished. As time, aided by the scrutinizing finger of Truth, points out with impartial fairness what each did in this gigantic grapple between two Anglo-Saxon armies, we are enabled, even now, while thousands of participants remain, to judge, recount and chronicle with accuracy the most important events that marked this mighty struggle.

Cavalry played a most important part in the Civil War. In fact, without this arm of the service, the Confederacy could not have so long maintained the unequal contest; nor the Federal Army have prevailed as quickly as was done. The story of the campaigns of Stuart, Wheeler, Morgan, the Lees, Forrest, Hampton, Ashby, Mosby, Green, Van Dorn, Shelby and Marmaduke, and their associates, gave war a new glamour, opened to chivalry a wider field for operation, painted to adventurous genius more entrancing visions, and made the service of men who rode to battle a transcendent power of which warriors had hitherto not even dreamed.

So far as has been historically made known, there is no similar service performed by the cavalry of any period. General Morgan, with his command, made two distinct marches of one thousand miles each into a hostile country. Shelby is reported to have ridden fifteen hundred miles when he raided into Missouri in September, 1863. There were times, probably, when Stuart and Hampton and their associates had fiercer conflict, but the strain was never so long drawn out and the calls on nerve and muscle and brain were never so severely concentrated as in these marches of Morgan and Shelby.

General Wheeler, in his raid around Rosecrans, was twenty-five days in the rear of the enemy, menaced on every side, and his men fought with a courage that was simply transcendent. His marches were characterized by fierce fighting and covered a more limited territory, but his captures and his destruction of property have few counterparts.

No fair man, reading the story of General Dick Taylor's exploits, in the spring of '64, can come to any other conclusion than that he and his men were heroic, of abundant patience and exhibited almost unlimited physical endurance.

The same can be said of Forrest. He did not ride so far as Morgan, Marmaduke or Shelby on a single expedition, but what he lacked in distance

2

he made in overcoming difficulties and in the extent and constancy of conflict, and in the tremendous losses inflicted upon his enemy's property and troops.

Shelby's Raid into Missouri in September, 1863, which lasted thirty-six days and involved marching fifteen hundred miles, an average of thirty miles per day, is a story of extraordinary skill and endurance.

Stuart's Chickahominy raid around McClellan's army, his march to Chambersburg and return, and the Battle of Fleetwood Hill will ever command the admiration of cavalry students.

Hampton's Trevilian campaign, his cattle raid, and the management of General Lee's cavalry before Petersburg point to him as a leader of wondrous enterprise, a soldier of unbounded daring and a strategist of great ability.

The cavalry generals who have been chosen as the chief subjects of this book all possessed, in a remarkable degree, the power of winning the confidence of their followers and their loyal support under all circumstances. With Hampton, men followed wherever he led, they never reasoned why they should go, they only asked that they be informed as to the will of their leader. And so it was true of Morgan, Stuart, Forrest, Shelby and Wheeler. They all had the absolute trust of their followers. No man beneath them in command ever questioned their wisdom or their judgment in battle or march. But when it came to inspiring men with the spirit of absolute indifference to death and relentlessness in the pursuit of the enemy, few would deny that Nathan Bedford Forrest did this more effectively than any leader who was engaged in the struggle. Generals Lee, Stonewall Jackson, Albert Sidney Johnson, Joseph E. Johnston always commanded the respect, devotion, love and admiration of their soldiers to such an extent that at any time they would have marched into the very jaws of death, under their leadership; but those who study the life and the extent of Nathan Bedford Forrest's achievements will generally agree that in inspiring his soldiers to fierce, persistent battle and absolute indifference in conflict, few, if any, equalled him, none surpassed him. The conduct of his soldiers at Bryce's Cross-roads, where he fought first cavalry and then infantry, sometimes mounted, most generally on foot, would show that he could exact from men as superb service as any soldier who ever led his followers into battle.

This suggestion as to Forrest does not detract from the glory of any other Confederate leader. We meet this almost hypnotic influence in many phases of life other than military. Those who study the actions and characteristics of General Forrest and who looked upon the faces of the men following him could but realize that by his bearing, example and dash he got the best and bravest that it was possible for human nature in war to give.

Romance, patriotism and love of adventure inspired the cavalry of the Confederacy to follow their renowned leaders. No man who has calmly read the stories of the conflicts and marches of the Army of Northern Virginia, or the Army of Tennessee, or of the Army of the Trans-Mississippi Department can fail to be filled with wonder at the duties the soldiers of these armies so cheerfully and so willingly performed. Without pay, illy clad and poorly fed, yet they were always brave. Though hungry in battle they were always courageous; and in conflict they had only one aim, and that was to defend their country and destroy its enemies.

There was much in the narratives of the South's past to inspire cavalrymen with Lighthorse Harry Lee valor. Their fathers and grandfathers had ridden with Marion and Sumpter, had fought with Shelby, Preston, Sevier and Campbell at King's Mountain, or had gone with Isaac Shelby and General Harrison into Canada to fight the Battle of the Thames, or composed the dragoons who had gone with Scott and Taylor to Mexico. The boys and young men of the South had read and reread the accounts of what these horsemen of the long ago had accomplished, of the dangers they had faced and the laurels they had won, and these records of a splendid past filled their hearts with deepest love of their country, and fired their souls to make achievements the equal of those of their renowned ancestry. The most romantic and chivalrous side of both the Revolutionary War and the War of 1812 had their happenings with horsemen, and the most of those were either on the Southern soil or came from the states which sympathized with the South.

It was this antecedent history that gave such impetus to the Confederate youth to find, if possible, a place in the cavalry. The men of the South were not only familiar with the use of firearms, but a majority of them were skilled horsemen, and these two things combined brought to the Confederate cavalry volunteers, active, adventurous, daring, reckless, vigilant, chivalrous soldiers that were bound to perform the highest type of military work.

In the American war, cavalry was to change its arms, the sabre was to be almost entirely eliminated. In its place was to come the revolver and

4

the repeating rifle, the magazine gun and the short Enfield. The holsters were to be abandoned. Instead, the belt with the six shooters and the sixty rounds of ammunition. These new cavalrymen were not only to serve as scouts, but to act as infantry, to cover military movements, to destroy the lines of communication, to burn stores, to tear up lines of railway, to gather supplies, to fight gunboats, capture transports; all these without any equipment of any kind, except their horses, their arms and some horse artillery of limited range. In a large part, they were to feed in the enemy's country, rely upon their foes for arms and ammunition. They were to have no tents; no wagons, except for ammunition; no cooking utensils, other than a wrought iron skillet. These, with canteens and food found on the march, were to prove their only means of subsistence. They were to be trained to ride incessantly, charge stockades, capture forts, take their place alongside of the infantry on the battle line, and to build or defend hastily constructed fortifications. No cavalry before had performed these services and none will ever perform them again. The newer conditions of warfare will change altogether the work that will be required of cavalry. The improvement in firearms, particularly in the artillery, would render the oldtime cavalry superfluous and its use, under the past methods, a simple slaughter without benefit.

These men, carried by horses with great celerity from place to place, were to perform a distinct and different service in war; sometimes in a single night they would march fifty miles. Sometimes in a day they would march seventy-five to ninety miles. They would destroy stores of supplies, wreck railroads, burn water stations, demolish trestles, attack and burn wagon trains. Their best living was to be obtained by victory and the popular application to the fortunes of war the maxim—"That they should take who have the power, and they should keep who can."

To fit them for such service, a new system of drill was instituted; half cavalry and half infantry, fighting on foot, in open rank; the charge on infantry on horseback was to become practically obsolete. They were, if occasion demanded, to be dismounted, fight in entrenchments alongside infantry, and charge batteries and abattis, the same as the infantry. With boundless energy, unlimited enthusiasm and a measureless love of adventure, the horseman was to meet these new requirements and frequently do all that infantry could do and, in addition, do what cavalry had never done before. In the West, this combined and new call for cavalry obtained its birth and hold and received its first and most successful development. It is urged that to General John H. Morgan and his followers ought to be accredited the application and successful demonstration of these new methods, which were to add such immense value to cavalry work. No commander ever before undertook to commit such tasks to horsemen. But the Southern soldier, who first developed all these qualities and performed these varying tasks, was to open for the Southern cavalry service an unlimited field for harassing, delaying, starving and even destroying opposing armies.

The marvelous endurance of the men who followed Forrest and Stuart and Morgan and Wheeler and Hampton and Shelby and Green and McCullough and Price has never been equalled. Storms and floods had no terror for these. No enemy was safe from their avenging hand and no vigilance could defy their enterprise. There were no alarms in any work for these brave and tireless riders. Single riders and even small troops of cavalry had made marches of a hundred miles in a day, but it remained for generals like Wheeler and Morgan and Forrest and Stuart and Hampton and Shelby and Marmaduke and Green to demonstrate the potency and tremendous value of cavalry in war, and lengthen the possibility of a day's march.

For the first two years of the conflict, the Confederate cavalry were practically supreme. Their enemies were slow to absorb these new methods and to apprehend the advantages of this new system. Stuart's Chickahominy raid, his march from Chambersburg; Morgan's two marches of a thousand miles each; Forrest's pursuit of Streight and his raid into Kentucky and Tennessee, under the most adverse physical difficulties, in midwinter or early spring, and his ride into Memphis, read more like fairy stories than the performance of men composed of flesh and blood. Wheeler's raid in Rosecrans' rear, his expedition into East Tennessee and the endurance of his men are almost incredible. These do not read like the performance of real soldiers, but more like the make-up of a military dreamer. One may call over the names of the great battles of the war, either east or west of the Mississippi River, and while the account of these engagements lose none of their brilliancy in comparison with those of any war, yet they cannot surpass, nor in some respects equal, the work performed by the cavalry. Fleetwood Hill (Brandy Station), Trevilian Station, Hanging Fork, Chambersburg, Hartsville, Cynthiana, Shiloh, Mt. Sterling, Bryce's Cross-roads, Parker's Cross Roads and Dug Creek Gap. Marmaduke's and Shelby's Missouri raids and the pursuit of Stoneman, Garrard and McCook, during the Atlanta siege, are stories of valor, endurance and sacrifice that lose nothing in comparison with the deeds of any other organization of the armies of the Confederate States. In exposure, in daring, in physical privations, in patience, in cheerfulness under defeat, in willingness to do and dare, the horsemen of the Confederacy must always command the admiration of those who study military records.

An unusual proportion of the Confederate cavalry came from eight states,—Virginia, Kentucky, Missouri, Tennessee, Texas, Alabama, Mississippi and South Carolina. When we call the cavalry roll, its names awaken memories of some of the most heroic deeds known among men. Every Confederate state furnished a full quota of horsemen, and none of them failed to make good when the crucial test came.

Alabama sent into this branch of service Generals William Wirt Allen, James Hogan, Moses W. Hannon, John Herbert Kelley, Evander M. Law, John T. Morgan and P. D. Roddy.

Kentucky furnished Generals Abram Buford, George B. Cosby, Basil W. Duke, Charles W. Field, James N. Hawes, Ben Hardin Helm, George B. Hodge, Joseph H. Lewis, Hylan B. Lyon, John H. Morgan, John S. Williams, W. C. P. Breckenridge and R. M. Gano.

Missouri brought as part of her offering Generals John S. Marmaduke, Joseph O. Shelby and John G. Walker.

Tennessee gave Frank C. Armstrong, Tyree H. Bell, Alexander W. Campbell, Henry B. Davidson, George G. Dibrell, Benjamin J. Hill, W. Y. C. Humes, W. H. Jackson, John C. Vaughn, Lucius M. Walker and Nathan Bedford Forrest.

Mississippi sent Generals Wirt Adams, James H. Chalmers, Samuel G. Gohlson, W. T. Martin, Peter B. Stark and Earl Van Dorn.

Georgia, Generals Robert H. Anderson, Charles C. Crews, Alfred Iverson, P. M. B. Young.

Florida, General G. M. Davis and Colonel J. J. Dickinson.

South Carolina, M. C. Butler, Thomas F. Drayton, John Dunnovant, Samuel W. Ferguson, Martin W. Geary, Thomas M. Logan, Wade Hampton.

North Carolina gave Lawrence S. Baker, Rufus Barriger, James B. Gordon, Robert Ransom, William Paul Roberts.

Maryland, Bradley T. Johnson and Joseph Lancaster Brent (the latter only an acting brigadier).

West Virginia, William L. Jackson, Albert Gallatin Jenkins, John McCausland.

Virginia, Turner Ashby, Richard L. T. Beale, John Randolph Chambliss, James Dearing, John D. Imboden, William E. Jones, Fitz Hugh Lee, W. H. F. Lee, Lumsford L. Lomax, Thomas Taylor Munfod, William Henry Fitzhugh Payne, Beverly H. Robertson, Thomas L. Rosser, J. E. B. Stuart, William C. Wickham.

Louisiana, Daniel W. Adams, Franklin Gardner, Thomas M. Scott.

Arkansas, William N. R. Beall, William L. Cabell, James F. Fagan, James McQueen McIntosh.

The Indian Territory, Stand Watie.

Texas, Arthur Pendleton Bagby, Hamilton P. Bee, Xavier Blanchard De Bray, Thomas Green, W. P. Hardemen, Thomas Hamson, Ben McCulloch, James P. Major, Samuel-Bell Maxey, Horace Randal, Felix H. Robertson, Lawrence Sullivan Ross, W. R. Scurry, William Steele, Richard Waterhouse, John A. Wharton, John W. Whitfield.

This one book must, in the very nature of things, be limited to a few hundred pages.

It does not and cannot undertake to tell all that was glorious and courageous in the service of the men who led and composed the Confederate cavalry. There will doubtless be some who will ask why certain battles and experiences were omitted. The author may have selected, in some instances, what would appear to many critics and readers not the most notable events in the Confederate cavalry work.

He may have inadvertently left out names that ought to have been mentioned, campaigns that were of vast importance, and battles that were full of sublime sacrifice and marked by the superbest skill.

The book is written with the bias of a cavalry man. It is written by a man who knows, by personal experience only, some of the things that happened where Forrest, Wheeler and Morgan fought. He only knew personally three of the men whose leadership and skill are detailed in the book. He never saw Stuart but once, and Forrest a few times, but he loves the fame of all these splendid men and has endeavored to do each the fullest justice.

There were one hundred and four Confederate generals, from brigadier up, who at various times led the horsemen of the South. A volume could be written of the services of each. A majority of them were equally brave and valiant, but fate decreed some should pass under the fiercest light, and win from fame its most generous awards. It may be that hereafter other volumes will be written to tell, if not who, what the Confederate horsemen were. One of the chiefest aims of this volume is to give Confederate cavalry leaders and their followers their just place in the history of the great war. There is neither purpose nor desire to take aught from any other branch of the service. The Confederate infantry, artillery and navy have each a distinct place in the struggle of the South for its national life. Every Confederate loves every other Confederate and glories in all that he did to win the immortality of the Confederate armies. The cavalryman asks that his work may be recognized and that his proper place shall be assigned him in the phalanxes of the brave who stood for Southern independence. He covets none of the fame that justly belongs to his comrades in other lines. He only seeks that what he did may be honestly told, and his achievements be truly recorded. He feels that he did the best that he could and that he is entitled to a complete narrative of that which he did and endeavored to do for his country. He does not claim that he was braver or more patriotic than his comrades who fought in other departments. He only asks that the world may know the dangers he had faced, the difficulties he overcame, the sacrifices he made, the sufferings he endured and the results his work accomplished. A true account is his only demand, and all the world will feel that this is his right.

The writer may not always be literally accurate in the things he undertakes to recount in this book about Southern cavalry. He may here and there have made slight mistakes in the description of the marches and battles he has essayed to describe. Relying upon books and participants, he could not always get the things just as they occurred. Eye witnesses often differ in discussing the same occurrence. There are hundreds of dates and names recorded in these pages. Error must have crept in, but in the main the history is what really happened, and these happenings alone will give Confederate cavalry fame and renown in all ages and amongst all nations.

They make up a great history of great leaders and valiant soldiers, and they must surely add something to the store of human heroism.

There is no desire to depreciate what men on the other side did. In the later years of the war, the Federal cavalry apprehended the tactics and the methods of Confederate horsemen, and they became foemen worthy of any steel. The third year of the struggle, the mounts of the Southern cavalry became less efficient and the disparity in arms and supplies more and more depressing amongst the Confederates. The Federal generals undertook then to cut Confederate lines of communication, and to destroy their commissary depots and to disrupt railway transportation. In such work, in 1864 and 1865, they laid heaviest burdens on the Confederate cavalry; and in many instances the jaded and starving horses, the illy-fed men, their scanty supply of ammunition put them at great disadvantage, but they were, in face of all these difficulties, game, vigilant, aggressive, enterprising and defiant to the end; and from April, 1864, to April, 1865, there was nothing more brilliant nor historic than the work of the Confederate horsemen, performed under the most unfavorable conditions, to stay the tide of Federal advance and success and to maintain to the end their nation's hope and their nation's life.

If the sketches these pages contain shall add one leaf to the Confederate Laurel Wreath, or bring to Confederate fame fuller recognition, the author will be many times repaid for the labor, expense and time expended in their preparation.

Bennett H. Young.
Louisville, Kentucky.
1914.

Chapter I

FORREST AT BRYCE'S CROSS ROADS, JUNE 10th, 1864

The spring and summer of 1864 in Virginia, Tennessee, Mississippi, Georgia and in the Trans-Mississippi Department proved one of the most sanguinary periods of the war.

During this time, Joseph E. Johnston made his superb retreat from Dalton to Atlanta, regarded by military historians as one of the ablest strategic movements of the campaigns from '61 to '65, and General Robert E. Lee, in his famous defensive campaign culminating in the decimation of Grant's armies at Cold Harbor, had killed or wounded more than eighty thousand of General Grant's followers, twenty thousand more effective men than Lee's whole army numbered!

In the Trans-Mississippi, between April and August, '64, General Dick Taylor at Mansfield and Pleasant Hill gained glorious victories in attempting to stay the advance of General Banks into the heart of Louisiana; and Kirby Smith, Price, Shelby and Marmaduke in Arkansas still maintained a courageous front to the foe. After three years of constant fighting, their soldiers were more thoroughly inured to the hardships of war, better trained to face its dangers, and men on both sides exhibited a recklessness in facing death which marked the highest tide of courage.

Early in the war the cavalry became one of the most effective arms of the agencies of the Confederates. With the vast territory in the West defended by the Confederacy, with a frontier line twenty-five hundred miles in extent, the marching speed of which mounted men are capable, the cavalry of the South, at this period, enabled them to do more, man for man, than any arm of the South's defenders. They proved not only the best allies of the Confederate cause, but later developed some of the most renowned cavalry leaders of the world.

There were many cavalry battles during the fifteen hundred and twenty days of the war—Trevilian Station, Fleetwood Hill, sometimes called "Brandy Station," Harrisburg, Hartsville, Okolona, Murfreesboro, Shiloh, Parkers Cross Roads, Reams Station, all of which gave resplendence to the fame of the Confederate horsemen. Over and above these cavalry battles, there was Bryce's Cross Roads, designated by the Federals as the Battle of Tishomingo Creek. Measured by losses, it stands pre-eminent; along strategic lines it is amongst the first, and counted by results to the defeated foe, it has no counterpart in any engagement fought entirely on one side by cavalry.

On the Federal side, two thousand officers and men, including the wounded, were made prisoners, and more than twelve hundred dead were left on the battlefield or in close proximity thereto, if Forrest's contemporary reports be correct. The Confederates lost a hundred and forty killed and three hundred wounded. General Forrest held the battlefield. His forces buried the dead, and his count was based upon the fullest knowledge of the tremendous mortality of this sanguinary engagement. There were differing statements concerning the casualties. The numbers here given are from men who saw the havoc on the field.

At Fleetwood Hill, the Confederates lost five hundred and twenty-three killed and wounded, and the Federals nine hundred and thirty-six killed and wounded. At Trevilian Station, a purely cavalry engagement, June 11th, 1864, Hampton carried into battle four thousand seven hundred men against nine thousand Federals. After the battle and in ten days' subsequent fighting, his losses in killed, wounded and prisoners were less than seven hundred. He captured six hundred and ninety-five Federals, including one hundred and twenty-five wounded. Hampton's killed numbered less than seventy-five. In the Trevilian campaign, continuing fifteen days, Hampton's losses did not exceed seven hundred and fifty killed, wounded and missing, while the Federals report a loss of one thousand five hundred and twelve, more than twice that of the Confederates. At Hartsville, the Confederates lost a hundred and twenty-five killed and wounded, and the Federals four hundred and thirty, with eighteen hundred captured. At Harrisburg, Mississippi, one thousand two hundred and eighty-seven Confederates were killed and wounded. At Bull Run the Federals lost in killed and wounded one thousand four hundred and ninety-two, with one thousand four hundred and sixty missing. The Confederates lost one thousand eight hundred and seven. On both sides approximately fifty-six thousand men were engaged. At Shiloh, April 6th and 7th, 1862, the Federal death roll was seventeen hundred and that of the Confederates seventeen hundred and twenty-eight, and yet on both sides ninety thousand men were engaged in the struggle. At Wilson's

Creek, the Federal loss was one thousand three hundred and seventeen, the Confederate loss one thousand two hundred and eighteen. There the forces were nearly evenly matched, and there were about ten thousand in the struggle. Accepting General Forrest's report to be true that more than twelve hundred men were killed and wounded in the six hours of fighting at Bryce's Cross Roads, then more men were killed and captured on that day than in any two other purely cavalry engagements of the war.

By June, 1864, Forrest had reached the full tide of his fame. He had improved every opportunity to develop his genius, and he never failed to make use of all the fighting opportunities that came his way. He did not always get the best the quartermaster had, and he had been hampered by interference from headquarters. He had long since ceased to rely upon his government for his mounts, clothing, arms and food. He had months before learned from actual experience that the Federals had better supplies than it was possible for the Confederacy to distribute, and that capture from his enemies was a quicker and surer way of getting what he wanted than to risk the red tape and poverty of Confederate quartermaster regulations.

Beginning as a private, Forrest had reached most distinguished rank. Both friends and enemies awarded him a high place among the great commanders of the war, whether in infantry or cavalry. Fort Donelson, Shiloh, Nashville, Murfreesboro, his raid into West Tennessee, his capture of Streight, and conflicts at Brentwood, Harper's Bridge, Chickamauga, his raid into middle Tennessee, West Point, Mississippi and the capture of Fort Pillow, had woven about him and his work a crown of romance and glory, and had justly, on his absolute merits, made him one of the most renowned leaders of the Confederacy.

His enemies feared and hated him as they did no other general of the South. War with Forrest was not only "hell," but savagest hell. His idea of war was to fight and kill and destroy with fiercest energy. It has been said that he considered the raising of the black flag as the most economical and merciful way of ending the war. His methods were not calculated to impress his foes with admiration. The many reverses they had suffered at his hands, the wholesome fear of his presence, his desperate courage, boundless resources, rapidity of movement, rapidity of onslaught, recklessness in facing death, and insensibility to fatigue made failure practically unknown in his campaigns, and he became a terror to his foes and a tower of strength to his comrades.

There was no Federal commander that did not count Forrest as a power to be considered, or a potent factor against which it was wise to calculate. General Grant and other Federal commanders did not hesitate to declare that Forrest had the Federal forces in Tennessee, Alabama and Mississippi hacked. They called him "scoundrel" and "devil," and put a price on his head, but this did not drive fear out of their hearts, or prevent some degree of tremor when they knew of his presence in the places where they were going, or where they thought he might happen to come.

Prior to and shortly after the battle of Bryce's Cross Roads, all the Federal generals were devising ways and means for the destruction of Forrest. On June 24th, 1864, General Sherman sent President Lincoln the following despatch:

"I have ordered General A. J. Smith and General Mower to pursue and kill Forrest, promising the latter, in case of success, my influence to promote him to Major General. He is one of the gamest men in our service. Should accident befall me, I ask you to favor him, if he succeeds in killing Forrest." Signed, William T. Sherman, Major General.

This was the highest price put on any Confederate officer's life during the war, and there is no other instance in American military history where one general found it necessary, in order to destroy an opposing major general, to offer a premium for his life and to openly declare that his death was the highest aim to be sought.

It will be observed that the offer was not for dispersing Forrest's forces; it was not for his capture; but "to pursue and kill." General Sherman did not want Forrest alive, else he would have framed his murderous suggestion in a different form. The idea of a possible surrender was ignored. Sherman seems to have proceeded upon the idea that dead men cease to fight or destroy communications. He told Mower to take no chances, but to "kill." This is the only instance among the Confederate or Federal commanders where a superior incited a subordinate to murder. He said once before in speaking of Forrest, "That devil Forrest must be eliminated, if it costs ten thousand lives and breaks the treasury." See despatch. Twice, in his telegram to President Lincoln, he lays stress upon the word "kill." First he says, "if he pursues and kills I promised him a major generalship;" second, "if he succeeds in killing Forrest, and aught happens to me so that I cannot make good, I ask you to favor him and give him the promotion which is the price of Forrest's death."

How transcendent Forrest's success must have been in his operations along the Federal lines to have produced this degree of fear in General Sherman's mind! Sherman was a brave and skillful general, but he seemed to consider that General Forrest's ability to injure the Federal armies was greater than that of any other living man, and with malignant hate, extreme fear, and almost barbarous cruelty, he offered a major generalship to an ambitious young brigadier general, if he would pursue and kill the Confederate leader. War amongst civilized nations is carried on against commands or organized bodies, not individuals. General Sherman reversed this well-recognized principle and declared war on an individual and offered a price for his destruction. He asserted that he had better sacrifice ten thousand of his countrymen and expend all its treasury contained than to let one man live to fight. The pressing exigencies invoked by Forrest's campaigns silenced the traditions and usages of war, and made his destruction, in Sherman's mind, justifiable by any means, foul or fair, and at any cost, however extravagant or hurtful, to rid his department of a brave and aggressive foe.

This proposition to reward General Mower was not to General Sherman's credit. He declared "war was hell," but at no period of the war's history and by no other Federal general was the death of any one man made a patriotic duty, or recommended and encouraged in the service of the Federal army. The South never had any reason to love General Sherman. He and Sheridan never respected as did other Union generals the rights of non-combatants. His subsequent burning of Columbia created in Southern breasts the harshest memories, but the incitement to killing Forrest, as the surest means of promotion and success for his subordinate added much to the grounds of the South for the bitterest hate. With half a century to calm passion, to still prejudice and restore reason, it is difficult to realize what a frenzy of fear and hate Forrest had aroused in the hearts of his enemies.

After failures, not necessary to recount, one last effort was made to run Forrest down and to annihilate or cripple his command. Forrest had been transferred to the Mississippi and West Tennessee Department. It was known as Forrest's Department. General C. C. Washburn, in command at Memphis, was ordered to send six thousand men in a final effort to rout General Forrest. Instead, he says he sent eight thousand, but he really sent ten thousand five hundred. Colonel George E. Waring, who commanded one of the Federal brigades, says, "We were a force of nine thousand infantry and artillery sent as a tub to the Forrest Whale." Captain Tyler, who operated in Sturgis' rear, captured the returns made out for the day. These showed ten thousand five hundred present for duty.

Other Federal generals had been tried out and found wanting, and in this last effort General Sherman called an experienced soldier, General Samuel Davis Sturgis, who had won great reputation in other departments. He had seen service under Lyon in Missouri, and after the death of that general, succeeded to command at the Battle of Wilson's Creek. Assigned to the Army of the Tennessee, later he was ordered to the command of the Department of Kansas. In 1862 he was summoned to Washington and given charge of the defense around the city, and he commanded a part of the 9th Army Corps at the Battles of South Mountain, Antietam and Fredericksburg. For nearly a year he was chief of the cavalry in the Department of Ohio, and there he did most effective work for his country's cause. He was counted as "dead game," a man of great force and energy and of extended experience. He was born in Shippensburg, Pennsylvania, on the 11th of June, 1822, and was forty-two years old at the time of the Battle of Bryce's Cross Roads. With him was assigned General B. H. Grierson, who was just thirty-seven years of age. As early as 1862 he had been placed in the command of a cavalry brigade, and had been conspicuous in skirmishes and raids in North Mississippi and West Tennessee. Under General Grant's eye he had made what was considered a particularly fortunate raid from La Grange to Baton Rouge. In June, '63, he was brevetted a brigadier general of Volunteers, and was regarded as a most stubborn fighter.

To these brigadier generals was added Colonel George E. Waring. At twenty-eight he became major of the 39th New York Volunteers. In August he was sent West as a major of cavalry, and shortly afterwards he became colonel of the 4th Missouri Cavalry. In 1863 he was in command of the cavalry brigade in South Missouri and North Arkansas. In 1863 he had command of sixty-five hundred men, mainly cavalry. He had gone with Smith and Grierson, and was now to go with Sturgis. His experience was wide and his courage of the very highest order. He was a gallant, good-natured and fierce fighter, and was not ashamed to admit the truth when he was fairly defeated. It was said by General Forrest of Colonel Waring, that his cavalry charge at Okolona, Mississippi, some time previous to this date, was the most brilliant cavalry exploit he had ever witnessed.

It was unfortunate for the Confederates that General S. A. Hurlburt was not added to this trio. In one of his reports, found in the Official Reports,

Volume 31, Part 1, Page 697, after failing to capture General Forrest, he said, "I regret very much that I could not have the pleasure of bringing you his hair, but he is too great a coward to fight anything like an equal force, and we will have to be satisfied with driving him from the State." General Hurlburt studied the results of Bryce's Cross Roads and learned that, after all the abuse heaped upon him by his enemies, Forrest occasionally enjoyed a fight even though he was compelled to try out conclusions with his foes with an odds against him of more than two to one.

This boastful soldier, more bloodthirsty even than his associates, not only proposed to kill Forrest, but after death to scalp his fallen foe and lay at the feet of his superior a savage trophy like the Indians of old, in the pioneer days of Kentucky and Tennessee.

In addition to this array of distinguished and experienced officers, the most careful provision was made in arming of the troops that were to undertake the expedition. They were given Colt's five-chambered, repeating rifles or breech-loading carbines, and were also supplied with six-shooters.

Two cavalry brigades and three brigades of infantry made up the force which was deemed capable of coping with Forrest under all conditions. Curiously enough, there was added a brigade of colored infantry. The events at Fort Pillow, on the 12th day of April, 1864, sixty days before, had been used to arouse the animosity and fiercest hate of the colored troops. It was claimed that General Forrest had refused to allow the colored forces quarter and had shot them down after they had surrendered. While this was amply disproved by overwhelming testimony, it served a good purpose to make the colored troops desperate in any fighting which should fall to their lot, and to make them unwilling to surrender to Forrest's men under any possible circumstances.

Correspondence between General Washburn and General Forrest brought out mention of no quarter, and it was claimed that General Washburn, in dispatching these troops, had suggested to this colored contingent to refuse quarter to Forrest's command. If not actually advising, he certainly acquiesced in their wearing some badges pinned upon their lapels, upon which had been printed these fateful words: "No quarter to Forrest's men." To a man of Forrest's successes and with his wonderful record in the capture of Federal prisoners, this was a most unfortunate declaration for those who were to pursue him, considering the uncertainty that attended those who might engage him in battle.

The object of this expedition was to drive Forrest from Western Tennessee and fully restore communication from Memphis down the Mississippi River.

The Federal commander did not take into account the heat of a Mississippi summer nor the torrential rains that so frequently inundate that portion of the South in June and July. On the day of the battle, the thermometer rose to one hundred and seven degrees; not a ripple stirred the air; the leaves were as still as death itself; men panted for breath.

The thicket was so dense that no eye could penetrate its recesses for twenty feet, and vision was so circumscribed that foes were almost invisible. In its impenetrable and pathless precincts, black jack and small oak trees had grown up into a jungle, and the men entering this gloomy and perplexing battlefield were unable to even conjecture what a minute would bring forth. Every nerve was strained; every muscle tense. No one cared for a second to avert his gaze from the front. At any instant a foe might spring up and fire in the face of the man who was advancing. A single step might reveal a line of battle, and the flash of gun or crack of a rifle was momentarily expected. A movement of the branches and rustling of the leaves might draw fatal volleys from carbines, rifles or revolvers, and here and there the crash of shells and the roar of cannon added to the fearfulness of the situation. The dangers and dread of every step were accentuated by the harassing uncertainty of the surroundings.

The western Confederate cavalry at short range always found the revolver the most effective weapon. Enfield rifles were good enough up to three hundred feet, but closer than that Forrest's and Morgan's and Wheeler's men relied upon their six-shooters. The men under Stuart and Hampton loved "the white arm," the knightly sabre; they found that it helped at Fleetwood Hill and Trevilian Station. Mosby's greatest reliance was on "Colt's Navies," and there were but few swords ever found with the cavalry of the Army of Tennessee. To the western Confederate horsemen, their heavy revolver was a great equalizer. The Federal soldier, when it came to short range, had no better weapon. At close quarters, with a firm grip on a six-shooter, a Confederate soldier felt he was the equal of any foe from any place, and thus armed when it came where he could see the color of the other soldier's eyes, he considered the Navy revolver the choicest weapon man could make. It was a destructive weapon in the hands of brave, calm soldiers. The bayonet lost all terrors to those who possessed this effective pistol. No advancing antagonist could hope to safely reach a man of nerve with a pistol, amidst this black jack and heavy foliage. There, ears sharpened by battle's dangers, and eyes made brighter by hidden foes, gave great zest to the game of war.

Leaving Memphis on the 1st of June, the approach of Sturgis and his command was slow and careful, surrounded with every possible precaution against surprise. The leaders knew the character of the enemy they must face, and they resolved to leave nothing undone which should prepare them for his furious onslaughts.

Bryce's Cross Roads, or Guntown, was seventy-six miles from Memphis. Nine days were consumed in the march. On the night of the 9th, Sturgis and his forces encamped on the Stubbs farm, about six miles from Bryce's Cross Roads. At this point was a blacksmith's shop and a store, and two roads crossed each other, one running southeast and the other almost directly south. A mile and a half away was Tishomingo Creek, a slimy and almost currentless stream at this period, although it had been replenished by the rains two days before. The soil of the road was the friable bottom land of Mississippi, which churns quickly into slush and then soon dries out.

About the time that Sturgis left Memphis, Forrest had started on a raid in middle Tennessee to break up the railroad connection south of Nashville. At the same time General Sherman was trying to fight his way to Atlanta, and it was deemed important to destroy the railroads between Chattanooga and Nashville.

Forrest had only gone a short distance when he was notified by General Stephen D. Lee to give up his raid and return to face Sturgis and his command, which had left Memphis a few days before.

There has been a good deal of discussion as to whether General Lee was willing for Forrest to fight at Bryce's Cross Roads. Certainly General Lee hoped that Sturgis would be permitted to march farther down into Mississippi before the contact should be forced. It seems, however, from what General Forrest told General Buford that he had made up his mind to bring on the engagement just where it occurred. And yet his troops were not in position to justify his engaging in a great battle.

Lyon, with his eight hundred men from Kentucky, Johnson, with a small brigade of Alabamians, were six miles away from the scene of battle at Baldwin; the artillery was at Booneville, eighteen miles away. It rained heavily on the 8th and 9th. General Forrest had said to General Buford, "They outnumber me, but I can whip them; the cavalry will be in advance, and we can defeat the cavalry before the infantry can march to their relief. It is going to be as hot as hell. The infantry will come on the run into the battle, and with the muddy roads and hot weather, they will be tired out, then we can ride over them. I will go ahead with Lyon and my escort and open up the fight." The wily Confederate general knew that soldiers never do their best when they enter battle after great physical punishment.

Sturgis knew that Forrest was around, and he felt sure that if he did not find Forrest, Forrest would find him. The night before the battle, Sturgis had intuition of disaster. Caution warned him to go back, and the temptation was very strong, but he had promised General Washburn and General Sherman much before he had started. He had boasted what he could do, or would do, and the instinct of courage prevailed over his instinct of fear and bade him go on.

At break of day Forrest's forces were all moving. They were converging to Bryce's Cross Roads. Grierson, in command of the Federal column, had left Stubb's farm to march toward Bryce's Cross Roads. The Federal infantry cooked their breakfast in a leisurely way, and were not ready to march until seven-thirty. Experienced and faithful scouts were bringing to Lyon, who was in the Confederate front, the accurate information of the movements of General Waring, who led the Federal advance with his brigade.

On the road, a mile and a half away from Tishomingo Creek, General Lyon had placed a strong picket. Two videttes were at the bridge that spanned Tishomingo Creek. These were not particular upon the order of their going. They fled southward, pursued by Waring's advance guard, which was followed by his entire command, and also by the other brigade of Federal cavalry. Lyon needed no commander to tell him what to do. To him belongs the credit of having opened the greatest of all cavalry battles, and to have done more than any one Confederate officer, other than Forrest, to win the crushing defeat of the Union forces on that historic field.

Forrest, with his men all counted, had only forty-seven hundred cavalry. This was the most he could rely on when more than half of them should gallop eighteen miles. Deducting horseholders, one in four, and the men who could not keep up in the mad pace necessary to get into position, Forrest could not have more than thirty-two hundred fighters in any period of the battle. Against these were Sturgis' cavalry and infantry and twenty-six pieces of artillery—all told, over ten thousand effectives. At the opening of the engagement, Forrest had eight hundred men with Lyon, eighty-five men as escort, and fifty men in Gartrell's company, making a total of nine hundred and thirty-five.

Forrest resolved to have what he called "a bulge" on the enemy. In his plain, untutored way he had said "bulging would beat tactics." Forrest had with him leaders who knew their business, and who understood his methods. They had been apt scholars in his school of war, and they were now going to put their teaching into practical effect, and under his eye and leadership win applause and glory for centuries to come.

One of Forrest's favorite maxims was, "Keep your men a-going." With a fierce feint, he undertook to deceive General Grierson, the Federal cavalry leader, as to his real strength. He had two-thirds less men than Grierson, and he was afraid that Grierson would attack him and rush his line, which he could have done, and scattered his forces.

With his limited numbers, he made the greatest possible show. Lyon had entrenched his men behind brush heaps, rail fences and logs. This was very warm, but it was much safer than out in the open. Finally Forrest ordered his soldiers to cross the open ground, and doubling his skirmish line, boldly marched out. They were widely overlapped by Waring and Winslow with their brigades, and for an hour Lyon bravely and fiercely kept up his feint, and then retired behind his entrenchments. A great burden was on Lyon's mind, but when it was most oppressive, the glad sound of the rebel yell fell upon his ears and then appeared horses flecked with foam, with their mouths open, breathing with stentorious sounds, panting as if ready to fall. Rucker and his tired troops, after a ride of fourteen miles, were on the ground, and quickly dismounting they went into line. Haste was the order of the hour. Lyon, to be saved, must be strengthened. Alone he had faced the thirty-two hundred Federal cavalry, and while he maintained his ground, no idea of running away had ever come into his mind. Three and one-half to one man had no terrors for Forrest with these Kentucky men. They were mostly mounted infantry, who had often heard the storm of battle.

Forrest patted Lyon on the back, and commended him for the splendid stand which he had made. Rucker, brave, gallant, chivalrous, had heard the roar of cannon, and although his tired horses were supposed to have reached their limit, he pleaded with his men to force them to still greater effort. He could hear through the cannon's roars the voices of comrades calling. He knew they were outnumbered nearly four to one and were being hardly pressed, and that he was their only hope of rescue.

The scene changes! They are now only two to one, and Forrest again advances and presses his lines close up to the Federal position. Before, he was afraid his enemies might realize his inferior numbers and rush him; now, with Johnson and Rucker, he had one to two. Before, nine hundred men had constituted his fighting force; now, sixteen hundred were hurried to the front. The lines of anxiety disappeared from Forrest's face; he never doubted when he could count one to two. At eleven, the fighting had been going on an hour and a quarter. Time was precious. The Federal infantry, struggling through the heavy mire and panting under that awful heat, were pressing on as fast as human strength and endurance would permit. General Bell was not yet in reach; he had to ride twenty-one miles to get on the ground and join in the fray. If Waring and Winslow could be swept out of the way, Forrest felt sure he could take care of the infantry when Bell came. Prudence might have dictated delay until Bell was on the scene, but the exigencies of the moment called for instant and decisive action. Morton, with his invincible artillery, was slashing his horses and with almost superhuman energy was urging his beasts to the highest tension to join in saving the day, but the longing eyes of Forrest, Lyon, Johnson and Rucker could not detect his coming, and no sign of Bell's shouting riders came through the murky air to tell them that succor was nigh at hand.

The time for feinting was past. Forrest understood that the crisis was upon him, and he always grasped the crucial moment. Riding swiftly in front of his forces through the jungles, he told his men that the time had come to win, that when the bugle sounded every man must leave cover, cross the open space, where it was open, and charge through the thickets where they prevailed, and rush their enemies. He rode like a centaur, giving his orders along the line. The comforting, encouraging word, the hardly pressed soldiers speaking bravely together, was ended now. Action, sharp and decisive, was the watchword. The clear, sharp tones of the bugle cut the murky air; the sound waves drove its inspiring notes across the battle front and, like a crouching beast springing upon its prey, every Confederate bounded forward. The sharp rebel yell filled the surrounding space and fell ominously upon the expectant ears of their foes.

The men of Waring and Winston braced themselves for the coming assault. Their fire was reserved to the last moment, and then the repeating rifles with their unbroken volleys, increasing in volume every moment, created a din that was appalling. The Confederates had only one fire, and that they reserved to the end. Their enthusiasm was at fever heat, and rushing on to close with their foes, fear was cast aside. The enemy was in front; tiger-like, the men in gray sprang forward. The keen, sharp whistle of the carbine balls and the buzz of the bullets filled the air in their passage, and cut the leaves and branches from the trees so that they fell like showers of dew upon the rushing Confederates. The Federals hurled their deep-toned battle-cry across the narrow space. They had come so close that they could now see face to face, and each line shouted defiance at the other. The blue and gray rushed upon each other with the ferocity of uncaged lions. The single shots from the Confederate Enfields, so long held, were now by pre-arranged command fired, and then the Confederates were ordered to draw their six-shooters and rush upon their foes. And quick as thought, the sharper sound of the six-shooters filled the air.

The Confederates had momentarily recoiled before the first terrific fire so unexpectedly poured into their ranks, but the Federals, in the face of the six-shooters, began to waver. One or the other must yield. The Confederates were pushing the conflict. Waring ordered up two new regiments to halt the advancing tide. The contest was short, but it was vehement. At close range, nothing could equal the six-shooter. The sword and carbine could not stay its murderous effect in the hands of the brave and determined Confederates.

Hand to hand, the conflict went on, but flesh and blood could not withstand such an assault. The Federal line began to yield. Lyon, Rucker, Johnson and Forrest urged their brave men to supreme effort. The tide was still for an instant, but only an instant. The reinforcements of Waring were brushed away, his lines broken. The apparent yielding of the Union cavalry encouraged and emboldened the men of the South, and now they drove forward with increasing energy and ferocity to the death grapple. Ammunition failing, the men used the empty rifles and carbines as clubs. A hand to hand fight cannot last long. Decimation of numbers soon weakens its intensity, but the proximity of men, looking each other in the eye, shouting defiance into the very faces of their foes, proves a tremendous strain upon any soldiers, and such fearful tension weakens enthusiasm and one side or the other begins to consider yielding. Rucker, Lyon, Hall and Johnson of Alabama were terrific fighters; they had caught Forrest's spirit and they advanced with such vehemence that it was almost impossible for any line to withstand them. The moment Waring's men began to give way, victory deserted the Federal standards. The piercing of the Union lines, the loss of its initial position, gave the Confederates added impetuosity and intensity in their advance. Nature was adding renewed difficulties to the conflict. The fierce summer sun was almost scalding. Perspiration burst from every pore. Men, under the intense heat, panted for breath. Forrest's men knew they must win at once or fail in the struggle. Not waiting even to be called, they pressed forward over the bodies of their fallen comrades and enemies. The Southern troopers seemed imbued with an insatiate thirst for the blood of their opponents. They remembered what Forrest had told them to do when the bugle blast brought them out from cover, and bade them press the fighting, and drive the Federals back. Thus, impelled by the necessity of immediate victory, answering the summons of their well-beloved commander, and thrilled by the memory of their past glorious achievements, they became almost a line of demons. They cared nothing for wounds or death; they were bent only on the defeat and destruction of their foes, and for the accomplishment of this were ready to win or fall, as fate should cast the die.

Forrest, within fifteen minutes of the time when the first shot was fired, had sent one of his most trusted staff officers to meet General Tyree H. Bell and bid him "move up fast and fetch all he's got," and to this he added a word to his beloved boy artillery man, Captain Morton, to stay not his coming but to bring up his horses at a gallop. Forrest's keen eye was watching with deepest anxiety to catch some sight of the coming ones, his ears attuned to catch the echo of the cheers of Bell's men or the rushing tramp of the tired steeds; but nothing was heard of his allies, needed so badly at this crucial moment.

He knew that Sturgis with his infantry would soon be on the ground, and that his tired and powder-grimed men could not withstand this new ordeal, when four thousand fresh infantry would change the alignments and render resistance of their impact impossible. A thousand conflicting emotions filled Forrest's heart, but Forrest was not to be stayed. "Forward, forward!" he cried to his men. Slowly, then quickly, the Federal cavalry yielded, and then Forrest pressed them back in disorder.

The spirit of resistance was broken. Waring and Winston could not, with all their courage and skill, stay the work of Forrest's battalions. They rushed from the front, giving to the men in gray complete possession of the coveted battlefield.

24

General Sturgis, in advance of his panting infantry, had arrived at the scene of the struggle. Message after message of emergency had come to him by swift-riding couriers. His infantry were forced all that nature would allow. These Federal soldiers were weighted down with their accoutrements, and suffering the almost resistless heat of the burning rays of a fierce summer sun and an atmosphere so sultry and humid that human lungs inhaling it were weakened rather than refreshed.

The Federal cavalry were glad to ride away, and, hurrying from such scenes of carnage and woe, disorganized and beaten, they tried to reform behind the upcoming infantry. It was with a profound sense of relief that they gave over the field to the footmen and let them face, in the bushes and jungle, the Confederate cavalrymen, who with such devilish fury had worsted them in the fighting of the past three hours and thinned their ranks by killing and wounding a large percentage of their number.

The Federal cavalry, in this brief struggle, had pushed their magazine guns and carbines to the highest pressure. Their ammunition was gone, and without bayonets they could not halt the Confederate assailants, who behind their six-shooters let no obstacle, even for an instant, stay their progress.

Forrest's prediction that he would whip the Federal cavalry before the infantry could get up was verified, but unless Bell with his reserves and Morton with his artillery were quickly at hand, his success would avail nothing.

The Federal infantry was quickly put in line, and even Forrest felt for an instant a sense of doubt, as he surveyed his tired followers, and scanned their faces, worn and sharply drawn by the harrowing experiences of the past three hours.

However resourceful, he could not immediately reach a conclusion as to what was best. His soul abhorred yielding now that he had won glorious victory, and the thought of abandoning it all at last and leaving his dead and wounded followers on the field and the triumph of his hated foes, filled his soul with keenest anguish. For himself, he would rather die a thousand deaths than to do this hateful thing. At his command, by superhuman courage, his boys (as he called them) had discomfited and driven away their foe, and as he looked down into the pale faces of the dead, who lay amidst the bushes and debris of the torrid forest, as he heard the groans of his gallant wounded and dying, burning with thirst and fever, as they pleaded for water, he dared not forsake them. The whistle of the rifle balls, the screech of the shrapnel again beginning to play upon his position urged him to speediest decision.

At this critical moment, while the firing on his side was spasmodic and occasional, he heard cheers and shouts. A moment later, from the woody recesses of the thicket, he caught sight of the face of Tyree H. Bell. The message he had sent two hours before had been heard. Bell had "moved fast and fetched all he's got" and Morton had "brought on his artillery at a gallop." True, many of the artillery horses had dropped dead by the wayside, overcome by the terrific punishment they had received in hastening to the scene of action, but as the dropping beast breathed his last, the harness was snatched from his dead body and flung upon another beast who had galloped or trotted behind the guns. These brutes had seen their fellows belabored with whips to increase their speed to the utmost, and if they reasoned at all they reluctantly assumed the burdens of their dead brothers and regretfully and sullenly took their places in front of the guns, made so heavy and so oppressive by the heat and by mud of the slushy roads.

When the supply of horses, in this mad rush of nineteen miles, gave out, cavalry men were dismounted and despite their protest, their horses were harnessed to the guns and caissons, which now at the highest possible speed were being dragged and hauled to the front, where Forrest was holding his foes at bay, or driving them in confusion from the field.

The first act of the grim drama had come out as Forrest had expected, and now the second was begun. He had vanquished the Federal cavalry and now he must destroy the Federal infantry. Bell had brought him two thousand men who, although wearied by a twenty mile ride during the past seven hours, had fired no guns and faced no foes. He had tried these newcomers in the past, and he did not fear to trust them in this supreme moment.

The Confederate chieftain did not long hesitate. He knew whatever was done must be done quickly. The Federal cavalry would soon be reorganized; the clash with the infantry (if they withstood the onslaught from the Confederates) would give the defeated horsemen new courage, and they would come back into the struggle far fiercer than before, for as brave men they would long to wipe out the memories and avenge their humiliating defeat with final victory.

The Federal infantry did not reach the battlefield until 1 p. m. They came under the most trying circumstances; the roads and the weather together were against them. The human body has its limitations. The Federal infantry did all men could have done; a majority of them were unaccustomed to the dreadful heat of the Mississippi thickets and swamps; they had been forced to the very highest efforts on the way; the sounds of battle were ringing in the ears of their leaders—the sultry air did not conduct the sound waves distinctly, but they heard enough to know that a desperate struggle was already on, and they were soon to participate in its dangers and its experiences. Aides came riding in hot haste from where the noise of strife was heard; the messages were delivered to the advance guard, but the hard-riding couriers were hastily escorted to the Federal leaders, and the solemnity of their faces and the seriousness of their visage unmistakably proclaimed that sternest business was being enacted at the place from which they had in such haste so furiously ridden.

The Federal cavalry, in squads and disorganized masses, was retreating from the front. No shout of victory or cheers had come from the horsemen to urge the infantry forward to the conflict, which had gone sorely against those who rode. Here and there an ambulance bearing wounded officers and privates told in unmistakable terms what losses were awaiting those who were pressing toward the conflict, and bandaged heads and bloody faces, and wounded arms and legs told the story of carnage where these sufferers had been.

Regimental and company officers were commanding more rapid marching. These men in blue had suffered, on the way, dreadful punishment from the sultry heat, still they were bidden with loud and vociferous orders to press forward. They were now beginning to catch sight of the wreckage, an overturned ambulance, a dead horse, streams of disabled men, broken wagons, fleeing teamsters, riding detached animals with the harness swinging about their legs, all made a depressing scene.

The Federal infantry were of good stuff. When within half a mile of the Confederate lines, they vigorously responded to the command "double quick march" and ran forward to meet a foe of which they could see but little. The buzz of the rifle balls they heard on every side, and the defiant yells, which came from the bushes and recesses of the thickets, into which the men in blue were being hurried to find somebody to fight, were no pleasant sounds.

As the Federal infantry swung into line, yells and cheers from the Confederate forces came across the short space between them. Something important was happening. Some relief and mitigation was at hand. The shouts were of gladness and not those of grief or even of battle. The Confederate artillery was swinging out to the front. The Confederate cavalry always had good artillerists, Pelham, Chew, Cobb, Rice, Morton, Thrall and Freeman were men whom any commander might covet and in whose services they might glory.

Forrest had two wonderful qualities. He made all his associates recklessly brave. They absorbed the touch of strange and ever-masterful courage that came oozing from his every pore. He was, besides, a wonderful judge of men; all his staff were men not only of intrepid spirit but of quick intelligence and infinite patriotism. They knew Forrest's limitations, but they understood his marvelous greatness. That Forrest was sometimes harsh, even cruel and bitter in his judgment and in his words and acts, none knew better than the superb men on his staff; but his transcendent genius, his matchless courage and his immeasurable loyalty overshadowed his faults, so that the light which came from his greatness so magnified his presence and power as to dwarf and blot out that which in many men would have been hateful deformities.

The battle line was not an extended one. Well for the Confederates that this was so. With no reserves and outnumbered two to one, the shorter the range of action the better, for the smaller force.

Three thousand six hundred fresh infantry were now thrown into the whirlpool of battle. The Federal cavalry cowered behind their allies, who had walked and then ran in that dreadful summer heat to help them in their extremity. The heavy fire of the infantry, the constant peal and boom of the artillery notified Forrest that the best reliance of the Federal general was at hand. It looked gloomy for the Confederate commander, but while the character of men and the fire on the Federal side had changed, General Forrest also had a present help in this trouble. Brave, gallant Tyree H. Bell had come. True, his troopers with jaded steeds had trotted or galloped for nineteen miles under the blaze of the torrid sun, but the poor beasts who had carried the men could calmly rest while the fighting part of the outfit were now ready to take their place in the freshening fray.

Bell had a noble record. He had been from the first captain of the 12th Tennessee Infantry. He had acted as colonel at Belmont, and on the bloody field of Shiloh again commanded this splendid regiment. Made its colonel, he had won fresh laurels at Richmond, Kentucky, in the great victory there under Kirby Smith, and still later he had become commander of a cavalry regiment, and at Murfreesboro and Chickamauga had furiously hammered the Federal flanks. In January, 1864, Forrest, who knew good fighters by instinct, gave Bell a brigade with five regiments. The most of these on this glorious day at Bryce's Cross Roads were to give another good account of themselves. At Fort Pillow, Bell with the rifle and revolver had assailed and won a very strong position, and now again in this conflict, and in many afterwards, he was to win his great commander's admiration and trust.

The pace set by the Federal infantry was fierce, but Bell's men made it fiercer. General Buford had come to join in the battle. Forrest trusted this Kentucky general as probably he trusted no other man under him. With an immense body, weighing three hundred pounds, he had a sharp, quick, active mind, a fearless soul and splendid military instincts. A West Point graduate, he won a brevet at Buena Vista and was in the Santa Fe expedition in 1848. He gave up a captaincy in the First United States Dragoons in 1854, and settled on a splendid blue-grass farm in Woodford County, Kentucky, the asparagus bed, as Tom Marshall called it, of the blue-grass. Made a brigadier in 1862, he led a few hundred Kentucky boys from the State with Bragg, and with General Joe Wheeler had thoroughly demonstrated his great ability as a cavalryman.

Those who kept pace with Wheeler and Forrest must not only be great fighters, but they must be great cavalrymen. He placed great store by three Kentucky regiments of infantry, whose longing to ride was at last gratified by the War Department at Richmond, and on mules and broken down artillery horses, they had come to fight with Forrest. These men with Buford had passed through the roughest military training as infantry, and when the romance and glamor of cavalry service came their way, with abounding gratitude for being allowed to become cavalrymen, they had the manliness and appreciation to show their government that they fully deserved the great favor that had been bestowed upon them.

The Federal men were sturdy Westerners. They were as brave as the bravest. They had trotted three miles, double-quicked another mile and marched four miles; and they had borne this severe punishment without a murmur. They longed for victory. To defeat Forrest would give them the approval of their government and the applause of their comrades; and they were very anxious to crown the conflict with one crushing blow at the hated Confederate chieftain who, with his followers, had not only evaded the Federal forces sent for his capture, but very often had dashed their hopes of victory and driven them discomfited from many fields of strife. These men in blue trusted that fate would now deliver him into their hands, and though they feared, they hoped, and this gave firmer tone to their onslaught.

There was no cleared space for maneuvering. Men who fought in this battle must go into thickets and through underbrush to find the foe they sought.

Forrest was too wary a general to allow the Federals to rest sufficiently long to recover from the depressing effects of their heated and wearying march. He well knew that in immediate and decisive attack lay his only hope of defeating his assailants, who so greatly outnumbered him. He had genius for finding the places where the fiercest fray would take place. Grierson's cavalry had, like worsted gladiators, sought refuge behind the men whom they jocularly called "webfeet." They had borne the brunt of the battle from ten to two, had been worsted, and were glad enough to let the walking men test the mettle of the foes they had failed to defeat.

Lyon, Johnson and Rucker had fought with the men under them, with vigor, against Waring and Winston, and they had longed for a breathing spell, but as Bell's brigade, after their twenty-one mile ride, swung into line, tired though they were, they were yet indisposed to unload on the newcomers, and so gathering themselves together, they resolved not to be outdone by their comrades who had on that dreadful morning not felt battle's grievous touch nor hunted through the heated thickets for those who sought their undoing.

Buford was ordered to slowly press the Federal right. Fronting Forrest and Bell the Federals were massing, and here Forrest realized must come the "tug of war."

Cautiously, but quickly, Bell's men sought the newly aligned Federal infantry under Colonel Hoge. As Bell's men advanced, with acute vision, born of expected danger, they could not even see the men in blue as they stood with their guns cocked, waiting for a sight of those who so fearlessly were seeking them in the recesses of the jungle. They heard the silent, stealthy approach of the Confederates. The rustle of the leaves, the pushing aside of the bushes told them the Southern soldiers were coming. In an instant, without a single note of warning, the murderous, blazing fire of a thousand rifles flashed in their faces. Many brave men fell before this terrible discharge. The dead sank without noise to the earth and the unrepressed groans of the wounded for an instant terrorized the Confederate line. The instinct of safety, for a brief moment, led them to recoil from this gate of death, and a portion of Bell's brave men gave way. The Federal officers quickly took advantage of the situation and made a strong and valiant rush upon the broken line. With a shout of victory upon their lips, they fixed their bayonets and rapidly pushed through the thicket to disorganize those who, under the dreadful shock of an unexpected fire, had momentarily yielded to fear. This was Forrest's time to act. The expected had come. Tying his own horse to a tree, he bade his escort do likewise, and he and Bell, calling upon their men to follow, revolvers in hand, rushed upon the vanguard of the Federal line. Quick almost as thought itself, the Tennesseeans came back to the front. Wisdom, with two hundred and fifty of Newsom's regiment, leaped also to the rescue, and those who for a brief space recoiled now turned with fury upon the line that had dealt them so sudden and so grievous a blow. Rucker, hard pressed, bade his men kneel, draw their trusty revolvers and stand firm. It was now brave infantry with bayonets against brave cavalry with revolvers. No charge could break such a line, and the men of the bayonet drew back from impact with this wall of revolver fire. Hesitating for a brief space, they recoiled before the charge of the gallant Confederates. Hoge's men crumbled away in the face of the short range and effective aim of the Southern cavalry. A fierce dash of Forrest, Bell and Rucker completed their demoralization, and the men with the bayonets, vanquished, pulled away from further conflict with these revolver-firing cavalrymen.

At this moment, war's sweetest music fell upon the ears of General Forrest. Away north he heard the sound of conflict. Miles away from the scene of battle, Forrest had ordered Barteau's regiment to proceed west and strike the rear of the Federal forces. The Federal commanders deemed it wise to hold the colored brigade in reserve. They were about the wagon train. Forrest was again to astonish his enemies by a flank and rear attack. This was unexpected, but it was none the less decisive. No Federal cavalry could be spared to reach the front. Whipped in the morning, they were not even now, in the middle of the afternoon, ready for a second tussle with those who had vanquished them. Barteau had been well trained by his chieftain, for whom he had aforetime made daring assault under similar circumstances. The wagon train guard sought safety in flight, and the colored troopers began to tear from their breasts the badges printed with those fateful words, "Remember Fort Pillow. No quarter to Forrest's men." These boastful exhibits were good enough at

Memphis on June 1st, but they became most unsatisfying declarations at Bryce's Cross Roads on June 10th. It made a great difference where they were shown.

A stampede began among these black-skinned warriors. Vigorously they pulled the badges from their stricken breasts and trampled them in the dust, ere Barteau and his furious horsemen could reach their broken phalanxes. The Federal front was still stubborn and sullenly refused to yield further ground. To win it was necessary that this front be broken. With startling rapidity, Forrest again mounted his horse, rode the entire length of his line, declaring that the enemy was breaking, and that the hour of victory was at hand. Two hours of carnage and conflict had passed since Bell came. Finding his boy artillerist, Morton, he ordered him, at a signal, to hitch his horses to four guns, double shot the pieces with grape and canister, rush them down close to the enemy's line, and deliver his fire. There were no reserves to protect the artillery, and Morton and Buford spoke a word of caution as to this extraordinary movement, but Forrest was firm in his resolve to test out the movement, if it cost him one-third of his artillery.

Tyler, with his two companies of the brave 12th Kentucky, Forrest's escort and Gartrell's company of Georgians, were to go west and charge around the Federal right, forcing their way to the Federal rear, on Tishomingo Creek, and engage with pistols any Federal force that might resist their progress.

Barteau, further east, was pounding the Federal rear, while Tyler, Jackson and Gartrell with great fury were hammering the Federal right. One-sixth of Forrest's fighting men were now in the Federal rear. Morton, doubtful, but brave, drove his four guns into the very face of the enemy, advancing upon them amidst a storm of fire. His men, leaving their horses behind, as a small measure of safety, pushed the guns along the narrow, muddy road with their hands, firing as they moved. They seemed the very demons of war, courting death or capture in this grapple for mastery. The roar of the guns quickened the hopes of the Confederates, and all along the entire Confederate line a furious rush was made upon the Federal position. So close were the opposing forces to each other that they exchanged words of challenge, and at every point the Confederates forced the fighting and doubled up the Federal advance. The game was too fierce to last long. The brave and daring men in the rear, with Tyler and Barteau, were riding with a vengeance in every direction, and with their revolvers were doing deadly work upon the fleeing foes. This charge was aimed chiefly at the colored troops, who, with visions before their eyes and echoes in their ears of Fort Pillow, were ready to flee away, without standing upon the order of their going.

Of this eventful moment, General Sturgis said, "I now endeavored to get hold of the colored brigade which formed the guard of the wagon train. While traversing the short distance to where the head of the brigade should be formed, the main line gave away at various points, order soon gave way to confusion and confusion to panic. The army drifted toward the rear and was beyond control. The road became crowded and jammed with troops; wagons and artillery sank into the deep mud and became inextricable. No power could check the panic-stricken mass as it swept towards the rear. The demoralization was complete." Even General Sturgis proposed to take the 19th Pennsylvania Cavalry as an escort, and through the cross roads of the country, to seek shelter in Memphis. The bridge across Tishomingo Creek became blocked by overturned wagons, the fleeing Federals found climbing over the wagons too slow, and waded or swam the Creek. Impeded in their flight, great numbers were shot down as they attempted to pass the stream. Morton's artillery rushed to the bank, and hundreds of the Federals, still exposed to fire, were cut down at this point. Forrest was as relentless in pursuit as he had been furious in battle.

As the closing scenes of the battle were concluded, the sunset came on. Now was the hour of the greatest triumph. The foe was fleeing, and the horse-holders, mounted upon the rested beasts, were rushed forward to gather up the fruits of the splendid victory. There was to be no let up even in the coming darkness, and the Confederates who were able, cheerfully hurried to the front. The Federals formed line after line, only to see them crushed and broken, while weary fugitives, driven by increasing fear, pushed on with all their remaining strength, to find some place of safety and rest. The Federals dared not stop for an instant during the lengthening hours of the dark, dark night. With sad hearts they kept up their flight, and when the sun dawned they had reached Ripley, twenty-two miles from the dreadful scene which long haunted the memories of the vanquished men in blue.

At 3 a. m., Buford, a few miles from Ripley, came upon the remnant of the Federal wagon train and the last fourteen pieces of artillery. General Grierson, at earliest dawn had attempted to stay the pursuit until he could reorganize his beaten battalion, but Forrest and his escort, with the 7th Tennessee, closed in upon them, and they dispersed in the by-roads and through the plantations. All semblance of order was gone. No genius could evolve a complete organization that would for one moment resist the foe.

The Confederates seemed as demons, relentless and insatiable. All through the day and night of the 11th of June, the tired Confederates followed, and, with boundless energy, pursued the fleeing foes.

The retreat began at 4 p. m., June 10th. The next morning the Federals were at Ripley, twenty-five miles away, and the night of the same day, they reached Salem, forty-eight miles from Bryce's Cross Roads. Nineteen pieces of their twenty-six cannon had been captured with twenty-one caissons, two thousand men, including the wounded and captured, and twelve hundred lay dead on the field of battle and along the ways by which the Federals had retreated. It took nine days to march from White Station near Memphis to Bryce's Cross Roads. The fleeing Federals had traveled the same road in one day and two nights. No pursuit was ever more vigorous or effective. Forrest gave the fugitives no rest or peace. Changing his pursuing column from time to time, he made every moment count, the Federals scattered through the fields and forests and the Confederates scoured the country to take in those, who, forgetting the first principles of a deserting and defeated army to keep together, fled into the byways and through the wooded country, in their mad effort to hide from Forrest and his avenging huntsmen.

There was no reasonable explanation of the stupendous victory. General Sturgis tried to excuse it by saying the Confederates had twelve thousand men, including two brigades of infantry, but the only infantry there were, were Lyon's troopers, who for more than a year had fought on foot in the campaigns of the Army of Tennessee.

General Sherman frankly said, "Forrest had only his cavalry, and I cannot understand how he could defeat Sturgis with eight thousand men."

Later he said, "I will have the matter of Sturgis critically examined, and if he should be at fault, he shall have no mercy at my hands. I cannot but believe he had troops enough, and I know I would have been willing to attempt the same task with that force; but Forrest is the devil, and I think he has got some of our troops under cower. I have two officers at Memphis who will fight all the time, A. J. Smith and Mower. The latter is a young brigadier of fine promise, and I commend him to your notice.

I will order them to make up a force and go out to follow Forrest to the death, if it costs ten thousand lives and breaks the treasury. There will never be peace in Tennessee until Forrest is dead."

The Kentucky brigade opened the battle, bore its brunt for more than three hours, and this gave to five Kentuckians a prominent and important part in battle on that day. First came General Hylan B. Lyon. Born in Kentucky in 1836, he entered West Point in 1852 and graduated in 1856. He first saw service against the Seminole Indians in 1856 and 1857, and after frontier work in California was engaged in the Spokane Expedition and in the battle of September 5th-7th, 1858. On April 3rd, 1861, he resigned his commission in the United States Army and was appointed First Lieutenant of Artillery in the Confederate Army. He organized and became captain of Cobb's Battery, but in ten months was made lieutenant colonel of the 8th Kentucky Infantry. He led this regiment at Fort Donelson, surrendered and was exchanged; and became colonel of the 8th Kentucky. At Coffeeville, Mississippi, he acquitted himself well. In 1864, he was promoted to be brigadier general and assigned to the corps of General Forrest, his brigade consisting of the 3rd, 7th, 8th and 12th Kentucky Regiments. They were brave, seasoned, fearless soldiers, and were prepared with their distinguished brigadier general on that day to give a good account of themselves.

Edward Crossland, Colonel of the 7th Kentucky Cavalry, did not go to the front in this great battle. Lawyer and legislator, he was one of the first men in Kentucky to organize a company for service in the Confederate Army, and for a year was in the Army of Northern Virginia. A lieutenant colonel for one year, he became colonel of the 1st Kentucky Infantry in May, 1862. He was at Vicksburg and Baton Rouge and Champion's Hill with Breckinridge. He was with Forrest to the end. He had the unfortunate habit to stop the flight of a bullet in almost every conflict in which he was engaged. Wounded again and again, he survived it all, and was with Forrest at the surrender. Upon his return, he was made judge, then congressman, and then judge again.

He had been wounded at Paducah, and if he had been at Bryce's Cross Roads, he would surely have drawn another wound. It always grieved him that he was not present at this greatest triumph of his idolized leader. This day found Colonel Crossland's regiment under command of Henry S. Hale. In the blood-stained thickets, Major Hale won deserved distinction. On one occasion his men hesitated, but he seized the colors and ran forward, flaunting them in the face of the enemy. No soldier could run away after such an exhibition from his commander, and they returned with exceeding fierceness and cheerfully followed their valiant leader.

This and like intrepid conduct on this glorious day added another star to Major Hale's rank, and he became lieutenant colonel of the 7th Kentucky Regiment, a just tribute to a gallant soldier. Kentucky sent none braver or truer to fight for the Southland.

Among the officers who proved themselves heroes on that day, none deserved higher honor than Captain H. A. Tyler, of the 12th Kentucky Cavalry. His assault on the flanks and his charge on the rear of the enemy were noble and superb exhibitions of the highest courage. He played havoc with the colored reserves who were protecting the wagon train. His voice was heard above the din of firearms and at the head of his squadron; he descended upon the black soldiers with such furious war-cries as to chill their blood and set in motion the retreat, which soon developed into an uncontrollable rout.

Chapter II

GENERAL HAMPTON'S CATTLE RAID, SEPTEMBER, 1864

General Wade Hampton, in the history of the Civil War, must ever be acknowledged to be one of the really great leaders. Of distinguished ancestry and high personal character, and endowed with sublime courage, he early entered the contest, and it was not long before his aptitude for cavalry service was so developed and amplified as to induce the War Department to confine his talents entirely to that branch. As the second of J. E. B. Stuart, he not only earned renown for himself, but was also one of the potent factors in helping his chief to carry out his cherished plans and to win the conspicuous place he occupied in the annals of the great war. To succeed so brilliant a leader and so thorough a cavalryman as General Stuart, imposed upon General Hampton most perplexing tasks and placed him in a position which would thoroughly try out the metal that was in him. It may justly and truly be said of General Hampton that he met all the conditions which surrounded him in the arduous work which his talents had won for him.

By the summer and fall of 1864, the obstacles which confronted the Confederate cavalryman had been largely augmented. Living upon the enemy had become practically impossible. Raids, in which wagon trains, provisions, army ammunition and clothing had hitherto been so successfully captured, were now seldom successful, and outpost duty and the punishment of the Federal cavalry, which undertook to destroy the transportation agencies south of Petersburg, engaged all the time and the energies and more completely developed the genius of the Confederate cavalry leaders of the Army of Northern Virginia.

Supplies of food had now become one of the most important, as well as the most difficult, of all the problems which faced with unrelenting grimness the armies of the Confederacy. The Federal raids west and north of Richmond, and frequent interruption of lines of communication about Petersburg and Lynchburg and up the Shenandoah Valley, had rendered the food supply uncertain. Three and a half years of war overwhelming the agricultural sections tributary to the Capital of the Confederacy, had greatly cut down the necessary quota of provisions.

For neither infantry nor cavalry was there much chance during that period to forage upon the enemy. The lines of investment and defence between Petersburg and Richmond kept the cavalry too far south to foray for supplies north of Richmond. The Atlantic Ocean—free to the Federals, but blockaded to the Confederates—formed a water route ever open and impossible of closure, giving the Federals perfect safety in moving food and supplies upon the currents of the mighty deep, where there could be no chance for the men of the gray to attack or appropriate them.

General Wade Hampton, always resourceful, had learned that on the James River, five miles east of City Point, the Federal army had corralled a large herd of cattle, kept upon such pastures as had been left by the environments and demands of war. Fortunate in the possession of most trustworthy scouts, who were entirely familiar with the topography adjacent to the James River and the Confederate and Federal lines at Petersburg, General Hampton knew with absolute exactness the place where these beeves were being fed and kept ready for Federal slaughter. He well understood that in any dangerous and hazardous undertaking, the men who followed him would never hesitate, but would cheerfully go where he led. These men were always well assured if he carried them into the midst of danger, he had genius to extricate them with masterful skill, and their cheers, when ordered to advance, were the best response which a commander could receive from the loyal hearts of his followers, and nerved his arm and quickened his brain for great exploits.

To succeed in this unique and difficult cattle raid, it was necessary to make an incursion to the rear of the Federal army within a very short distance of City Point, the headquarters of General Grant and his subordinate commanders. City Point had become the center of operations as well as the base of supplies of the Union forces, and even the most sagacious and cautious Federal soldier hardly deemed it possible that Confederate cavalry could march in the rear of the great army that then lay beside the James, or could, with impunity, pierce the lines covering Federal headquarters and drive off the large supply of beeves which had been gathered for army use.

On September 4th, 1864, General Hampton set out on this perilous undertaking. He took with him men who were tried and true, men who feared to take no risk, to brave no danger and who were capable of achievements deemed wellnigh impossible by those unaccustomed to the daring enterprises of war. He had with him General W. H. F. Lee's division, Rosser's and Dearing's brigades, and a hundred men from General P. M. B. Young and General Dunnovant. W. H. F. Lee's division was composed of three brigades: General Beale's, General Barringer's and General Dearing's—the last named having only one regiment and one battalion! There could be little choice among those who composed the cavalry of the Army of Northern Virginia. They were all and always to be depended upon. In this extraordinary expedition, those who were chosen were measured not so much by the individual courage they possessed above their fellows, as by the condition of the animals to be subjected to such extreme hardship as awaited the expedition.

The three thousand men mustering for this foray were told only that the service was both daring and important. These men did not deem it necessary to inquire where they were going and what the service was. They knew that Hampton planned, that Lee and Rosser, Beale, Young, Dunnovant, Barringer and Dearing aided their chivalrous commander, and they had sublime faith in the skill, as well as the courage, of these intrepid leaders. There is something in the cavalry march that exhilarates men, stirring and stimulating the spirit of adventure. Visions of glory give quickened powers to the men who ride to war. Those who composed the long line behind General Hampton were cheerful, patient and hopeful, and inspired by patriotism and courage, they rode out southeastwardly with the confidence born of chivalry and implicit belief in the ultimate success of their cause.

After a march of thirty miles southeastwardly, the little army bivouacked at what was known as Wilkinson's Grove. Undiscovered, they had now traveled eastwardly far enough to steer clear of the extended lines of the Federal army which lay between them and the ocean. With the break of day, the march was resumed. The heads of the horses were now turned north, and before daylight had receded the adventurous command had reached the Black Water River. These movements had brought General Hampton entirely around the left flank of the Federals, and he had now come close to the place where he had intended to force the enemy's lines. The bridges had long since been destroyed, and it was necessary to erect temporary structures. There was no rest for the engineers or their assistants. They had ridden all day, but now they must work all night. A torch here and there was occasionally lighted to help the men adjust a refractory timber, but in the velvety darkness of the still night, cheerfully and heroically, these brave men hurriedly erected a rude bridge across the stream, whose currents flowed between the narrow banks, as if to defy or delay these patriots in their efforts to provide food for their hungry comrades, who, in their beleaguered tents around Petersburg, were longing and watching for supplies which would give them strength to still withstand the vigorous assaults of an ever-watchful and aggressive foe.

Leaving only the pickets on watch, the command bivouacked upon the ground, and horses and men in mingled masses—side by side—slept until midnight. Cooked rations had been brought with them, and no camp fires were kindled which might reveal their presence. No trumpet or bugle sound was used to wake the soldiers, the low-spoken commands of the officers instantly aroused the slumbering troopers whose ears were quick to hear the low but stern orders of those who called them to renew their wearying march. Long before the darkest hours that precede the dawn, the men mounted, and before the sun had risen had ridden the nine miles which lay between the bridge and the largest detachment of the enemy's cavalry, which guarded the pasturing cattle. The coveted beeves were feeding just two miles farther on.

North and south, there were several bodies of Federal horsemen, but General Hampton believed that if he could distance the larger force it would prevent the small detachments from having any base upon which to concentrate. To General Rosser, always spirited, gallant and aggressive, was assigned the duty of making an assault upon this force, and he was ordered immediately after the dispersal of the Federals to corral and drive the cattle away.

The march from the bivouac where the Confederate cavalry had rested and obtained a few hours' sleep, consumed five hours, but before the sun had well risen, Rosser attacked with fiercest energy. To General Lee was assigned driving in the videttes. A cavalry regiment from the District of Columbia, as soon as attacked, entrenched itself behind barricades and gave notice that they proposed to dispute Rosser's right of way and to resist him to the last. The coming of light had renewed the enthusiasm of the horsemen, and with the rising sun, their courage rose to the sublimest heights. This feeling of determination to win at all hazards permeated the entire Confederate commands, and when Rosser called for sharp, impetuous, decisive, gallant service, his men rode and rushed over all obstacles, and in a very few moments defeated the Federal command opposing them, all that were not killed or captured riding off in wild dismay.

General W. H. F. Lee and General Dearing were directed to disperse and ride down everything which wore a Federal uniform wherever met with. Pickets, troops, regiments, whatever opposed, and wherever opposing, they were to assault and drive away. Particularly were they to look after couriers, who might bear any messages to Federal commanders of the presence of these headlong and apparently reckless Confederates. In fact, a courier was captured and a dispatch taken from him, giving the exact location of the herd, which had been moved only the day before.

As soon as General Rosser had dispersed the detachments of Federals which he was ordered to destroy, he immediately dispatched a portion of his command to secure the cattle, which was done without either delay or difficulty. The guards, panic-stricken by the presence of enemies whom they thought were forty miles away, were overpowered and made prisoners before they realized that Confederates were in their midst. A few horses and all the beeves, numbering 2,486, were corralled. There was no time for parley, delay, congratulations or cheers. Safety required an immediate movement southward and away from the presence of the numerous Union forces, who would soon learn of this bold and aggressive raid and set about the punishment of the audacious aggressors. But the spirit of war and destruction could not be stilled. Dangers could not deter the cavalry from proceeding to burn camps, to destroy great quantities of supplies, and immense storehouses of clothing and provisions. There was many times more than enough to meet all the wants of the foraging troopers. They were quick to appropriate such of the enemy's goods as met their needs, and then the torch did its destructive work and rendered useless the immense stores of food, clothing and munitions of war which Federal foresight had garnered and gathered for the use of the troops and camps south of the James River.

The campaign was so mapped out and planned that each man fully understood the duties he was to perform. The secret of the marvelous success which had so far attended the expedition was the result of perfect orders communicated to the men who had ridden fast and far on this splendid adventure. The Confederate troops were necessarily scattered, the cattle had been rounded up, couriers had been intercepted, videttes had been driven away. These movements covered a large territory, but it was all done so systematically and so thoroughly that it looked as if some machine had been adjusted and set for this task. There had been no mistake in the distribution of the orders, and no officer or man failed to carry them out. The troops were elated by their superb success. Their victory lifted them to the greatest heights of enthusiasm, and its glory seemed to fill the very air and yet, amid all the fascination of their splendid success, prudence told everybody that now was the hour of their extremest peril, and that the greatest task of all, that of driving away this splendid herd of cattle and delivering them to the Confederate commissary, was yet to be accomplished.

It was a trying work to which these soldiers were now subjected, but one which the experience and courage of these men had fully trained them to perform.

In the later months of the war, the sphere of action of the cavalry became very much broadened. Earlier, raiding and scouting had been their chief business, but now in emergencies they were used, not only as cavalry, but as infantry; and their lengthy military training fitted them to perform their part as soldiers in any enterprise and in any line of service. Extraordinary scenes were now witnessed, for the situation was weird in the extreme. The beeves, alarmed by the shouts of the soldiers and the firing, had become frightened and unmanageable, for their new masters were not only strangely garbed but acted in a way that they had never before witnessed. To quiet the beasts in this emergency, the Federal herders were called upon, whom the terrified animals recognized as their former masters and keepers, while they looked with fear and suspicion upon the noisy and dust-stained cavaliers who now claimed them as their property.

The Confederates soon found that if the cattle were driven in one herd, the difficulties of moving them would be much increased, their speed would be much lessened and the animals in great crowds might become panic stricken, and so with the help of the herders and captors, three or four hundred cattle were placed in one bunch or detachment; these were surrounded by the horsemen and forced forward as rapidly as the condition of the beasts would permit. Celerity of movement was one of the important elements in this splendid enterprise. No one understood this better than General Hampton and General Robert E. Lee, and even down to the youngest private this knowledge quickened the movements and steadied the arms and braced the hearts of every soldier who composed the command. Within three hours from the time General Rosser fired the first gun, General Hampton had accomplished all his purposes and was ready to withdraw. With the self-possession and calm of a great leader and without semblance of fear or apparent solicitude, he began the task of extricating himself from the dangerous and hazardous conditions into which the necessities of General Lee's army and his energetic zeal had involved him.

No Federal general or soldier had dreamed that such a campaign could or would be undertaken. Even had it been thought of, the hazard and the danger of it would have convinced the most cautious Federal officers that nobody could or would essay to enter upon such a perilous and reckless expedition.

General Hampton, though, had friends who knew of this brilliant undertaking. General Lee counted the hours which intervened from the time Hampton formed his lines and marched away. He knew that only vastly disproportioned numbers could stay the men who rode behind his adventurous cavalry associate. He could not hear Hampton's guns, but a soldier's instinct, the telepathy of genius, had whispered to him that Hampton had done his work. He felt that failure was almost impossible; that Hampton might be annihilated by overwhelming forces, but General Lee knew the men who followed the man, and so when Hampton began his march southward the Confederate commander, behind his lines at Petersburg, began a demonstration upon the entire Federal front. With fierce assault, pickets were driven in, troops at double-quick were moved from position to position; the whole Confederate forces were under arms, and so far as military foresight could discern, everything indicated that General Lee was preparing to make a strenuous assault upon every vulnerable Federal position. The cavalry, left behind with General M. C. Butler, also began to skirmish with the enemy's pickets and outlying posts, and between the movements of the cavalry and infantry, the Federal officers were firmly impressed that a crisis in the defense of the Capital of the Confederates was on and that General Lee was now going to force a battle which would decide the fate, not only of the Army of Northern Virginia, but of the Confederacy itself.

Fortunately for General Hampton and General Lee, General Grant was absent. He had gone to Harper's Ferry to consult with General Sheridan about a movement down the Shenandoah Valley. Telegram after telegram began to pour in upon him; he had hardly time to read one before another was forced into his hands, and they all bore tidings which disquieted his calm. The Federal cavalry, which had been completely scattered, brought in with them marvelous stories of the overwhelming forces that had attacked and dispersed them. Their distorted imaginations had increased the numbers of Confederate troops until it appeared to them that every man in General Lee's army had been mounted and was charging down upon the lines about City Point with a fierceness that indicated that the furies had been turned loose and that the unleashed dogs of war were ready to attack all that could oppose them. The communications which had passed between General Meade and General Grant and the Federal subordinates during this period are most amusing. The quick and unexpected onslaught had completely dismayed the Federal Army. Its officers believed that so much ado being made along the lines in front could not possibly have occurred, unless General Lee really intended some important and decisive movement. Along the wires were flashed the stories from the fleeing cavalry that the Confederate forces counted more than fourteen thousand men. Those who were sending these messages did not stop to figure that this was more cavalry than General Lee had in his army. Hour by hour quickened these fancies born of fear, and each fleeing horseman painted in more lurid terms the pursuing foes, which they declared were close behind. The gunboats were ordered to cover City Point for the defense of the immense supplies there stored. Reserved troops were quickly pushed forward, and a universal spirit of alarm and uncertainty prevailed throughout the Federal camps.

In a few hours, the results of General Hampton's incursion dawned upon the Federal leaders. Chagrined and surprised at the success of the Confederates, and determined to punish and resent their temerity, vigorous measures were taken to release the cattle and disperse or annihilate their captors. They understood that the march and drive of the cattle would be difficult and slow, that the Confederates had the long line and their pursuers the short one.

The Federal cavalry, under Generals Kautz, Gregg, Davies, all ambitious and restive under the just criticism of their superiors for permitting such a coup, with fierce resolution and quickened energy, set their followers in motion and hunted their receding foes.

General Rosser had the cattle and could protect the narrow line along which he was passing. His brigade was a wall of fire in his immediate rear, but the converging pursuers from the north and west, quickened at every step by the appeals of their officers to avenge what they regarded as an affront, must be held back by Generals W. H. F. Lee and Dearing. Those who followed these officers always gave a good account of themselves, and General Lee, while active in his retreat (an activity strictly limited by General Rosser's ability to move the cattle), while not seeking battle, stood with iron will between their hot pursuit and the coveted droves, which were forced to their utmost speed by the whips of the captive drovers and the shouts and belaboring of the bold horsemen whose every stride was haunted by the fear of the following Federal cavalry, now galloping to punish the audacity of the Confederate raid.

With eager eyes and ears, General Lee and General Dearing scanned every angle of the horizon, and every sound that passed southward, every cloud of dust that rose heavenward, every object that dimmed the perspective was scrutinized with earnest gaze. Eyes and glasses united in finding the position of every coming foe, and the quick ears of these trained horsemen were turned to catch each breeze, and to detect if possible the earliest tidings of those who were bent upon their destruction.

General Hampton rose to the call of the hour. Anxious well he might be, but despite the throbbings of a heart aroused to mightiest effort, he bore himself with the calmness of a skilled leader and fearless soldier. To him and those he led, the issues were momentous. Capture, imprisonment, the humiliation of defeat and the loss of prestige, were grievous burdens to carry, but behind him there was a splendid past and before him a future big with patriotic hope, and he waited the orderings of fate with sublimest confidence.

Along his lines he rode with words of encouragement and cheer, and none could discern in his demeanor the tumult of dread that disquieted his soul. No word or act of his was necessary to tell the men who with unquestioning loyalty were ready to do his bidding the grave dangers of the hour. Intelligent and watchful they shared with their leader the knowledge that the situation was fraught with utmost peril and that nothing short of the noblest courage, quickest perception and unfailing steadiness could avert threatening disaster.

Hampton, Lee, Rosser and Dearing were splendid leaders, they had with them great soldiers, and combined they wrested from fate a great victory. General Davies was the only Federal cavalryman that was able to force any sort of a battle, but General Lee was quick to resist his interference. Halting to feel General Lee's line, Davies and Gregg sent a flanking detachment to strike the retreating columns five miles away, but when they came the Confederates were gone and this proved the last real attempt to stop the march of Hampton's forces.

General Hampton, the master mind of this splendid movement, by the aid of his faithful scouts and ever alert guides, kept fully in touch with each part of the ever-changing field. Self-reliant, confident of his soldiers, and a believer in his ability and destiny, nothing escaped his oversight and care. If he feared, none knew it. If his brave heart ever trembled, there was no external sign of his apprehension, and his unruffled countenance was a constant inspiration to those who, if needs be, would follow to death at his call, and who had not even a momentary doubt of his ability to safely deliver them from the tremendous risks of the hour and the terrifying difficulties of their hazardous expedition.

Uncertainty as to the number of men engaged in this movement dampened the ardor of the attacking Federal cavalry. They did not know really what to expect. They could hardly believe that a force so small would have dared strike their rear, and if it was as large as military science suggested, they had no real taste for grappling a foe equal in numbers to their own. Lee and Rosser were fighting the Federal cavalry and holding them at bay. The cattle, now divided, with soldiers and herdsmen pressing them forward, were traveling farther and farther south. The hours no doubt seemed long to the Confederate horsemen, but the excitement of the battle and the presence of the enemy had sustained them through all the experiences of the day. With such mental surroundings, minutes had greatly lengthened, and all the Confederates were glad when they saw a little ahead of them Nottoway River and recognized that Freeman's Ford, where they were to pass that stream, was safe from the enemy's grip. As the lowing beasts, the shouting drivers, the tired riders and the weary horses took the stream and passed safely over to the other side, to a point where they were safe from attack, generals, line officers and privates took renewed strength and all congratulated each other that a kindly providence had guided their feet and brought them safely under the protecting wing of the legions of infantry and artillery, for whose sustenance they had endured such tremendous suffering and faced such extraordinary dangers.

Hampton, with his matchless courage, felt that his full task had not been performed, and leaving the beasts to browse and later under lessened guards to pursue their journey leisurely towards General Lee's fortified

46

camp, he, himself, summoning such of his followers as were yet able to ride to still greater tasks, recrossed the stream and began, now tigerlike, to hunt his pursuers. He felt that these men, who had had the temerity to pursue him and his great commissary stores, should be punished for their audacity, and so, turning northward, he set out to search for the enemies who had attempted to take from him the rich prizes which his superb intrepidity and magnificent daring had won for the Confederate army.

The Federal cavalry, far from their infantry supports and with magnified ideas of the strength of the Confederate forces, were not impatient to try conclusions with the Confederate troopers who had so audaciously possessed themselves of their cattle, and so Hampton's weary men, with more weary and tired horses, turned their faces in pursuit of the Federal cavalry. They found that those who had pursued were now ready to retreat, and the Federal cavalry was willing to leave them alone to enjoy the spoils of victory and the splendid meat supply which they had so courageously won.

General Hampton and his men had marched a hundred miles in three days, part of this time encumbered with twenty-five hundred beeves; he was far removed from the support or help of his friends, except so far as General Lee, by his movements in the face of the Federal lines, could intimidate the army which was opposing him and which was creeping hour by hour closer and closer to Petersburg and endeavoring day by day to find the vital and weakest points in the wasted Confederate lines. The infantry and artillery who were keeping at bay the besiegers who were pushing forward to throttle the Confederacy and wrest its Capital from its control and to drive Lee and his army from Virginia soil, upon which had flowed such torrents of the best blood of the South and on which had been won such laurels by the Army of Northern Virginia, heard strange rumors that day, as the first couriers brought the tidings of Hampton's Raid.

Fatigued men and jaded beasts mutely appealed for rest and sleep, and so when General Hampton found that his foes, unwilling to hazard a battle, rode away northward as he appeared from the south, he gave the command to face about, and by easy stages he led his troopers across the river where they might, for a brief while, enjoy the rest they had so richly earned and receive the plaudits of their comrades, to whom they had brought such needed and healthful supplies in their extremity and hunger.

For a little while, it was impossible for the Confederate army to realize what General Hampton had done. The cavalry, always sufficiently boastful, were not slow to tell of the difficulties and dangers of the march, of the excitement and adventure which attended every hour from the advance until the retreat. They were real heroes, and there was no reason for them to be modest about their exploits, and to the amazed infantry they repeated, probably oftentimes with more or less exaggeration, the experiences and events of this strange, successful and wonderful expedition. Here and there the infantry had questioned the steadiness and courage of the trooper under fire, but as this famished army enjoyed, with gratitude and satisfaction, the delicious steaks which their cavalry friends had brought them from the Federal depot, they assigned this commissary achievement to a high place in war's annals, and accorded to Hampton and his troopers in this raid unsparing and unmeasured praise. If General Hampton had done nothing else than inaugurate, organize and successfully promote this marvelous raid, he would be entitled to high rank among the cavalry leaders, not only of the Civil War, but of the ages.

Chapter III

KENTUCKY CAVALRY FIGHTING WITH ROCKS, DUG CREEK GAP, MAY 8-9, 1864

General Joseph E. Johnston had one of the most varied and eventful careers of any general officer in the Confederate service. General Robert E. Lee was born January 19th, 1807; General Johnston was born February 3d, of the same year, making a difference in their ages of fifteen days. They were both Virginians, and graduated from West Point in the same class.

General Johnston held the highest rank of any officer in the United States army, who resigned to take service with the Confederate government. Of the really great leaders of the men who wore the gray, he was perhaps criticized more than any other. Whatever were the charges against General Johnston, he was always able to defend himself with forceful ability, and with extreme plausibility to present both his theories and the conduct of his campaigns in a strong and vigorous way. Oftentimes, a student of the history of military operations will question, in his own mind, whether General Johnston was really a great soldier, or an unfortunate victim of jealousy, or a brilliant leader, against whom fate had a bitter and lasting grudge. Whatever critics may say, he maintained to a wonderful degree the confidence and esteem of his men, and his Atlanta campaign will attract attention through all ages and demand admiration for the man who successfully planned and carried it out. It unquestionably takes high place among the great campaigns which were conducted from 1861 to 1865. The seventy-four days that Johnston passed in the immediate presence of the opposing army were days of incessant fighting, great mortality and immeasurable toil; and of such a character as to hold to the highest tension the nerves and hearts of his followers. Probably no officer who followed the stars and bars ever had a more difficult task assigned him than that which was given to General Johnston in northern Georgia, in the spring and summer of 1864. General Bragg's failures, whether justly or unjustly, had called forth the sharpest criticism, and while a great soldier, he did not retain in defeat the love and faith of the men he led. In these matters, General Johnston never failed.

General Johnston was placed in command of the Army of the Tennessee, by the authorities at Richmond, with the distinct understanding and positive order that he must advance and stay the tide of invasion which was slowly but surely moving southward and sapping the sinews and the life of the Confederacy. All knew that if the Army of the Tennessee should be destroyed, and the Federals should take possession of Alabama, Mississippi and Georgia, with the Mississippi River as a base, it would not be very long until whatever may have been General Lee's resources, he would be taken in flank and rear and his armies annihilated.

General Johnston, while confessedly a man of genius, was also extremely tenacious of his rights, and resented what he considered a slight; and he did not hesitate in the most emphatic way to criticize that which his knowledge as a general condemned.

The Confederate government, on two occasions, at least, was forced over the judgment of its executives, by popular clamor, to give to General Johnston most important commands. Twice removed, he was subsequently reassigned to the positions from which he had been retired. In each case, and whenever removed failure followed, he calmly and with the most abundant reasons was enabled to tell those who deposed him, "I told you so."

It may be that General Johnston frequently asked of the War Department what it was helpless to give. He was wise and experienced enough to see the overwhelming needs of the armies. He was sagacious enough to fully estimate the power and strength of the enemy. He loved the cause of the South so thoroughly that he hesitated to stake its destiny on one battle, the outcome of which was extremely doubtful. He refused to risk the life of his country on a single throw "of the wild, grim dice of the iron game." Those in authority charge that he was over-cautious and afraid to take the chances that the surrounding exigencies and dangers demanded, and that he put his own judgment over and above the orders of his superiors. He never realized that they fully appreciated and understood the needs of the situation, and he never fully recognized that those above him had the right to demand that he should subordinate his judgment to the authority from which he derived his power. He felt that he had closer and more complete view of the entire field; that he knew better than those five hundred miles away of the desperate chances they called upon him to assume, and he believed that the South could not afford to take such forlorn risks when by the caprices of fate the life of the Confederacy was hanging by a most delicate thread.

General Johnston had personal reasons which caused him to distrust the fairness and justness of the War Department in the treatment of himself. The order in which the generals were named, whereby he was made the fourth in rank, was extremely distasteful to him, and he did not hesitate to say that he felt he had been wronged.

His conduct of the Army of Northern Virginia had given him much reputation, but in the momentous struggle around Richmond, the cruel destiny, which appeared to overshadow him, brought him a wound on the 31st of May, 1862, when, humanly speaking, victory was within his grasp.

He was succeeded on that day by General Robert E. Lee, and from that time, General Johnston's connection with the Army of Northern Virginia ended. During the term of his service, he was wounded ten times. He was brave to a fault, but never to such an extent as unnecessarily to imperil the life of a commander.

Many opportunities came, but the fair-minded student must admit that, with the exception of Bull Run and Seven Pines, he never had an equal chance.

The correspondence between General Johnston and the authorities at Richmond shows that the government had good reasons to feel that General Johnston was not a very obedient commander. And while he may have known better than those who gave the orders, they considered it was his business to obey rather than to question or complain.

From May, 1861, to June, 1862, General Johnston was in active and constant service. He was often charged with over-caution, but his admirers say this resulted from his great loyalty to the South and his eager desire to see it win its independence.

After his wound, on the 31st of May on the James River, he was forced to remain inactive until the summer of 1863, when Vicksburg was in peril—again his country called, and he responded cheerfully and promptly.

His campaigns in Mississippi and his failure to relieve Vicksburg have been widely and sharply discussed. That the operations in behalf of Vicksburg and for the defense of Mississippi failed, could not, by those unbiased, be attributed solely to any fault on the part of General

Johnston. He protested that disobedience of his orders, by inferiors, marred his plans, and on December 18th, 1863, he was directed to turn over the army of Mississippi to General Leonidas Polk. He was naturally not sorry to be relieved from a situation that had been associated with so many embarrassments, and in which there were so many unfortunate misunderstandings.

The Confederate government again called him a second time to take command of the Army of the Tennessee; but he was relieved on the 22nd day of July, 1863; and on the 3d of December, 1863, he was again instructed to lead the forces which were attempting to stem the advance of the invaders towards Atlanta, and the further progress of which, into the heart of Georgia, was regarded as an impending death blow to Confederate hopes.

General Johnston, with his knowledge of equipment, realized how inferior were those of his men to the armies that wore the blue, and most earnestly and insistently pleaded for better equipments and more troops. It must be said that he knew better than any living man the condition of the forces, which he was called to command. The failures of his predecessors only quickened his desire and hope, out of the wreck, to win victory, and it may be that a patriotic spirit, united with ambition, also pointed out to him in an attractive form the fact that he was to save Atlanta from the grasp of the Federal forces, and become the leader in the West that General Lee was in the East.

There must have been a feeling of intense satisfaction to General Johnston in the resolution of the Confederate government to appoint him anew to the second and most important command in the Confederate armies.

Those who put themselves in General Johnston's place are bound to admit that he had some ground of justification for his feeling towards the Confederate authorities. We can look at these conditions more clearly after a lapse of nearly fifty years, and even the friends of the men who composed the War Department, and the friends of General Johnston, are forced to the conclusion that there were two sides to the controversy.

When, on December 27th, 1863, he assumed command of the Army of the Tennessee, General Johnston undertook a Herculean task. From all the reports of those connected with the department, it is shown that General Johnston made the best of the situation when matters were turned over to him. General Johnston had assumed a burden which would press hard upon his shoulders. Persistently and even fiercely, he called for more troops, more horses, more guns, more feed, more men in the infantry. It was his desire to be able to stop the invasion. He was not satisfied with the meagre resources of the government at Richmond, but asked more. When called to the command of the defeated army, it was with the understanding that he should make an offensive campaign. The authorities felt that a Fabian policy was the forerunner of ruin, and that Napoleonic methods, with even desperate odds and chances, was the only plan which suggested or held out the least show of victory. He had a right to expect such resources as would give him some sort of chance in the desperate battle which his country had called upon him to wage. He was facing an army twice as large as his own, probably the best equipped army that ever marched on the American continent, commanded by a general who, as even those who disliked him admitted, was a great soldier, who had behind him practically unlimited resources, against which General Johnston was to go with comparatively few and badly provided men, and he constantly and with increasing emphasis made demands on his government for more troops. The people at Richmond felt the crucial moment was at hand and the chances of battle must be risked even though the chances were very largely against the Confederate troops. They said, in substance, to the leader of the Army of the Tennessee:

He either fears his fate too much
Or his desert is small,
Who does not put it to the touch
And win or lose it all.

So soon as the rains of the spring had ceased and the roads had dried, the Federal general set out with a force of eighty-five thousand men to force his way down through Georgia to Atlanta; he had already gone through Chattanooga, he was well on his way from Chattanooga to Atlanta, and between him and his destination only stood Johnston with as brave men as ever faced a foe; men who were ready and willing to die, if needs be, to save their country. The fierce campaigns of the winter which had been imposed upon the cavalry had weakened their force, many of them were dismounted, and many more of them were poorly mounted, and in that depleted condition were not equal to the tasks that this important march was now to lay upon them.

Forrest and Wheeler and their subordinates had done all that men could do. They had pushed their columns to the limits of endurance. Their presence now became necessary to protect the flanks of General

Johnston's army and stand off Federal raids. They were too busy at home to justify attacks upon the enemy's rear.

In the first few days of May, General Sherman began to feel his way towards the Confederate position. The Army of the Tennessee had wintered at Dalton, a place that General Johnston could not see was of any strategic importance, but its surrender would mean another disappointment of the national hopes, and a further impairment of confidence in the Confederate forces to resist the apparently relentless destiny that was pursuing the decimated legions that had so long and fearlessly challenged a further advance into a state, the possession of which was vital to the nation's life.

Among the forces composing the cavalry of General Johnston's army was Grigsby's Brigade, composed of the 9th Kentucky, led by Colonel W. C. P. Breckinridge, and Dortch's and Kirkpatrick's battalions. These soldiers were among the best that Kentucky furnished. They were largely young men from the Bluegrass, few of them exceeding twenty-five years in age. They had come out of Kentucky in July, 1862, and October, 1862; had now received more than a year's seasoning, and were by their military experiences fitted for the hardest and fiercest conflicts. They had left Kentucky well mounted. Grigsby had been on the Ohio raid and escaped the catastrophe which met General Morgan's command in July, 1863, at Buffington Island. A portion of his regiment and a part of the 10th Kentucky Cavalry alone came back from that fatal ride. The 9th Kentucky, under Colonel Breckinridge, had not gone upon the Ohio raid. Grigsby was one of the best of the Kentucky cavalry colonels. He was born in Virginia, September 11th, 1818. He was just forty-four years old when he entered the Confederate service; brave, determined, fearless, enterprising, he established a splendid reputation, and when the Army of the Tennessee was before Chattanooga, he was given command of a brigade by General Wheeler, including the 1st, 2nd and 9th Kentucky Cavalry and later Dortch's and Kirkpatrick's battalions. In the retreat from Missionary Ridge, General Bragg designated Grigsby and his Kentuckians to cover the rear, and they did it with preeminent valor and intrepidity.

Later on, General Wheeler became so much attached to General Grigsby that he made him chief of staff; and in Tennessee, Georgia and the Carolinas, during the darkest and closing scenes of the nation's struggle, he won superb commendation and became one of General Wheeler's most trusted and vigilant lieutenants.

The 9th Kentucky Cavalry was essentially a central Kentucky product. It was recruited partly during General Morgan's raid of 1862, in Kentucky, and was completed during Bragg's occupancy of the state, in the summer and fall of 1862. It was commanded by Colonel W. C. P. Breckinridge who, when a mere lad at college, won a reputation as one of the most eloquent of the young men Kentucky had ever known.

He had been practicing law four years when the war began. In July, 1862, he recruited a company that became part of the 2nd Kentucky Cavalry, under General John H. Morgan.

When the Confederates returned to Kentucky, under Bragg, Captain Breckinridge was enabled to recruit a battalion, and this was subsequently consolidated with Robert G. Stoner's battalion and became the 9th Kentucky Cavalry Regiment, of which Breckinridge became colonel.

By December, 1862, he was in command of a brigade in General Morgan's famous Kentucky raid, which covered the Christmas of 1862 and New Year of 1863. Saved from the wreck of the Ohio raid, his regiment was part of the brigade commanded by Colonel Grigsby in Kelly's Division of Wheeler's Cavalry Corps.

The Kentucky brigade was engaged in many brilliant operations in Tennessee and Georgia. Part of it rode with Wheeler in his raid through Tennessee, in Sherman's rear. General Wheeler, in his reports, was generous in the praise of the distinguished young colonel, afterwards known as the "Silver-Tongued Orator of Kentucky," and representative of the Henry Clay district for a number of years in the United States Congress.

Two of the services rendered by the Kentucky brigade are to be sketched in this book. First, the brilliant fight at Dug Creek Gap, at the opening of the Atlanta campaign, and, second, its work in capturing General Stoneman, some weeks later.

The Kentucky brigade, at the Dug Creek Gap, did much to give inspiration to the army under General Johnston, which, while generally retreating, was always cheerful and, even though constantly retiring, never lost its courage or its fortitude.

This brigade was not overly fond of discipline, against which there was always a silent protest; notwithstanding which they were always ready to grapple with any foe that fate brought across their path. They bore the hardships of every campaign without a murmur or complaint. In July, September, October, November and December, no raids, however trying, had been able to bring from these splendid cavalrymen a sigh of regret or a murmur at the arduous work that their country and general had assigned them. When General Johnston, with complete reliance upon their courage and fidelity in the face of the most imminent danger, designated them for a difficult and hazardous service, they accepted it with great joy, and marched out with defiant shouts and enthusiastic cheers to obey his commands and fulfill his expectations.

While General Johnston, through January, February and March of 1864, was appealing for more men, more guns and more equipments, Sherman had orders from General Grant to "move against Johnston's army, break it up, and to get into the interior of the enemy's country as far as he could, inflicting all the damages possible on their war resources." General Johnston had directions to strike the Federal army in the flank, attack it in detail, or do anything that, by a bold and aggressive forward movement, would inspire the people of the Confederacy with yet more patience and more willingness to make still further sacrifices for Southern independence.

As to how many men Johnston and Sherman each had at this particular time, there has been much calculation and superabundance of figuring. General Johnston said that on the 30th of April, up to which time no serious losses had been inflicted upon his forces, he had forty-two thousand eight hundred and fifty-six men. Some Federal writers insist that the Confederates had eighty-four thousand.

By the 1st of May, 1864, the roads had dried sufficiently to warrant an earnest advance, and on the 5th of May, General Thomas, under direction of General Sherman, made a movement on Tunnel Hill. On May 7th, the Confederate forces were withdrawn, and then commenced the famous Dalton-Atlanta campaign.

Four miles southwest of Dalton, on the great road from Dalton to Lafayette, a little distance away from Mill Creek Gap and Snake Creek Gap, was Dug Creek Gap, a mere road cut out of the mountain side, and the steeps rising up beside the road provided splendid opportunities to resist those who might undertake to force a passage over the mountain by this narrow precipitous defile. It was not a place to deal much with artillery, but it was a spot where close range or hand-to-hand fighting alone was to settle the conflicts of the day. Oftentimes, the Confederate soldiers had marched through Dug Creek Gap, and in February, preceding Sherman's advance in May, it had been seized by an Indiana regiment, which held it until the gallant Cleburne drove it away and repossessed it for the Confederacy.

Dug Creek Gap had not been fortified and when, on May 5th, General Sherman began his famous march, it was guarded by a small number of Arkansas troops under Colonel Williamson, numbering not more than two hundred and fifty. General Sherman was constantly and cautiously pushing his way southward. He had three armies, under three skillful and experienced generals: Thomas, with sixty thousand; McPherson, with twenty-four thousand five hundred; and Schofield, with fifteen thousand five hundred. These, like the waves of the sea, were slowly but surely spreading and reaching southward along the highway to Atlanta.

Starting at Bowling Green, not more than a year before, it had gradually advanced fifty miles into the heart of Georgia, all this while pushing the Confederates before its victorious marches and incessant attacks. It, as yet, had not reached its goal, and more than one hundred thousand men had, by wounds or death, paid the penalty of its fortitude and endurance. Composed largely of men from the West, who were made of stern stuff, the rebel yell had no terror for its legions. When the rebel yell was given, there was always a response, sharp, quick, defiant, which meant, "We are not afraid, and we are ready to grapple with you in deadliest combat."

On the night of the 7th of May, Grigsby's brigade, after having been driven through Mill Creek Gap, had gone into camp. The marching, fighting and riding of the day had wearied all its troopers, now so far removed from their Kentucky abodes. As they laid down upon the soil of Georgia, tired and weary, they had visions of their homes, and were reveling through dreamland, in joyous anticipations of some day joining those they loved in the far North. War's sorrows, its deaths, its dangers, its sufferings were lost in the peace of sleep. These dreams were rudely awakened by the harsh, shrill tones of the bugle. Turning over on their hard beds on the ground, a number of them asleep on rails and brush, they essayed to believe that the call was only a fancy of weary brains and pulled their blankets more tightly about their heads. They tried to hope that the sound of the trumpet was only a delusion and not a real command to rise and ride. They rubbed their eyes and wondered why this untoward night summons.

War, relentless, cruel and pitiless, turned a deaf ear to nature's pleadings for rest for her exhausted children. Hesitation was only for a moment. The worn animals were quickly saddled, the Kentucky troopers mounted, and out through the darkness of the night they trotted, not knowing whither they were bound. Their commanders had orders that they were to defend Dug Creek Gap, eight miles away, but they kept the secret of their destination hidden in their own hearts.

McPherson, young, brave, vigorous, was leading the Federals; he was hunting for Snake Creek Gap, some miles south and west of Dug Creek. A corps of the Army of the Cumberland were covering these movements and marching forward down the railroad. Hooker was ordered to seize Dug Creek Gap, and then push south, so as to protect McPherson, who, marching west, then south, then east, was to pass through Snake Creek Gap and strike the railroad in the rear of Johnston.

The position at Dug Creek once taken would necessitate an immediate retreat from Dalton, and with this Gap in the mountains held by the Federals, Gen. Johnston's left flank would be severely exposed.

Before the break of day of the morning of the 8th, scouts of the 9th Kentucky Cavalry had told the story of McPherson's flank movement and of Hooker's advance on Dug Creek Gap. To the experienced eyes of the cavaliers of the Kentucky brigade, the large infantry forces being massed along the line left no doubt that serious work was ahead, and that Dug Creek Gap was an important point and the key to the present situation, and for its possession the Federals had begun a vigorous movement.

Across Dug Creek, at the foot of the mountain, the Kentucky cavalry had advanced north and picketed the road against the enemy. Eight hundred Kentucky cavalrymen and two hundred and fifty Arkansas infantry were to hold this now important position. It was a difficult and a dangerous task, but these men in gray felt they were able to answer the summons and hold the defile.

Later, when it was dark (full moon), Granbury's Texan footmen would come up, but in May, in Georgia, it was a long while from two o'clock in the afternoon until the shades of night should cover the sides of the mountains, and the sun would hide its face behind the western slopes of the eminences through which nature had cut the gap for the passage of man. So strategic had this position become that it was now well settled in the minds of the Confederates that it was one of the doors into Dalton, and these thousand and fifty fighting men were to hold it against four and a half times their number, composing Geary's division of Hooker's corps.

The Federal forces seemed impressed with the idea that they would take the Confederates unawares. They had not calculated the sort of stuff that made the men who held the Gap. The Federal signal corps, at the dictation of an assistant adjutant general, flagged General Sherman, "The infantry has just formed and started to attack the Gap. The artillery is in position and I hope to be able to send you word within half an hour or an hour that the Ridge is taken." General Geary admitted that he was assaulting with forty-five hundred men, four and a half to one, without counting his batteries.

The advance guard and picket line of the Kentuckians that had crossed the creek were slowly but surely driven in. They retired sullenly, and at each favorable opportunity stopped, turned and showed that they were not disposed to run away, and with fierce volleys disputed every inch of ground. The Federals had not supposed that any important force would be there to oppose their march, and when the thin line of skirmishers receded from the advancing wave of blue-coated marchers, they felt that the conflict was practically ended, and that Dug Creek was theirs. Crossing the creek and up the mountain side, the Confederate cavalry retreated, until at last they found their comrades and backers, the remainder of the brigade, awaiting the final grapple on the mountain crest. The gray line was thin, very thin, but what it lacked in numbers, it made up in grit, and now that the limit of retreat was reached, they set about the more serious business of teaching the enemy of what material the defenders were made.

The brave infantry from Arkansas and the chivalrous cavalry from Kentucky stood side by side, and no sooner had the head of the Federal column come within reach of the cavalry Enfields than a hot and incessant fire was poured in upon the advancing line. All through the day, these cavalrymen had been hard at work, but as the shadows of evening were falling, they were less prepared for the vigorous and lusty attack that was now to be made.

Up and up the mountain side came the men clad in blue; above them the weary Southrons, long without food, either for man or beast, were waiting their onslaught. The Confederates had largely the best of the position, and they improved it to the fullest. It soon dawned upon the Federals that, instead of having undertaken an easy task, they had assumed a most arduous work, and that their progress would be resisted with great skill, unyielding tenacity and dauntless persistence.

A sense of danger and strategic instinct had brought General Hardee and General Cleburne to aid, by their counsel and their presence, in the defense of this valuable position. Intently and eagerly they watched the

Kentucky cavalry and Arkansas infantry face the superior forces, but it was not their presence that made the fighting spirit of these Confederates rise to the highest plane—it was the fact that they knew they were holding a stronghold of importance and that General Johnston, over at Dalton, was expecting and believing that they would beat back the foe.

Again and again the infantry assaulted the Confederate line, but each time they were driven off with loss. When probably the struggle was more than half over, the ammunition began to grow scarce in the cartridge boxes of the Confederates; in a spirit of more dare-deviltry than intention to do any great damage to their foe, some of the Kentuckians began to hurl stones down the mountain side into the midst of the Federals. It took a few minutes to catch the import of this new style of warfare, but as the great stones began to rush down steep declivities, gathering impelling forces from every foot of descent, tearing the tops of trees and breaking limbs and cutting down saplings, the men on the hill began to take in the effectiveness of these improvised engines of war. It is true, they had no catapults, like the Romans of old, with which to fling them far down the mountain, but they had strong arms, guided by brave and fearless hearts. They caught, with soldierly impulse and sagacity, the effectiveness of this new plan of defence, and stone after stone was seized and sent crashing below, until along the whole line went up the shout, "Throw down the rocks, throw down the rocks," and a great hail of stones began to fly from the heights and sides of the eminence into and through the ranks of the ascending Federal legions.

General Geary, under whose immediate order the assault was made, in his report, said, "Hand to hand encounters took place, and stones as well as bullets became elements in the combat."

For a little while, the Federals thought that these stones were cast down by accident, that some soldier by a misstep had turned them loose. But quicker and faster and fiercer fell the stone storm, and with terror they realized that their enemies above them were turning loose these strange emissaries of death, and their souls and hearts were shadowed with a touch of panic at this new method of defending the pass, adopted by their enterprising foes.

With diminishing ammunition, but yet without decreasing courage, the fierce and unequal contest was maintained. Those who had no cartridges threw down the stones. Those who had cartridges sent bullets below to stop the advance of the brave and adventurous assailants.

In a little while, the gloom of night began to brood over the baleful scenes around Dug Creek Gap. As darkness finally set in, the stone-throwing cavalry and infantry heard the rebel yell creeping up the southern mountain side. In their rear, closer and closer, the inspiring voices sounded. They wondered from whence the gladdening sound came, and who were these assailants, from whose vigorous lungs, were speeding messages of help and cheer, and bidding them still longer defy their foes. They heard the tramp of horses, the rush of horsemen, and the cry of battle. And, in a little while, up from the mountain on the southern slope emerged Granbury's Texan Infantry. These men were born horsemen. They had all their lives ridden across the prairies of Texas, and they were at home in the saddle.

Under orders from General Cleburne and General Hardee, the infantry had been rushed forward to carry encouragement and bring succor to these valiant Kentuckians and Arkansans who, with such superb courage and unlimited patience, were defending the Gap with unfaltering vigor.

As the Texans at double-quick speeded to the scene of the conflict, at the foot of the slope they saw, in charge of the horse holders, the steeds of the cavalry, who had dismounted to go forward on the mountain height to battle. With a wild whoop, the astonished horse holders were commanded to turn their bridles loose, and upon the steeds, waiting now through the long day for their riders to come, at once sprung these sturdy, brave and resolute Texans. Mounted in the saddle once more, they felt war's delirium and seemed to catch the spirit of the chainless winds that swept across the prairies of their state, and shouting and yelling they galloped forward at a breakneck speed to the succor of their hard-pressed comrades on the mountain top.

For a little while, the dismounted cavalry could not understand the changed situation. They looked upon the animals and knew they were theirs, but they had strange riders, the saddles were filled with soldiers they had never seen before, whose names they could not call, whose regiment they could not distinguish. But the Texans had come for war and, quickly dismounting, they turned over the steeds of the Kentucky men to their rightful but tired owners, and took position in the battle line in Dug Gap to defend its now renowned and blood-stained heights. They had come to succor and to relieve these Kentucky and Arkansas soldiers, who for twenty-four hours had known neither rest nor food. They had come to tell them to go down the mountain side, and in sleep recuperate their wasted and tired energies, while they watched and defended the place now made illustrious by their valor. Granbury's Texan Brigade came ready to share all the danger of the place and hour, but the assaults were over and the victory had been won ere they had in such startling fashion appeared on the scene. In the darkness of the night, the men who so splendidly and so patiently had stood throughout the day against great odds, to save the destruction of the left flank of General Johnston's army, marched down into the plain below. They had fought a great fight with the help of their Texas allies. They had set a splendid example of noblest endurance and heroic gallantry. They had given the first notice to General Sherman that the way he was to march would be a path of blood, and that if he won, it would be at a tremendous sacrifice of his best and bravest troops, and that in facing the oft-defeated, but not dejected, Army of the Tennessee, he was to encounter men worthy of any cause and whose defense of their homes and firesides would dot the mountains and valleys of northern Georgia with many thousands of Federal graves, and if he did reach Atlanta, it would only be when his losses would equal even those his soldiers had witnessed at Shiloh, Murfreesboro, Perryville, Chickamauga and other fields upon which already fearful sacrifices had been the price of victory. It was a success that declared that the Army of the Tennessee had lost none of its courage and that in the coming seventy days more than sixty thousand Union men, in death or with wounds, should fall by the way, on the road to Atlanta.

The Kentucky brigade and the two hundred and fifty Texans had set the standard. Their comrades would accept the measure. They had outlined the manner of conflict that Sherman's army must expect. It was to be a series of battles where "Greek would meet Greek," and there would not be a single mile of the entire distance to Atlanta traversed without the copious shedding of the blood of brave and true men.

Chapter IV

GENERAL JOSEPH WHEELER'S RAID INTO
TENNESSEE, FALL OF 1863

General Joseph Wheeler's raid into Tennessee in October, 1863, has few parallels in cavalry campaigns. Removed from the excitement and delirium of war, many of its happenings appear incredible, and were it not for official reports of both sides, the account of it when read would be declared unbelievable, and deemed the result of highly wrought imaginings, or the Munchausen stories of some knight errant, whose deeds could not measure up to the creations of his ambitious fancy.

Half a century between these occurrences and their narration only increases our wonder and admiration at the exploits of these courageous horsemen, who seemed to have known neither fatigue nor fear in the pursuit and punishment of their country's foes. Viewed from either a strategic point, or considered in relation to the losses inflicted upon those who opposed them, this raid stands out in military history as one of the wonders of war, and assigns its masterful leader and its no less masterful men a very high place among the world's cavalry heroes. Hard riders, fierce fighters, insensible to fear, they hesitated at no undertaking assigned them, and they never questioned, but were glad to go where their gallant leader bade them march.

Wheeler, himself, seemed immune from death. Engaged in two hundred battles and in six hundred skirmishes or smaller conflicts, he escaped injury. Like Forrest, he led wherever he was present, and he never hesitated to charge any line or assail any force that came his way.

A partisan cavalry leader can never know fear or doubt. His chiefest hope of success is based on the surprise of his foes, and quick, reckless dash and bold onslaughts make up oftentimes for lack of numbers. A soldier, who at twenty-five years of age had risen to be a brigadier general, at twenty-six, a major general and commander of a corps, and a lieutenant general at twenty-eight, and achieved such great success and renown as General Wheeler, could neither be the product of favoritism nor the output of accidental promotion. Behind such rapid advancement, there must have been magnificent genius, coupled with the fullest improvement of every opportunity that crossed his path. He had no real failure in his career. Victory after victory came to him as if sent by a biased fate; and a calm review of his life by a just and impartial critic must force to the conclusion that he was one of the most remarkable men of the wonderful period in which he acted.

The Battle of Chickamauga, one of the fiercest of the great conflicts of the war, was marked by an unyielding courage, a sullen and intense obstinacy on both sides. That engagement again proclaimed the determination of both sides to fight out the issues which the war involved, until one or both antagonists, in the awful destruction of men and resources, should be unable to longer continue the struggle. The results, beyond the immediate relief from pressing invasion, certainly did not compensate the Confederate armies for the dreadful loss Chickamauga involved. Whether the Confederate leaders thoroughly improved the partial advantages gained will remain an open question, but the outcome imposed upon the Confederate cavalry new and greater labors, which all history will declare were met with a courage and enterprise, which added new laurels to their hitherto nobly earned fame.

With Chattanooga still in possession, and with the Tennessee River behind them, the Federal armies now were to face one of war's most dreadful foes. Hunger is a most potent general that no antagonist chieftain can ignore. Supplies for the Federal armies were to reach them either by the Tennessee River, or by the wagon trains starting from points on the railroad, operated from the territory north in Tennessee, and against these slow and tedious methods of feeding an army, the Confederate cavalry were now turned loose, to burn, scatter and destroy.

General Wheeler was given the entire command of the Southern horsemen operating in this territory. Barely twenty-seven years of age, wisely or unwisely, he was given prominence over Forrest and other cavalry leaders, who had on many fields demonstrated dazzling genius and exhibited sublime courage. Brave and patriotic as were the armies of the Tennessee Department, yet as always where human ambitions and services are involved, jealousy is bound to arise, and no sixty thousand men can be aligned under a flag for any cause, where some differences will not occur and where in leadership and assignments some animosities will not arise. Some men are born to lead and some to follow, and neither in Virginia, Tennessee, nor in the farther West were the soldiers of the Confederacy exempt from those ills that ever attend army organizations. This was somewhat intensified in the army of Tennessee, which by the summer of 1863 had developed three great cavalry leaders, Wheeler, Morgan and Forrest. General Wheeler's youth made against him in the consolidation of the cavalry by General Bragg. His real virtues were obscured by the suggestion that his almost unparalleled advance over the older men was the result of official partiality, and not the just outcome of military skill and his achievements. For a long while, this unfortunate condition hampered both Generals Forrest and Wheeler. General Bragg saw the solution of this most serious problem later and removed it so far as he could, but there are those who think he unduly delayed action in so critical a period and where transcendent opportunities were at hand. With such a leader as General Forrest, at the time of the October raid (which was led by General Wheeler), also turned upon the enemy's line of communication, it appeared to the men of that time that only one result could have come to Rosecrans' army, and that would have been practical starvation and annihilation.

These personal differences were at the most acute stage when General Wheeler was assigned a difficult and almost impossible task. It is but fair to General Wheeler to say that, under these trying circumstances, he acquitted himself with most commendable modesty and delicate tact and, except in so far as he was required by unpleasant orders, he did nothing to add to the seriousness of the complications then existing. He was to accomplish a Herculean task, one involving supreme risks to his own command and to General Bragg's entire army. The capture of General Wheeler's cavalry at that time meant calamitous results to the cause of the Confederacy,—reckless courage, untiring work and supreme daring, with quickest perception and thorough comprehension of surrounding conditions, made the call upon the young general such as had never come to a man of his age before.

The events succeeding the Battle of Chickamauga had placed upon all the cavalry, under General Bragg, demands that were wellnigh insupportable and which involved personal privations and soldierly effort, which few men could endure. Both men and beasts had felt the burden of these tremendous exactions during this brief but important period. Less than two weeks had elapsed since that great engagement, and from the horror of its closing scenes the cavalry, led by Generals

Forrest and Wheeler, had known neither rest nor release from diligent and vigilant service.

Horses, unshod and broken down, driven to the limit of endurance; men, illy fed and emaciated by the demand of those horrible hours, were allowed no season of quiet, so necessary for physical recuperation. Pity for their beasts, rendered dear to them by common sacrifice and common danger, had a depressing effect upon the minds of even those brave soldiers, now well trained to the difficulties which war brings to every brave soul.

It was under these circumstances that General Bragg called upon General Wheeler to cross the Tennessee and destroy the wagon trains, which in long white lines dotted every road north of Chattanooga and upon which, for food and ammunition, the Union forces were compelled to rely. Calling his subordinates, and explaining to them the work that General Bragg had mapped out, almost without exception they pleaded for mercy to man and beast and for a brief season of rest before such arduous and difficult tasks were assumed. Not a few declared that it was impossible to meet such demands and that to require such service, under existing circumstances, was not only unwise but inhumane.

One of General Wheeler's marked characteristics was absolute obedience to orders, and he never permitted anything short of the impossible to prevent their fulfillment. The quick answer to all these objections was a general order to his command to prepare for the raid and to cross the Tennessee River at once. In the early dawn, with less than two thousand men, he forced a passage of the river at Cottonport, thirty miles east of Chattanooga, in the face of a force twice as large as his own, and with such vigor did he press the enemy, who stood in his pathway, that he captured more than a hundred prisoners and brushed them aside from his chosen line, as the wind drives straw from its path.

Before the shades of night came on, two brigades under peremptory orders joined him. They promptly followed in the path that he had opened, and now, with three thousand eight hundred jaded horses and tired men and a limited supply of ammunition, he stood alone, defying a great army both in his rear and his front, and with a mighty river flowing between him and his supports and comrades.

No soldier heart ever faced more difficult conditions or assumed greater responsibility, and none ever met them with calmer courage or more cheerful complacence. His men measured up to the demand of their leader. In the past they had always taken care of themselves when beset by enemies and danger, and now, under the valiant leadership of General Wheeler, sustained by their indomitable will and unfailing gallantry, they believed that in the end all would be well.

If there were hesitation and doubt, these were immediately flung to the winds. There was no time to scan the darkening horizon. Gloomy enough was the outlook if they listened to fear, but fear these gallant men had never known. Some spoke of disaster, but the orders of their superior stood out before the mind, and misgivings were quickly drowned by the prospect of vigorous action. The brave man, seeing danger, braces himself to face it and with resourceful powers lays his plans to avoid it. General Wheeler's pessimistic advisers pointed out the consequences of failure and gave expression to their serious fears of the result of so hazardous and so uncertain a movement. Caution suggested to turn back while the way was open, but General Roddy, with his brigade, had crossed the river some miles below, and if all the enemy should concentrate upon him, they would annihilate his command. The cavalry leaders of the Confederacy were always faithful in the succor of their comrades, and no danger could deter them from going to the help of those who were sorely pressed. Stuart, Morgan, Forrest, Wheeler, Marmaduke, Shelby and Hampton never forgot this cardinal principle of cavalry faith; and Wheeler declared that he would not desert Roddy in this emergency because of any risk that was open before his vision, and bidding fears begone, he ordered a forward march through darkness of the night in a drenching rain. He had encountered a Federal regiment of cavalry and, pushing these aside, the appetites of his men, like tigers tasting blood, were whetted for still fiercer work. On the morning of October 2nd, hours before daylight came, he started out in search of richest prey. One hour's ride revealed the presence of thirty-two wagons and two hundred mules and horses. There was nothing General Wheeler's command needed more than horses, and those welcome additions to his mounts were to his troopers sure omen of greater victories. This capture was concluded before the full orb of day had come to cheer the victorious marchers. As the sun in glory rose over the mountain tops, from a lofty elevation, there burst upon the view of Wheeler and his followers a panorama of beauty and joy. Twelve hundred wagons, with their covers whitened as snow, spread like a gleam of silver down through the valley and across the hillsides and over the mountain ridges, were crawling along the highway, laden with supplies of the most tempting kind and weighted down with ammunition, designed to take the lives of the men in gray, brothers of Wheeler's followers, who across the Tennessee were holding in check the Federal army invading the Southland.

To many starving men, with but scant supplies in their cartridge boxes, and still scanter in their haversacks, and now already aware of the but short delayed breaking down of the steeds they were astride, this scene presented an enrapturing vision.

But this glowing perspective had in it a gruesome and darkening setting. A brigade of Federal cavalry marched in its van and another in its rear, and to make the work still more repellent, a brigade of infantry marched alongside its huge serpentine body and behind the infantry rode a third brigade of cavalry, all intent upon the safe delivery of this precious cargo to the Federal army, a few miles away, camped beside the Tennessee River.

These Confederates had come out to hunt the tiger, and it was no unreasonable or traitorous thought to fear that the conditions might be reversed and at the end, the tiger might hunt them. What Wheeler had searched for, Wheeler had found. The game was tempting if dangerous to play, and when Wheeler, in the past, had come upon the object of his search, he had never before in all his marches and campaigns let it escape without a fight. There was neither time nor occasion for arguing with fear. True, he was outnumbered two to one, but he had never before counted that too great odds to grapple, and so without even hesitation, he bade his following go in. It was a long space, and many times the Federal guard could not protect at every point—it measured at least twelve miles. Three columns simultaneously broke in upon the slender line. The teamsters, never very brave, terrified by the shout of battle and the din of rifle and pistol shots, sought safety amidst the cargoes of the wagons, or springing from the mules, ensconced themselves in the depth of the surrounding hills and mountains and, from behind stones and trees, watched the struggle for the ownership of the huge train they had believed to be safe from any onslaught. Contact with the foe had been so quick and so unsuspected that neither they nor their soldier friends had opportunity for introspection, to figure out just what was best to be done under the supreme scare that had without warning pressed upon their minds. The Federal guards were not disposed to run away without a fight. They had no time to mass and General Wheeler gave them no opportunity of combining, so as to get the fullest advantage of numbers, and in hammer and tong style both sides went at each other, by gage of battle, to determine who should have the immensely valuable train. The Confederates were a real hungry lot, and their supply of horses greatly limited. They much desired bread and steeds to ride, and the need of something with which to shoot gave vigor to their every movement. Hunger and the possible contingency of walking are a great incentive to a horseman's fighting qualities, and for two hours the contest went vigorously on. In this case the hungriest were the gamest. They had also before their minds a well-defined fear of languishing in northern prisons, in case they failed to win, and with all this flood of thoughts coursing through their minds, the men in gray fought with a desperation that presaged victory, and after two hours the Federal guards gave up the contest and retreated from the scene of struggle. With a thousand prisoners in the hands of the ragged, hungry, reckless Confederate soldiers, the whole wagon train was at their mercy. The victory won, the savage work of destruction was now at hand. War, always dreadful, was now to witness most distressful scenes. The imagination of countrymen and frightened teamsters magnified the number of wagons composing this immense train. Some said three thousand, some two thousand, but it certainly contained more than one thousand, not counting the sutlers, who, under the protection of this numerous military convoy, were seeking the front to realize large profits from hunger and want which depleted army supplies would pour into their capacious and avaricious coffers.

As General Wheeler had not much more than two men to each wagon to be destroyed, the burning of these became a gigantic task. The story of the engagement would soon be noised about. Swift-riding couriers would carry the details of the disaster and in a short while, Federal reinforcement would be at hand to punish these adventurous and daring horsemen, who in apparent disregard of both prudence and wisdom had journeyed so far from their supports and so recklessly undertaken to operate in the rear of a great army, which had two and a half times as much cavalry as those bold raiders numbered and enough infantry to watch and guard every ford across which they might undertake, in their return to their own army, to reach the south bank of the Tennessee. Needed supplies were quickly pulled from the horseless wagons, rifles and ammunition were seized from prisoners or hunted in the depths of the "Prairie Schooners," and then the torch began its baneful work. Wagons, mules and mounts for the victorious horsemen were safely corralled. Mules, now as the engines for handling supplies, had become contraband of war. The dumb, helpless creatures were ready to adopt the victors as their masters and, without raising constitutional question of the relation of the States to the Federal government, would patiently take upon themselves the tasks and hunger that the new ownership would demand. They could help the enemy, they meant loss to the Federal treasury, they looked with their innocent and inoffensive eyes into the faces of the powder-grimed captors and seemed in their docility to plead for life and toil beyond the Tennessee River, in the wagon train of the army that had risked so much in the change of their ownership. Selecting the strongest, the largest and best fed for use, the remainder were doomed to death. All things, animate and inanimate, which could help the foe must be destroyed. The supply wagons were all fired, the ammunition wagons were reserved for later action. The smoke of burning timbers, cotton covers and harness sent up a huge signal that betrayed the presence of an adventurous foe and wrote upon the very heavens that fiercest destruction was turned loose. This warning could not be stayed and so, if escape was meditated, quick work must go on. The helpless brutes were led aside, and those which were not to serve the new master were condemned to a speedy death. A rifle ball at close range was driven into the hearts of the beasts, or, held by the bridle, a sharp bowie knife was drawn across their throats. The command withdrew to a safe distance. A few chosen messengers were sent to fire the wagons containing the ammunition. A feeble, flickering flame started as the Confederate destroyers ran to each wagon and touched its inflammable tops and sides, and then, with a speed quickened by the fear of a fierce explosion, the torch bearers fled in haste from the coming dangers, inevitable from a combustible outbreak. General Rosecrans, when the huge column of smoke stood out against the sky, seeming to pierce its very battlements, promptly sent out reinforcements to help the guards who had in their custody treasures of food, more valuable to his armies than a treasury filled with gold. The Confederate horsemen stood these off until eight hours had elapsed from the time of capture. The whole earth seemed to feel the vibration of the millions of cartridges that were exploding with the fierce heat, and the bursting of thousands of shells filled the atmosphere with their hissing tongues of fire and shook the earth with their ceaseless detonations.

Ere the sun, which rose in splendor upon the mighty train, as it

70

wound its way to the relief of its friends and owners, had set behind the mountain height on its western side, the savage work of destruction was accomplished. Its defenders were scattered. Its beauty had vanished, only ashes and carcasses told the story of its greatness and its destruction, and darkness closed in about the weird surroundings, and the fateful events of the day were ended; and Wheeler and his men, happy in victory, well supplied, and with a new crown of laurels, in the stillness of the night rode away in search of other and new adventures and in quest of more glory and increasing fame.

Chapter V

GENERAL JOHN H. MORGAN'S RAID INTO
KENTUCKY, JULY 4-28, 1862

At Huntsville, Alabama, John H. Morgan was born on the 28th of June, 1825. He was descended from Virginia ancestry, his father having moved from Virginia to Alabama in early manhood. His father married a daughter of John W. Hunt, of Lexington, Kentucky, a man of wealth and high standing. The father moved to Kentucky in 1829 and purchased a farm close to Lexington. At that time his son, John H., was four years of age. The young Morgan grew up proud spirited, brave, manly, enjoying and rejoicing in the best things of life. He became a very companionable man. He distributed kindness wherever he went, and none ever came to him in need and went away empty handed. He was extremely generous in his judgment of men and sincere in all his friendships. In military dress, he was among the handsomest of men, six feet tall, weighing about one hundred and eighty-five pounds, erect, handsome, graceful. In uniform he attracted attention wherever he went. He was a lieutenant in a Kentucky cavalry regiment in the Mexican war.

In 1857 John H. Morgan organized a militia company in Lexington called the "Lexington Rifles." Later, they became a part of the Kentucky State Guard. This company was thoroughly drilled and comprised many of the best young men of the State. Its uniform was handsome and striking.

It was not until near the end of September, 1861, that General Morgan undertook service in the armies of the Confederacy. He would have been earlier in the conflict but for the serious illness of his wife, who died in the summer of 1861. The authorities suspected the loyalty of the State Guard and an order had been issued for its disarmament. This was resented by many of the companies and led a majority of its men of military tastes to take sides with the South. After concealing the guns of the Lexington Rifles, early in the evening of September 21st, General Morgan left Lexington with two-thirds of his company, and passing through Anderson County, camped at Lawrenceburg, twenty-

72

two miles away. John Crepps Wickliffe, later lieutenant colonel of the 9th Kentucky Infantry, also had a company of State Guards, and these resolved to take service in the Confederate army. Wickliffe had captured a few Home Guards in Nelson County, and this put him in conflict with the Federal authorities. He united his men with those of Morgan and together they numbered three hundred. The interference with the Home Guards rendered further stay in Kentucky dangerous. After two days' hard marching, this force came to Green River, which was then the dividing line between the Federal and Confederate forces, and here the newcomers were enthusiastically welcomed. Captain Wickliffe attached his company to the 9th Kentucky infantry, then being organized by Colonel Hunt. Half of Morgan's infantry had come out mounted. The remainder managed to find mounts, and there were numerous horsemen scattered around the Confederate camps who quickly took service with Morgan. In order to employ his men and to give them experience and steadiness, he used them as scouts, sometimes, on such expeditions, reaching fifty miles into territory occupied by the Federals. During the winter two other companies came to Morgan, under command of Captain Thomas Allen of Shelbyville and James W. Bowles of Louisville. These made Morgan's original squadron, which by the daring and genius of its commander quickly won fame and renown.

In 1859 a railroad was completed from Louisville, Kentucky, to Nashville, Tennessee, a distance of one hundred and eighty-six miles. Its chartered name was the Louisville & Nashville Railroad. All the streams in Kentucky run northward into the Ohio River. The Louisville & Nashville passed southwestwardly, and in pulling away from the Ohio, of necessity it ran perpendicular to the course of the streams, all of which entered the Ohio or were tributaries of streams that did. Salt River, Rolling Fork, Green River, Nolin, Barren, Cumberland and numerous smaller streams all traversed the pathway of this railroad. The topography of the country through which the Louisville & Nashville Railroad was constructed naturally demanded many bridges and trestles of great length. Few railroads were ever built that offered better facilities for destruction by cavalry raids.

A man of General Morgan's boldness, intense activity and prevalent courage could not long remain idle. The enemy in front of him were the people he had come to fight. All who wore blue were his foes. To destroy lines of communication and harass and kill these men was the purpose for which Morgan had enlisted, and he was never idle when he could get permission to assail and punish them.

In December, 1861, when he was a captain, he won reputation by the destruction of the bridge over Bacon's Creek, twenty miles south of Elizabethtown. At that time the immediate command of the Confederate troops on the south side of Green River was held by General Thomas C. Hindman. He and Morgan were kindred spirits and he aided the cavalryman in many ways in these incursions. General Morgan was overjoyed when he received permission from General Hindman to undertake the destruction of the bridge over Bacon's Creek. In this enterprise, he was compelled to march for fifty miles in a country well garrisoned by Federal soldiers. His squadron at that time numbered two hundred. Apprehending serious work, he took all his men with him who had mounts that would pass inspection. Nobody could tell what moment Morgan would be compelled to fight, and he aligned every available man. The Confederate forces, by this time, were south of Barren River and it was thirty miles from the Barren to the Green River. Morgan camped the first night a few miles away from Green River, and concentrated his forces in a forest on the top of a hill. He waited until night to resume his march. He crossed the river just above Woodsonville, in Hart County, and riding until midnight reached Bacon's Creek and was glad to find that there were no guards. His followers at that time were not as experienced in the destruction of bridges as they became later, but after kindling the fires and doing all in their power to aid its destructive agencies, in three hours the bridge crumbled into ruins and its burning timbers told the story of his success. The results from a military standpoint were not great. It delayed the advance of the Federals a few days, but to Morgan and his men it was a great object lesson. They now began to realize how easy it was by these long marches to do immense damage to the means of transportation on which the Federals relied to supply their forces, now slowly but surely making their way southward.

On the 20th of January, 1862, General Morgan undertook a still more perilous task. With five men he left Bell's Tavern in Barren County, found a ferry where he could cross the Green River, and rode into Lebanon, sixty miles distant, with this small force. Several hundred Federal troops were encamped near Lebanon and there were many blue-coated stragglers in town. Morgan rode furiously up and down through the streets, destroyed supplies and paroled a number of prisoners. Far within the Federal lines, it became necessary for him to resort to strategy. He took from the Federal prisoners their blue overcoats, and he and his soldiers donned these and this enabled him to pass where, if his identity had been known, he would have been captured or killed. Unwilling to return empty-handed after this hazardous journey, he decided to bring with him five prisoners. Mounting them on horses, he added to his trophies some flags. He made a vigorous forced march. This was his only hope of escape from the dangerous situation into which he had fearlessly come.

Pursued by two companies of cavalry he brought his prisoners and trophies to the banks of the Green River and crossed it and turned the ferryboat loose, as the Federals arrived on the opposite shore. These two expeditions, so successful and accomplished under the most difficult surroundings, not only tried the mettle and the courage of Morgan's followers, but gave their leader a wide reputation for daring. Morgan thus early acquired a taste for such work, which he afterwards carried out on a much larger scale, and with such success, which in a little while would mark him as a great partisan leader.

Between the Green River and the Nolin River, or Creek, was twenty-one miles. Morgan and his scouts had become thoroughly familiar with every foot of ground, and frequent dashes were made by them into this territory. There is nothing can create so much enthusiasm in a soldier as activity and success. The entire command became confident and courageous in such undertakings, and were impatient for their constant repetition.

General Albert Sidney Johnston evacuated Bowling Green on the 14th of February, 1862, and on the 16th of February, Fort Donelson was captured and fifteen thousand Confederate soldiers and a large amount of supplies were surrendered to General Grant. A few days later Nashville, Tennessee, was evacuated. This transferred the operations of the Confederates south and east of Nashville. From the ruins of Fort Donelson, General Nathan Bedford Forrest had brought out his command, and the Confederate cavalry, under Forrest and Morgan, became a part of the garrison at Nashville, immediately preceding its evacuation. When Nashville fell the Confederates moved back to Corinth, Mississippi, and from thence General Johnston advanced against General Grant and on the 6th of April, 1862, fought the Battle of Shiloh. At the termination of this struggle such a ratio of mortality was exhibited as the world had never before seen. At Shiloh two hundred and eighty men in every thousand were struck, and twenty-four thousand dead and wounded was the dreadful echo which came from this scene of havoc, to tell the world the earnestness of the purpose which moved and led the men who had entered into the Civil War.

Change of locality brought no cessation of activity to Morgan and his men. Two days before the Battle of Shiloh he was commissioned a colonel and given authority, which was to him far more pleasing than rank,—to act independently. He had now attained his chiefest ambition. He had a squadron of brave, chivalrous, dashing young men who would follow wherever he led the way and go wherever he told them to go, and he could use them where in his own judgment he could do the most damage to the enemies of the Southland. In the Battle of Shiloh General John C. Breckinridge, so wonderfully beloved by Kentuckians, commanded a division. To this division Morgan's squadron was now attached. In this battle there was little for the cavalry to do, but they performed every service bravely and cheerfully. Morgan's losses were slight.

A little while after Shiloh, Morgan received permission to make an expedition into Tennessee. His force had increased to three hundred and twenty-five men; marching with a swiftness that his enemy had not time to calculate, he captured Pulaski, Tennessee, and took four hundred prisoners. Later he made an effort to capture the city of Murfreesboro. Here he met reverses and it required some time for him and his men to recover from the shock of this defeat. Later he made a raid through Tennessee, reaching as far north as Cave City, Kentucky. Early in the spring, Captain John B. Castleman of Lexington brought a company of eighty men, and in May, 1862, two cavalry companies, commanded by Captains Gano and Huffman, came to Morgan. With intense joy he saw his command now increased to five hundred men.

Prior to June, 1862, no really striking cavalry raid had been made. Small forces had succeeded in limited forays, but they had accomplished very little, and the panic produced by the appearance of such squadrons was mild compared with what such expeditions would later develop.

On the 13th of June, 1862, Stuart had ridden around McClellan's Army, making what was known as the Chickahominy Raid. Before Morgan had heard of this he had secured data for making an expedition into Kentucky, which in the length of march, in the terrorizing of the enemy and in the destruction of property was to be one of the famous cavalry expeditions of the war. A partisan ranger regiment from Georgia, under Colonel A.

A. Hunt, had been assigned to Morgan's command, and he now had, all told, eight hundred and sixty-seven men. A few more than half of this force were Kentuckians. Hope beat high in the bosom of the Kentucky contingent when, on the 4th of July, 1862, they rode out of Knoxville, Tennessee, and took the highway for Sparta, one hundred miles northwest. The portion of Tennessee then compassed by the command was not in sympathy with the Confederacy. It was mountainous, sparsely settled and full of bushwhackers, who improved their skill as marksmen by firing from behind rocks and trees into Morgan's followers. On the 7th of July they encamped a few miles from Livingston, Tennessee, and by the middle of the day following, the Cumberland River was forded near the village of Selina. Tompkinsville, the county seat of Monroe County, Kentucky, was only eighteen miles distant and here was a portion of a battalion of the 9th Pennsylvania Cavalry. Morgan thought this would prove easy of capture. His presence was unsuspected by the enemy. Sending forward his scouts to investigate, he held his troops on the banks of the Cumberland until darkness came. This gave his men a few hours' rest and at midnight he resumed the march. He calculated that he could make three miles an hour over the roads, which were extremely rough. A short distance from Tompkinsville, Morgan detailed Gano's company and a company of Mississippi rangers, under Captain Harris, to take the road to the right and get in the rear of the enemy on the main road which led from Glasgow to Tompkinsville. Just after daybreak he found his enemies. They had intimation of his approach and had made preparations to give him a warm reception. A few volleys were fired, and the 2nd Kentucky regiment, dismounted, assaulted the enemy's position. In a little while it was all over. Twenty of the enemy were killed and thirty wounded. Some prisoners were taken, but Gano and Harris were in the rear and put themselves across the pathway of the fugitives and Major Jordan, Commandant, and a portion of his command were made captives. Curiously, only one Confederate was wounded. Colonel Hunt, commanding the Georgia regiment, was shot in the leg and the bone shattered. He was left behind and died in a few days. Wagons, arms, munitions of war, the very things Morgan wanted, were found in abundance. As General Morgan set out with two hundred unarmed men, this was a great windfall. Saddles and cavalry equipments were found for many of those who were in want of these essentials.

It took some hours to destroy the property, parole the prisoners, and at three o'clock in the afternoon General Morgan set out for Glasgow. At one o'clock at night he reached that city. These night marches were hard on his men, but they mystified and terrorized the enemy. The roughness of the road reduced the speed to three miles an hour. Captain Bowles' company, of the 2nd Kentucky, had been largely recruited at Glasgow. This made a glad and happy reunion between a portion of the command and their friends. Marching ten miles to Bear Wallow, General Morgan rested until his telegraph operator, George A. Ellsworth, could ride to the Louisville & Nashville railroad near Cave City and attach his pocket instrument to the wires and get the necessary information as to the disposition of the Federal forces in front. Heavy storms of rain beat down, and the men as well as the mounts were drenched to the skin. Riding all night, by eleven o'clock next morning the command camped within fifteen miles of Lebanon. For military purposes a railroad had been constructed to Lebanon from the main line of the Louisville & Nashville at Lebanon Junction. Detachments were sent out to destroy bridges along this line. This delayed the march a little while, but at ten o'clock in the night Morgan surrounded Lebanon, and of the garrison, two hundred surrendered. The forces sent out to burn the bridges between Lebanon and Lebanon Junction had no easy sailing. They stopped a train bearing a large number of soldiers which had been sent to the relief of Lebanon, and this brought on a battle, in which nobody on either side was seriously hurt. At Lebanon great treasures were found. Hundreds of Enfield rifles had been stored there, and buildings filled with cartridges and ammunition of all kinds which had been stored away. The two little brass pieces that had received such rough usage over the narrow and uneven roads, in order to keep pace with the cavalry, were supplied with all the ammunition they could need. The hungry were fed and the badly clothed received unlimited supplies and the tired horses, which had now marched something like two hundred miles, were replaced, where necessary, with fresh steeds belonging to the United States Government.

Colonel Morgan issued a stirring proclamation calling upon the young men of Kentucky to rally to his standard. These were sent forward by scouts and placed where they thought they would do the most good. Reaching up to Springfield, ten miles away, another march in darkness was determined upon, and after tramping all night, at nine o'clock on Sunday morning Morgan appeared in Harrodsburg. It made but little difference to these men following Morgan if night was turned into day.

The moon and stars were bright enough for their guidance and the well-graded and smoothly-packed turnpikes made plain the paths they were to follow and gave their horses, which had suffered so severely on the rocky, mountain roads, some rest after the harassing experiences of the five days before. Here was plenty of southern sentiment and southern sympathy. A number of Morgan's men had come from Harrodsburg, and the people were glad to see a Confederate force. No time could be allowed for reunions with loved ones. Marching part of the night, the command reached Lawrenceburg, where it was necessary to gather more information. Three hundred and twenty miles had now been put behind these adventurous horsemen. It was eight days since they left Knoxville. They had averaged forty miles a day. Ordinarily this terrific strain would have affected the men seriously, but the pleasure and delight of home-coming to the Kentuckians and the excitement of those who had never been in the State kept all the men as fresh and bright as the day, when, with quickened pulses, they rode out of Knoxville. Stables along the line supplied some mounts, and the Federal Government had supplied more. Captures had given arms and ammunition, a few recruits had come in, and full of hope and full of courage, there were now nine hundred soldiers; and there was no nine hundred men on the other side that could have stopped the victorious advance of this daring column. The three and a half weeks allowed for this journey was so brief that extended sleep was not considered, and at the dawn of day, the next morning, stock had been fed and breakfast cooked and the column was in line on the road from Lawrenceburg to Versailles. Four miles from Lawrenceburg was the Kentucky River. At the ferry where the turnpike crossed it was not fordable. The ferryboat had been sunk; the men quickly raised and repaired it. The whole country was thoroughly demoralized and frightened by reports of the number of men Morgan had with him, and the sending out of detachments in many directions had multiplied in the Federal minds many times the number of his command. Kentucky was full, at the time, of Home Guards, citizens who had been armed for the purpose of intimidating the southern sympathizers. These Home Guards made haste to seek safety and refuge in cities like Frankfort and Lexington. Every town was looking out for itself. The country people would make no opposition, for the larger portion of them were sympathizers, and so Colonel Morgan gave his men a good rest at Versailles until ten o'clock the next day.

Eight miles from Versailles was the town of Midway, the halfway point between Lexington and Frankfort, through which a railroad had long been operated. This railway was used to run trains from Lexington to Louisville, through Frankfort, a distance of eighty-three miles, to carry soldiers to impede Morgan's march. The authorities at Frankfort and Lexington did not know exactly where Morgan was and so the advance guard rapidly entering Midway, captured the telegraph operator. No cavalry commander ever had a more skillful telegraphist than George A. Ellsworth, and he was a most important factor in Morgan's success on these expeditions. He thus tells the story of his operations at this place:

"At this place I surprised the operator, who was quietly sitting on the platform in front of his office, enjoying himself hugely. Little did he suspect that the much-dreaded Morgan was in his vicinity. I demanded of him to call Lexington and inquire the time of day, which he did. This I did for the purpose of getting his style of handling the 'key' in writing dispatches. My first impression of his style, from noting the paper in the instrument, was confirmed. He was, to use a telegraphic term, a 'plug' operator. I adopted his style of telegraphing and commenced operations. In this office I found a signal book, which proved very useful. It contained the calls of all the offices. Despatch after despatch was going to and from Lexington, Georgetown, Paris and Frankfort, all containing something in reference to Morgan. On commencing operations, I discovered that there were two wires on the line along this railroad. One was what we term a 'through wire,' running direct from Lexington to Frankfort, and not entering any of the way offices. I found that all military messages were sent over that line. As it did not enter Midway office, I ordered it to be cut, thus forcing Lexington onto the wire that ran through the office. I tested the line and found, by applying the ground wire, it made no difference in the circuit; and, as Lexington was headquarters, I cut Frankfort off. Midway was called, I answered, and received the following:

"'Lexington, July 15th, 1862.

"'To J. W. Woolums, Operator, Midway:

"'Will there be any danger in coming to Midway? Is everything right?

"'Taylor—Conductor.'

"I inquired of my prisoner (the operator) if he knew a man by the name of Taylor. He said Taylor was the conductor. I immediately gave Taylor the following reply:

"'Midway, July 15th, 1862.

"'To Taylor, Lexington:

"'All right; come on. No sign of any rebels here.

"'Woolums.'

"The operator in Cincinnati then called Frankfort. I answered and received about a dozen unimportant dispatches. He had no sooner finished than Lexington called Frankfort. Again I answered and received the following message:

"'Lexington, July 15th, 1862.

"'To General Finnell, Frankfort:

"'I wish you to move the forces to Frankfort, on the line of the Lexington railroad, immediately, and have the cars follow and take them up as soon as possible. Further orders will await them at Midway. I will, in three or four hours, move forward on the Georgetown pike; will have most of my men mounted. Morgan left Versailles this morning with eight hundred and fifty men, moving in the direction of Georgetown.

"'Brigadier-General Ward.'

"This being our position and intention exactly, it was thought proper to throw General Ward on some other track. So, in the course of half an hour, I manufactured and sent the following dispatch, which was approved by General Morgan:

"'Midway, July 15th, 1862.

"'Morgan, with upward of one thousand men, came within a mile of here, and took the old Franklin road, marching, we suppose, for Frankfort. This is reliable.

"'Woolums—Operator.'

"In about ten minutes Lexington again called Frankfort, when I received the following:

"'Lexington, July 15th, 1862.

"'To General Finnell, Frankfort:

"'Morgan, with more than one thousand men, came within a mile of here, and took the old Frankfort road. This dispatch received from Midway, and is reliable. The regiment from Frankfort had better be recalled.

"'Brigadier-General Ward.'

"I receipted for this message, and again manufactured a message to confirm the information General Ward received from Midway, and not knowing the tariff from Frankfort to Lexington, I could not send a formal message; so, appearing greatly agitated, I waited until the circuit was occupied, and broke in, telling them to wait a minute, and commenced calling Lexington. He answered with as much gusto as I called him. I telegraphed as follows:

"'Frankfort to Lexington:

"'Tell General Ward our pickets are just driven in. Great excitement. Pickets say force of enemy must be two thousand.

"'Operator.'

"It was now 2 p. m., and as Colonel Morgan wished to be off for Georgetown, I ran a secret ground connection, and opened the circuit on the Lexington end. This was to leave the impression that the Frankfort operator was skedaddling, or that Morgan's men had destroyed the telegraph."

General Morgan was the only cavalry commander who extensively or successfully used the telegraph to learn the plans and position of his enemies and to thwart their arrangements for disturbance of his progress, or to place troops in his front. The country through which he operated did much to aid him in this respect, but it was also due in great part to the marvellous skill of his operator, George A. Ellsworth. The story of how he misled his foes, and deceived them as to his intentions and line of march, is not only one of the most amusing but one of the most surprising of the war's happenings. He passed through four years of war, followed telegraphy and died in Texas about 1910.

The Federals were so thoroughly alarmed that they were unwilling to risk engines and cars and men on the road. Reports of atrocities and barbarities of Morgan's command were circulated through the country. They were called murderers and thieves and assassins and horse thieves. Bad names did not worry Morgan's followers. They cared little what they were called if they could harass their foes. They settled down to a feeling of pride that they had been able to excite in the minds and hearts of the enemy such bitter and malignant hate. Neither Morgan's nor Forrest's command were much troubled over Federal abuse. They knew that if their foes cussed them, their foes must have suffered to arouse such maledictions, and they rode on and fought on, oblivious of what reports were circulated about their doings. Those who did not have southern sympathies escaped hurriedly from the contemplated line of march and hastened to Lexington and Frankfort for protection. Having obtained all the information that was necessary, at sundown Morgan appeared at Georgetown, the county seat of Scott County, twelve miles from Midway.

With Lexington demoralized and Frankfort terrorized and with the Federal commanders at both places afraid that Morgan was going to attack them, he sat down at Georgetown to have a really good rest. A detachment had been left at Midway to delay operations between Lexington and Frankfort, and Captain John B. Castleman of Company D was sent to destroy the bridges between Lexington and Paris on the Kentucky Central Railroad. Captain Castleman did thorough work. He was ordered to proceed up and down the railroad, tear up the track, and burn the bridges. The country outside of the cities was now completely dominated by Morgan. Lexington and Frankfort were too fully garrisoned to justify their assault. Captain Castleman, after fully carrying out his orders, marched to Winchester. These were ready heroes when the highest daring was demanded, and the young men who served under Morgan were equal to any emergency. On reaching Winchester, after the destruction of the Kentucky Central Railroad, Captain Castleman would pass near the home of his parents. He had secretly entered Lexington in disguise and obtained full information as to the numbers and position of the enemy. Safely performing this hazardous work, he rejoined his command.

On the way to Winchester he ran afoul of the advance guard of Metcalf's brigade. Without a moment's hesitation he ordered his eighty men to charge the three thousand Federals. The boldness and fierceness of this assault demoralized the enemy. They judged that no sagacious leader with such odds against him would undertake such reckless work, and they receded before the assault, leaving their dead and wounded behind. The valiant young captain, not satisfied with the morning's experience, returned to Horeb Presbyterian Church, a few miles away. Here his family had worshipped for many years. Behind the structure his command were hidden when a company of Federal cavalry came down a cross road. These also outnumbered the company which had, with such reckless valor, dispersed their comrades a few hours before. With the recollection of their previous splendid success, they did not hesitate to assault this new column. Waving their hats and filling the air with the rebel yell, they rode at the advancing foe. Visions of Morgan's entire regiment flashed before their surprised minds, and not waiting for the moment of impact, they turned and rode away, leaving as testimonials of the fierce courage of the Confederate assailants a number of dead and wounded.

With these thrilling experiences attesting the intrepidity of his boys, a large proportion of whom were born and reared in the neighborhood, the youthful commander withdrew his company and pushed on to Winchester, where later Colonel Morgan found him awaiting his arrival.

Morgan was now alone in the face of his foes. He could depend upon no aid from his fellows. Insofar as help was concerned, he had "burned the bridges" behind him. There were none upon whom he could fall back. He was as far from all supports as it would be from Richmond to New York. The supreme audacity of such a campaign had never been known before. In no country, in no war, had any leader ever undertaken such a hazard or invited such peril. There were Federal troops three hundred miles south of him and thousands around him. The way he had come was lined with Federal garrisons, and urgent calls were made for Federals to face him and equally as urgent for those behind him to prevent his escape and crush the little company he had brought with him so far into the Federal lines. He was smashing all military precedents. The books written for the guidance of soldiers contained nothing like the history this bold rider was making, and there was, in all military annals, no parallel to what he had now accomplished. This new soldier Daniel had come to judgment, and there were none who could fathom or interpret his decrees. Later, others would rise up to emulate him in the pathway he had blazed. He was the pioneer, and the first cavalryman who had undertaken such marvellous marches, or defied the formulas and maxims that military authors had written for the guidance of those who went to war. Sage generals decreed him reckless, rash, heedless and prophesied destruction, capture, failure. They reread the books generals read and in all these there was nothing, they said, for this knight errant, but sure and certain disaster. But Morgan's great mind had taken in all the chances he must face. He knew the country and the people whither he had come. He knew the courage and almost superhuman endurance of the youths who rode behind him, and so he bade defiance to axioms and precedents and pushed on where his genius and daring told him he would win victory and discomfit his foes, make new records for his horsemen, show others the effects of bold, dashing movement, and give to cavalry a power and efficacy of which the soldiery of the world had not hitherto written or prophesied.

With Federal forces about in every direction, in Frankfort, Lexington, Falmouth, Danville, Winchester, Cynthiana, it looked as if escape was well-nigh impossible. Morgan had now fully carried out his plans and so he turned his eyes toward Cynthiana, the county seat of Harrison County.

It was twenty-two miles distant from Georgetown over a beautifully-graded macadam road. It was sixty-six miles from Cincinnati, and if Morgan could reach Cynthiana and capture it, this would still further disquiet and disturb Lexington and alarm the people of Cincinnati.

A force was sent to drive in the pickets at Lexington. This was promptly done, and the outposts went scurrying back to proclaim the near approach of these desperadoes, and while Lexington was vigorously defending itself from a present foe, Morgan was marching on Cynthiana.

The Federal authorities at Nashville, three hundred miles away, were frantic with fear, and Cincinnati was in the throes of chaos and fright. General J. T. Boyle was then in command of Kentucky with headquarters at Louisville, and he kept the wires burning, telling the story of Morgan's performances. On the 10th of July he wired General Buell: "The rebels under Starnes, over two thousand, with three pieces of artillery, crossed from Sparta, Tennessee, into Kentucky, cut to pieces Major Jordan at Tompkinsville, and are moving on Glasgow." General Buell, calmer, tried to allay the fears, and so he wired General Boyle: "Force of the enemy doubtless greatly exaggerated. A regiment of your cavalry, properly managed, will force him to cross the Cumberland or destroy him." General Buell at this time did not seem to be acquainted with Morgan's ways of doing things. By the 12th of July the situation appeared much more serious to General Boyle and so he wired General Buell: "Morgan has fifteen hundred men. His force is increasing. All the rebels in the State will join him if there is not a demonstration of force and power sent in cavalry. The State will be desolated unless this matter is attended to. The city is so endangered that I am bound to keep force here. Send me cavalry and other reinforcements. I know more of Kentucky than you can possibly know, and unless it is proposed to abandon Kentucky, I must have the force." On the 15th of July he telegraphed General Buell: "The secessionists have lied for Morgan and magnified his forces. He has divided them up and is burning bridges on the Central Railroad between Paris and Lexington. Only the low and evil will join him." On the 12th of July he telegraphed: "The whole State will be in arms if General Buell does not send me force to put it down. Morgan is devastating with fire and sword." On the 13th of July Mr. Lincoln telegraphed General Halleck at Corinth, Mississippi: "They are having a stampede in Kentucky. Please look to it. A. Lincoln." On the 13th of July Mr. Lincoln telegraphed General Boyle: "I have telegraphed him (Halleck) that you are in trouble." On July 15th Richard Smith, at Cincinnati, telegraphed: "Danger of serious trouble here, external if not internal. Men enough for emergencies but no arms, no head. Military commander should be appointed for this post. Press this upon Stanton at once." On the 19th of July General Boyle telegraphed: "The boldness of Morgan's raid gives reason to believe that he has been reinforced and that they will fall upon Kentucky in her helpless condition." The mayor of Cincinnati telegraphed that he had called a public meeting. He wired on July 18th: "Cynthiana surrounded at 5:30 p. m. Boyd Station, this side of Cynthiana, expects to be attacked any moment. Morgan reported to have twenty-five hundred men. We have no organized forces here." On the 19th of July General Boyle, still more excited, wired the Secretary of War: "There is a concerted plan between the traitors at home and the rebels in arms. Morgan's force has increased. It is estimated at from twenty-five hundred to three thousand. I do not believe it is so large. Every species of falsehood is being circulated by the traitors at home, producing consternation among the people to get the people to rise. Morgan proclaims Breckinridge is coming with thirty thousand men. Traitors throughout the State circulate it." On July 24th Buell telegraphed General Boyle: "I approve of punishing the guilty, but it would not answer to announce the rule of 'no quarter' even for guerrillas. Neither will it be judicious to levy contributions on secessionists for opinions alone.... I approve of your preventing any avowed secessionist from being run for office," and then so as not to show disregard of the military situation, with a touch of sarcasm, General Buell telegraphed the same day: "Is it true your troops surrendered to Morgan at Cynthiana?"

It was impossible for any command with the limited number of men composing General Morgan's diminutive brigade to maintain itself much longer, surrounded as it was, not only by garrisons but pursuing forces on every side, and from Nashville, Munfordsville and Bowling Green, troops might be sent to cut off his escape through Southwestern Kentucky. These home-comers would have been glad to have pitched their tents around the Bluegrass and remained there forever, but dangers rose thick, fast, plenteous on every side and the question of escape now began to loom up as the greatest problem of the hour. As if to defy fate and to show his enemies the extent to which he could go, General Morgan determined to capture Cynthiana, thirty-two miles north from Lexington and twice that distance from Cincinnati. When he should once reach Cynthiana,

86

if the game became too strong for him to return along the direction through which he had come, he might go around by Pound Gap, or up along the Big Sandy and reach Virginia, and then march down to the place from whence he had started. Several hundred men under Colonel Landram of the 7th Kentucky cavalry and a number of Home Guards were defending Cynthiana. The Confederate commander was anxious to give the Federals once more a touch of his skillful and avenging hand and let them feel once again the impress of his power and he rapidly marched to Cynthiana. The guards of the town had a twelve pound brass howitzer. This had been sent out from Cincinnati in charge of a company of firemen. Morgan thoroughly understood the topography of Cynthiana. The Federal pickets were attacked a mile and a half from the town and an advance guard chased them to the edge of the city.

To get into Cynthiana, troops would have to cross the Licking River. An old-time, narrow, covered wooden bridge led over the stream, but by its side there was a ford waist-deep. Above and below, one mile each way, there were fords. Gano's battalion was sent up and the Georgian regiment down, with the command to attack the town from the directions along which they were ordered to move. The 2nd Kentucky, deemed the steadiest of those with Morgan, was to enter the town by the Georgetown road. The Federals had, with great skill, placed their men on the opposite bank of the river, and no sooner had the regiment come in sight than they opened a brisk fire. One thousand feet from the bridge the little Confederate howitzers were placed and they opened their fire upon the houses which had been occupied by the enemy. The Federals' one piece of artillery had been fixed to sweep the bridge. Two companies marching up the banks of the river opened such fierce fire across the stream that the Federal troops at that point were glad to throw down their guns, and it was one of the curious episodes of war that their captors made them wade across the river to complete surrender. As the space through the bridge was in the line of the Federal guns and the approach protected by sharpshooters, it became apparent that to proceed in that direction would entail a large loss, so without further ado Company A of the 2nd Kentucky, raising their guns and ammunition above their heads, waded the stream and established themselves behind houses on the opposite side and poured in heavy volleys upon the Federal column. The "bull pups" were brought forward, but as the lines were then not more than one hundred and twenty-five feet apart, the fire from the sharpshooters was so fierce that it drove the gunners from the pieces. The bullets of the Federals, striking the horses, attached to one of the limbers, they ran away carrying it within the Federal lines. A game so tense could not last long, and Company C, of which Captain James W. Bowles, ever valiant—and at that moment thought reckless—was in command, charged across the bridge and up the main street. However reckless the movement, it turned the scale for the Confederates.

In a few moments the Federals were driven from their positions and forced back to the center of the town. The Texans under Gano and the Georgians under their lieutenant colonel now began to make themselves felt, and all three assailing parties met at the same moment around the piece of artillery which the enemy had fired with such rapidity and with great effect, and all three claimed the honor of its taking. The stream was passed, the Federals routed. The attack upon the depot in which the Federals had taken refuge was effective, and Colonel Landram, who was commander of the garrison, was chased ten miles on the Paris road.

Before the victory was won the new recruits, picking up guns which had been thrown down by the Federals, inspired by the courage of the veterans, rapidly rushed to the front and received their baptism of fire. Company A, which with such gallantry had waded the river to get at the enemy's head, suffered great loss. The captain, first lieutenant and second lieutenant had been wounded and the command of the company fell to the third lieutenant.

The day was filled with stirring incidents. The march of twenty-two miles from Georgetown had been made to Cynthiana, and the first act had been closed by its capture before noon. Morgan had wounded and killed one hundred of his enemy; he had lost forty, killed and wounded, and had captured four hundred prisoners. With sorrow and grief he left a portion of the severely wounded behind, and the dead were abandoned and remained in the hands of kind and sympathizing friends, to be laid away in the cemetery on the hill.

If it had been difficult to get so far into Kentucky, the danger of getting out was hourly increasing. By two o'clock the march was begun for Paris, and Morgan turned his face Dixie-ward. It was fourteen miles from Cynthiana to Paris. A long way out from Paris, a deputation from the town met General Morgan, offering to surrender the place. As the sun went down, the command went into camp a short distance east of Paris. The day had been a vigorous one. Twenty-two miles to Cynthiana, a fight, captures, destruction of property, fourteen miles to Paris, was not a bad day's work, and in the beautiful Bluegrass woods, with an abundance of food for man and beast, the hours of the night were passed. The bold riders had earned sleep and no fears of the morrow disturbed their tranquility. They had learned to let each day's trouble care for itself. If they were not sleeping the sleep of the just, they were enjoying the repose of the worn and weary.

Early in the morning a large Federal cavalry force, estimated at three thousand, commanded by General Green Clay Smith, drove in Morgan's pickets. These were not very hungry for Confederate work, and they did not push the fighting. The prisoners had been paroled, but a long line of buggies and carriages were sandwiched in between the commands composing Morgan's following, bearing away the wounded who had met their fate at Glasgow, Cynthiana and other points along the line. There was a sort of brotherhood oath among Morgan's men that the wounded would never be left, and it was only under extreme circumstances that this obligation was voided. The failure to find the usual number of wounded after a battle encouraged the belief that Morgan had taken the lives of his wounded to prevent their being made prisoners. If the Confederates could keep the Federals behind, there was not much danger. Morgan's force had been camped on the Winchester road, and this was the way he intended to take on his march southward.

Well out on the Winchester Pike, Morgan waited for General Smith's force, two and a half times as numerous as his own. The Confederate commander had no fear of those who should follow. He doubted not that he could outride any pursuers. His chief concern was about those who should get in front, not those who might come from the rear. From Paris to Winchester was sixteen miles, and though he was occasionally attacked by General Smith, he proceeded leisurely along the macadam highway between the two places, and rested his men at Winchester from twelve to four o'clock in the afternoon. A twelve hour march, including the night, brought Morgan to Richmond. He here found awaiting him a complete company of new recruits under Captain Jennings. Half a day's rest at Richmond and another night march brought the Confederates to Crab Orchard.

Morgan had intended to remain for some time at Richmond and recruit as large a number of new soldiers as possible, but Smith was behind him, other detachments were converging toward his path, and the Federal colonel, Frank Woodford, was collecting forces to intercept his march southward and troops were being rushed by rail to Lebanon. Notwithstanding all this, General Morgan exhibited neither fear nor haste. He preserved the dignities of a complacent withdrawal from scenes, though full of danger, not yet so imminent as to make him rush away as if not willing, if necessary, to try out the wage of battle. A few hours' rest at Crab Orchard and at eleven o'clock the march was commenced to Somerset, about twenty-eight miles distant. By sundown the space had been covered. Here the Confederates again found large quantities of stores, the telegraph office was open. More than a hundred wagons were captured and burned, and ammunition, shoes, blankets and hats, in great quantities, were stored in warehouses in exceeding abundance. There was lavish appropriation. A few wagons were loaded with the things which were most needed in Dixie, and the torch was applied to the others and they were reduced to ashes.

At Stigall's Ferry, six miles from Somerset, the Cumberland River was passed, and that night the command camped at Monticello, twenty-two miles southwardly. All need of hurry was now past. There was no likelihood that the Federals would cross the Cumberland River. Morgan had outmarched them and out-maneuvered them and he was safe. With satisfaction and peace of mind born of noble achievement, he could look back upon the events of the past twenty-four days. He summed it up in these words: "I left Knoxville on the 4th of this month with nine hundred men and returned to Livingston on the 28th inst. with twelve hundred, having been absent twenty-four days, during which time I have traveled over a thousand miles, captured seventeen towns, destroyed all the government supplies and arms in them, dispersed about fifteen hundred Home Guards, paroled nearly twelve hundred regular troops. I lost in killed and wounded and missing of the number that I carried into Kentucky, about ninety."

At Somerset, Ellsworth, the operator, had telegraphed for Morgan and himself several messages to the Federal leaders in Kentucky, and concluded his telegraphic work with the following despatch: "Headquarters Telegraphic Department of Kentucky, Confederate States of America. General Order Number 1. When an operator is positively informed that the enemy is marching on his station, he will immediately proceed to destroy the telegraphic instruments and all material in his charge. Such instances of carelessness as were exhibited on the part of the operators at Lebanon and Midway and Georgetown will be severely dealt with.—By order of G. A. Ellsworth, General Military Superintendent, C. S. Telegraphic Department."

The story of the successes, victories and strategies of this wonderful expedition was quickly spread abroad throughout the entire Confederate States. The minds of many of the young men were stirred by the strange exploits of Morgan on this raid, and their hearts were thrilled with the story of his adventures and his triumphs. Many who had not enlisted were inclined to seek service under the Kentucky chieftain. They longed to have experiences such as he and his followers had enjoyed on this marvellous raid. What was accomplished by General Morgan set other Confederate cavalry leaders to thinking and inspired them with patriotic ambitions to emulate the tactics of the Kentucky cavalryman.

Chapter VI

FORREST'S RAID INTO WEST TENNESSEE, DECEMBER, 1862

To the great Volunteer State, Tennessee, belongs the credit of having produced, in many respects, the most remarkable cavalry leader in the world—Nathan Bedford Forrest. He was born near Duck River, at a little hamlet called Chapel Hill, then in Bedford County, Tennessee, but now comprised within the boundaries of Marshall County. Scotch-Irish and English blood flowed through the veins of this great warrior. This strain rarely fails to produce courage, fortitude and enterprise.

When Nathan Bedford Forrest was thirteen years of age, the financial affairs of his father, William Forrest, had gone awry. Leaving Tennessee with seven children, he entered a homestead in Tippah County, North Mississippi, a region which had just been opened to settlement through a purchase by the Federal Government from the Chickasaw Indians. The magical hand of immigration had as yet done little for this region. The Indians had hunted over the lands, but civilization had not given it prosperity and fitted it for the homes of peaceful agriculturists.

Death, with rude hand and pitiless dart, cut down the father, William Forrest. His oldest boy, not sixteen years of age, became the head of his family, including his mother, six brothers and three sisters, and then four months after the father had passed away, there came a posthumous boy, Jeffrey, who, on the 22nd day of February, 1864, was to die a soldier's death at Okolona, Mississippi, resisting Sooy Smith's raid. In the supreme moment of dissolution his valiant and heroic brother pressed his dying form to his heart and imprinted upon his cheek, now damp with the death sweat, a last kiss of affection and love. The death of this young brother, upon whom Forrest lavished an immeasurable wealth of tenderness, was the greatest blow the war brought to his fearless heart.

Forrest, deprived of education by the calls of filial duty, secured only such learning as could be obtained at a primary school in Middle Tennessee and in Mississippi in 1836 and 1837, which was scant enough, and which was won between the fall harvest and spring planting seasons.

Within three years, by his indomitable will, his great industry, his shrewd judgment and unceasing labor, he had won for his mother, sisters and brothers agricultural independence.

Typhoid fever, with malignant fierceness, had stricken down two of his brothers and his three sisters, one of these last being a twin sister of Forrest himself.

When twenty years of age, the war spirit of Forrest was moved by the struggles of the people of Texas in their contest with Mexico for independence, and among the adventurous and gallant boys of the South, who cast in their lot with the people of Texas, was this young Tennessean. After reaching the scenes of war, lack of transportation and of necessity for their services forced these young men to either settle in the new republic or to return to their homes. Forrest was penniless, but he split enough rails in a little while to pay his passage to his home in Mississippi, which he reached after an absence of four and a half months.

In 1845 Forrest involuntarily became an actor in a tragedy in Hernando. Four men, grieved at some act of his partner and uncle, Jonathan Forrest, undertook to kill him. Single-handed and alone, Nathan Bedford Forrest severely wounded three of the assailants and drove the fourth from the field. In the conflict, the uncle was mortally wounded, although he had taken no part in the affray.

After reverses in business, Forrest left Hernando, in 1852, and established himself as a broker in real estate and dealer in slaves in Memphis.

In 1861, General Forrest was a cotton planter in Coahoma County, Mississippi, growing a thousand bales of cotton per annum, and with his fortune increasing every year.

He now stood high among the most successful and active business men in Memphis. He had won a fortune by sagacity, integrity and sobriety, and though lacking in education, there was something in his personnel that impressed men with his right to be a leader. He was a born captain, and nature wrote his right to command on his face.

In April, 1861, his foresight assured him that war was inevitable, and he proceeded to arrange his affairs for the impending conflict. His whole soul was centered in his desire to make the South free, and the independence of the Confederate states, he firmly believed, was the only guarantee for a permanent peace.

After a visit to Mississippi, he returned to Memphis and immediately became a private in the Tennessee Mounted Rifles, under Captain Josiah H. White. He sought no rank. His highest aim was to serve his country, and, resolved upon the utmost effort to uphold her cause, he was willing to face all dangers where duty pointed the way. The pupil soon taught the master, and within a month Isham G. Harris, Governor of Tennessee, and General Leonidas Polk urged and commissioned Forrest to recruit a regiment of cavalry. A hurried visit to Kentucky enabled him to purchase five hundred Colt's navy pistols and a hundred saddles with their equipments.

While in Louisville, he learned that a company of cavalry was being organized for him by Captain Frank Overton, at Brandenburg, Meade County. Hastening thither, he mustered in the Boone Rangers, ninety stalwart sons of Kentucky, which became the first company of the regiment.

Forrest was not long in reaching Bowling Green with his Boone Rangers. A skirmish or two on the way demonstrated his marvelous genius for war, inspired his men with absolute faith in his leadership, and left behind him an ominous warning to those who later in the struggle should be so unfortunate as to cross his path.

A company was organized in Memphis during Forrest's absence, called the Forrest Rangers, under Captain Charles May,—and the Boone Rangers became the nucleus of Forrest's famous regiment, which in a few weeks grew to be a battalion of eight companies, and, which in a few days by active operations, laid the foundations of their leader's astonishing reputation and success.

Two of Forrest's companies were from Kentucky, one from Meade County and one from Harrodsburg. Alabama contributed four, Texas one, and Memphis one, so that as far as his fame was to become coextensive with the South and West it would seem as if fate had spread over Kentucky, Tennessee, Alabama and Texas a call for these men who were to make their commander renowned.

In a little while, Alabama sent two more companies, and the regiment became of sufficient numbers to make Forrest lieutenant colonel. Alabama troops predominated in his own regiment.

Many skirmishes and marches marked the career of this active and aggressive command prior to February, 1862, and then Forrest was ordered to repair to Fort Donelson, where as senior officer, he assumed command of the cavalry of the army here concentrated. The cavalry consisted of Forrest's regiment, Colonel Gantt's Tennessee Battalion, and three Kentucky companies under Captains Huey, Wilcox and Williams, counting, all told, eight hundred men.

Twenty-five thousand Federals surrounded fourteen thousand Confederates at the eventful siege of Fort Donelson. By the exigencies of war these men were surrendered. Whose fault brought about this unfortunate result has long been one of the most fiercely discussed of Confederate military problems.

When a council of war had decreed that a surrender was inevitable, Forrest entered an earnest protest; and at the suggestion of General Pillow, he was allowed to effect his escape, upon condition that he should do so before a flag of truce had communicated with the enemy. The sequel shows upon what slight events human destiny hinges. Had Forrest been less courageous or determined, his future would have been entirely changed. His pluck and his pride revolted at a cavalry soldier yielding without a vehement wrestle with the god of chance; and his brave soul cried out against becoming prisoner without one impetuous appeal to fate for a juster determination of the conflict which raged at this crucial hour.

In the darkness and frost of a cold winter night, Forrest immediately laid his plans to bring his horsemen out of the beleaguered fort. By four o'clock in the morning, with five hundred men and officers, he undertook to ride away. He could only conjecture as to what was ahead. He had no time to send out scouts to reconnoitre as to the presence or position of his foes. He was not so much concerned as to who and where they were. The only anxious inquiry that crossed his mind was how many they were and whether the waters that traversed his path were too deep or too swift for him and his followers to ford or swim in their struggle to find a way of escape from the clutches of their enemies. He had no guides to point the road. He knew that safety beckoned for a southward march. A great host was encamped somewhere in the vicinity. He knew they were ready to dispute his going. He had never traveled the road he was to follow. His keen vision could only pierce a few feet into the blackness of the night. He had only one plan and that was to fight and ride over whatever obstructed his chosen track. With one hand to guide his steed and the other grimly gripping his faithful revolver, he led his followers cautiously and yet speedily amidst the oppressive silence. Every slip of his floundering steeds amidst the gloom of the cold and dreary night, seemed full of awful portent and danger, and yet, amidst all these depressing conditions, the gallant leader entertained no thought of a retreat and sternly ordered all to go forward. It required an iron will and an invincible soul to thus lead five hundred men on this desperate and difficult ride. A few wounded Federal soldiers, crouching by the fires of the rails they had kindled into flames to keep the warmth of life in their maimed bodies until their comrades with the dawn of day should bring succor, were the only sentinels that called to the riders to halt. These were not disposed to question Forrest's right to pass on into the outlying darkness and he was glad to leave them alone in the cheerless hours of that dread night, which the misfortunes of war had forced them to face.

Once, back water seemed to stop the course of the gallant troopers, but it was only for a moment. His advance guard hesitated, but calling them to clear the way, he fearlessly crushed the ice with his sword, and bade those behind to follow where he so promptly and confidently led.

This sally and escape of Forrest, in the face of almost insurmountable obstacles, gave him a reputation for courage and enterprise that betokened how great his future would be. That this determined cavalryman marched safely away, was to the ambitious and glory-seeking youth of the Southwest a special invitation to enlist under his banners; and decided many of the bravest and most patriotic men of middle Tennessee to enlist under the guidons of such fame-winners as Forrest, Wheeler and Morgan. Succeeding events would only magnify his promise and his skill. Forrest had already shown himself in the briefest while to be a great cavalry leader, and his genius, to those who watched and interpreted it ever so slightly, shone with transcendent brilliance and indicated that he would win renown and attain the highest rank.

On the 16th of March, 1862, two other Tennessee companies came to the regiment; these gave it a full roster, and by acclamation he became colonel; Kelly, lieutenant colonel; and a private, R. M. Balch, major.

When General Bragg marched into Kentucky in the summer of 1862, he left Nashville behind him, under the control of the Federals. After returning from Kentucky, in October, through Cumberland Gap, by degrees he marched westward, and in early winter at Murfreesboro, thirty miles south of Nashville, established his lines.

General Bragg, in December, deemed it important for General Forrest to make a raid into West Tennessee, destroy connections with Memphis, apparently threaten the Louisville & Nashville Railroad between Louisville and Nashville, damage the railroads and break up, if possible, the lines of transportation which enabled the Federals to maintain themselves at Memphis and the adjacent territory.

General Wheeler had been promoted and assigned to the chief command of the cavalry, with headquarters at La Vergne, and Forrest was ordered to report to General Bragg in person. Thereupon, General Forrest was assigned to the command of a brigade of about eighteen hundred men, consisting of the 4th, 8th and 9th Tennessee Regiments, Russell's 4th Alabama and Freeman's Battery. This promotion of General Wheeler over Forrest and Morgan greatly disappointed both of these leaders and excited much criticism amongst the rank and file. Not only with the cavalry, but with infantry, was this action most severely condemned. At this time General Wheeler had won neither the record nor the fame which later excited the admiration of all the men in the armies of the South. Morgan's two Kentucky raids and the Battle of Hartsville, one of the most brilliant achievements of the war; Forrest's escape from Donelson, his magnificent service at Shiloh, and his assault on Nashville and capture of Murfreesboro, had already made both marked men and given them the admiration and love of the entire army, and there was much indignation at the apparent subordination of Forrest and withdrawal from his forces of the men who had been taught in his campaigns his methods of fighting, and who had learned to believe in him as one of the most wonderful soldiers of the Confederacy.

General Bragg received, with some degree of impatience, General Forrest's complaints as to either insufficient equipment or undisciplined troops, and directed General Forrest to march westward, to cross the Tennessee River, and operate north and west of Memphis, up to the Kentucky line as far as Moscow, some hundred and sixty miles away.

Taking his final orders on the 10th of December, 1862, and reviewing his command, at the risk of being reprimanded for insubordination, in writing he again called the attention of General Bragg to the lack of ammunition and supplies, and proper arms for his men.

The soldiers under him were largely raw new levies, armed chiefly with flintlock rifles, many without flints. They possessed ten caps per man, and a very meagre and scanty supply of ammunition.

In response to his second demand for better guns and more ammunition, he was curtly and peremptorily ordered to march without delay and take his chances with what had been assigned him for the raid.

Forrest keenly felt this treatment. His best troops had been taken from him. Only four old companies remained with him, men who had already shown great aptitude for partisan work and knew his method of fighting, and were prepared to follow him under all conditions.

To the untrained student General Bragg's orders bordered on cruelty, and Forrest fiercely resented in his heart the great wrong thus inflicted upon him. He was proud, brave and profoundly patriotic, and no man in the South was more deeply attached to the Southern cause than he. For awhile he brooded over this injustice, but he loved his country too much to falter or hesitate even if he felt and believed that this treatment was indefensible. General Bragg, to him it appeared, had sent him upon the most dangerous mission of the war, and as if to render the task doubly hazardous, had taken from him the men he so much needed for the work he was required to do, and had given him instead men whose inexperience and lack of drill and discipline would render his success full of uncertainty and well-nigh impossible.

He was commanded to undertake and possibly to force the passage of the Tennessee River, when it was swollen by the winter rains, and without even the semblance of a pontoon bridge, he was expected to cross his men, horses, artillery and supplies as best he could. He was either to construct ferry boats, or raise those that had been sunken to hide them from Federal eyes; to search in the creeks or thickets for a few skiffs, or to fashion them from the boards he might pick up in a country already impoverished by the ravages of war. He was to cross the river in face of a vigilant and expectant foe whose garrisons were ordered to be upon the alert for his coming; and were a long time before urged to watch for the presence of the man whose fear was in every heart and whose desperate courage and resistless onslaught had made him a very terror to the peace and quiet of those who were to prevent his coming, or expected to punish his appearance in the country, the holding of which was an essential to the safety of their operations on the Mississippi River below Memphis. Thereafter, he was to move into a region filled with large Federal garrisons, all thoroughly armed, very many times more numerous than his own force, and to ride over roads softened by the winter rains, which by the travel of his horses and guns, were churned into slush, reaching above the knees of the animals, and through which his artillery could only be drawn at an average speed of less than a walk. The conditions of these highways would not only disspirit his followers, but subject them to such physical strain as would possibly render them unable to perform the duties that the campaign necessitated.

He had eighteen hundred troops and four guns. Baggage was reduced to a minimum. Marching westward from Columbia, Tennessee, he reached a place called Clifton, on the Tennessee River. An old, leaky ferryboat, "a tub," raised from the bottom of the stream where it had been sunk to save it from Federal destruction; a hastily constructed similar craft made from hewed logs, and a half dozen skiffs, were his only means of transportation across the deep stream. The boats were either rotten or leaky, and all dangerous. Horses and mules were driven into the stream and forced to swim, while the men with their saddles, blankets, frying pans, guns, cannon caissons and ammunition wagons, were with the constant fear of Federal gunboats, Federal cavalry and infantry ever in their minds and with constant apprehension of resistance, as speedily as possible, under these adverse conditions, ferried to the western bank of the swollen river.

Only a great soldier and a great leader could have maintained his own equanimity with such adverse surroundings, or could have kept his followers under control with destruction every moment staring them in the face. On the shore, now on the western bank, now in the turgid waters, again on the eastern side, he calmly directed every movement, and his presence gave his followers hope when hope seemed absurd, and imbued them with a sublime courage they themselves could not fathom or understand. That he was there quieted every impulse to fear, and that his eye was upon them spurred every man to the noblest endeavors. Before him, every thought of cowardice became a retreating fugitive, and his example taught every trooper in the brigade that no foe was invincible and no task impossible. Morgan and his men crossing the Cumberland to reach Hartsville, Wheeler and his men forcing a passage of the Tennessee to destroy Rosecrans' trains, were full of sublime heroism, but Forrest's passage of the Tennessee River at Clifton, on December 16th and 17th, 1862, will long live as one of the most persistently courageous achievements of cavalry in any age or war.

The strain on man and beast was almost unbearable. Forrest had with him many officers as brave as he but less experienced; but Starnes, Dibrell, Russell, Jeffrey Forrest, Freeman, Morton, Biffle, Woodward, William M. Forrest, Cox, Gurley and many others in this command held up the hands of their beloved leader and aided him in giving even the humblest private a spirit of devotion that made every man who wore the gray jacket an intrepid hero, and a soldier who was without fear, even unto death.

Scouts above and below, ever vigilant, watched for coming gunboats. Pickets, hastily sent out on the western side of the stream, guarded every road that led to the ferry, and eager eyes, quickened by impending danger, scanned every hilltop and watched every avenue of approach. Two nights and a day were consumed in this arduous undertaking. The gunboats could not safely travel at night and Forrest availed himself of this to further his difficult work. He was crossing, with most inadequate means, the fifth largest stream in the United States. The distance from shore to shore was more than half a mile, the current was rapid, and while poling flatboats is a slow and tedious process by day, by night the difficulties were much enhanced. Forrest and his men successfully defied and overcame these natural obstacles, and by the morning of the 17th his men and equipments were all over, the boats were poled back to the western shore, sunk, committed to the care of a few guards, who protested at being left behind for what they esteemed an inglorious task, and with a questioning gaze, Forrest looked across the stream, wondering if he could later repass its currents, and with a wave of his sword, launched forth on his hazardous mission. Aligning his small command, he bade them go forward, not doubting that even with such odds against him, fate would lend a helping hand and safely bring him back from sure yet unknown dangers and fierce battles to his own, again.

This tremendous task accomplished and his scattered forces united, he marched eight miles to Lexington, Henderson County, and encamped for a little while, to allow his wet, hungry and tired soldiers to dry their clothes, inspect their guns, and to relieve their minds as well as their bodies of the great strain to which they had been subjected in the extraordinary and eventful experiences of the past forty-eight hours.

On examination, it was found that the greater part of the ammunition, in crossing the Tennessee River, had become wet and consequently unserviceable, and while this loss of the slight supply of ammunition which had been assigned to his command was being considered, a blockade-runner who had been sent through the lines, appeared with fifty thousand caps.

Forrest had sent forward his agents to secure this supply of ammunition. Already the Federals had had warning of Forrest's coming, and he had barely advanced a mile until he had encountered squadrons of the Federal force moving along the same road to check his farther advance. Prepared or unprepared, Forrest had come to fight. He viciously assailed the Federals and quickly captured or routed one, a Federal Tennessee regiment, and the other the 11th Regiment of Illinois Volunteers, in which last Robert G. Ingersoll became a Confederate prisoner.

Refreshed and strengthened by Federal supplies, and new and better mounts, he pursued the fugitives furiously, and three days after crossing the river reached Jackson, Tennessee (fifty miles away). He had rested only a day, and his march was never without opposition from his foe.

The Federals quickly concentrated troops at Jackson from the North and South. The railroads from the north were immediately torn up, isolated stations were captured, and guns and ammunition provided for thoroughly arming the Confederates. Forrest was not slow and by the removal and bending of the rails, he cut off further succor or supplies to the garrison at Jackson from the north.

At this time, the force at Jackson was estimated at fifteen thousand. Maneuvering so as to create the impression of an army of a larger force than was really at his call, and with only one regiment apparently in front of Jackson, he started northwest to Humboldt, and here found his richest booty. Two hundred prisoners, four gun caissons, five hundred standard muskets and three hundred thousand rounds of ammunition, and equipments of all sorts here fell into Forrest's hands.

Reserving the best for himself, the torch was applied to the remainder and the insatiable flames ate up the property that Federal foresight had collected to feed the garrisons that now filled every town of any importance in the adjacent country. His force, had now become steadied by the influence of his example and by his brilliant success. The experiences of a few days had made them veterans, and taught them the ways and genius of their resourceful leader and he too now began to realize that even these new and hitherto untried men were dependable soldiers in any crisis that his daring might invoke.

Five days out from the Tennessee River, General Forrest reached Trenton, and prepared for its capture. A man of intensive action, he quickly surrounded the town. It did not take long to drive the enemy into their breastworks. A charge from Forrest and his escort completed the work. With two hundred and seventy-five men, some of them inexperienced volunteers, General Forrest had captured four hundred prisoners of war, including two colonels, many field officers, a thousand horses and mules, wagons and ambulances, and ammunition, and two hundred thousand rations of subsistence, all worth a half million of dollars.

Flintlock muskets and shotguns were now thrown away. Enfield rifles, the best possible Confederate arm of that period, were issued to his entire command, and with an equipment, the same in most respects as that of their foes, the new soldiers caught the true spirit of war and were eager to meet their adversaries upon more equal terms. Recruits had more than made up for the losses which Forrest had suffered, and well-equipped and well-armed, he still numbered eighteen hundred men and officers.

With the exception of the Tennessee Federal Regiment, all other prisoners were paroled, required to march to Columbus, Kentucky, under an escort, and there turned over to the Federal commander.

The way was now clear, and General Forrest marched toward Union City, on the line between Kentucky and Tennessee. Stockade after stockade was taken, and the real and greatest work of the expedition was now begun. He had come to destroy the railroads. A few of his companies had done such work before, and with eagerness and spirit they gleefully set about the pleasing task. Spikes were drawn, rails were stacked on piles of logs, and the fiery flames assisted in the work of demolition. The iron rails, under the influence of the savage glow, began to twirl and twist and, bent in all directions by the increasing heat furnished by renewed giant piles of wood, they seemed almost alive in their strange contortions; and curved, crooked and ill-shapen lengths of iron were soon all that remained of the tracks that were so essential to transport food supplies for the armies which encamped toward the south, who were dependent upon these rails for their daily bread. He followed the line of the Mobile and Ohio railroad and destroyed it, and tore up its track for fifteen miles, burning down trestles, removing cattle guards, and inflicting tremendous losses upon the line.

In the meanwhile, the forces at Jackson had gotten their second breath. They undertook now to intercept Forrest and prevent his recrossing the Tennessee River. Short work was made of Union City; two hundred and fifty officers and men entrenched, surrendered with their arms and supplies. Here three hundred more prisoners were paroled.

General Forrest had now reached the northern limit of the lines of his expedition, at Moscow, a few miles over the Kentucky border. Several days were spent in demolishing the heavy trestles on the north and south forks of the Obion River.

Twelve thousand Federal soldiers had now been concentrated at Trenton. Forrest had not been out from his crossing of the Tennessee River nine days. Marching twenty-six miles to Dresden, and realizing the work that was before him, he resolved to give his animals and his men a day's rest to prepare them for the well-nigh superhuman tasks which were before them.

The Federal commanders resolved to prevent General Forrest from recrossing the Tennessee River, and to this end, they applied all the means at their command. They had plenty of men, but the trying problem was to anticipate Forrest's track and to cope with his wonderful methods for outwitting his foes.

With the keen mind of the great cavalry soldier, it did not take General Forrest long to understand that his enemies were concentrating their forces to prevent his re-passage of the river. He fully understood that it was impossible for him to escape south, that he must go east, and in going east, he must get over the Tennessee River. Before he could start well upon his return, it was necessary for him to cross the Obion River, which empties into the Tennessee, but this was now full with winter floods. All the bridges but one had been destroyed. Across this dangerous and uncertain stream, the bridge had been partially torn out, and it was left undefended because it was regarded as impassable.

Within an hour, the men were at work getting together timber with which to repair the bridge, so as to admit of the passage of artillery. The seemingly hopeless task was accomplished in the briefest period. Within an hour, the causeway was made passable. It was a cold, dark midnight, and a sleeting, drizzling rain was falling, chilling the bones but not the hearts of the Confederate command.

General Forrest, in order to nerve his soldiers for the dangers of slipping from the tottering bridge, himself mounted the saddle horse and drove over the first wagon. Catching the inspiration of their great leader's courage, two teamsters attempted to follow. They slipped or fell from the bridge and plunged into the deep stream and freezing mud, from which they were with difficulty released.

Men, who had hitherto looked on with undisturbed hearts, now began to question if the crossing of the stream could be made, whether in the gloom of the dark hours which precede the dawn, and the dawn was far off, it would be possible to carry over his sixteen hundred soldiers now present with their equipments. But there was no difficulty or danger that could quail the heart of Nathan Bedford Forrest. The muddy, slushy roads made the passage more dangerous. Conscious of the lack of supplies in the territory into which he must return, Forrest was endeavoring to carry a number of wagon loads of flour, coffee and sugar. The safety of his command and the lives of his soldiers rose higher than all thoughts of the commissary, and the mud and chuck holes were filled with sacks of flour and coffee, and along these and over these the wagons passed.

The trains, by three o'clock, had been gotten over the bridge, but the muddy, sloppy condition rendered it impossible for the artillery horses to draw the guns and caissons. The horses were knee deep in mud, and the men waded in slush half way up their limbs. Fifty men were detailed with ropes to pull each piece of artillery, and only by these superhuman efforts, at three o'clock in the morning, the Obion was passed.

The only rest that could be allowed after the awful experiences of the night was a short halt for food; and hardly had men and beasts satisfied nature's craving until the scouts informed General Forrest that twelve miles away were several thousand men, converging upon his small and valiant force.

General Forrest had no idea at this time of giving any intimation where he would pass the Tennessee River. And he pursued his way southward toward Lexington, over a wild, rough, hilly, rocky road. The tramp of the horses and the cutting of the wheels of the artillery and the wagons made the road a veritable bayou. The friable soil, stirred and cut by cannon, caisson and wagon wheels, and mixed by the six thousand hoofs of the cavalry horses, became a canal of freezing slush. The animals and their equipments were bespattered with this horrible material, and the clothing, necks, faces, saddles, blankets and guns of the riders were covered with mud, making the march extremely distressing. With grim courage, they ceased endeavoring to wipe the disgusting slime from their faces or clothing. They gritted their teeth, clenched their reins with a stronger grip, and, uncomplaining, rode on in the dark stillness of the awful night; they could at least, they believed, endure the horrors of the situation until dawn of day. This, they hoped, would bring some relief and somewhat assuage the dreadful punishment of this night march. The scouts reported one brigade of the enemy within six miles of General Forrest, another, six miles from this force. Resting until four o'clock, his men were aroused, ordered to saddle and prepare for the advance upon the Federal armies.

General Forrest determined to force the fighting, and he had only a brief time to form a line of battle. Biffle, with his regiment, had moved towards Trenton, but the soldierly instinct told him that his chieftain was calling for him, and so he paroled his prisoners, destroyed his supplies, and turned his face toward the battlefield which was now to decide the fate of the command. General Forrest believed he could destroy one brigade, under Colonel Dunham, before the other, under General Sullivan, could march six miles over the terrible roads along which it must advance, and he resolved to try his fortunes with Dunham first.

The Federals were quite as eager for conflict as General Forrest, and as soon as they felt the impact, pressed forward with great vigor. General Forrest had six pieces of artillery and about fourteen hundred available fighting men; he was hunting a fight, and he was to get quite all that he desired.

Both sides felt the importance of the issue, and both were eager to secure the advantage in positions. Forrest's artillery, always well placed, was now concentrated upon the Federal lines. The men in blue advanced resolutely to within a hundred and eighty feet of the artillery, but they only came to be repulsed with great slaughter. The Confederate leader thought it was better to make this first an artillery fight, and to reserve his small arms for the later period, when the second force should try issues with him.

Colonel Dunham, in command of the Federals, showed himself to be a fighter. Repulses did not weaken the courage of either himself or his troops, and they renewed charge upon charge. At last his lines were broken, and his men left their cover and ran across the field, where many of them were captured and slain.

Colonel Starnes attacked the enemy in the rear. He had been detached for making this kind of assault; always one of Forrest's chief maneuvers, who often declared that one man in the rear was worth two in the front. On Starnes' arrival in the field, white flags were hoisted and Forrest and his troopers were masters of the situation.

While Forrest was congratulating himself upon his safety, Colonel Carroll, a staff officer, rose up to inform him that a superior number of Federals had come into action and were now in his rear. This was a great surprise and an unlooked-for emergency. A full brigade of fresh troops, now behind him, pressed on with remarkable vigor and spirit, and the attack was so sudden and fierce that two hundred and fifty of Forrest's men were captured, four caissons and two brass cannons were disabled in an attempt to withdraw from the field, and these were abandoned, with a loss of a number of troopers and some artillery.

The newcomers were quite as game as the men who had withstood Forrest's several assaults. They poured a heavy fire into the Confederate line sustained by their artillery and fiercely and furiously assailed the several Confederate positions. It looked as if the wily Confederate leader had been caught napping, and that favoring fortune, which had so often and so propitiously come to his rescue, was about to desert his standard and give the victory to his enemies.

With only a hundred and twenty-five men, Forrest made one of his characteristic dashes upon the artillery of the enemy, which was being served in such efficient manner as to inflict great loss. Fortunately the horses attached to three of the pieces took fright and ran in the direction of the Confederate lines, where they were seized and driven away.

In the meantime, Colonel Starnes had attacked Dunham's rear and this halted him, and enabled General Forrest to capture General Dunham's wagon train with all his supplies, and this was skillfully carried from the field.

General Forrest had now all the fighting he wanted for one day. He had put in nine hours. Twenty-five officers and men had been killed, seventy-five wounded and two hundred and fifty captured. Three caissons, five wagons and mules and seventy-five thousand rounds of ammunition had been left with his enemies.

The Federals had fared even worse than the Confederates. A colonel and lieutenant colonel and one hundred and fifty rank and file had been wounded; fifty dead lay on the ground.

Forrest, with twelve hundred fighting men, had whipped eighteen hundred and then finally stood off a fresh brigade. It was not often that General Forrest was taken unawares, and those who knew his marvelous ability to get information wondered how General Sullivan with a fresh brigade could approach his rear and attack it without notice. Forrest, however, had not forgotten to look after this end of the line. The directions were misunderstood by the officer. He, hearing the guns, deemed it necessary to make a detour in order to reach Forrest. Had this officer promptly reported the presence of Sullivan, Forrest would have been able to destroy Dunham before the arrival of fresh Federal forces, and then with his usual vehemence turned upon the Federal reenforcements and chosen his battlefield with his fresher foes. For once the Confederate chieftain was glad to get out of reach of his enemies. He felt that he had fully enough of conflict, and his best thoughts and energies were engaged in devising ways and means to extricate his command from what even he, chief of military optimists, must admit was a most difficult and dangerous situation.

The engagement at Parker's Cross Roads, where the commands of Dunham and Sullivan felt that they had severely battered General Forrest, gave the Federals some grounds for believing that even he was not invincible, and encouraged them to seek another trial; and they were, though with many precautions for safety, anxious to again fight out the wager-of-battle.

Twelve miles away from the battlefield, Forrest halted to feed his men and dress the wounds of his patient followers. They had passed the highest physical tests and had come forth victorious, but even Forrest's followers had limitations and reached a point where nature revolted and peremptorily called a halt.

The Confederate chieftain now determined to recross the Tennessee at Clifton, the same point at which he had passed it fifteen days before. In his hazardous position, this was the only hope of emerging in safety. He had left his sunken boats to rescue him in a last emergency. At no other point was there a substantial chance to find even the crudest means of passing the swollen stream, which, like a great spectre, stood out on the horizon to haunt his dreams and to thwart his escape.

The Federals were glad to leave Forrest alone, and Forrest was glad to leave them alone. With all the vigor and courage the Federals had shown in the pursuit of the Confederates, their failure at the last moment to pursue and attack him while crossing the river is one of the strange and inexplicable delinquencies which now and then appeared in the tactics of both armies, during the four years of the struggle.

When close to the river, the scouts brought information that ten thousand infantry and cavalry were moving from the direction of Purdy and towards Clifton, and this gave General Forrest new cause for apprehension and solicitude.

A few miles from Clifton, across Forrest's only path leading to the river, he found a regiment of Federal cavalry drawn up in battle line. There was no time for maneuvering, and Dibbrell, always gallant, was ordered to charge down the road across which the Federals had been placed. Dibbrell, realizing the situation, was quick to act, and furiously assaulted the line, cut the Federals asunder, and then Starnes and Biffle, one on the right and the other on the left, went after the detachments, and in a brief space they were scattered and driven from the field.

Strange to say, twenty men were killed on the Federal side and fifty prisoners taken, and only one man struck on the Confederate side. This was General Forrest's forage master, who was standing by his side, and called his attention to some object. While speaking, he was struck by a spent ball, which flattened on his forehead without penetrating the skull, and the officer fell stunned, but soon revived and only suffered the inconvenience of a severe headache.

Every nerve was now strained to reach the river. The sun was at its meridian when General Forrest rode up and looked across the currents that swirled between him and safety. The skiffs on the other side of the Tennessee, and the flatboats which had been sunk after the passage on the 15th, had been raised, under the direction of Jeffrey Forrest, who, with the speed born of the extremities of the hour, with a small following had galloped forward to put in readiness the meagre flotilla with which the retreating Confederates might cross the river and find safety from their numerous and aggressive foes.

When General Forrest arrived, the boats were ready to move, the horses were detached from all the wagons and artillery, driven into the river and made to swim across. The same process was gone through with the cavalry horses. It was a wonderful sight to a looker-on,—hundreds of horses struggling in a swollen stream. All understood what even an hour's delay might mean. The beasts could swim, but no man could endure the freezing waters, or hope after half a mile of immersion under its chilling currents to emerge on the other side alive. Logs were searched for in the drift, fence rails were hunted. These were lashed together with grape vines, halter ropes or bridle reins, and on these improvised rafts, bushes and drift were piled, and with poles or board paddles, pushed and pulled across the stream.

The artillery and wagon horses and a majority of the cavalry mounts were animals which had been captured from the Federals. The supreme hour was at hand. Only the speediest action could hold out the slightest hope of escape. One section of artillery, under Captain Douglass, and one regiment were posted a mile away from the ferry. These were directed to fortify their position as best they could, to hold it in the face of all odds, under all circumstances, and to fight even to annihilation. Only brave

108

men, who have received such a command, can realize how calmly human courage rises to its very zenith under such conditions. No one detailed for this important duty sought relief. Forrest himself told them they must stay and if need be, die to save their comrades. They made no excuses, they asked no exemption. They were ready to serve as told and, had the occasion required, every man was ready to fall where his country, at that hour, called him to stand.

The river was eighteen hundred feet wide, but it had banks which were favorable for the escape of the animals from the stream.

From twelve o'clock until eight o'clock at night, the flatboats pulled up stream half a mile and were then permitted to drop down with the current, and were drifted and poled across, and after eight hours the five pieces of artillery, six caissons, sixty wagons and four ambulances, equipments of all kinds, and the whole command had been carried over the swollen stream and were landed on the eastern side of the river. Thirty-six hours out from Parker's Cross Roads, where Dunham and Sullivan and Fuller had raised such a rough-house with Forrest, he had marched forty miles, and safely passed all his forces with their horses and trains over the Tennessee. This remarkable feat again demonstrated Forrest's wonderful wealth of resource, and served notice on his enemies that there was nothing he would not dare and few feats that he could not accomplish.

Fourteen days had elapsed since the passage of the river, but what marvelous experiences had Forrest and his raw levies passed. They had traveled over three hundred miles, had been in three sternly contested engagements, with daily skirmishing, had destroyed fifty large and small bridges on the Mobile and Ohio Railroad, and had burned trestles, so as to make it useless to the enemy; had captured twenty stockades, captured and killed twenty-five hundred of the enemy, taken and disabled ten pieces of artillery, carried off fifty wagons and ambulances with their teams, had captured ten thousand stands of excellent small arms and hundreds of thousands of rounds of ammunition, had returned fully armed, equipped and mounted; had traversed roads with army trains which at that season were considered impassable, even by horsemen. Only one night's rest in fourteen days had been enjoyed, unsheltered, without tents, and in a most inclement winter, constantly raining, snowing and sleeting; but these wonderful men had endured all these hardships, neither murmuring, complaining nor doubting, but always cheerful, brave and resigned to do any and every duty that sternest war could bring.

This one campaign had made Forrest's new troopers veterans. There was now no service for which they were not prepared. They were ready to follow their leader at any time and everywhere, and thereafter no troops would perform more prodigies of valor or face a foe with more confidence or cheerfulness; and yet before them were many of war's sacrifices, dangers, disasters, toils and trials, which would call for the best that was in man.

Chapter VII

TEXAS HORSEMEN OF THE SEA,
IN GALVESTON HARBOR, JANUARY, 1863

General John Bankhead Magruder was born in Winchester, Virginia, on the 15th of August, 1810. He came of not only a distinguished but a martial family. Singularly attractive in personality, he entered West Point and graduated from that institution in 1830.

Thirty-six years of age when the Mexican War began, he was not without a wide military experience, and on many battlefields had exhibited the superb courage which marked his entire career as a Confederate officer. He won fame at Palo Alto in the Mexican War, he earned a brevet at Cerro Gordo, and at Chapultepec and in the City of Mexico he added still more largely to his splendid reputation for gallantry and dash. Imbued with all the patriotic state pride and love of a native born Virginian, he early resigned his position in the United States army and took service under the Confederate government.

By March 16, 1861, he was colonel; ninety days later a brigadier general; less than four months afterward he was a major general; and, with probably one exception, when it was claimed he was tardy, he justified the opinion of his friends and superiors that he was a great soldier, an eminent strategist, with extraordinary aptitude for all phases and departments of war.

In the Virginia-Yorktown campaign in 1861, he fought the Battle of Big Bethel. He was then only a colonel, but there he ranked such men as D. H. Hill and others of great future renown.

Big Bethel was not much of a battle after all, but it served to stimulate and nourish Southern pride, and helped also to arouse Northern patriotism. With one man killed and seven wounded, it is with reluctance that it can be called a battle at all. The most that General Magruder could enumerate as a loss on the Federal side (with all the bias of a general anxious to promote hope in his countrymen), was from twenty-five to thirty killed and a hundred and fifty wounded.

On this field fell the first martyr to the Southern cause. He was a member of the 1st North Carolina Infantry, and volunteered with four others to cross the firing line and burn a house, from which it was supposed the Federals would have superior advantages in their assault on the Confederate position. When he fell, his companions were recalled.

North Carolina, with the noble impulses of a great state, and with commendable pride in its magnificent reputation in the Confederate War; has builded a monument to the first, not only of her sons, but all the South's sons, who laid down their lives for the life of the Confederacy.

This young man was Henry L. Wyatt, only a private in the 1st North Carolina Regiment, yet he won imperishable fame by his service, which, while not more glorious than the thousands of others who later made the great sacrifice for their country, became preeminent because he was the first to shed out his blood for the Southland.

From this battle, so ably directed by General Magruder, comes North Carolina's claim, "First at Bethel."

Not only in the United States army, but in the Confederate army, General Magruder was known as "Prince John." Careful of his person, inclined to stylishness in dress, even before the war, at Newport, Rhode Island, he was considered among the handsomest, as well as the most courteous and gracious of American soldiers.

In the seven days' battle around Richmond, and at the sad finality of that wondrous campaign, Malvern Hill, Magruder bore a distinguished and valorous part.

In the fall of 1862, matters had reached almost a crisis in Texas. Jealousies, which calmer judgment now declares unfortunate though not unusual, among proud and patriotic men, had seriously affected the success of Confederate arms west of the Mississippi. A head was needed, and so, of the general officers in the East, General Magruder was selected by the government, not only as a successful soldier, but as a high grade organizer, to assume charge of the affairs of the great territory west of the Mississippi. This department had boundless possibilities. It had material for great soldiers. Its men, accustomed to hardships, trained to the highest physical endurance by their daily surroundings, and accustomed to danger and adventure, were ready to volunteer with readiest alacrity, and to fight without fear. The splendid achievements of the trans-Mississippi volunteers will stand the closest scrutiny, and the sharpest comparison with any of those heroes, who by their courage and endurance won renown for the armies of Tennessee and Northern Virginia. Their deeds, though not yet justly and fully chronicled, will, when truly recorded, add still more resplendence to the name of "Confederate Soldier."

It was believed that the generals, hitherto operating with separate commands, would recognize General Magruder's superior ability and justly earned reputation, and that under his guidance, wide experience and honorably won fame, would co-operate in the campaigns in Arkansas, Louisiana, Texas and Missouri, and when massed under a man of General Magruder's genius and skill would stay threatened Federal invasion and produce the results their fighting qualities might reasonably be expected to evolve.

After starting upon his journey, circumstances arose which recalled him temporarily; but toward the end of October, in 1862, he reached Texas.

General Magruder early realized the necessity of holding the line of the Rio Grande, which for more than twelve hundred miles was the boundary between the Confederate states and the Republic of Mexico. Along so many hundreds of miles of waterway, and a line which presented a great many military difficulties, it was impossible for the United States, without a base on the Gulf of Mexico, to interrupt or prevent the transportation and sale of cotton and the return of supplies through Mexico, which at that time were almost absolutely necessary to maintain an organized army in Texas. The preservation of this territory was a military necessity. It divided the Federal forces and kept a great number of men engaged in defending the flanks of the armies operating along the Mississippi River and the Gulf of Mexico.

Up to the time of Magruder's coming, those in command in Louisiana and Texas had practically conceded that a full defence of the Texan coast was impracticable. Galveston, by reason of its peculiar topographical position, had been abandoned. A small Federal force was quartered on the wharves, close to the limits of the city, while the Federal fleet, outside, prevented egress and ingress to the harbor, and only waited reinforcements to make a more permanent and extensive occupation and by closing the avenues to Mexico, make complete the blockade of the entire borders of the Confederacy.

General Magruder was considered one of the best strategists in the Confederate army. By quick movements and the rapid disposition of troops, he had delayed General McClellan's march along the Yorktown Peninsula several weeks, and he was now resolved to rid the coast of

Texas of Federal invasion and to restore Galveston to Confederate control. He had but few of the more powerful resources of military arts at his command; his artillery was limited; he had no gunboats and no material from which to make a gunboat that could ride the ocean storms; but his coming with a magnificent past of military achievement, and his personal confidence and courage, quickly inspired the people in the proximity of Galveston with the highest opinions of his talents and gallantry, and created hope where the surroundings declared there could be no hope.

It is fifty miles from Houston to Galveston, and the Brazos River, together with the bayous, afforded communication with the Gulf, through the harbor at Galveston to that city. Prompt in action and resolute of purpose, General Magruder reconnoitered the situation at Galveston, and determined to re-take the place. He only proposed to make this attempt after a very careful survey and an equally careful arrangement of his plans. The Federal fleet blockading Galveston was not very extensive, yet was so out of proportion to anything that the Confederates could bring to bear upon it, that an attack on it was considered absolutely foolhardy.

General Magruder had brought with him from Virginia a few hundred Enfield rifles. These proved of tremendous value in the operations he was to undertake at Galveston. Shotguns and ordinary hunting rifles were not very satisfactory, unless at very close range, and while General Magruder may not have anticipated such service as they should render at Galveston, it was deemed by his followers extremely fortunate that he had the foresight to introduce, with his coming to his new field of operation, these English guns.

Among Federal vessels blockading the port at Galveston was the Harriet Lane, commanded by Captain Wainwright; she carried four heavy guns and two twenty-four-pounders. The Westfield, mounting eight guns, was a large propeller, and the flagship of Commodore Renshaw, in command of the blockading fleet. The Owasco, another propeller, carried eight heavy guns; the Clifton, a propeller with four heavy guns and an armed schooner were among the vessels which composed the fleet which General Magruder, with the most inadequate means, proposed to attack and destroy, or put to flight.

As early as the beginning of 1863, the Confederate cavalry had been taught to be ready for any service, whether in scouting, raiding, assaulting infantry or defending forts. In the demands upon cavalry, the Confederate authorities were no respecter of persons, and that a man belonged to the cavalry gave him no exemption from any service that infantry or artillery could perform.

By the 1st of November, 1862, General Magruder issued a call for volunteers. Hand bills were distributed throughout the city of Houston, calling for enlistments. It had been given out that Captain Leon Smith would have charge of the operations by water. These calls received few responses. Some said it was the hazard of the expedition, others were unwilling to volunteer under Captain Smith, a stranger. Call after call fell on deaf ears, and incredible minds and unwilling hearts, so far as the citizens and the sailors about Houston were concerned.

General Magruder's plans seemed doomed to failure, when Lieutenant Colonel Bagby of the cavalry suggested to General Magruder that Colonel Tom Green was a man of boundless courage and also of unlimited resources. The history of General Green's intrepidity, fortitude, and superior ability in extricating his brigade from New Mexico a few months before had spread abroad through Texas, and after this superb performance, many people thought there was nothing that General Green could not accomplish.

General Magruder promptly sent for General Green and unfolded to him his plan of attack on Galveston, and suggested to him to take three hundred volunteers from his cavalry, and with these, on board two steamboats under command of Captain Leon Smith, aid in General Magruder's attempt to recapture Galveston. But General Green, conscious of his power and confident of his ability as a leader of men, declined to embark on boats under the command of Captain Smith, insisting that, as he was supreme on the land, he must also be supreme on the sea; and then it was that General Magruder, pleased with the spirit of the man, entrusted to Colonel Green the command of the two river steamers, the Bayou City and the Neptune, which had been rudely converted into marine rams with a few cotton bales to protect their wheels and engines.

It required immeasurable courage in such frail and unseaworthy boats to pass out into the Gulf of Mexico, or into the harbor at Galveston, and attack war vessels. General Green, now fifty-one years of age, had led a most strenuous life, and it was too late for him to take counsel of fear. He went back to his command full of the excitement and glamour of glory's calls and issued the following order:

"Soldiers, you are called upon to volunteer in a dangerous expedition. I have never deceived you, I will not deceive you now. I regard this as the most desperate enterprise that men ever engaged in. I shall go, but I do not know that I shall ever return; I do not know that any who go with me will, and I want no man to volunteer who is not willing to die for his country and to die now."

None could say that they misunderstood the purport of this laconic but stirring and impassioned appeal. The 5th and 7th regiments had been recruited to a full quota. Not five in a hundred had ever been to sea; they knew nothing of the management of any sort of seagoing vessel, but they did know that General Green wanted them to go and they did go, largely because he was going with them. When the two regiments were drawn up in line and volunteers called for, be it said to the renown of Texas and to the honor of the Confederate soldier that, without an instant's hesitation, or a moment's delay, every man in these two regiments stepped forward and declared his willingness to take the chances of war in an expedition of which they knew nothing, except that their beloved commander told them that while it might lead through the paths of glory, it also might lead to the grave.

In all the history of the Confederate armies, so replete with the highest and noblest heroism, there is no record of anything grander or more inspiring than this act of the men of these two regiments, offering, in the face of the warning of their beloved commander, to go with him, if needs be, even unto present death, to serve their country.

A cavalryman never likes to give up his horse. There is a sense of safety, as well as a sense of pride in the cavalry mount. And when those valiant Texans went away and committed their steeds to the care of their comrades, it added a new radiance to their courage and valor. Ready to leave their beasts to enter upon an element of which they knew nothing and engage in an enterprise of which they were profoundly ignorant, all because, through the voice of their commander, they heard the call of country bidding them go to meet the foes of the land they loved, was both an unusual and an extraordinary exhibition of patriotism and of obedience to duty's demands.

But, like those with Gideon of old, three hundred alone could assume the dangers and win the honors of this peculiar engagement.

Some members of the 4th Regiment heard of the expedition, and these hurried forward to offer their services, but they were reluctantly denied the valued privilege, and ordered back to their command. Satisfied to obey, they were filled with grief which later became even more poignant when they understood the result of the splendid victory of which they were denied a share.

It was a difficult task to determine who should go, in face of the universal and intrepid desire manifested by these volunteers, to take part in this desperate and dangerous enterprise.

With that abandon of courage that marks the really brave, these three hundred soldiers, one-half from the 5th and one-half from the 7th Regiment, marched down to the wharf at Houston, and took passage on the Bayou City and Neptune.

General Green remained with the Bayou City. The Neptune, the faster boat, was commanded by Lieutenant Colonel Bagby, on which were volunteers from two artillery companies. But the main fighters and the great fighting machine, the real men behind the guns, were those who handled the Enfield rifles which General Magruder brought over from the far East.

With such unworthy seagoing vessels, protected with a few bales of cotton, likely to be blown up by the first well-directed shell, only the most valiant of men would have undertaken so hazardous an enterprise. The remaining men of the 4th, 5th and 7th Cavalry, composing Sibley's brigade, had been dispatched to Galveston to engage in the assault by land and the defense of the guns on the beach.

General Magruder led the land forces in person. Along the wharves and shores of the bay, all the Confederate artillery was put in position. There was little, if any, protection to the guns or gunners. They were coming out in the open to fight the men who were protected in ships, and they were eager for the unequal fray.

General Magruder had announced that he would fire the first gun, and that when this was heard, all the artillery should turn loose upon the Federal fleet.

Under Colonel Cook, five hundred men plunged into water waist deep, carrying upon their shoulders the scaling ladders, upon which to climb upon the barricades held by the Federals on the remains of the City Wharf.

Neither wind nor wave had aught of terror for these splendid knights of the sea, who, in the darkness of the night, guided only by the pale stars, encumbered with guns and ladders, were hunting for their foes, who, safely barricaded, were waiting to send death-dealing missiles into their ranks. On land, such an assault had terrifying elements, but wading out into the sea, with neither beacons nor torches to guide their steps, carrying or pulling scaling ladders, by which alone they could hope to engage an enemy entrenched high above them upon wooden wharves, reaches to the sublimest heights of human courage.

The dismounted cavalry had been brought within a short distance of Galveston, and when the first gun was fired, with brave and steady heads and fleet of foot, they pressed forward to the front, on the line held by the venturesome artillery.

The Federal ships were not slow to take their part in this magnificent night pageant. Shells and bombs and shot plowed through the walls and over the fortifications and played hide and seek amongst the guns and caissons, that stood out on the land with distinctness, when the flashes of the cannon lit up the weird scenes of the fateful hour. The men in line on the shore were unable to reach their enemies, who were safely anchored out in harbor. Though their position was made uncomfortable by the fierceness of the fire, none flinched and none sought to avoid the consequence of the unequal affray.

So close were the combatants together that shells alternating with grape and canister speeded forth from the Federal gunboats, and from midnight until morn this contest was waged. From two o'clock until the dawn of day, fierce and fast flew the shells; and the roar of artillery and the flashes of the guns made the bay a scene of terror.

Magruder turned his eyes anxiously towards the direction from which his navy should come. The men aboard the steamboats heard the sound of artillery and, catching the inspiration of the hour, with illy suppressed anxiety and impatience, urged that they push forward into the midst of the conflict. They had waited from midnight until four in the morning for the sign which would bid them to enter the arena, and when at early morn they heard the call for them to come, it was with difficulty that their commanders could restrain their impatient ardor.

As they sailed down the Bayou, they caught sight of the flashes which marked the place where the artillery duel was being fought out. The clear starlight, with the moon gone down, was a splendid background upon which was painted the illuminations created by rapidly firing ordnance. This was more brilliant and more beautiful than any display that fireworks might produce.

The roll of the cannon was sweet music to the patriots now afloat and being propelled with quickening revolutions of the wheels into the turmoil and excitement.

The Federal ship, Harriet Lane, being nearest the shore, was the first to receive the attention of the Confederate navy. The Neptune, the fastest of the flotilla, came quickly within range of the Federal fleet, and in swinging around to the side of the Harriet Lane, was struck amidships and quickly sank. The water was so shallow that it did not reach the upper part of the vessel. Without being deterred from the serious business in which they were engaged, the cavalry mounted on the highest portion of the boat and with their Enfield rifles poured a deadly fire upon every part of the Harriet Lane, and practically drove her gunners from their posts.

The Bayou City, not so swift, but manned by none the less determined soldiers and sailors, swung promptly into action. Compared with the Lane, she was helpless in an artillery fight, but those aboard of this frail ship had no dread of any danger that the exigencies of the hour could precipitate. As she advanced into the battle, her best piece of artillery burst and the valiant captain, Wier, who had volunteered to direct the guns, fell dead by their side.

Disregarding all ideas of prudence, and casting to the winds or the waters all fear, the Bayou City, with her improvised ram, made straight for the Harriet Lane and drove her iron nose into her sides. The blow was given with such force that it disabled the Harriet Lane; the vessels appeared as one forum of raging conflict. With grappling irons, the Confederates held the two vessels fast together, and then in obedience to the call of General Green, every man from the Bayou City sprang upon the deck of the unfortunate Lane.

There were no words of parley, there were no calls for surrender, but the brave Texans, under their valiant commander, with Enfield rifles and their swords, made quick work of the crew of the Federal ship, and in the briefest period the storm quieted to the stillness of death.

The commander of the Lane, Captain Wainwright, was killed. Lieutenant Lee, his junior officer, was mortally wounded. There was nothing to do but ask for quarter. The Federal troops on the wharves, who, by reason of the shortness of the Confederates' scaling ladders, had escaped capture, now surrendered, and fate with relentless and pitiless edict, gave the Federals over to complete defeat.

When Captain Lee, a Confederate officer, one of those manning the Bayou City, looked into the faces of the Federal prisoners, he was shocked to see that the dying lieutenant on the Harriet Lane was his own son.

Commodore Renshaw, in command of the Westfield, was not disposed to rush away and leave his comrades on the Harriet Lane unsupported. The shallowness of the water and the limited space in which these vessels had maneuvered caused the Westfield, Commodore Renshaw's boat, to run aground. The Mary Boardman, one of the transports, gamely essayed to help the Westfield, and the Clifton, another propeller, tendered her assistance in her extremity. The laurel wreath had been woven for the brow of the daring, fearless Confederates, and no effort of the brave Federals could stay the losses. When the enterprise was first considered, only hope stirred the hearts of the men in gray. They scarcely calculated that, under the most favorable conditions, any such consequence could come from the expedition. Brave and fearless, they were not prepared for such a wonderful result. True, they were guided by Magruder's genius, aided by Smith's skill, led by Green's immeasurable courage, helped by Bagby's experience, impelled by Scurry's valor, encouraged by Cook's dauntless bravery, and inspired by McNeill's calm and imperturbable gallantry; but none dared to believe that so much could be accomplished in so brief a period, or such transcendent success crown even the bravest of men, facing such difficulties with such splendid reward. The Federal vessels which escaped sailed away. They left Galveston a Confederate possession. The survivors were glad to go beyond the reach of horsemen, who were as reckless and enterprising on the sea as they had proven themselves on the land.

It was a great victory. It cost the Confederates twenty-six killed and one hundred and seventeen wounded, but the success of the enterprise and the flight of the Federal vessels from Galveston set abroad a great wave of enthusiasm and patriotism. Few could realize that such glorious results could be obtained by men, handicapped by insufficient resources, even when sustained by the highest courage and noblest spirit. What had been done stirred the hearts of all the people of Texas. They recognized in General Magruder an illustrious soldier, and in the Texas cavalry, whether on land or sea, an invincible host, which had the apparent power to wrest from fate victory under any conditions, however adverse or stormy.

Chapter VIII

COLONEL ROY S. CLUKE'S KENTUCKY RAID, FEBRUARY-MARCH, 1863

On the 14th of February, 1863, a small brigade of Kentucky cavalry assembled at McMinnville, Tennessee. Seven hundred and fifty men constituted the organization. The 8th Kentucky cavalry, of which Roy S. Cluke was colonel, Major Robert S. Bullock commanding, was to form the basis of the men to be used in an expedition into Central Kentucky. Lieutenant Colonel Cicero Coleman of the regiment had been seriously wounded at Hartsville on the 7th of December, and still suffering, was unable to go. In addition to the 8th Kentucky cavalry, the 9th Kentucky cavalry furnished two companies under the command of Colonel Robert G. Stoner, who was one of the bravest and most enterprising of Morgan's men. These constituted the first battalion. Companies C and I of Gano's regiment and Company A of the 2nd Kentucky, under command of Major Theophilus Steele, constituted the second battalion. Later, in Wayne County, Companies D and I of Chenault's (the 11th) regiment, were added to Stoner's battalion. Colonel Cluke was allowed a couple of brass cannon, howitzers, affectionately called by Morgan's men the "bull pups." They never did very great damage, but they made a loud noise. They looked to an enemy much bigger than they were, and if they were not very effective with their shots, they were oftentimes extremely forceful with their "barking."

No seven hundred and fifty men were ever more ably commanded. Colonel Cluke was not only a brave but a brilliant officer.

General Morgan furnished his two brothers as part of the staff. The best possible material was designated for this service. The men chosen for this raid were thoroughly acquainted with most of the territory through which Colonel Cluke would necessarily have to pass. The companies of the 11th would know Madison and the adjoining counties, Companies C and I of the 3rd Kentucky (Gano's) would know Scott and Franklin Counties. Company A of the 2nd would be familiar with almost the entire Bluegrass, and Cluke's own regiment would know Kentucky from Maysville to Springfield and Somerset. He started out with the advantage of men who had full and complete knowledge of the country through which he was to operate. This added much to the efficiency of the little brigade. Lieutenant Shuck, of the 8th Kentucky, was given the command of the advance guard. The importance of the advance guard in cavalry campaigns cannot be over-estimated. It requires officers of great coolness, of much dash, dauntless courage, and men who never counted the cost and who would follow in the face of any danger wherever they were ordered to go. In such an expedition scouts would also play a most useful and prominent part. To Lieutenant Hopkins, of the 2nd, and S. P. Cunningham, of the 8th, were given the choice and control of the scouts. Neither the advance guard nor the scouts made a very large force. All told, they did not exceed forty, but these were men upon whom any commander could rely at any hour of day or night and in any place whither they might come.

At McMinnville a hundred rounds of ammunition were counted out and six days' rations were issued to the men upon the morning that they marched away. Nature did not appear to be in harmony with the purposes of this expedition. The weather was extremely inclement, and, for that part of Tennessee, extraordinarily cold. Hardly had the line been formed until sleet and rain and snow came violently down. These, with the tramping of the horses' feet, soon made veritable sloughs of the dirt roads over which the march was progressing. The line pursued ran through Sparta, Obey City, Jamestown, in Tennessee, to the Kentucky border. This country presented a scene of universal desolation. In times of peace it was not fully able to supply the needs of its own inhabitants, and now that armies had traversed it for more than a year, there was not sufficient forage at any one place to feed one company of horsemen. The six days' coarse rations given the men in their haversacks at McMinnville would keep them from want, but the horses, with hardest possible service in the midst of fearfully disagreeable weather, could only hope for scantiest and most insufficient provender. The entire one hundred and ten miles from McMinnville to the Cumberland River had been, before this period, practically eaten out of house and home, and there was little left for the strangers who might pass these mountain ways.

The Cumberland River was the only real barrier to this small force as it entered Kentucky. Once it was passed, there would be so many roads for the invaders to take that it would be impossible for the defenders to either stop their march or seriously impede their journeyings. The banks of the Cumberland were full. The Federals on the north side had taken all boats across to prevent passage by an enemy. Luckily, a canoe was found hidden away, large enough to convey Colonel Stoner and Lieutenant Hopkins and several men over the stream. These silently and stealthily paddled across. Some countryman, without the fear of "blue coats" before his eyes, had stored this craft in the bushes along a small tributary. He had probably used it in secret ferrying of goods to the south bank. With plenty of everything on the north side, it was not treason to keep a canoe hidden, with which, when no picket was present, or his eye not open, to run across the boundary calico, sugar, coffee or other necessities, so essential to the war-despoiled women and children on the south side, upon whom starvation and want had laid heavy hand.

Colonel Stoner and his cavalry comrades were fortunate and shrewd enough to surprise and capture the Federal pickets who were posted to guard Stigall's Ferry, a short distance north of Burnside, where Colonel Cluke had proposed and now determined to cross. A couple of flatboats and a coal barge were discovered amongst the Federal possessions, and these were quickly brought over. Now, in the face of vigorous foes, action was the watchword of the hour. With their saddles and guns, the men hastily rushed into the flatboats and poled and paddled over the stream. A more desperate mode of crossing was assigned to the horses. It was still bitter cold, and the poor beasts were forced into the river and compelled to swim its rapid currents. They could not speak, and they hesitated to plunge in; but the shouts and belaborings of their apparently cruel masters were more potent than their fears, and with only their noses above the water, and their bodies beneath the frigid waves, lapped into motion by the piercing winds, they swam diagonally across to the opposite shore. Already weakened by a trying march of more than a hundred miles, so great was the shock to the animals that a number of them were chilled to death and died upon the bank as they emerged from the water.

The severity of the winter rendered very rapid marching impossible. On the 19th of February, the little army reached Somerset, the county seat of Pulaski. A strong Federal force was stationed there, but alarmed by reports of an army of Confederates approaching from Knoxville, they hurriedly retreated to Danville, forty-five miles away and left a clear road for Colonel Cluke. Here a full supply of stores had been collected. Their guardians were in such a great hurry to ride to Danville that they forgot, or neglected, to destroy them. This was a gracious windfall for the Confederates. The Government and the sutlers had the very things these benumbed men and horses most needed. After supplying his tired beasts and hungry soldiers with all that was necessary to comfort, warm and feed them, and burning the remainder, Colonel Cluke made a forced march of twenty-eight miles to Mount Vernon. If he accomplished his work it was important to surprise his enemies, and in such work Colonel Cluke was a master hand. Finding nothing here, he pushed on to Richmond, Kentucky. The roads were wet, sloppy, slushy, and still blinding snowstorms and heavy rains with chilling currents, rushing down from the north, attempted to bid defiance to these sturdy riders, to stay their advance and render their march more harassing and tedious.

Lieutenant Cunningham, who was with Lieutenant Hopkins in command of the scouts, was a man of almost superhuman courage and of a genius and resource that entitled him to higher command. A few miles out on the pike from Richmond, advancing with eight men, he found a picket post of the Federals, consisting of four videttes. Challenged, he declared that he and his followers were friends. Dressed in blue coats, such as they were wearing, and which were a part of the Somerset find, he persuaded the Federals that they were a detachment of Woolford's Federal cavalry which was returning from Tennessee to Kentucky to assist in repelling the raid of Morgan's men. He told the questioning videttes that all the Federal forces were now concentrating at Lexington, that General John C. Breckinridge, by way of Cumberland Gap, had already entered the State with ten thousand Confederate infantry. The sergeant quickly became communicative and gave Cunningham a statement of the location and strength of all the Federal commands, and finally invited the Confederates to go to a house a short distance away, where the remainder of the picket detail was stationed. Cunningham cheerfully accepted the proffered hospitality of his new-made friends, but upon reaching the house he was somewhat embarrassed to find that twenty-four soldiers constituted this outpost. He persuaded the commander to send back one of his men with two of the Confederates to get information about some other of the Federal forces that were coming a short distance behind. The Federal, thus despatched, when out of sight of the post, quickly found himself a prisoner. Hopkins, Cunningham's associate commander of scouts, in a brief while, arrived on the scene with eight new blue-coated riders. The Confederates, now two-thirds in number of the Federal garrison, without parley or argument immediately announced their identity and attacked their hospitable and surprised friends, and killed one, wounded two, and made all the others prisoners. The generosity of the course pursued by Cunningham was open to serious criticism, but warriors do not carry copies of Chesterfield's rules in their pockets and find little use for their precepts and teachings on cavalry raids.

No outpost was ever captured more cleverly or more completely surprised, and few similar incidents reflect more credit on the actors.

Ten miles away there were two hundred and fifty Federal cavalry. This was just exactly what Cluke wanted. Fresh horses, cavalry saddles and ammunition would be a great comfort to the men who rode with him, but the story of Breckinridge's coming had reached Richmond. Rumors traveled in those days on the winds—and the Federal cavalry hastily decamped. Major Steele, with three companies, pursued these fleeing troops. He overtook them at Comb's Ferry, on the Kentucky River, twelve miles from Lexington, and, fighting and running, drove the Federal column into the city. In attempting to capture some videttes, who had indicated they would surrender, one of the Federals fired his rifle at Steele's breast, but a thick Mexican blanket folded about his body saved his life and protected him from injury except a broken rib. It was a serious misfortune that a man so brave and enterprising, so thoroughly acquainted with the geography of the territory over which the operations of the next thirty-five days would extend, should at this critical moment, became incapacitated for active service.

Colonel Cluke was now far into Kentucky. He was over two hundred miles from where he started. He had been out nine days. He had no easy job. He had worked his way, he had seen much of the enemy and at every point had mystified and alarmed the Federal commands. He and his subordinates had managed to escape from very serious battle. Detachments were sent in every direction to increase the terror of the Federal forces at Lexington, Mount Sterling, Paris. They threatened, attacked and captured several important positions, and his enemies, magnifying his forces, sat down inactive until they should determine whether Breckinridge and the ten thousand infantry behind this dashing cavalry advance were really coming, and until they could count Cluke's followers and figure up just what they would go against if they might force him to battle.

Cluke's men who lived in the immediate vicinity of Lexington, Mount

Sterling, Winchester and Richmond were granted temporary furloughs in order to visit their friends, renew their wardrobes, and, if desirable, replace their mounts, and enjoy the association with their loved ones whom they had left four and a half months before. Only the complete mystification and demoralization of his foes could justify so astute a leader as Cluke in risking such a proceeding. Happy days for these bold riders. The four and a half months of absence had been full of excitement, adventures and war experiences. The march out of Kentucky, the Battle of Hartsville, the Christmas raid, were stories that sounded well in the telling and impressed those who stayed at home with the courage and marvelous achievements of the narrators who, in the partial eyes of home folks, at least, were transformed into real heroes,—these boys who had gone away to fight for the South.

Ceaseless activity marked every hour of those who had not been furloughed. Demonstrations on Paris confined the garrison there, while Stoner, moving back to Mount Sterling, found a Federal Kentucky cavalry regiment, which, with a small force, he promptly attacked and drove away. He captured many prisoners and the road by which these Federals retreated was strewn with overcoats, guns, haversacks and wagons, which unmistakably demonstrated that some of those who were hunting Cluke did not just now desire a formal introduction.

On the 24th of February Colonel Cluke had concentrated his command at Mount Sterling, and the whole day was spent in collecting and distributing horses, equipments and arms. By this time the Federals had become somewhat doubtful and inquisitive about the strength of the invaders. The ten thousand infantry did not show up from Cumberland Gap, and they began to realize that the Confederate detachment, which had given them all this trouble and hard riding and had alarmed them so terribly, was probably not, after all, a very great army. All sorts of dreams and visions came to the Federal pursuers. Colonel Runkle of the 45th Ohio Regiment, Acting Brigadier General, reported: "I was confident of cutting the enemy to pieces between Richmond and the Kentucky River." Of his march to Winchester he wrote, "The inhabitants reported that they threw their dead into the stream (Slate) and carried off the wounded."

A Federal cavalry brigade made a dash at Mount Sterling, Cluke's headquarters. Only two hundred men of the command were on hand at that particular moment. Furloughs had decimated Cluke's forces and they were glad to get out of the town, but they were gladder still

126

that the Federals did not pursue them. A Federal officer, reporting the occurrence, wrote: "The rebels had a heavy guard out here and made a show of fighting, but when we fired on them they rang the bells in town and all went out in a huddle. The rebels burned their wagons and threw everything away they had stolen." He also said, "We heard heavy firing yesterday below here in direction of Jeffersonville. Suppose Miner has cut them off, which I ordered him to do." The cutting off was more imaginative than real.

The sound of the Federal guns had not died away before four hundred of Cluke's furloughed men hastened to the relief of their retreating companions. The Federal cavalry established itself at Mount Sterling but left Colonel Cluke in command of the surrounding country.

Oftentimes in partisan war, strategy is as important as men. Lieutenant Cunningham was sent to threaten Lexington. Among the scouts was Clark Lyle. Young, vigorous, brave and enterprising, he now undertook a most perilous mission. Cunningham had sent a spy disguised in Federal uniform to the headquarters of the officer commanding at Mount Sterling, and this shrewd messenger was smart enough to put in his pocket some blank printed forms which lay upon the table of the commandant. One of these was filled up as an order purporting to be from the commander at Lexington, Kentucky, directing the commander at Mount Sterling to march instantly to Paris, twenty miles north of Lexington to repel a raid which was impending by the Confederates against the Kentucky Central Railroad, which connected Cincinnati and Lexington.

Lyle, dressed in full Federal uniform, rode into Mount Sterling at the top of his speed, lashing his horse at every step. The animal was reeking with foam. He rushed to the headquarters of the commander, Colonel Runkle, and delivered the orders. The bugles were instantly sounded, and the Federal cavalry brigade moved out to Paris. Hardly had the sound of the jingling sabres ceased along the macadam road which led from Mount Sterling to Paris, before Cluke, with his reorganized force, re-entered the town and captured the garrison and the stores. He found Mount Sterling a most delightful place to remain. It was only twenty miles from Winchester and only a few more from Richmond. The predominating element was Confederate, and Colonel Cluke remained for some eight days, enjoying the hospitality of his people and feasting upon the good things with which the Bluegrass was replete. The Federal commander, concerning this, said: "Found order false on 27th. I received order to pursue Cluke and use him up, which I proceeded to do." A Federal major, not to be outdone in giving an account of his past, said that he had received orders to find Cluke and that he "moved forward like hell." Somehow or other these active and ferocious commanders never got where Cluke was. The Federals, however, became dissatisfied with Cluke's occupation and coming in full force, they drove him across Slate Creek into the Kentucky Mountains. Detachments with Stoner, coming past Middletown and around Mount Sterling, were roughly handled by the Federals, but with small loss they reached the main force, when Cluke, hearing that Humphrey Marshall with three thousand soldiers was advancing into Kentucky, fell back to Hazel Green, Wolfe County, thirty-five miles southeast.

Established for a few days at Hazel Green, an epidemic, a cross between erysipelas and measles, appeared, and half of Cluke's small command were disabled with this dangerous and treacherous malady. Had the Federals pursued him at this time they would have captured a large portion of his command in bed or camp, and certainly they would have made prisoners of the sick, and if hard pressed would surely have either forced him to return to the mountains or be himself made a captive. Though so many of his men were sick, Cluke sent Colonel Stoner back to Montgomery County, in the vicinity of Mount Sterling. This was done just to let the Federals know that he and his men were around and if necessary would show fight. No better man than Stoner could have been found for such a mission. The Federals, getting increased courage from the Confederate retreat, began to demonstrate themselves and advanced upon Hazel Green. Cluke, not to be outdone, moved further east, thirty miles to Salyersville in Magoffin County, still deeper into the mountains. The season was unpropitious. The fountains of heaven seemed to open. Rains came down in torrents. There were days when horses and men, with cold, chilling rains, were almost incapacitated from service. On the 19th of March, Cluke, through his scouts, discovered that he was apparently entirely surrounded. Fifteen hundred Federals had marched by his front and gained a position in his rear. Eastward, from Louisa, one thousand men were rushing upon him, and westwardly, from Proctor, on the Kentucky River, in Lee County, eight hundred more Federals were moving to crush this bold and defiant Confederate raider. The forces had not fully recovered from the attack of the disease at Hazel Green, and at this time Cluke had not more than five hundred effectives.

It was a bold thought, but with true military instinct, he concluded that the only thing to do was to attack his enemy where he was least expecting it. He was only sixty miles from Mount Sterling. The roads were almost impassable, and these would render the march extremely difficult, trying and laborious. He assumed wisely that the enemy would not suspect that he would reappear at Mount Sterling. Rapidly as possible, marching through slush and rain and across swollen streams, he passed through and around his foes. The combination of rain, cold and the spattering of men and horses by the slush created by the tramp of the column, rendered the conditions surrounding this march almost unbearable. Either of the three elements would have been distressing, but combined they became well-nigh intolerable. The author had many experiences of war's hardships but, in common with his comrades, he considered this ride from Salyersville to Slate Creek the most arduous and disagreeable of all things that touched the life of Morgan's men. The ride around Lebanon in January, 1863, on the Christmas raid, brought almost incomparable suffering. Those who endured the cold of that dreadful night believed that they had reached the limit of human endurance. There the awful freezing was the chiefest element of suffering; but the men who rode with Cluke from Salyersville to Slate Creek declared that the hardship was even more terrible for man and mount than the ride around Lebanon.

Before leaving the sick men, Cluke's men scattered out into the mountains. A majority of the people of Wolfe County sympathized with the South, and it was not difficult to find friendly homes for the convalescent fugitives. The Licking River and all its tributaries were full and in many places over the banks, but the horses could swim and the men could go over in canoes and flatboats, and in a real emergency they could and did swim with their mounts. Colonel Cluke made a fierce and hard drive at Mount Sterling. On the morning of the 21st of March he appeared before the town and demanded its surrender. This was firmly declined. Heading one of the columns himself, he charged into the very heart of the city. The Federal garrison was driven back into the Court House. The Federals away from the Court House had posted themselves in residences along the streets, but the torch, the axe and the sledge hammer soon made a passway up to a hotel which was occupied by a number of Federals with the lower story used as a hospital. Here a flag of truce was run up. Cunningham and Lieutenant McCormack and six men advanced under the flag. Upon reaching the building, they were jeeringly informed that it was the sick who had surrendered and not the well soldiers, and these threatened to fire upon Cunningham and his comrades from the upper rooms, if they undertook to escape from the building. The outlook was extremely gloomy. Lieutenant Saunders suggested that each Confederate take a sick Federal soldier and hold him up in front while they escaped from the position into which their courage—and some might say rashness—had brought them. Putting this plan into immediate execution the retreat was begun. It was impossible for the Federals to fire without killing their sick comrades, but Cunningham and his friends were inconsiderate enough to set fire to the hospital before they so unceremoniously left, and in a little while, through charging and fighting, the men who had refused to surrender and had threatened to fire on Cunningham, found themselves in a most unfortunate predicament. The lower story was beginning to blaze. The sick were carried out, but the well men who had declined to respect Cunningham's flag of truce, must either burn up, jump out of the windows, or be shot down. No men ever more gladly surrendered, and the captive Federals and the Confederates all united in a common effort to save them from their impending doom. The Federal prisoners and the Confederates together worked to quench the flames which had been started under the hospital.

Time was of the very essence of victory. None could tell at what moment the Federals, left behind at Salyersville, might put in an appearance. Garrisons at Lexington, Paris and Winchester would soon hear the news of Cluke's coming and might ride to the rescue of their friends. Every man caught the spirit of haste. True it was Sunday morning, but war does not respect any day of rest. To have lost, after the brilliant strategy of the dreadful march from Salyersville would leave regrets that no future success could palliate. Every Confederate was terribly in earnest, and no laggards on that otherwise peaceful day of rest were found in Cluke's following. Captain Virgil Pendleton of Company D, 8th Kentucky, was mortally wounded and died shortly afterwards. No braver soldier or more loyal patriot ever gave his life for the South. Captain Terrill and Lieutenant Maupin of Chenault's regiment were seriously wounded. Both brave officers, they fell at the front.

The work was short, sharp and decisive. In six hours the agony was past. Two hundred and twenty wagons, five hundred mules and one thousand stand of arms were the reward the captors had for their heroic services. Three killed and ten or fifteen wounded was the penalty paid by

Cluke for his victory. The enemy lost a few more, and three hundred and one were paroled.

The forces which had been sent to catch Cluke were not long in finding that their enemy had evaded them and, rapidly leaving the mountains, had gone down into the Bluegrass and won a victory. They promptly followed on, searching for their agile foe.

Cluke's successful work incited spirited criticism of the conduct of the Federal commanders. Colonel Runkle and General Gilmore appear not to have agreed about the work done in this campaign. Colonel Runkle, with great complacency, reported: "As for my men, they have ridden day after day and night after night, without sleep or rest, and have pursued eagerly and willingly when so exhausted that they fell from their horses." On this report General Gilmore endorsed: "How his men could have been without sleep and his horses without rest during the two days he halted at Paris, I cannot understand." Captain Radcliffe, Company E, 10th Kentucky Cavalry, who capitulated at Mount Sterling, was, by the department commander, dishonorably dismissed from the military service, subject to the approval of the President, for his disgraceful surrender of the place.

Later he was honorably acquitted by a Court of Enquiry and cleared of all imputation upon his character as a soldier and restored to his command. Somebody had blundered and a scapegoat must be found.

So far as written reports are concerned, Colonel Cluke made only one return, which is as follows: "Rockville, Rowan County, Kentucky, March 24th, 1863. I reached the above place last evening, just from Mount Sterling. On the morning of the 21st I moved with my command direct to Mount Sterling, where I learned there were between three hundred and four hundred of the enemy guarding a large supply of commissary and quartermaster's stores, together with the good citizens of the place. After crossing Licking River I found the road in such condition that it was almost impossible to move my artillery. I placed three companies to assist and guard it, with directions to move on without delay to Mount Sterling. I then moved with my command to Mount Sterling, which place I reached about daylight the next morning, where I found the enemy quartered in the Court House and adjoining buildings. I immediately demanded a surrender of the place, which request they refused to comply with. I then gave them twenty minutes to get the women and children from town. That they refused to do also, and fired upon the flag of truce from the Court House and several other buildings immediately around the Court House. My artillery, not coming up in time, I was compelled to fire the town to dislodge the enemy. After several houses had been burned, they surrendered the place; but before surrendering, they kept up a continual firing from the buildings upon my men, who were protected by the fences, stables and outbuildings around the town. I paroled two hundred and eighty-seven privates (14th Kentucky cavalry) and fourteen officers. I paroled them to report to you within thirty days, which I herewith send you. The property destroyed, belonging to the enemy, will reach I think five hundred thousand dollars. I occupied the town about six hours when my scouts reported a large force advancing from Winchester. I immediately moved in the direction of Owingsville. I had not proceeded more than five miles when they made their appearance some two miles in my rear, numbering about twenty-five hundred men, with several pieces of artillery. They would not advance upon me and I quietly advanced on to Owingsville, without pursuit, and from thence on to the above place. When I left West Liberty for Mount Sterling, the enemy, numbering thirteen hundred men with four pieces of artillery, were at Hazel Green, in pursuit of my force. They reported and despatched a courier to Mount Sterling stating that they had me completely surrounded, but I surprised them by making my appearance where not expected. General Marshall is within forty miles of this place, moving on with sixteen hundred cavalry. He lost his artillery the other night. The guard placed over it went to sleep and some Home Guards slipped in on him and carried off the gun, leaving the carriage and caisson.... I send you three prisoners of which you will take charge until you hear from me again.... My command is elegantly mounted and clothed, in fact in better condition than they have ever been. If your command was here, you could clean the State of every Yankee."

Marching over from Southwestern Virginia, General Humphrey Marshall had driven the forces which had gone to capture Cluke at Salyersville back into Central Kentucky. This left Cluke an open way for the return to Monticello, Wayne County, Kentucky.

After maneuvering with his enemies for some days, he received orders from General Morgan to march southward by way of Irvine, McKee, Manchester and Somerset, to Stigall's Ferry, where he had crossed the river some weeks before. He had not been away more than seven weeks; he had traveled, all told, eight hundred miles, almost altogether within the line of the enemy. He was always operating with an inferior force, but he was ever ready to fight. The history of war furnished nothing superior to the skill and strategy of Colonel Cluke in this expedition. He was campaigning over two hundred miles from his supports; he had larger, active forces and many strong garrisons about him, and these were threatening and covering at all times the only way by which he could return to his starting place. His daring and skill had braved his enemies at every turn. He played with them as a cat with a mouse. Leading them far into the mountains, he slipped away before they realized that he was gone, and in the darkness of the night, amid storms, and over roads believed to be impassable, he made a tremendous march and pounced down upon an intrenched garrison more than half as great as the force he carried into the fight, and then escaped in the immediate presence of a Federal force five times as large as that which he was commanding. He destroyed more than a million dollars' worth of property. For weeks he defied and evaded his pursuers and then crossed the Cumberland River at the same point he had passed it, with his command well equipped, and reported to his superior commander the brilliant experiences without a serious mishap or defeat during his long stay amidst his enemies.

POSTSCRIPT

Roy Stuart Cluke was born in Clark County, Kentucky, in 1824. His mother died when he was only three weeks of age and he was reared by the family of his grandfather, James Stuart. This grandfather had served in the Revolutionary War under Washington. Allotted a large tract of land for his revolutionary services, he settled in Clark County and had for his homestead a thousand acre farm near the junction of Clark, Bourbon and Montgomery Counties, by the side of a great spring, known as "Stuart Spring." In the early days of Kentucky, water was even more valuable than rich land.

James Stuart had four sons, and all were soldiers from Kentucky in the War of 1812.

After such education as the local schools of his period could give, he was sent to a military school at Bardstown, Kentucky. Shortly after attaining his majority he volunteered for service in the Mexican war, and went with a company of Kentucky cavalry commanded by John Stuart Williams, his cousin, afterwards brigadier general in the Confederate army and United States Senator from Kentucky. The company made a most enviable record in Mexico. Briefly before the commencement of the Civil War, he organized and trained a company of cavalry which was attached to the State Guard. This company was noted for its thorough drill, its magnificent mounts, its splendid equipment and its dashing riders. When General Bragg invaded the State in 1862 he organized a regiment of cavalry composed largely of men from the Bluegrass counties. More than eight hundred men enlisted in this regiment, which was called the 8th Kentucky. When only a portion of his regiment had been enlisted, he was sent to harass General George W. Morgan, the Federal officer who was making his masterly retreat from Cumberland Gap, through the mountains of Kentucky. The 8th Kentucky subsequently became a part of General John H. Morgan's command. His regiment was actively engaged in service from August, 1862, until his capture, July 26th, 1863. He was at Hartsville on December 6th, 1862, on the Christmas raid, and led an independent expedition into Kentucky in February and March, 1863. He was captured on the 26th of July, 1863, with General Morgan, at Salineville, Columbiana County, Ohio, and was conveyed to the Ohio penitentiary with the other officers of the command, and kept there for some months and subsequently removed to Johnson's Island, Sandusky, Ohio. He loved the excitement and din of war. He chafed under his confinement in the penitentiary and at Johnson's Island. It was reported that he had been poisoned in prison. This, however, was denied and later was discredited. He died under distressing circumstances in December, 1863. There was an epidemic of diphtheria among the Confederate officers at Johnson's Island about the time of Colonel Cluke's death. A man of marvelously prepossessing physique, he enjoyed the friendship of the officers of the prison. He had been allowed to visit the office and read the newspapers. While thus employed one morning, with his strong, silvery voice, with military calmness, he said, "Gentlemen, I will be dead in a few minutes. I have only one request to make of you as soldiers and gentlemen. Leave my arms folded across my bosom like a warrior and tell them to place my Mexican War sabre by my side. Telegraph my cousin and foster brother, Samuel G. Stuart, of Winchester, Kentucky; request him to come for my body and bury me next to my mother in the old Stuart graveyard at home." He folded his arms, the paper fell from his now nerveless grasp, his head drooped on his breast. Even his enemies were impressed at his calmness and courage in the presence of the great enemy. They rushed to his side. The prison physician felt his pulse and lifting his head from his chest, where he was listening for the heart beats, he turned his face to those aside and said, "He is dead." The drama was ended and in pathetic gloom the curtain fell on the brilliant and gallant soldier.

Six feet, four inches tall, splendidly proportioned, with a magnificent suit of brown hair and whiskers, graceful as any man who ever rode to war, as brave as the bravest, calm, cool, fierce in danger, his presence was always an inspiration to his followers. He was idolized by his men. He had won the confidence and admiration of General Morgan and all who were associated with him in the division. Had he escaped on the Ohio raid, he would have been made a brigadier general. There was universal sorrow that so splendid a life should go out with such darkened surroundings. His remains were brought to his native State and deposited first where he asked, in the old Stuart graveyard, and then later removed to the Lexington cemetery. In this wondrously beautiful "City of the Dead" he rests close to his great leader, Morgan, within a stone's throw of the grave of General John C. Breckinridge, just across the way a little bit from General Roger W. Hanson and Colonel W. C. P. Breckinridge, and under the shadow of Kentucky's memorial to Henry Clay.

Those who loved and followed him have built a simple granite monument on which is inscribed:

"Roy Stuart Cluke. 1824-1863.

Colonel of the 8th Kentucky Cavalry, C.S.A.

Erected by his Comrades."

Chapter IX

SHELBY'S MISSOURI RAID, SEPTEMBER, 1863

Certain parts of Missouri were settled, almost entirely, by Kentuckians. In the earlier days there had been a tremendous emigration from Kentucky to Indiana and Illinois, and when these States had received a large quota of inhabitants from Kentucky, the overflow from that State then turned to Missouri. Its counties and towns were designated by Kentucky names which were brought over by these new people from their home State. In and around 1850 this tide of emigration flowed with a deep and wide current. Among those who left their homes to find an abiding place in the new State, marvelous accounts of the fertility and splendor of which were constantly being carried back to Kentucky, was Joseph O. Shelby. He was born at Lexington in 1831, and when only nineteen years of age joined in the great march westward and found a home on the Missouri River at Berlin, one hundred and fifty miles west of St. Louis. These Missouri-Kentuckians carried with them one of the important manufactures of the State,—hemp, which for many years was chiefly a Kentucky product. In the rich, loamy lands of Missouri, this staple grew with great luxuriousness, and the introduction of hemp seed from China both improved the quality and increased the production per acre. Not only did the fertile land and the salubrious climate turn these people westward, but a love of change also aroused this spirit of emigration.

Young Shelby was fairly well educated. He was a born leader, and no braver heart ever beat in human bosom. Warrior blood coursed through his veins. His grandfather was a brother of Isaac Shelby. This guaranteed patriotism and valor. He had great dash, a spirit of unlimited enterprise, willing and ready to work, with a vigorous body and a brave soul, he became a Missourian and was an ideal immigrant. He had come from the very center of hemp manufacture in Kentucky. This product was made into bagging and bound with hemp ropes. The cotton country of the South was largely dependent upon Kentucky and Missouri for these two things so essential in marketing cotton. It was a most profitable and remunerative manufacture and was largely carried on by the use of negro labor. Modern machinery had not then been invented for the use of weaving the bagging or of twisting the ropes. To produce these products so important in cotton growing, it was necessary to rely upon the crudest implements.

Sixty miles east of Kansas City, Shelby selected a location at Waverly, Lafayette County, and there began his operations as a bagging and rope manufacturer. It was easy to ship the product down the Mississippi and from thence to scatter it throughout the cotton districts by the waterways over Arkansas, Louisiana, Mississippi, Tennessee and Alabama. Shelby was successful from the very inception of his new enterprise. He was hardly well settled in his new home before the difficulties in Kansas began. Strongly believing in slavery, his views as well as his interests and his proximity to the Kansas line intensified his opinions. Loving adventure, brave in war, he returned to Kentucky to recruit there for the Kansas imbroglio. In these days it was not difficult to find in Shelby's native State men who loved adventure, who were always ready for war, and were overjoyed at the chance to get into a fight. With Clark, Atchison and Greene, Shelby did his full share in the Kansas fighting. It gave him experience that was valuable to him a few years later in the great war. He won reputation with his Kentucky fighters, and when the truce was patched up he went back to the peaceful surroundings of his rope walk in Waverly. This place was noted for its uncompromising Southern sentiments. The anti-slavery settlers who went by it, ascending the Missouri River, always steered away from it. They knew there was neither comfort to be obtained nor security to be assured when they passed this point. They could not buy anything they wanted there, and they were likely to find trouble.

When the troubles of 1860 began to develop, no one was more enthusiastic for the South or more willing to fight for its rights than Joseph O. Shelby. There was no section, even in Confederate States, more loyal to the South than the immediate territory about Waverly. With sentiments fixed and embittered by the Kansas War, the young men of that portion of Missouri were not only brave and ambitious, but they were anxious to go to war. With his prejudices quickened and enlarged by his nearness to Kansas, which was even then a bitter State, in so far as slavery was concerned, Shelby organized and equipped a company of cavalry at Waverly. It was easy to fill up its ranks with enthusiastic, dashing young fellows who were only too happy in taking the chances of battle, and they were charmed to find a leader of Shelby's experience, of his enthusiasm, and of his intrepidity.

Independence, Missouri, the county seat of Jackson County, was only twelve miles from Kansas City. A vast majority of its people were intensely southern, and when Independence was threatened with the presence of Federal dragoons, Shelby and his company lost no time in marching forty miles from Lafayette County to see that their friends and sympathizers at Independence had a square deal from the Union soldiers. It soon was spread abroad that if the dragoons did come there was trouble ahead and they stayed away. Shelby, now in for the war, rode to join Governor Jackson and General Price in defense of Missouri.

In these days it did not take long for fighting men in Missouri to find people who were willing to fight them. The southern part of the State was much divided in political sentiment, and the bitterness of a civil war found full development in that territory. At the Battle of Carthage, July 5th, 1861, Shelby and his men did splendid service, and their excellent discipline, their superb courage, did a great deal, not only to create, but to intensify the spirit and steady the arms of the entire Missouri contingent. Beginning as a captain, rising to brigadier-general in three years, Shelby had an activity and experience that few enjoy. He fought in the Army of the Tennessee, and he fought in the Trans-Mississippi Department, and he was never more delighted than when fighting.

Wilson's Creek, one of the sanguinary battles of the war, was fought on the tenth day of August, 1861, and there Shelby again demonstrated that the only thing necessary to make a reputation and fame as a great cavalryman was the opportunity.

General John H. Morgan, in Kentucky, and Shelby were close friends. They began their careers in much the same way. Morgan had his company of Kentucky riflemen: Shelby his company of Missouri cavalrymen. Morgan died in the struggle: Shelby lived thirty-six years after the close and died in 1897. These two soldiers had grown up in Lexington, and while Morgan was five years Shelby's senior, they were intimates. Shelby's career did not close until May, 1865. At the end, unwilling to accept the results of the war, he marched into Mexico with five hundred of his followers and undertook to found an American colony. This project soon failed. The wounds of the war began to heal, and Shelby and his colonists were glad to come back and live under the flag they

138

had so bravely and tenaciously fought. No man in the Confederate army marched more miles, and, with the possible exception of General Joe Wheeler, fought more battles. His activities were ceaseless as the seasons, and his capacity for riding and fighting had no limit. The Trans-Mississippi Department had more difficulties to face than any other part of the Confederacy. They were styled "The Orphans." They were the step-children in supplies of provisions and munitions of war, and, but for the trade in cotton which was arranged through Mexico, its conditions would have been difficult and well-nigh hopeless. Far removed from Richmond, the seat of the government, it was the scene of jealousies and disputes as to the rank of officers. Covering a territory greater than the remainder of the Confederate States, separated by the Mississippi River from the armies of the East, assailable by the ocean on the south, pierced by many navigable streams, with few manufactories, and with contentions caused by conflicting claims, it was the theatre of much mismanagement; but, through all, its soldiers were brave, loyal and patriotic, and lose nothing in comparison with the best the Confederacy produced. Considering the means at hand, the men in Missouri, Arkansas, Texas, Louisiana and Indian Territory did much to win the garlands with which fame crowned the brows of those who immortalized the gray.

In 1862 and the beginning of 1863, when the call became more urgent from the East, Shelby was among the Missourians and other soldiers from the Trans-Mississippi who crossed the Mississippi River. Leaving their own territory unprotected, these thousands of Arkansas, Missouri and Texas men cheerfully and bravely took their lives in their hands and went over to help their brethren in Mississippi and Tennessee who stood with hands uplifted, crying, "Come over and help us." Shelby, with his company, gladly crossed the stream. They left their horses behind them and went to aid Beauregard and Bragg, Hardee, Van Dorn and Polk, who, with their armies, were so sorely pressed by the descending avalanche, which, coming down through Kentucky and Tennessee and along the Mississippi and up the Tennessee River, was surely and quietly destroying the life of the Confederacy. The pressure, in the absence of these men who had been transferred into Mississippi and Tennessee, became so tense in Missouri, Arkansas, Texas and Northern Louisiana, that additional measures were taken to enlist soldiers who would prevent the occupation of the western bank of the Mississippi, and among the men commissioned to raise regiments, Shelby was the first named. It was not much to do for a man to tell him that he might raise a regiment when he was a thousand miles away from anybody he could hope to enlist. He had a hundred trained, disciplined and gallant men, and with these, hope made the future attractive. Difficulties in those days did not discourage Shelby, and so, taking his one hundred men—whose terms of enlistment had expired, they found their way by railway and on foot to the Mississippi River, at a point opposite Helena, Arkansas. At this time, that part of the Mississippi River was under control of the Federals, except Vicksburg and Port Hudson. It required an unusual man to meet the conditions that now faced Shelby. He was a wonderful man, and by January, 1863, he had entered the State of Missouri, then within the grip of Federal forces, and almost entirely under Federal control with garrisons in every center over the State. With fifty thousand Federal soldiers controlling that Commonwealth, he passed through all these; he safely evaded the enemies in the southern part of the State, carrying his one hundred men for two hundred and seventy-five miles through territory thoroughly occupied by his enemies, In a very brief while, he was not only able to get together a regiment, but a brigade. He was unwilling to take any more chances on twelve months' enlistments, and he swore his recruits in for the war. The men who had been with him gave him the best possible credentials among the young men along the Missouri River. Threatened Federal conscription and persecution by their foes had made them desperate, and they were only too glad to find a leader who had come from Corinth, Mississippi, with fame in battle, to organize and lead them. It was splendid material, and Shelby's success was not only surprising to him but to all the commanders further south in Arkansas. Such an experience was an unusual one in the life of any man, and only one of great resources and iron will could have succeeded when going into the enemy's country garrisoned on every hand and made liable to arrest and even death, and secure three regiments of a thousand men each and march them three hundred miles into friendly territory. Having no arms, except such as they could find at home, consisting of shotguns and revolvers, they furnished their own mounts and gladly went where Shelby asked them to go.

Only a man who had the essential qualities of a cavalry leader could have won in the face of such difficulties. Shelby improved every opportunity that came his way. There were constant jealousies which opposed his promotion. After he had organized and disciplined his brigade, it was nearly twelve months before his commission as brigadier-general came. This he was to win by his raid into Missouri in September, 1863, but he got it later. Waverly, the most northerly point which Shelby was to reach on this raid, was, as the crow flies, two hundred and seventy-five miles from the Arkansas line. From Arkadelphia, where Shelby started, it was two hundred and fifty miles to the Arkansas line. He had been long teasing his superiors to let him make a raid. There were many inducements for him to take the chances of such an expedition. He felt sure in the first place he could carry his men in and safely bring them out. He felt extremely confident that he could enlist a large number of recruits, and he was not devoid of ambition, so he longed to demonstrate his power and his capacity as a leader. He had been a colonel for nearly two years. He had self-confidence, he had marvelous resources, and he always won the admiration of his associates. General Schofield was in command of the department of Missouri. The State covered an area of sixty thousand square miles. To defend this, he had fifty thousand soldiers, and Missouri herself had enlisted many of these, which, while in the employ of the State, were subject to Federal jurisdiction.

On the 10th of September, 1863, Little Rock had been evacuated and a few days later taken possession of by the Federals. This was a great blow to the men of the Confederacy. Fort Smith also had fallen, and these two towns on the Arkansas River gave control to the Federals of one-half of the State. Through the White and Arkansas Rivers it opened up means for transporting men and supplies four hundred miles south of St. Louis. To Arkansas the loss of the Arkansas River was what the loss of the Mississippi River was to the Confederacy. It was yet, however, a great task for the Federals to move supplies from the White River or the Mississippi River when the stages of the Arkansas River prevented the passage of boats along its waters. The loss of Little Rock and Fort Smith and the shutting off of the Confederate troops from easy access to Missouri had done much to depress the spirit of the men who, west of the Mississippi, were struggling for Southern independence. For months Shelby had entertained the idea that if he were but turned loose with one thousand men he could ride to the banks of the Missouri River, do much damage to the property of the Federals, and bring out a large number of recruits. In Missouri the conditions had rendered it unsafe for men who sympathized with the South to express their sentiments, and anxious again to turn his face towards his adopted home and meet his friends and family, and longing for the glory which he felt would come to the successful prosecution of such an expedition, he pleaded with Generals Holmes and Price and Governor Reynolds and the other officials in the Trans-Mississippi to give him this permission. The Confederate authorities looked at the thing more calmly than the young military enthusiast. He assured them that recruits would be abundant and that he could fill up his ranks, dismay his enemies, and inflict severe loss in every way upon his foes. They felt that he was taking a tremendous risk to make such an expedition. Some suggested that he was hot-headed, that he lacked the experience as well as the poise for so grave an undertaking. He had been a colonel for twenty-two months. None could deny that he was courageous, that he had faith in himself, that he was possessed of unlimited enthusiasm. These were a splendid equipment for the work he essayed to do. Shelby's persistence at last availed, and on September 10th, 1863, consent was given for him to make the attempt to carry out his plans. He was allowed eight hundred men, twelve ammunition wagons, and two pieces of artillery. Only six hundred of his men started with him from Arkadelphia, two hundred recruits he was to pick up later further north. Arkadelphia, in Clark County, Arkansas, was one hundred and fifteen miles south of Ozark, at which point Shelby had determined to cross the Arkansas River. From Fort Smith, as well as from Little Rock, scouting parties had gone sixty miles south of Ozark, so that in fifty miles from where Shelby started it was certain he would meet opposition, and that the Federals would attempt to thwart his plans. Once permission was given, there was nothing short of death could stop Shelby's march. He had pleaded to go, and no dangers, no opposition, could deter him from his purpose. It was true that gloom and doubt had settled in the hearts and minds of many of the leaders who at that time were gathered in and about Arkadelphia, but this spirit, either of hesitation or fear, never touched the soul of Shelby. The people who permitted Shelby to go had forebodings of the outcome, and permission was only granted when it became apparent that nothing would satisfy Shelby but an opportunity to work out his plans. The limited number of soldiers allowed him showed that the Confederate leaders were not willing to risk very much on his undertaking. Marmaduke, always ready to take risks, assented, but he gravely doubted the result. The men who were to go with Shelby were as enthusiastic as he. It was "Home-going," it was an opportunity to try out chances with the militia over in Missouri, whom Shelby and his men

142

hated with greatest bitterness. The autumn sun was shining brightly when Shelby aligned his small force, placed himself at their head, and waved adieu to Governor Reynolds. The other troops, watching the departure of these gallant and dashing raiders, experienced deepest sorrow when they realized that they were to be left behind. There was no man among the thousands who witnessed the going of these brave boys who would not have willingly taken chances with them. There were no fears of what the future would bring forth. One man in every six of those who rode away would not come back, when at the end of thirty-six days Shelby would return.

Two hundred men taken each from four regiments lacked in some respects homogeneity, but all shouted and waved their hats and guns as the command to march passed down the line. From that moment they became brothers with a common purpose and common courage. The fact of going had by some subtle telepathy, which always marked cavalrymen, gone out among the entire brigade, and from that moment there was universal eagerness to ride with Shelby, and when the assignments were made and the columns formed there were two thousand disappointed men who felt most keenly the dealings of fate which deprived them of a place in the moving column. If the selection had been left to Shelby he would most likely have taken his entire regiment. These had become with him so dependable, and between themselves and Shelby there had grown up not only affection but completest trust. They believed in him and he believed in them, and they felt that no emergency could arise and that he would make no call upon them that was not demanded by duty. As these six hundred brave men mounted into their saddles and the column started, cheer after cheer greeted each company as it passed by. Governor Reynolds and General Price forgot the formality of military etiquette, and with those who went and those who stayed they joined in vociferous cheers. Benedictions came from every heart as out into the unknown dangers and experiences of the expedition these men rode, souls all aglow with patriotism, joy and soldierly valor. When Shelby held the hand of Governor Reynolds, the expatriated governor prayed him to be cautious, begged him to save as far as possible the lives of the young heroes under him and to be watchful even unto death. As this kindly admonition ended the governor pulled the leader close to him and whispered into his ear, "Joe, if you get through safely, this will bring you a brigadier-general's commission."

An ugly wound received eighty days before at the assault upon Helena, July 4th, still gave Shelby intense suffering. It was unhealed and suppurating. A minie ball had struck his arm and passed longitudinally through the part from the elbow down. It was still bandaged and supported with a sling. With his free hand he gathered up the reins of his bridle and ignoring pain and danger, he looked more the hero, as thus maimed and yet courageous he started on so long a ride and so perilous a campaign. With his great physical handicap, the admiration was all the more intense, for the spirit and the grit of the man who was undertaking one of the most dangerous and difficult expeditions of the war. Shelby's body was subordinated to the beckonings of glory and the splendor of the opportunity which had now come in obedience to his pleadings to serve his State, his cause, his country. Other men, less brave or determined, would have hesitated. Some men, possibly equally chivalrous, would have taken a furlough rather than have sought new dangers and more difficult service.

None of these boys marching away cared to peer into the future. Along the roads and the paths of the ride and in the midst of battles they were to fight, one in six was to find a soldier's grave, or, struck down by wounds or disease, might meet death under the most distressing circumstances at the hands of the bushwhackers and home guards who then filled the garrisons of Missouri towns. The joy of home-going eliminated all thought of misery of the future. These men were to ride two hundred and twenty-five miles to the Arkansas State line and two hundred and fifty miles from the Arkansas State line through Missouri to Waverly, in all four hundred and seventy-five miles. The return made nine hundred and fifty miles, even if they marched by an air line.

A little way out on his journey Shelby met Colonel David Hunter with a hundred and fifty men, recruits who were coming out from Missouri to join the Confederates in Arkansas. Hunter and Shelby were kindred spirits. The persecution of some of Hunter's family had rendered him an intense fighter. He was considered one of the rising infantry officers, but cavalry work suited him better, and so he gave up his rank of colonel with a regiment of infantry in order to take the chances of recruiting a cavalry command. Hunter was bringing out with him several hundred women and children who had been driven from their Missouri homes. Turning these over to a portion of his command, he chose the more promising of his followers and fell into line with Shelby. At Caddo Gap, on the fourteenth day, it was learned that a company of Confederate deserters and Union jayhawkers were in the mountains close by. With a horror and deepest hatred born of the crimes of these men, outlaws from both armies, it was resolved that the first work of the raid should be their extermination. Major Elliott, commanding one of the battalions under Shelby, discovered the lair of these men later in the afternoon, and as soon as it was dark he attacked them with great vigor. Seventy-nine of them were killed and thirty-four captured. Their leader was as brave as any soldier in either army. Puritan blood coursed through his veins. Condemned to death for his crimes, he was left with Major Elliott while the remainder of the force marched forward. The captain of the firing party with a small squad was left to finish up reckonings of justice with this bloody robber and murderer. There had been no court martial. These men were to be killed by common consent. They had been taken in the act, and their crimes were known. The captain in charge of the execution thought it would not be unreasonable to allow any of those who were to be put to death a brief time for prayer. Lifting up his voice, so that all his captors and executioners could hear, the condemned captain prayed—"God bless the Union and all its loyal defenders. Bless the poor ignorant rebels; bless Mrs. McGinnins and her children; bless the Constitution which has been so wrongly misinterpreted, and eradicate slavery from the earth." The increasing distance between the command induced the captain to cry out, "Hurry up, hurry up, old man, the command has been gone an hour and I will never catch up," to which the captain, so soon to die, responded, "I am ready, and may Heaven have mercy upon your soul." The order was given, and the death of twenty old men who had been murdered by this man in the immediate neighborhood shortly before, was avenged, in so far as human law could mete out punishment for horrible crimes. Both sides hated these outlaws, and Federal reports are full of similar condign punishment inflicted upon this class of marauders, who plundered and killed without the least regard for the laws of God or man.

When near Roseville, a short distance south of the Arkansas River, Shelby encountered the 1st Arkansas Federal Cavalry. In northern Arkansas, by the summer of 1863, Union generals had been able to induce enlistments among the residents of that part of the State, and naturally the feeling between these so-called renegades and the Missouri and Arkansas Confederates was extremely bitter, and whenever they faced each other in battle there was no great desire to hear the cries or calls of surrender.

These Federal Arkansians and a battalion of the 3rd Illinois Regiment undertook to dispute Shelby's right of way. They were speedily ridden over and the road cleared of this impediment. The river was forded near Ozark, and here again Shelby found some old acquaintances of the 6th Kansas Cavalry. This regiment had seen much service in southwest Missouri and northern Arkansas. It had hunted Shelby and Shelby had hunted it, and neither avoided an opportunity to measure swords with the other. Shelby disposed of this new menace in short order. He had now gotten far up among the mountains, and he traveled a hundred and forty miles, with two fights to his credit, and concluded to give his men one day's rest.

On the 21st of September, Shelby received authority to make the expedition, and on the 22nd he promptly started on this tremendous march of fifteen hundred miles. Cutting the telegraph wires north of the Arkansas River, Shelby planned to enter the Boston Mountains, from which, northwardly, no intelligence of his coming could be disseminated. It did not take Shelby long to find Federal forces. Within four days from the time he left Arkadelphia, he had learned that his advance would be fiercely contested. His chief concern was to pass the Arkansas River. He found it fordable, but treacherous, and by the 29th, seven days after starting, reached Bentonville, Arkansas. By the 4th of October, Shelby had marched two hundred and fifty-five miles to Neosho, Missouri, where there were three hundred Federal cavalry. These were quickly surrounded and forced to surrender. Their equipment was tremendously valuable, but their horses were a real godsend.

So soon as Shelby passed Neosho, his enemies were fully aware not only of his presence but of his plans. They argued reasonably that he would seek to reach his own home at Waverly and that he would not diverge from a straight line more than twenty or thirty miles. The Federal forces then in Missouri were concentrated at points between Neosho and Waverly over a space twenty or thirty miles wide. By this time, the passions of the war had been fully aroused. Life became no longer a certain thing, the law having been suspended and the southern part of Missouri having been greatly divided; hates had been aroused, excesses committed, men killed, families driven from their homes. McNeil's disgraceful order for the deportment of Southern sympathizers from a large portion of the State had been savagely enforced, and so, on reaching Bower's Mills, a place where the militia had been particularly offensive, the town was sacked and then burned. Along the route Shelby traveled the next day, after leaving Bower's Mills, every house belonging to a Southern family had been burned and, in many instances, the inhabitants put to death. On the 7th of October Shelby captured Warsaw in Benton County, far up towards the point he was attempting to reach. Here, too, Federal forces attempted to dispute his passage of the Osage River. By this time a spirit of highest enthusiasm had taken deepest hold upon the men. Nothing could chill their spirits. Soldiers dashed into and across the river. Neither nature nor man could stay their progress. At Warsaw vast quantities of all kinds of stores and supplies, including horses, had been concentrated and these all fell prey to the hungry raiders, and what they could not use were turned over to the remorseless touch of the flames.

By the 10th of October, Tipton was reached. On an air line, this left Shelby only fifty miles from Waverly, to which place, the abode of his dearest friends, he purposed in his heart to go. From Tipton for thirty miles in every direction rails were torn up, bridges destroyed, wires cut, and cattle guards and water tanks obliterated. When leaving Tipton, Shelby found opposed to him Colonel T. T. Crittenden, a Kentuckian, whom Shelby had known in earlier days, and who had a thousand well-armed and well-drilled mounted men. Shelby had two reasons for destroying Crittenden: first, he hated him, because he was a renegade Kentuckian, according to Shelby's standard; second, because he stood across his pathway to Booneville. The artillery was brought into line with the cavalry, and Shelby's whole command, with his artillery in the center, made a galloping charge at Crittenden's regiment. The Federal regiment melted away, leaving the killed and wounded behind and a few prisoners as hostages.

Booneville, on the south side of the Missouri River, had been a place from which many expeditions had been sent out and from which many orders had been issued for the persecution of the Southern people. The town authorities, pleading for mercy, gladly surrendered. It looked as if Shelby had disregarded all prudence and brought himself into a trap from which it would be impossible for him to escape.

Hardly had Booneville been passed when General Brown, a Federal commander, with four thousand men, came up. Brown was a vigilant general, an impetuous fighter and a soldier of both renown and courage. He was not afraid of Shelby. In this respect he was better off than some of his associates. Game, ambitious and enterprising, he thought it would

147

be a splendid stroke to bag Shelby in his territory and take him a prisoner to Jefferson City—Missouri's capital. To accomplish these ends, he carefully laid his plans and bent his utmost energies. He well understood this meant real fighting. He lost no time in assailing Shelby's pickets. He resolved to push his foes at every point, and fight whenever he could find a Confederate.

Shelby had broken an axle of his rifled gun. This he felt would be extremely useful to him later on. He ordered Colonel Hunter to hold the enemy in check until he made the necessary repairs on his cannon. By ten o'clock at night, stores had been removed and the gun repaired. The night before had been one of a great downpour of rain. This prevented much sleep. Shelby, not unmindful of the tremendous work that was immediately before him, determined to give his troopers a night's rest, so that they might be better prepared for the strenuous experiences that the morrow and the next three days had in store for them. General Brown was fiercely persistent and assailed Shelby's rear furiously and incessantly. The Federal authorities were clamoring for Shelby's destruction or his capture. At the crossing of the Lamine River, Shelby ambushed the Federals and inflicted serious loss and routed the assailants; but only momentarily, and then they came back more savagely. To reach Waverly, it was necessary to pass through Marshall, and, as Shelby approached that place, he found four thousand more Federal soldiers under General Ewing, drawn up ready for the gage of battle. With Brown in the rear and Ewing in the front, it looked gloomy for the Confederates. Shelby was now five hundred miles from any real hope of succor. General Sterling Price and Governor Reynolds at Arkadelphia, Arkansas, however much they might desire to help the dashing raider, could do naught for his rescue. A few scattered companies far down in Missouri had neither the will nor the chance to help him. He was four hundred miles inside the enemy's lines, and these enemies were hunting him with extremest vigor. His capture meant fame for the captor, and his destruction meant temporary peace in war-torn Missouri. Every available man was being thrown across Shelby's pathway, and every possible obstacle put along the road he was of necessity compelled to travel. His march from Marshall and Waverly, from a military standpoint, was both audacious and reckless, and appeared to be the act of a man trifling with fate. To his enemies, it seemed that Shelby's impetuosity and the longing for home-going had destroyed all sense of safety, and they were congratulating themselves that he had gone

148

into places from which escape was impossible. Measured by the ordinary standards of military prudence and foresight, Shelby had pursued a most unwise course, and the omens were bad for him and his small brigade. Shelby conceived the idea of destroying Ewing before Brown could come up in his rear, and then take his chances with Brown, and so, with his twelve hundred cavalry he attacked four thousand infantry. In a short while Ewing had been roughly handled, and his rout was inevitable. Fate seemed propitious, and hope rose high in Shelby's breast. The battle with Ewing was almost won, and with him out of the way, with shouts of victory on their lips, Shelby would, he believed, make short work of Brown. An evil destiny now intervened. Brown had overwhelmed Shanks' two hundred and fifty men left to delay his crossing the Lamine River, and he had rushed on to help Ewing at the moment when Shelby's genius and vigorous attack had nearly completed victory. Shelby needed no interpreter to tell him that; the firing in his rear demonstrated that he had miscalculated the rate of Brown's approach and that six pieces of artillery and four thousand fresh troops were upon him.

In such an emergency there was only one course left open and that was to retreat. Shelby had left a valiant lieutenant to dispute the crossing of the Lamine River with Brown, and to hold him while he whipped Ewing. Well did this gallant soldier, Colonel Shanks, perform this task. He stood the test as only a brave man could, but the storm he faced was more than any two hundred and fifty men could withstand. There was nothing left for Shelby but to cut his way through the lines of Ewing. This was a dangerous undertaking. Even to so brave a man as Shelby, it was a hazardous task. He looked and saw a weak place in the Federal line. Only instantaneous action could save him. A Federal regiment stationed in a corn field with skirmishers well to the front, and safely ensconced behind corn shocks, seemed to be the best chance for a hard drive and successful onslaught. He was too far from his base to give up his ammunition. He hated to abandon his meagre supply of cannon. If he stood still between the two advancing Federal armies of four thousand men each, annihilation or surrender was the only fate that could befall him and his men, however brave they might be. The flash of the eye and the resolve of a practiced warrior decided the course he would follow. Escape he would or die in the attempt. Widening the front of regiments and placing a rider on each horse of the ammunition wagons and artillery, he dashed furiously at the Federal forces. The Federals met the shock with courage and stout resistance, but the fierce riding Confederates were too much: they yielded sufficiently to allow Shelby to pass through with his wagons and his cannon. Hunter's regiment, becoming entangled in the thick woods, did not keep well closed in, and the Federals rallied and cut off Hunter while Shelby rode triumphantly away. Hunter, true to the necessities of the occasion, turned squarely to the right and galloped through another part of the Federal line and made his escape. Shelby's force was now divided, but it had left the enemy behind. It was impossible for any troops to out-march them. Shelby, hoping against hope, waited two hours for his separated forces to join him. Prudence told him longer waiting meant destruction, and he retreated to Waverly. For eight miles the Federals pressed his rear with relentless zeal. By three o'clock in the morning Shelby passed through his home town. The desire of his heart was gratified. A few moments were spent in greeting, and now he was ready to find his own again, and so, turning squarely south, he started on his long and ever-lengthening march to the place from whence he had come.

A little way from Waverly, at Hawkins' Mills, Shelby concluded that his wagons and his artillery would be troublesome, and so he sunk them in the Missouri River and reduced everything to the lightest possible weight. It was of the highest importance that he should safely pass the Osage River. It was a long march from Waverly to this river. Sleep and rest were out of the question. The tired beasts were allowed to feed a little and the men took an hour or two for repose. Even an hour's delay might bring disaster. Nature pleaded for repose and rest, but safety pointed her finger forward, and fate, willing to extricate the bold horseman, bade him stay not his hand nor speed. Leaving Waverly, on the morning of the 14th, to the evening of the 16th, he had marched more than one hundred miles. He had gone through from the Missouri to the Osage River in two days. This was a tremendous spurt. Nothing now, short of bad management, could prevent Shelby's escape, and so he began to move somewhat more leisurely. Along by the road at Warrensville, there were two thousand Federals waiting to hold him up; but he passed a few miles west without alarming them, and proceeded on to Johnson County, to which point they pursued him. One of the Federal commanders reported that Shelby's men were "running like wild hogs," and another, that, bareheaded and demoralized, they were making their escape in detached parties through the woods, thickets and byways. Even though hard pressed, and with no time to spare, Shelby could not refrain from one effort to punish those who had so vigorously and so sorely pressed upon him. He ordered a dash at his foes, and they, quickly realizing that it was not wise to press Shelby, even if he was running, fled at his coming. On the 17th, 18th and 19th of October, men and horses were put to the utmost limit. The Federals were loth to permit Shelby's escape, and they hung on to the Confederate rear with the grip of death. With such odds in their favor, they held it a great misfortune to let him get away, and they judged that all sorts of inquiries and criticisms would follow, if, with fifty thousand Federal soldiers in Missouri, even so resourceful and dashing a cavalryman as Shelby could march nearly through the entire State in the face of so many pursuers, and then safely ride away. Energies were redoubled, orders of concentration kept the wires warm; but warm wires, circulating orders and relentless pursuit could not stop the mad speed and the ceaseless tramp of Shelby and his men. They had better reason to urge them escape than those who were following had to run them down. On the 20th of October, he was safely on the Little Osage River in Arkansas, and there, to Shelby's gratification and surprise, he found the remainder of his command under Colonels Hunter, Hooper and Shanks. Reunited, their spirits rose to the highest pitch of enthusiasm. They had been battered and hammered and pursued, but they were all safe. One hundred and fifty of the eight hundred men who started were either wounded or dead along the line of march; but the expedition was completed, and the apparently impossible was accomplished.

Fate dealt more generously with Hunter and Hooper and Shanks than with Shelby. At Florence and Humansville and Duroc, on the Osage, they had had their troubles with the First Arkansas cavalry. They had a fight with McNeil's two thousand men at Humansville, but he was held in check. The Federal forces were fierce in their attacks, and they marched with the greatest strenuosity to block the way these men were taking to avoid capture. Artillery with cavalry in a forced march is never a thing to be desired. Guns and caissons make heavy pulling, and no horses can for many miles keep pace with horsemen who are pushed to their highest speed. The help of the cannon had now lost much of its value and as it might retard the speed in some slight degree, it was destroyed and abandoned and the last of Shelby's battery went down before the aggressive pursuers. It was abandoned at Humansville, and the fleeing horsemen were glad to get rid of such a grievous burden.

The greatest sufferers on the tremendous march had been the horses. They were goaded, tired and driven to the greatest effort. Half starved, with reduced flesh, their speed was ever-decreasing. Mercy was so incessant and so insistent in her appeals that the beasts were given three days' rest. Not a single soldier was willing to scout except when absolutely necessary to keep in touch with the movements of the enemy. The Federals, under John Cloud, hearing that Shelby had escaped from Missouri, left Fayetteville and went out to hunt him, but Cloud was not very anxious to find Shelby. He followed slowly and at a safe distance and pursued Shelby to Clarksville on the Arkansas River where Shelby crossed the stream twelve miles east of Ozark, where he had passed thirty days before.

A great march was ended, and Shelby, in his reports, claimed that he had in the thirty days killed and wounded six hundred Federals; he had taken and paroled as many more; he had captured and destroyed ten forts, about eight hundred thousand dollars' worth of property and he had captured six hundred rifles, forty stand of colors, three hundred wagons, six thousand horses and mules, and destroyed a million dollars' worth of supplies. At one place in Arkansas he had dispersed eight hundred recruits and destroyed fifty thousand dollars' worth of ordnance. At the time Shelby left Arkadelphia, Rosecrans was calling for help, and one day after Shelby started, the Battle of Chickamauga had been finished and Rosecrans, with his army driven back and discouraged, was at Chattanooga, crying for help. Ten thousand men were kept from reinforcing Rosecrans. All this was accomplished by eight hundred men. Shelby's superiors had led him to believe that this was a forlorn hope. The young Confederate colonel had shown them they were mistaken in their estimate of him and that he was worthy of the wreath on his collar which would make him a brigadier-general.

Chapter X

BATTLE AND CAPTURE OF HARTSVILLE
BY GENERAL JOHN H. MORGAN, DECEMBER 7th, 1863

In October, 1862, General Braxton Bragg, after the campaign in Kentucky, had brought his army out by Cumberland Gap, and, resting a brief while in East Tennessee, moved his forces to Murfreesboro, thirty miles southeast of Nashville. During General Bragg's absence on his Kentucky campaign, the Federals had a large garrison at Nashville. General John C. Breckinridge, too late to enter Kentucky, with General Bragg, had been stationed at Murfreesboro with a small Confederate force to watch and hold this Nashville Federal contingent in check. By the 12th of November, General Bragg had brought his soldiers through from Knoxville to Murfreesboro. It then became apparent that somewhere in and around Murfreesboro, or between that place and Nashville, a decisive battle would be fought. The Nashville garrison, reinforced by the return of General Buell's army, would be ready for aggressive warfare south of that city, and as Bragg's army now intervened between these Federals and their advance southward, it required no wise military student to predict that a great struggle would soon be on. At that time few understood how great that struggle would be, or that when it was ended and the losses counted, it would rank as amongst the most sanguinary battles of the war, with a loss of two hundred and sixty men per thousand, making it, in ratio of losses, according to reports, the second bloodiest field of the Civil War. Forty days later this expected conflict took place at Murfreesboro in the Valley of Stone River.

Perryville, Kentucky, where, on the 8th of October, 1862, a battle had raged with such fierceness, had also proved a memorable conflict to the men of the Army of the Tennessee. There the Confederate loss was three thousand, two hundred and twelve, the Federal loss four thousand, two hundred and forty-one. For the number of men engaged, in proportion to the time the battle lasted, it stands in the very forefront of mortalities. General McCook, of the Federal Army, referring to it, said: "It is the bloodiest battle of modern times for the number of troops engaged on our side." On the Confederate side one hundred and ninety-six in every thousand were killed or wounded.

On the 20th of November, 1862, the army of Tennessee was organized with General Braxton Bragg as commander. The three army corps were officered respectively by Generals E. Kirby Smith, Leonidas Polk and William J. Hardee. General Don Carlos Buell, on the Federal side, on October 30th, 1862, had been relieved, and General W. S. Rosecrans had been put in his place.

At this period of the history of the war in Tennessee, Sumner County, of which Gallatin was the county seat, was one of the richest and most productive of the agricultural districts of the State. Gallatin was thirty-five miles from Nashville, northeast. Sumner County adjoined Davidson County, of which Nashville was the county seat. East of Gallatin, some fifteen miles, was Hartsville, a small town, now the capital of Trousdale County, one and one-half miles north of the Cumberland River. Lebanon, Tennessee, the county seat of Wilson County, was due east of Nashville. A line drawn from Murfreesboro a little east of north would pass through Hartsville a distance of thirty-eight miles. Bragg's army extended from Murfreesboro in the direction of Lebanon. A portion of his infantry was at Baird's Mills, a village twenty miles away. Castalian Springs was between Gallatin and Hartsville, nine miles from Hartsville and six miles from Gallatin. At Castalian Springs, the Federals, under John M. Harlan, had a force numbering six thousand men. At Hartsville was Dumont's Brigade, the 39th in the Army of the Cumberland, consisting of two thousand one hundred men.

General Morgan always maintained a very warm love of Sumner County. Some of the happiest hours of his military life were passed there. He was ever glad of an opportunity to return to Gallatin. Quite a number of his followers were residents of the county. His opportunities for scouting and getting information in that section were most excellent. He learned that the Federals had about thirteen hundred troops at Hartsville, and he calculated that their capture was not only possible, but easy, by a bold, quick dash. On August 17th, 1862, he had captured Gallatin, and with it two hundred prisoners, including Colonel Boone and the other commanding officers of the 28th Kentucky Federal Regiment. He had another remarkable experience there, of which he wrote: "... thus ended an action in which my command, not exceeding seven hundred men (one whole company being in the rear with prisoners), succeeded in defeating a brigade of twelve hundred chosen cavalry sent by General Buell to take me or drive me out of Tennessee, killing and wounding some one hundred and eighty and taking two hundred prisoners, including the brigadier-general commanding and most of the regimental officers."

The Federal generals were justified in the belief that it was unreasonable for the Confederate troops to march northward from Murfreesboro to Hartsville when there was a full garrison at Nashville, as such a force would be exposed to a flank and rear attack from that place. John H. Morgan, though not yet having a commission of brigadier-general, was in command of a brigade composed of five regiments and two battalions. He conferred with General Bragg and mapped out a plan by which he assured General Bragg that with a force of cavalry and infantry not exceeding eighteen hundred men, it was practicable to cross the Cumberland River, attack Hartsville and capture it before the Federal Army at Castalian Springs, which was three times as strong as the force Morgan proposed to take with him, could reach Hartsville and succor the garrison there. After some discussion and prolonged consideration General Morgan's enthusiasm overcame not only the fears but the objections of the Confederate commander, who did not fully appreciate the rapidity of cavalry movements under leaders like Forrest, Morgan and Wheeler. General Morgan devised the plan and assumed the responsibility for its success. He was willing to stake his reputation and risk his life on the outcome. He requested permission to select the force which should accompany him, and for the infantry he chose the 2nd and 9th Kentucky. These were part of what was known as the "Orphan Brigade," at that time under command of General Roger W. Hanson, who twenty-four days later, was to die from wounds received on the battlefield of Murfreesboro, where, with his last breath, he pathetically exclaimed, "It is sweet and pleasant to die for one's country." Colonel Thomas H. Hunt, who had made a splendid reputation for his regiment at Shiloh, Corinth and Baton Rouge, was designated commander of the infantry. The 2nd Kentucky, under Major James W. Hewett, on this occasion carried into battle three hundred and seventy-five men, and Captain James T. Morehead led the 9th Kentucky with three hundred and twenty men, making the infantry all told six hundred and ninety-five men. The cavalry consisted of Gano's, the 3rd Kentucky, Bennett's, the 9th Tennessee, and Cluke's, the 8th Kentucky, and part of Chenault's, the 11th. Together they counted close to fifteen hundred. Two Ellsworth rifled guns and two brass howitzers comprised the artillery outfit.

At Hartsville was stationed the 104th Illinois infantry, the 2nd Indiana cavalry, the 12th Indiana battery, Company E of the 11th Kentucky cavalry, and the 106th and 108th Ohio infantry. The brigade was commanded by Captain Absalom B. Moore, of the 10th Illinois, who had come to Hartsville on the 2nd of December to relieve his predecessor, Colonel Scott, of the 19th Illinois.

General Hanson's brigade, from which parts of the two Confederate regiments had been taken, was then at Baird's Mills, twenty-three miles from Hartsville.

Prior to this time the infantry and cavalry which composed this expedition had not seen much of each other. At Baird's Mills, on December 6th, for the first time, they came in real contact. The infantry looked a little askant at the cavalry. None of the horsemen going with the infantry had seen very extended service. Cluke's, Chenault's and Gano's regiments and Stoner's battalion were new and had been largely recruited in August and September in Kentucky, and Bennett's regiment was not much better, but it was worse off so far as discipline was concerned. Early in the morning of December 6th, the cavalry regiments were marched to Baird's Mills, arriving there at eleven o'clock. There was a macadam road from Lebanon to Hartsville. The ground was covered with snow, and the temperature was low. It was not a good day for infantry to march, and it was not favorable weather for cavalry to ride. At eleven o'clock these organizations, after a short rest, began the march out of Lebanon for Hartsville. The cavalry rode in the van with celerity, but it required three hours for the infantry to cover the eleven miles to Lebanon. By way of encouragement to the infantry, they were told that an arrangement had been made by which with the "ride and tie" system, they would be mounted half the way. Under this method the cavalry would ride five or six miles forward and leave their horses and then march five or six miles on foot. In the meantime, the infantry would come up on foot and mount the cavalry horses and then ride forward several miles and leave the horses to await the coming of their owners. Theoretically this seemed a reasonable proposition. At least it looked fair. A short distance from Lebanon the infantry felt the time had come for them to change their method of transportation. They had patiently trudged along through the wet snow, and they were sure if they could get out of the slush that the

156

tread of the infantry and the wheels of the artillery and the tramp of the horses had created, they would be happier—at least more contented. The swap was made. The shoes of the infantry were thoroughly soaked and the freezing cold after they were mounted, benumbed their limbs. This was particularly hard on their wet feet. Unaccustomed to the methods of cavalry, they did not know how to keep warm, and in a little while they declared they would rather walk. The cavalry had gotten their feet wet while they were playing the infantry act, and slipping and sliding in the slushy material which covered the pike, they were glad to remount, but the same biting cold which so severely punished the infantry seriously troubled them. To make matters worse, the horses got mixed, and this set their owners to cursing and abusing everybody connected with the expedition. The cavalry cussed the infantry, and the infantry cussed the cavalry, and between them they cussed everybody they knew anything about. The situation was so extremely ridiculous that after awhile everybody lapsed into good humor. It was a gloomy opening for so glorious a campaign. Nature, unpropitious, appeared implacable, but the purpose and plans of the expedition soon leaked out and the entire command became at once enthused with the prospect of a fight and victory. In a brief while, with all the discomforts which surrounded them, the horsemen and the "footmen" made up, jollied each other, and swore they were glad they had come. They were assured that with Morgan, Hunt, Duke, Chenault, Cluke, Gano, Bennett and Stoner as their leaders, something really great was about to be achieved, and triumph, glory and renown were in their grasp.

General Morgan had calculated to assault at daylight. He estimated that his fighting force would be considerably larger than that of the enemy he was to attack and attempt their capture, and as they might be intrenched, he must not only take advantage of strategy, but also of the opportunities which would come from sudden and vigorous onslaught in the dark upon unprepared soldiers.

In marching the artillerymen had much the best of it, but when the fighting began they got much the worst of it. The drivers were riding, and the gunners, perched on the caissons, were removed from all contact with the slush, and by rubbing and stamping they kept their feet and hands warm enough to prevent them from getting down to walk. They looked with complacency upon their less fortunate fellows who were trudging the pike.

The Cumberland River in this locality was the dividing line between the Federal and Confederate territory. General Morgan, through his scouts, had managed to procure a few small leaky flatboats at Puryear's Ferry, several miles below Hartsville. Around ten o'clock at night the advance guard and artillery reached the river. The infantry, beginning their marching at eleven o'clock in the morning, now, after eleven hours, had covered seventeen miles. They could almost see the lights of the camp fires at Hartsville.

From the time of the reconnaissance of Morgan's scouts, the Cumberland River had made a material rise, and to put across the artillery between ten o'clock and three o'clock, five hours, with the inadequate equipment, was no light task. General Morgan was in immediate command of the infantry and artillery, and Colonel Basil W. Duke in charge of the cavalry. There was of necessity a great rush to get over the river in order to enable the infantry to march five miles quickly enough to strike Hartsville at daybreak, and every energy was bent to accomplish this herculean task. Finally this was safely accomplished and the infantry and artillery, full of hope, and though naturally wearied from a long, difficult march of over twenty-one miles, were inspired to new efforts when they realized that only a short distance away was the game in search of which they had come, and for the bagging of which they were undergoing such severe physical punishment.

After recovering their horses as far as possible, the cavalry left the pike and marched through the country to a ford several miles below the ferry, where the infantry and artillery had been put over. Haste and complete co-operation were equally essential in the successful issue of this perilous undertaking. Generals Morgan and Duke had calculated that the stream would be fordable, but fate again seemed to intervene to protect the Federals, quietly sleeping in their tents on the heights about Hartsville. The darkness, the severe cold, the rapid currents and the leaky, inferior boats, the difficult landings and still more difficult fords, all combined to try out the courage and metal of the men now going upon one of the most hazardous enterprises of the war. These obstacles did not shake the determination of General Morgan or the patience or courage of his men. They had come to win glory and punish their enemies. Prudence may have suggested to turn back. Morgan, believing in his destiny and relying upon the valor of his followers, resolved to go on and succeed or meet direful defeat.

In this perplexing and uncertain hour, General Morgan measured up to the highest standard of a great cavalry leader. Calm, fearless, confident, undaunted, he supervised the troublesome crossing. With Colonel Hunt of the infantry he appeared to be everywhere. His valiant spirit chafed at the unavoidable delays, but a kindly word of encouragement to his toiling, tired and half-frozen men warmed their blood into a new glow and gave them quickened action and expanded hope. The leader's indomitable will stilled every doubt or fear and made every man in the ranks an invincible hero. The darkness, relieved only by a few flickering torches, made ghastly shadows on the muddy, sloppy banks. Pickets, hastily sent in the piercing cold, were in the silence watching for any foes who should be skulking at these unseemly hours in search of enterprising enemies, and they could hear in the Federal camps the commands spoken in relieving guards who were unconscious of the presence of Confederate legions which at earliest dawn were preparing to swoop down upon them with defeat and capture, and who by the rising of the morrow's sun would bring death and wounds to many and captivity to all the sleeping hosts for whose defense and protection they were, with ceaseless tread, pacing the frozen and snow-clad earth.

By reason of recent rains further up the river, its currents were increased and quickened, and when the advance guard of the cavalrymen undertook to cross the river at the appointed ferry, to their dismay they discovered it was impassable at that point. Nothing daunted, however, by this unlooked-for obstacle, General Duke learned that there was a ford farther down the stream, where it was likely he could get his men and horses across, and rapidly and silently the cavalry trotted through the fields to the new ford. When this was reached it also presented most serious difficulties. It was an unused crossing, and it was impossible to get to the river except by a crooked bridle path along which the men could proceed only in single file. When the river was reached, it was found that the descent into the water was almost impossible. It was necessary to spur the horses into the stream over a bank several feet high. As a result, both men and horses were submerged in the water, and with the thermometer low in the scale, in the night time, and in the gloom of the darkness preceding the break of day, such a bath would have a fearfully chilling effect upon the ardor of any patriot. With several hundred horses tramping over the narrow path which led to the bank of the stream, the slush was churned deeper and deeper. Wet to the skin, with their clothes muddy and dripping, with their saddles, blankets and saddle pockets in the same condition, as these horsemen emerged from the stream on the north side, they found equal difficulties there. The ascent was steep and slippery and the pathway rough, and the shivering mounts with difficulty bore their riders to the open land.

Even the horses, with the vision of the misfortunes to their fellows ahead, were reluctant to make the plunge down into the river. The brutes saw the sad plight of those who were just in front, and watching them struggling in the water, they hesitated to follow in such difficult role. Spurring, pushing, driving, belaboring drove them one by one into the stream. The soldiers, shaking with cold, almost wished they were back by their happy firesides in central Kentucky, but they were game enough for any contingency war might develop, and as the leaders rode into the stream none hesitated, but all took the plunge. Those who were first over managed to build a few fires by which they might create some heat for their soaked and shivering bodies. So depressing was the temperature of the water and so great the strain on the nervous system that, after the plunge, quite a number of the command became so benumbed as to be unable to go forward. Notwithstanding the untiring efforts of General Duke, aided by the regimental officers, it was found impossible to get all the command over in time to enable the approach to Hartsville by daybreak. With part of the cavalry on one side and part on the other, General Duke, who was always prompt, at four o'clock in the morning took such men as had already passed the stream, consisting of Cluke's, Chenault's and Bennett's regiments, and rode with accelerating haste to the appointed meeting place, a mile and a half from the camp of the enemy. He picketed the line of march from the ford to the junction point so that no Federal forces could prevent the remainder of the column which had been left behind from reaching those who had gone before. Six miles was between him and the spot where he had agreed to meet General Morgan, and after this union they would still be nearly three miles from Hartsville. The infantry was over, the artillery was over, and three-fifths of the cavalry, and when these were united, General Morgan decided that he could wait no more for the other regiment (Gano's), but must take his chances with what men he had and rush the enemy. He knew full well it would not take long for the Federals to march double quick from Castalian Springs to Hartsville. This could be done under stress in two and a half hours, and when this force should reach Hartsville, General Morgan understood he would have an enemy in his rear three times as strong as his fighting men, and a body in front largely outnumbering the men he proposed carrying into the engagement. This was a period of tremendous physical and mental strain. It required supreme courage and unfailing nerve to enable even the greatest of leaders to calmly face such an emergency. The seven hundred infantry were now shut in by the river, which a short while before under great difficulties they had passed. If Colonel Harlan at Castalian Springs and the Hartsville garrison should unite, even the courage of the "Orphan Brigade" would be severely tested to face such tremendous odds. In a crisis, the cavalry might scatter and ride away, but the infantry would have no chance of crossing the Cumberland, or marching through the country on foot. Victory, and victory quick, was the only solution of the grave problems of the hour. Boldness, promptness, intrepidity, desperate courage might save the situation, and it was not without serious, but silent misgivings that General Morgan ordered the command forward. In his calm and unruffled countenance, in his self-possessed and undisturbed demeanor, none could detect the conflict and struggle that was filling his mind and heart. There were no preliminaries that required a moment's delay. Instant and fierce fighting might win. Hesitation or doubt would bring certain disaster. In the silence and gloom of the night, led by the guides, familiar with every foot of the way, those who walked and those who rode pressed on to find the sleeping foe. Few commands were necessary. The column covered more than a mile, but the horsemen in front followed hard upon the guides, and the infantry with quickened steps, kept a pace that left no intervals between the mounted men who in the vanguard held the place of danger and honor.

As the day was breaking, the cavalrymen in advance struck a strong picket force half a mile south of the Federal camp. The outpost fired and retreated. This awakened the sleeping Federals. Aroused, they immediately got ready to receive these early, unwelcome morning callers. General Morgan had not expected to capture the pickets. He hoped the cavalry would capture most of the camp, ride down the sentinels, and the infantry coming up would thoroughly finish what the cavalry had begun.

In the incredibly short space of time that intervened between the attack and the real fight, the surprised Federals formed a line of battle. They had been taken unawares, but they were not disposed to run away without a conflict. They were on an elevation which slightly raised them above the surrounding fields through which the Confederates must approach.

The report brought to Morgan made the numbers of the Federals at Hartsville somewhere around thirteen hundred, but through the dim light of the morning, when he saw twenty-one hundred men instead of thirteen hundred spring into line, immediately it was suggested to his mind that maybe it might have been wiser for him to have remained on the south side of the Cumberland. As they rode into the line of battle, Colonel Duke casually remarked to General Morgan that he had gotten more than he had bargained for, to which Morgan quickly replied, "We must whip and catch these fellows and cross the river in two hours and a half or we will have three thousand men on our backs." Then he did not know how greatly the army under Harlan outnumbered the little force with him, which his faith in them and in himself had led him to venture into such perilous surroundings. Had he known all he might even have hesitated and he would surely more strenuously have hastened the destroying hands of his followers in burning and wrecking the stores he had captured. If the men at Hartsville could hold off the attack a sufficient length of time to enable the men from Castalian Springs to reach the scene the seven hundred infantry and six hundred cavalry in line would make the issue very uncertain. At that time, General Morgan did not have more than twelve hundred men with which to go after the enemy. Brave, defiant and hopeful, he had sent Bennett's regiment into the town to prevent the escape of the Federals. It really looked for a moment as if nobody would have to look after the escape of the Federals, but that Morgan would have to look sharply after his own escape. The Federal officers could hardly believe that so small a Confederate force would dare approach the position they were now attacking, and the audacity of Morgan's movement created the impression of a very large force, and this did much to demoralize the Federal garrison. In sight of each other the two opposing armies formed their lines. The Federal force was composed of nearly all infantry. They had only a small number of cavalry. The lines were formed about twelve hundred feet apart, and the skirmishers from these two armies filled the intervening space and promptly opened a spasmodic fusillade.

Cluke's and Chenault's men, riding swiftly upon the scene, instantly dismounted and gallantly sprang into the fight. Although they only numbered four hundred and fifty men, they looked like several thousand to the affrighted Federals who, rushing out of the tents, were not in a frame of mind to calculate with mathematical exactness the number of those who, intent on conflict, were rapidly and fearlessly rushing into their camp. The skirmishers at once became busy and annoying, but Cluke and Chenault double-quicked within three hundred feet of where the Federal skirmishers were. The Federals fired a volley and then retreated, but the dismounted cavalry rushed on as if nothing had happened. One hundred and eighty feet away another volley was fired, and still Cluke and Chenault were advancing. As Cluke and Chenault got within close quarters the 104th Illinois infantry fired at short range. They attempted to back and reload their guns, but a second volley from the dismounted cavalry caused them to break in great disorder. Within thirty minutes of the time Cluke's and Chenault's men began to fire, they had cleared their front of any organized resistance. In the meantime the enemy's artillery was hammering away at Cobb's two pieces. He had only two caissons, but one of these was blown up by an exploding shell from the enemy and his battery had suffered a loss of more than twenty per cent of its members. The Federal artillery was handled bravely and skillfully and inflicted severe damage upon Cobb's men and caissons.

The infantry had marched twenty miles over snow-covered, slushy roads, along every step of which incisive cold had partially benumbed their limbs. The warm work of battle gave them new physical energies. As the 2nd Kentucky dashed across the space that separated them from the Federals, somebody unfortunately gave the order to "Halt and dress." The enemy had been driven back before the impetuous charge of the cavalry, and the infantry lost no time in finishing the brave work of the horsemen. With victory just within their grasp, there was no need for "dressing." A number of officers sprang to the front and countermanded the order, and Captain Joyce, seizing the colors, waved them in the dim light of the early morning and bade the men to follow where he would lead. At this juncture a concentrated fire of the Federals resulted in great loss to the 2nd Kentucky Infantry. For an instant the line swerved uncertainly, and then this regiment with eager, resistless fury, rushed to the conflict again. The 9th Kentucky infantry now wheeled into action. Stirred with the battle sounds, they pressed upon their foes like lions released from their cages. Fortunately, at the critical moment, one hundred of Gano's regiment, which had later crossed the Cumberland River, precipitated themselves into the conflict. Their coming was timely. Their shouts and reckless charge added new terrors to the already disturbed garrison. The Federals, with the Confederates in the front and on their flank, were driven into a narrow space and suffered severely from the pitiless and well-directed fire of the men in gray. The incessant thud of the minie balls told the story of the havoc. It appeared to the affrighted Federals that there was no hope of escape. In seventy-five minutes from the time the opening shot had been fired the white flag was run up. The Federal garrison had surrendered, and the first act of the drama had been finished.

For the length of time the Confederates were engaged the losses were large. The 9th Infantry lost seventeen men, the 2nd lost sixty-eight, the 11th Kentucky Cavalry, seventeen, Cobb's battery, ten, and Cluke's regiment, thirty-two. More than half the entire loss fell on the 2nd Kentucky Infantry. With two hundred and thirty men engaged, Cluke's regiment reported a loss of thirty-two, making its casualties fourteen per cent of the men carried into the fight. Gano, Chenault and Bennett had twelve killed, wounded or missing. Lieutenant-Colonel Cicero Coleman, of the 8th Cavalry, ever chivalrous and gallant, while nobly leading a section of his regiment, was seriously wounded.

Two handsomer men than Colonel Cluke or Lieutenant-Colonel Coleman could rarely be found in any organization. Both over six feet, both splendid horsemen, always erect and graceful in their saddles, and full of magnetism, they communicated by their superb presence and their fearless conduct to the men of the regiment an enthusiasm in war's operations that was always inspiring and helpful, and made each man believe that the result of the conflict was dependent upon his personal valor.

To the Federals there came a heavy loss of killed and wounded. Eighteen hundred prisoners were forced across the Cumberland and were turned in to the Confederate headquarters at Murfreesboro.

Danger was now imminent on every side. One could breathe it in the air. An attack from the forces at Castalian Springs was momentarily expected, but General Morgan could not resist the impulse to destroy wagons and stores, and these things were quickly reduced to ashes. A large amount of clothing was seized in this fortunate capture. Boots and shoes meant much to some of the cavalry regiments, especially the 8th and 11th, who in the march had to reinforce their worn boots and shoes with pieces of blanket. In the face of impending and immediate attack the work of destruction was thoroughly completed. It was against the creed of Morgan's men to leave anything undestroyed that could aid a foe.

A suspicious firing was soon heard in the direction of Castalian Springs.

Quirk's scouts were doing their best and bravest to hold the Federals in check. They were retiring only because the numbers of the enemy were overwhelming, but the Enfield rifles were speaking defiance to their assailants, and if they were receding it was only because prudence bade them go. Colonel Cluke and his regiment were sent to aid in the show of resistance and the pressure, still increasing, became so great that Gano's regiment, which in the meantime had arrived, was sent to their support.

Time was never more valuable to any army than to this little Confederate brigade now leaving Hartsville. The Cumberland River, difficult of fording, was in front, and an enemy three times as strong was now pressing vigorously behind.

The artillery, which had been brought along, together with the captured guns, was placed on the south bank to protect the crossing. Courtesy to the conquered ceased to be the order of the hour. The captured were urged and driven forward at the highest possible speed. Some were hesitant about going, but war knows nothing of the law of politeness and their captors demanded double quick march from the crestfallen and distressed prisoners. The wagons were placed in front. Two captured Parrot guns made splendid companions for the "bull pups." These remained with the Division until General Morgan's capture in Ohio, July 26th, 1863. One of these was called "Long Tom" and was the object of great admiration and was held in truest affection by the whole force.

As the Confederates approached the river, the infantry began to be very chummy with the cavalry. At the highest possible speed and with great haste they had marched away from the scene of their splendid achievement. They had not been subjected to the bath which a few hours before had been the fate of the horsemen and they had no fancy to ford the icy stream, even under the Federal pressure behind them. A glorious victory had been won, in the winning of which every part of the brigade had borne a distinguished part. Heroes of a common venture, they were alike jubilant over the brilliant work of the morning, and when they got down to the stream it required neither pleading nor threats for the infantry to secure seats behind the horsemen, and so, two on each steed, with their legs lifted high out of the cold water, the patient, gentle, useful horses carried the victors to the south side of the stream.

Among the triumphs and congratulations, the cavalry was not indisposed to be generous to the unfortunate prisoners, and after the infantry had been delivered on the south side, where they might defend any attack

165

of the approaching Federals, now extremely annoying and persistent, they recrossed the stream, and each horseman took a prisoner behind him and thus ferried him over, but the pursuit became fiercer and stronger, and as the cavalry, which were fighting the advance from Castalian Springs approached the stream, the situation became so emergent that the unfortunate prisoners who had not gotten a seat behind the cavalry were forced into the stream, which reached their waists, and required a wade through the rapid, cold current. This was not done without some threats of violence, but the water was to be preferred to bullets, and reluctantly, and with loud protests against such violation of the laws of war, accompanied by all sorts of "back talk," the Federal prisoners were rushed through the water and with a close line of horsemen on either side were hurried across the stream. The victors had not thought of parole. Even if they had, there was no time to carry out the details of such a process. The eighteen hundred prisoners would look well in the column of the returning heroes when they reached Baird's Mills and Murfreesboro, and with grim grip, the Confederates held on to their prisoners. Here and there one dropped out, but almost the entire number was gotten safely over the river and finally delivered to the guards at headquarters.

The rear guard bravely defended every foot of the ground. They were anxious to get away, but prudence and pride alike required that they should make stubborn resistance, and with every expedient known to cavalrymen, they delayed the approach of the Federal forces. The Federal commander had some disquieting fears about the number of men that were engaged in the expedition, and he did not press the pursuit as savagely as he would have done had he known that less than seven hundred men were standing in the pathway he must travel to reach his adventurous foes, who were now divided by the rapid currents of the icy stream.

A part of the Confederate dead who so gloriously had died were left behind. Their enemies gave them burial. War destroys the tenderness of sentiment. The safety of their own lives was more important than the sepulture of the slain, however bravely they had gone down in the struggle. Most of the wounded were placed in wagons and ambulances, which were driven away from the scene of carnage and battle. The infantry, in defense of their wounded comrades, had the call been made, would have been extremely dangerous customers. The economics of war are ruthless. The living, the fighters, are to be considered, and then the maimed and dead. On the horsemen fell the burden of the defense of the rear. During all the expedition, the web-footed infantry had gotten the worst of the deal, and the cavalry, gay, happy and mounted, were disposed to place no unnecessary work upon their comrades who were trudging their way back to their comrades, who were longing to hear the tidings of what battle had brought to those who had been selected for so dangerous a mission.

If the infantry had looked with side glances at the cavalry when at Baird's Mills, they had now lost the recollection of such ungenerous feelings in admiration for the horsemen who, dismounted, had manifested a courage and valor equal to their own, and who, in the charge and advance upon the enemy at Hartsville, and in standing off the Federal pursuers, had displayed an intrepidity that was not unworthy of any Kentucky Confederates, be they men who walked or men who rode to battle. Whenever Hartsville was recalled or its experiences were freshened in their minds, there was no distrust of the steadfastness of the 3rd, 8th and 11th Kentucky Cavalry, and the gallant 9th Tennessee, and by common consent the 2nd and 9th Kentucky Infantry admitted these regiments which had been with them at Hartsville into the full brotherhood of war's heroes.

The captured guns and the four pieces brought by Morgan were pounding away on the south bank of the river and hurling shot and shell at the pursuers on the north bank, serving notice on the Federals that thus far and no farther could they come. It never entered the minds of the Federals that the Confederates were so few in number. They could not understand how any commander with the slightest prudence would expose his men to such risk as Morgan had dared. It would have been questionable for even cavalry to have undertaken such a campaign, but to jeopardize two of the best regiments of infantry in the army of Tennessee by marching and fighting so far from their military base, and with such liability to attack on the rear and flank, was inconceivable to the Federals who were pursuing. They concluded that there were at least three times as many in the battle as had captured their comrades at Hartsville. Colonels Harlan and Moore estimated Morgan's fighting force at five thousand, and Federal officers declared that they had seen several regiments of infantry and cavalry standing across the river awaiting the return of their comrades who had gone over the stream and won victory at Hartsville.

By eleven o'clock the agony was past. The pursuit was ended. Joy and complacency filled the hearts of the infantry as they tramped back to Baird's Mills. They did not ask to ride any more. The cavalry marched

167

in the rear and stood guard and waited for approaching foes. None came. After crossing the stream, courtesy and generosity prompted kindness to the blue-coated prisoners. There was no word of unkindness spoken.

Along the Confederate lines, they were received with surprise, and wonder staggered credence to believe how few could have accomplished so much or that any men in such rigorous weather could have so quickly covered so great a distance, or against such odds have won so marvelous a victory.

For a little while the Federal commanders were dazed. On December 7th General Rosecrans wired General George H. Thomas as follows: "Do I understand they have captured an entire brigade of our troops without our knowing it, or a good fight?" And at one thirty o'clock the same day there came from the President at Washington the following message: "The President to Major General George H. Thomas: The President demands an explanation of the Hartsville affair. Report in detail exact position, strength and relative distances of your troops between Gallatin and Hartsville, and causes of disaster as far as known to you."

On December 10th, the rage and indignation became more pronounced, and General Halleck wired from Washington: "The most important of the President's inquiries has not been answered. What officer or officers are chargeable with the surprise at Hartsville and deserve punishment?" Later General Halleck wired the President: "I respectfully recommend that Colonel Moore, 104th Illinois Volunteers, be dismissed from the service for neglect of duty in not properly preparing for the enemy's attack on Hartsville, Tennessee." Afterwards Colonel Moore was allowed to resign on the ground of disability after long imprisonment by the Confederates.

Meagre and exaggerated reports were spread among the Confederates of the number of men that had reduced such a numerous company to prisoners. The whole army with glad cheers along the line greeted the return of the victors. Much was said of the cavalry, but the chiefest and highest meed of praise was awarded to the infantry. In less than thirty-six hours they had marched forty-five miles over trying and difficult roads, had fought a battle, with their associates had captured eighteen hundred prisoners and brought these back across an almost impassable stream in the midst of fierce winter weather.

General Bragg, more or less phlegmatic, was moved to enthusiastic praise. He tendered to General Morgan his thanks and assured him and his troops of his unbounded admiration.

He said: "I take great pleasure in commending the endurance and gallantry of all engaged in this remarkable expedition." He predicted that such valor and courage had before it higher and yet more magnificent victories, and to appeal still more strongly to the pride of those who had been engaged in this wonderful conflict, he ordered that hereafter, upon the battle flags of all organizations which had taken part in this battle, the name of "Hartsville" should be emblazoned, to remind the world forever of the bravery, endurance, enterprise and courage of those who had there won such great distinction.

Chapter XI

WHEELER'S RAID INTO TENNESSEE, AUGUST, 1864

The tremendous exactions of the Confederate cavalry, in the summer and fall of 1864, gave severest test of both their physical resistance and their patriotism. Food for man and beast was reduced to the minimum of existence. As food lessened, work increased, and the dumb brutes felt more sorely than man the continual shortening of rations.

In July official reports showed that for three days the cavalry of General Wheeler received thirteen pounds of corn per horse. The regular ration was ten pounds of corn and ten pounds of hay. As against the amount experience had shown essential for maintaining strength and vigor, the Confederate horsemen saw the beasts that they loved even as their own lives cut to three and one-third pounds of corn, just one-third of what nature demanded, outside of rough provender, such as hay or oats. The horse could live, but that was all. To put these starving beasts into active work, to exact of them thirty miles a day, with an average of one hundred and eighty pounds on their backs, was only to leave many of them stranded by the roadside to die of starvation and neglect, or to be picked up by the country folks with the hope that a ration of grass or leaves would, in the course of months, bring them back to health.

The cavalryman often starved himself without complaint to help his horse. When it comes to work with insufficient food, as between man and brute, the man is the stronger. The spirit of the man, like the air plant, extracts life from his surroundings and thus begets a strength and virility to which the beast is a stranger. At this period there was a little green corn found here and there, in the patches planted by the women and children, who were fighting for life in the rear of the army, where war's relentless ravages had left for beasts little but the air, a sprinkle of grass, the branches of the trees, or the sprouts that had come up about the roots. These most frequently were the largest part of the ration served the southern cavalry horse. The men watched these animals grow weaker day by day, and when corn was issued to the soldiers to be parched, they took

170

a small portion for themselves, and patting the noses of the mounts with fondest touch, they would slip a part of their own food into the mouths of the steeds they had learned to love as if they were human.

Western Confederate genius was now engaged in wrestling with the destruction of Sherman's lines of communication. It was one hundred and fifty-two miles from Chattanooga, the real base of Sherman's supplies, to Atlanta. Bridges and trestles were numerous, and against these again and again Confederate ingenuity exhausted its power and its enterprise. Sherman was dreaming of a march to the sea. Hood, who succeeded Johnston, was dreaming of flank movements and marches to the rear, and while these leaders were figuring and counting the cost, upon the cavalrymen was laid the heaviest burdens of conflict. Former conditions had now been reversed. In the earlier stages of the War, the Federals were chiefly solicitous to repel cavalry incursions and raids, but now the Confederates were to swap jobs and thwart Federal assaults on lines of communication. This put upon the Confederates increased vigilance and demanded of them that they should make military bricks without the straw necessary to their manufacture.

The proper care of horses was now an important part of the martial regime. If the men were thoughtless enough to overburden their mounts, experience and necessity told the officers, responsible for results, that these details must be watched, and higher authority must intervene to protect the animals, now even as necessary as men in the operations of the hour.

On August 9th, 1864, an order was issued looking to a most rigid enforcement of this sane and wise regulation. No officer of any grade or any soldier was allowed to carry any article outside of his gun and his cartridge box, other than a single blanket and one oil cloth. Naught but something to warm the body and protect the skin would be tolerated, and once, every day on the march, inspection was a part of every officer's duty for the enforcement of this requirement. Ordnance wagons, caissons and ambulances were subjected to the same close scrutiny and the immediate destruction of all contraband was the stern and irrevocable order of General Wheeler.

General Hood was feeling the constant and relentless pressure of General Sherman around Atlanta. Wheeler and Forrest were his only reliance to lessen the hold that was silently but surely throttling the life of the Army of the Tennessee. Something must be done to relieve this acute situation and to Wheeler and Forrest, Hood appealed in the extreme hour asking if they could not cut off or shorten Sherman's supplies. If they could compel him to withdraw some thousands of his men, there might yet be a chance. Without these, it could only be a question of days, mayhap with good fortune, weeks. No one could foretell what a brief span might bring forth, and so, catching at faintest hope, these two wondrous cavalry soldiers were to take another turn at the wheel.

It was believed by General Hood, and in this General Forrest concurred, that if Wheeler could pass around Sherman's army, tear up the railroad north of Atlanta, then reaching to Chattanooga, force a passage of the Tennessee River, swing around towards Knoxville and thence down into Middle Tennessee and assail Nashville and wreck the railroads between Nashville and Chattanooga, this, accompanied by Forrest's assailment of the lines in Western Tennessee and Southwestern Kentucky, would, if it was within the lines of human possibilities, loosen Sherman's hold on Hood's throat.

General Wheeler had concentrated four thousand men at Covington, Ga., forty miles south of Atlanta. The best horses were selected. They were shod and fitted by every means at hand to enter upon one of the most wearying marches of the War. They would perforce rely on some captures of steeds. The Confederate cavalry never failed to count on the United States government to supply a full share of their wants, when thus in need. With the long, long tramps ahead, there were even some dismounted men who resolved to go on this expedition, willing to take the risk of capture, believing that the uncertainties of war and the certainties of striking some loose Federal cavalry force would stand them well in hand, and give them earth's now richest treasure, a horse. The warrior of old had cried out, "My kingdom for a horse," but these dejected and bereft horsemen were putting a higher value on such a priceless gift, and were placing their lives in the balance, to win, if mayhap they might win, the coveted prize.

General Hood had calculated that if Wheeler could safely trust to capture food and ammunition, that surely he would break Sherman's line, and that inevitably Sherman must pay not only some, but much heed to this active, devastating force in his rear.

No extended rations were allowed to go. A blanket and gum coat blanket were all the baggage permitted except a loose horseshoe and a frying pan. It required only the cooking of some water-softened cornmeal, made into soggy bread, to supply immediate wants.

172

The Confederate horsemen had long since learned the full import of the petition of the Lord's prayer, "Give us this day our daily bread." He had shortened it up to say, "Give us one square meal"; and he laid down on the wet or hard ground, covered his face with his worn hat or tattered blanket, and let no thought of the next meal disturb his dreamless sleep.

Starting on this long journey, General Wheeler swung eastwardly to avoid, as far as possible, Federal interruption. In less than twenty-four hours, he began to let his enemies know that he was in the saddle. He struck the railroad near Marietta, Ga., and proceeded to wreck it for miles. He and his followers were hungry. Their larder was empty. They felt certain that Sherman's supply trains were on the march between Chattanooga and Atlanta. Their horses needed corn, their bodies needed food, and they resolved to apply the old doctrine of "He takes who may; he keeps who can." A long train of cars was captured, but men and their horses could not eat engines and cars. Then came the comforting message, through friendly sympathizers, that a long wagon train, well guarded, was on the highway a little farther north. This glad news quickened hope and cheered body and soul. A short distance away, a great vision crossed their gaze. When it first stood out upon the horizon, the weary troopers rubbed their eyes, pinched their tired limbs, to discover if they beheld a mirage, or was it real things that loomed across their perspective. The men first saw horses and mules, as if trees walking. The white tops of the commissary schooners, led horses, trailing mules, and a vast horde of driven beeves moving southward, headed for Sherman's headquarters, developed into a reality. The only drawback was men in blue, some riding, many tramping alongside the wagons. All of these carried guns, and they had special orders to kill all who attempted to take these things from their custody. Necessity is a great incentive, and the Confederates, with patriotism and hunger impelling, without preliminary proceedings, made vigorous assault on the custodians of what to those attacking was the equal of life itself. The odds were against the Confederates, but these had so much at stake that the issue could not long be doubtful. They went after their enemies with such dash and determination that the guards soon fled and left to them the possession of the wagons, the beeves, the horses, the mules and great stores of good things to eat. The cravings of nature were quickly met, but, as with hands full, riders supplied their own bodies, bits were removed from the mouths of the faithful steeds, and with greatest dispatch a bountiful supply of shelled corn and oats was spread upon the ground before the enraptured vision of the jaded steeds. The lowing, restless cattle were corralled by the new masters. Doomed to an early death, it made but little odds whether they fed men who were clad in blue or gray.

General Hannon, with a guard, soon herded the precious drove and its course was promptly turned eastward to escape Federal interference. The captors hoped to run the gauntlet of Federal pursuit and with the glorious prize to bring gladness and relief to the hungry men who, in and about Atlanta, with unfailing courage, were hanging on to that citadel with the grim courage of a forlorn hope to save it from capture and destruction.

These cattle and their guards, although vigorously pursued, with favoring fortune escaped the imminent dangers about them and were landed within the Confederate lines. They would yield more than one million pounds of choice beef, thirty-five pounds for every soldier in General Hood's army. When these lowing beasts joined the Confederate commissary, there was universal delight, and many joys were added to those who so valiantly were defending the environed citadel about which so much of Confederate faith was now centered.

Emboldened by his success, the Confederate chieftain now followed the railroad, northward from Marietta. He was going over the ground with which he became so familiar a few weeks before on Johnson's retreat from Dalton to Atlanta. No Federal foresight could stay the avenging hand of the Confederate railway wreckers. Dalton, Sherman's starting point in the early days of May, was captured, and from Resaca to that point, in many places the track was completely torn up. There were Federals behind and Federals all about, but their presence did not disturb the game little southern general and his men in gray. Bridges, trestles, cattle guards, guns, ammunition, mules, horses, were the things he had calculated to capture and destroy, and to this work he bent all the energies of his willing and active followers. In crossing the streams, the ammunition of every soldier was inspected by officers and every man was compelled to tie his cartridge box about his neck to prevent contact with water. The man, the horse, the gun, the powder and ball must be kept in the best possible condition. On these, combined, depended not only the safety of the command, but the success of the campaign. A few sentences from General Wheeler's order of August 9th, 1864, will tell how stern was the demand for the protection of the horses who were to carry their masters on this strenuous march: "No soldier of any grade whatever will be permitted to carry any article of private property, except one single blanket and one oil cloth." Officers and men alike were to share these prevailing and bear these stringent exactions. There was no complaint against these drastic regulations. Rarely, if ever, were these orders disobeyed. With noblest patriotism and sublimest self-sacrifice, the volunteers under Wheeler recognized the necessity of such a call and there was no claim of self-denial and no call of physical privation they were unwilling to face or endure, if they only might win their country's freedom and drive its enemies from its soil.

When marching out of Dalton, the Federal general, Steedman, furiously assailed Wheeler's command, but he was beaten off, and a direct march was made on Chattanooga. This greatly alarmed the Federal leader, and he hastened to the rescue of that stronghold; and then General Wheeler, as if playing hide and seek, turned again to Dalton, to which place he was in turn followed by Steedman, only to find his wary enemy gone. These valuable days for Federal repair of the railroad were thus consumed in fruitless marching and countermarching, induced by General Wheeler's strategy. This interrupted the use of the railway for twelve days, and these two hundred and eighty-eight hours meant much to Sherman's one hundred thousand followers, camped on the Chattahoochee. The exactions of twelve months of war and alternate occupation of both armies had depleted the country along the railway of all that could sustain man or beast, and by the necessities for forage, General Wheeler was compelled to leave this ravaged territory, and marched eastwardly towards Knoxville. There he was sure of reaching supplies, and he quickly turned his steps towards the valleys along the Tennessee River above Chattanooga. Once before, he had crossed at Cottonport, forty miles above that city; but when he came to the scene of his former brilliant operations, floods filled the banks of the stream and prevented a passage there. He resolved to follow the line of the river towards Knoxville and search for some spot at which he might swim or ferry over. Leaving six companies of thirty men each along the railway to harass and alarm the Federals, with the remainder of his troops he rode away. Those left behind gave a good account of themselves. More than twenty loaded trains became victims of their matchless daring, and it was some time before the enemy knew that General Wheeler had moved his sphere of operations.

If one will take an enlarged map and start with a line beginning at Covington, Georgia, forty miles south of Atlanta, where General Wheeler concentrated his troops on August 10th, to begin this expedition, and trace through all the journeyings of his command for the next twenty-eight days, some idea can be obtained of the tremendous energies and wonderful skill that marked this raid. To make this ride without let or hindrance, within the period it covered, with the animals and supplies possessed by Wheeler's men, would be considered a reasonable march; but encumbered with artillery and ammunition wagons, the sick and wounded that always must follow in the train of a cavalry incursion make the difficulties appalling. Hidden dangers lurked on every side. The constant pursuit, as well as the constant change in the Federal disposition of both cavalry and infantry forces, rendered the game at all places and hours distractingly uncertain, and only a leader of consummate energy, combined with masterful skill, could hope to escape in safety from such desperate and perilous complications. To make the most conservative estimate of excursions from the main line of march would require something like six hundred and fifty miles of riding on this raid. No well-appointed commissary was present to feed man and hungrier beast. These must live from hand to mouth and either take food from the enemy or to impress it from people, loyal in most cases to the South, and already so impoverished by war that starvation was a real and ever present factor. In partisan warfare, soldiers do not care much for the taking of even the necessaries of life from those who oppose or do not sympathize with them; but to go into a farmer's barn lot and take his hay, corn and oats, shoot down his hogs and cattle for food, and clean up his chicken coops, because you are compelled to take these or starve yourself and your horse; and knowing all the while the owner loves the cause and country for which you are fighting, and probably his sons and relations are somewhere out in the army contending for that which is dear to you and them, is bound to create a profound sense of grief and sorrow and even shame in any honorable soul. These takings of food from sympathizers often leave in the hearts of true men bitter and more depressing memories then the death and wounds on the battlefield, or the pathetic scenes where comrades in the cheerless hospital are wrestling with disease in a combat for life.

If General Wheeler and his men could not find and take from Federals the things that were essential to life, then they were compelled to despoil in the struggle for self-preservation their own friends and countrymen.

There were but few soldiers in General Wheeler's four thousand men who rode out of Covington, Georgia, on August 10th, 1864, who, as between the consequences of battle and the taking from aged men, helpless women and dependent children their only food supply, would not have gladly accepted the alternative of battle with absolute cheerfulness and the chances it brought of death or wounding. Two-thirds of the territory to be traversed was a friendly country. In East Tennessee, Confederates found few supporters, or well-wishers, and here the southern soldier was not disturbed about discrimination; but Middle Tennessee and Northern Georgia were almost unanimously loyal, and ever greeted the legions in gray with smiles and benedictions, and so long as they had any surplus over starvation's rations, would gladly have shared it with the trooper who followed Wheeler, Forrest or Morgan on their arduous rides.

In all this long march and hard campaign, there was not one day, hardly one hour, in which there was not contact with the enemy. The Federals appreciated, as well as the Confederates, what the destruction of the railway between Atlanta and Chattanooga meant to Sherman and his great army camped southward in Georgia. If forced by lack of food and munitions of war to recede, it meant losing what had cost a year's vigorous campaigning and the waste of the thousands of lives that in battle or by disease had been paid as the price of winning the most important citadel of Georgia.

The twenty-four days, from August 10th to September 3rd, were eventful days in the history of the army of the Tennessee. Sherman sat down in front of Atlanta in July, and by slow degrees was endeavoring by siege and starvation to drive General Hood away. This proved a most difficult task. From Atlanta to Nashville was two hundred and eighty-eight miles, and while Sherman might hammer Hood's lines south of Atlanta, Hood had most potential wreckers in Forrest and Wheeler to operate on this three hundred miles, upon one hundred and fifty-two of which, from Chattanooga to Atlanta, he must rely for those things without which war could not be carried on. Against this line of Sherman's, the Confederate cavalry again and again were hurled, always with tremendous effect. Now and then they put Sherman and his men on half rations, and the ordnance department counted their stores to calculate what might happen if the pressure was not relieved. No phase of the war presented nobler evidences of skill, great self-sacrifice or physical endurance, as month after month, Wheeler and Forrest went out upon their errands of destruction and waste. Over in Virginia, Stuart and Hampton grandly met the conditions that faced them there. Across the Mississippi, in Arkansas, Missouri and Texas, brave spirits were fearlessly keeping up the conflict against ever-increasing odds; but along the Mississippi, the Tennessee and the Cumberland were surroundings that invoked a breadth of genius and a scope of operation that excited wonder and admiration everywhere the story was told. The distance here was so great, nature's obstacles so pronounced, that those who measured and calculated and mastered these, needed something almost above the human to forecast and overcome.

The War, from 1861 to 1865, developed many problems that no soldier in the past had ever faced. There were no experiences that the books described that could fully guide the men in this department as to the best means of harassing and defeating armies that came like Sherman's.

For the special work that the time and place had cut out for the South, Providence provided two men whose names must go down in human history as superb examples of skill, daring, resource and patience, which will always give them a proud place in the annals of war. Whether we write Forrest and Wheeler, or Wheeler and Forrest, it counts not. Different minds may gauge them differently, but at the end, all who study what they did and how they did it, must set them down as amongst the greatest soldiers of the world. Those who looked upon their faces might not catch at once the splendor of their powers. They were totally unlike in most of their physical makeup, but when once the beholder looked into their eyes, the only safe index to the soul and mind, there was in both of these remarkable men something that at once challenged admiration and proclaimed superiority. In both of their countenances, the Creator stamped valor, intrepidity, self-confidence, individual force and genius and power of achievement. To thus speak of these two extraordinary men takes nothing from the achievements or talents of other great southern cavalry leaders. Stuart, Hampton, Morgan, Marmaduke, Shelby and many others filled their spheres with a luminosity that age cannot dim. It may be that it is probably true that Forrest and Wheeler would have failed when Stuart, Hampton and Morgan won. Each takes, by his performance, an exalted place in the resplendent galaxy of the South's heroic world. One cannot be judged sharply by the other. There was so much that was brave, skillful and intrepid in them all, that the pen of criticism, by way of comparison, falls paralyzed by the wonder, love and admiration for the various achievements of these military prodigies.

Even during the last days of the War, men who wrote rather than fought, attempted to draw comparisons between the cavalry leaders and what they had accomplished; but the hour for this is now forever gone, and they who love the South and its precious memories sit and gaze in rapture and astonishment at what all and any of these men, with such meager resources, were able to accomplish in those days of darkness and trial, and what the men who followed the stars and bars were doing and daring so constantly in their struggle with an opposing destiny, to win a nation's crown for the Confederate States.

Some say that Wheeler's raid through Northern Georgia, into Middle and Eastern Tennessee, in the last days of August and the first days of September, 1864, is a performance so unique and marvelous that it takes a place in history by itself.

Others point to Forrest's raid into Middle Tennessee, which, succeeding that of General Wheeler, sets a mark on such campaigns that none other ever reached; but those who love Morgan, with the pride of his great achievements, point to Hartsville and the Christmas raid of 1862 as the most remarkable achievement of the great performances of southern cavalry. Another voice speaks of Stuart's Chickahominy raid and of his ride from Chambersburg to the Potomac, and the Battle of Fleetwood Hill (Brandy Station) as overshadowing all other cavalry triumphs, while others call to mind Hampton's cattle raid, his Trevilian Station battle and campaign with his jaded mounts, and cry out, "Here is the acme of cavalry successes"; but when we recall what all of these men and their chivalrous followers accomplished for the renown and glory of a nation whose life span was only four years, the human mind is dazzled with the wealth and extent of the glorious memories that gather about the pages which tell of southern cavalry achievement, service and fame.

When General Wheeler, on the 28th day of August, marched up almost to the gates of Nashville and terrified its defenders, he carried with him a motley crowd. The brigades of General Williams and General Anderson had not returned to General Wheeler. They moved east and did incalculable service for the cause in saving the salt works, in Southwestern Virginia, upon which the people and the armies of the Confederacy, west of the Mississippi River, depended for salt, which, next to bread, was the staff of life. But the defection, whether wise or unwise, reduced General Wheeler's force, already scant enough, to only two thousand men, and thereby imperilled the success of the incursion and threatened the destruction of General Wheeler's entire command, which at that time would have proven an irreparable loss to Hood's army. The rise in the Tennessee River had forced General Wheeler to extend his line far east of where he had intended originally to go. These unexpected currents carried him miles beyond Knoxville and out of his chosen path, and the detour south and east of Knoxville to cross the rivers greatly stayed the work of wrecking the railroads between Nashville and the South. Once he was over the Tennessee and its tributaries, the Holston and the French Broad, General Wheeler turned his face westward. The country through which he was to march was in some parts unfriendly. At Clinton, Kingston and other points on his way, he found scattered Federal camps and supplies, but what he needed most now was horses. He had come three hundred miles, and three hundred more must he traverse before he could draw a long breath or be sure that he could, without disaster, reach General Hood's quarters. Day by day, his beasts became more jaded. No animal, which could carry a man, was left behind, and what could not be taken from the enemy must be impressed from friend or foe along the road which he was passing. The extra shoe or pair of horseshoes with which every prudent cavalryman provides himself, where it is possible, when starting on these marches, had in most cases been exhausted. The company farrier or the comrade who could put on a horseshoe loomed up as the noblest benefactor of the hour. Some were already dismounted. Love, money and force were all beginning to be powerless to mount those who composed the columns. Then, too, ammunition was getting very scarce, and the few cartridges which now rattled in the partly emptied cartridge boxes were constant warnings to the commander to seek his base of operations. All these things spoke to General Wheeler with forceful emphasis, but he also remembered his work was not fully done. The long detour around Knoxville had changed his march, but it had not changed his plan or his purpose, and he could not be satisfied until he grappled again with the railroads which supplied Sherman and put out of commission some more bridges, trestles and cars and supply stations south of Nashville. The road by Sparta, McMinnville, Lebanon, Murfreesboro and intervening places was long, rough and rocky. It proved very trying to the speechless beasts who had now marched, counting the detours, an average of over thirty miles a day. The men had done the fighting, but the beasts had done the carrying, and the beasts in these raids always got the worst of it. The way home was not distressingly: beset with enemies until the vicinity of Nashville would be reached, but there was a sufficient sprinkle of foes to keep the southern riders aware that they were engaged in war, and no twenty-four hours passed without some evidence of the presence of the Federals. The march around Knoxville had mystified the Federal leaders. They were as surprised as General Wheeler that he had gone so far east, but now that he had turned north and westward, none had wisdom enough to prophesy where he would turn up in the very near future. General Wheeler had a wide, wide territory before him. He might strike in north of Nashville and pass around through West Tennessee, or he might follow the Louisville & Nashville Railroad north and destroy that great artery of commerce. Whither he would go, none could even guess, and when Grant at Washington, and Sherman at Atlanta, pleaded for some tidings of the aggressive Confederate and begged to know whither he had gone, the men watching Middle and East Tennessee could only answer, "We cannot tell where he is or into what place he will come." As the posts became scarcer General Wheeler traveled the harder, and he soon put in an appearance at Sparta and then at McMinnville, the last only sixty miles from Nashville. He was getting close to the danger line. At this juncture, General Wheeler's difficulties began to greatly enlarge. His fighting men, with the loss of Williams and Anderson, had been cut down, even with several hundred of recruits, to twenty-five hundred men.

On the 30th of August, he made a stirring patriotic appeal for every able-bodied man to flock to his standard. He pointed out what Georgia was doing in demanding the services of every male from seventeen to sixty-five, and he pleaded with all who could fight or were willing to fight, to gather under his standard and to go to the help of their fellow-Tennesseans, who, down at Atlanta, were meeting every call unreservedly and rendering every service to stay the tide of conquest.

This appeal did not fall on deaf or unresponsive ears. Two thousand came to join Wheeler and hundreds more to take place with other commands, and almost a mob followed his line of march. Some of them brought guns, most all of them horses, but twenty-five hundred men were to do the fighting for this unorganized host. Only twenty-five hundred could fight, but they could and all must eat, and the impoverished country could not maintain this hungry throng. A supply for all of these could only find sustenance in Federal storehouses, and to these General Wheeler turned his attention, ever keeping in mind that under all the pressure about him, he had come to harass and distress his foes, and this must not be omitted. Forcing his way northwardly from McMinnville to Lebanon, thirty miles west of Nashville, his enemies became almost desperate, and the commandant at Gallatin, twelve miles from Lebanon, burned up a great supply of stores and hastily decamped. Several other stations joined in this move for safety. Of what was ahead of him, General Wheeler had no accurate news. On a straight line, he was nearly three hundred miles from Hood, and if the pace became desperate, Hood in the end must become his best backer outside of his own gallant and intrepid followers. Cutting in behind Murfreesboro, thirty miles south of Nashville, with apparent indifference to consequences, he turned sharply to the north again and came up within eight miles of Nashville, and with his pickets in sight of the spires and smoke, he began to wreck the railroad leading to Chattanooga. The Federals did not appear to know just where the bold leader was and they did not care where he went if he kept out of Nashville, but in the very shadow of its domes, he set his wreckers to work demolishing the line which meant so much to Sherman. These experienced destroyers made haste in their work of ruin. Moving southward, they left savage marks to tell of their presence, and the burning ties and twisted iron informed the onlooker that experienced men were engaged in this mission. General Wheeler had only occasion to keep out of the path of large forces. Stockades were exempt, except where their occupants had fled, and for seventy miles south of Nashville, the wrecking went vigorously on. Rousseau, Steedman and Granger, who were managing the watch for Sherman, either did not know where Wheeler actually was or they did not appear overly anxious to stop his progress. Following the Tennessee & Alabama Railroad for seventy miles with leisurely movements, General Wheeler, seemingly regardless of his foes, pursued his appointed way to a position north of Florence, Alabama. General Wheeler's audacity apparently paralyzed the efforts of his pursuers. At Franklin, they had forced some sharp fighting, and here the chivalrous major general, John H. Kelly, fell. Rarely did the South, with its transcendent oblations on the altar of freedom, make nobler offering than this gifted army officer. A graduate of West Point, endowed with great military genius and burning with unbounded patriotism, few men with his opportunities did more for the South than he. In the full tide of a magnificent and brilliant career, he died, leading his men on to battle. Trusted and loved by General Wheeler, he had learned his leader's methods and, like him, always went to the front, and when it was necessary to inspire and enthuse his command, he led them in every assault upon the lines of their foes. It was in such work he fell.

Recruits, wagon trains, ambulances and wagons filled with wounded, dismounted men and broken down steeds, were the constant reminder to General Wheeler of the dangers of his perilous retreat. About him, all these disturbing difficulties and dangers momentarily stared him in the face. Behind him, vigorous foes were many times pressing his rear guard. What forces might be moved by the Federals to block his path, he could not foresee, but over and above all these disturbing complications, the Confederate leader, weighing not more than one hundred and thirty pounds, sat in his saddle, calm, self-possessed and fearless, awaiting with a brave heart and an undisturbed soul all that fate could bring across his path. He felt that with the brave men about him, war could bring no conflict and present no experiences from which he could not, with credit to his chivalrous command, emerge without defeat and destruction, and in which he would not punish his enemies and give them experiences that would cause them to regret that they had ever assailed his followers or disputed his pathway.

On this great raid, one hundred and twenty dead and wounded was all toll that the God of War exacted of General Wheeler's forces. He compelled General Sherman to send more than twelve thousand men to the help of his commands. He had destroyed the use of one of the railroads on which the Federals relied for twelve days, the other for thirty days, put General Sherman's forces on half rations and created in his army a dread and apprehension that did much to help depress their activities and awaken doubts as to the final outcome of the conflict for Atlanta.

Chapter XII

JOHNSONVILLE RAID AND FORREST'S
MARINE EXPERIENCES, NOVEMBER, 1864

October and November, 1864, covered the most successful and aggressive period of General Forrest's remarkable exploits. Volumes could be written describing the details of his marvellous marches and his almost indescribable triumphs with the means and men at his command. From August 23rd to October 15th, 1864, his capture of Athens, Alabama, the expedition into middle Tennessee, the destruction of the Tennessee and Alabama railway, the capture of Huntsville, destruction of the Sulphur trestles, the battle at Eastport, had presented an array of experiences and won victories enough to make him and his men heroes for the years to come. Within these fifty-three days the actual and incidental losses inflicted upon the Federals cannot be fully estimated. He had killed and captured thirty-five hundred men and officers of the Federal Army, added nine hundred head of horses to his equipment, captured more than one hundred and twenty head of cattle, one hundred wagons and their supplies, and possessed himself of three thousand stand of small arms and stores for his commissary ordnance and medical supplies, which made glad the hearts of his hungry, ill-clad and debilitated followers.

Six long truss bridges had fallen before his relentless destroyers, one hundred miles of railroad had been completely wrecked, two locomotives, with fifty freight cars, had been demolished, thousands of feet of railway trestles, some of sixty feet in height, had been hewn down and given over to flames, to say naught of hundreds of thousands of other property essential to Federal occupation. He had caught up one thousand men in Middle Tennessee for his own command and enabled six hundred men who had either straggled or been cut off from General Wheeler when he had raided the same territory a short while before to come out to the commands. It had cost Forrest three hundred men and officers, killed or wounded. Some of his bravest and best had died on the expedition. Many of them were men whose places could now never be filled, but according to the economics of war, the price paid was not too great for the results obtained. He had traversed over five hundred miles and left a savagely marked trail of ravage and destruction wherever he had come. Not a day was without some sort of contact with the enemy, and every hour was full of danger and peril, demanding ceaseless vigilance and wariest care. On January 13th, 1864, a new Department styled "Forrest's Cavalry Department" was organized out of West Tennessee and Northern Mississippi. Hardly had the new year been ushered in when the Federal Government, with ten thousand well-equipped and well-drilled cavalry, undertook to force a way down from Memphis to Meridian, taking in some of the Confederate strongholds like Pontotoc, Okolona, Columbus Junction and Macon, a distance of two hundred and fifty miles, to end at Macon. General Sherman was to move from Vicksburg with an army of twenty thousand troops. Co-operation of the cavalry was deemed of the greatest importance. To lead these horsemen, William Sooy Smith, not only a great engineer, but a successful soldier, was placed in command. Telegraphic communication had been opened between Vicksburg and Memphis, so that it was hoped these forces, thus co-operating, might keep in touch with each other. General Sherman made good his march to Meridian, playing havoc with railroad connections and other property in Mississippi. General Smith however failed to keep his engagement. He had been delayed in starting, until the 11th of February, from his rendezvous, Colliers Station, twenty-five miles southeastward from Memphis. He waited here for Colonel George E. Waring, who had been instructed to come from Columbus, Kentucky, with another brigade, under orders to unite with General Smith. Waring left Columbus with several thousand cavalry, and with the best arms of that period, and what was considered at that time amongst the most thoroughly furnished cavalry forces that had ever gone from the Federal lines. General Smith had informed General Sherman that Forrest would strike him somewhere in Northern Mississippi between Cold and Tallahatchee Rivers. After his invasion of West Tennessee, General Forrest had been enabled to get together four brigades under General Richardson, Colonel McCullough, General Tyree H. Bell and General Forrest's brother, Jeffrey E. Forrest. The Confederates were not inactive, and they prepared to offer strongest resistance to General Smith. The State Militia, under General Gholson, were brought into line. Smith marched for several days unhindered, and the absence of Confederate forces impressed him that it would not be long before he would come in contact with Forrest. Northwestern Mississippi was a great prairie country, producing the most grain of any section of the Southwest. When the Federals reached West Point, Mississippi, there were unmistakable signs of battle. There General Smith learned that three Forrests were about, General Nathan Bedford, Colonel Jeffrey E., and Captain William, and investigation disclosed that the number of men with Forrest was about two thousand. General Smith had now traveled half way from Memphis to Meridian, and Sherman was waiting and watching for Smith's coming. General Forrest had studiously circulated reports magnifying the number of men under his command. By the 21st of February, Smith felt that the impending blow was about to fall. He hesitated and was lost. He turned back, and Forrest's hour of advantage had come. Colonel Waring in his book, "Whip and Spur," of this moment speaks as follows: "No sooner had we turned tail than Forrest saw his time had come, and he pressed us seriously all day and until nightfall." The retrograde movement was just commenced when Jeffrey Forrest's orders were to fall in after Captain Tyler's battalion and to assail the Federal rear at every chance. Pursuit was vigorous and active, and General Smith's retreat became almost a stampede. It was in one of these charges that Colonel Jeffrey E. Forrest, commanding a brigade, the younger brother of General Forrest, was killed. For over sixty miles, night and day, a relentless pursuit was kept up. Forrest had four thousand men that were new troops. A majority of them had seen service less than six weeks. They were hardy men but mostly untrained soldiers, but they prided themselves that they were the equals of any veterans.

By the time General Smith reached Memphis he had more of a mob than an army. There was practically no organization left and it was almost a case of everybody for himself and devil take the hindmost. Not two weeks had elapsed since, in the pride of strength and full of ambitious hopes, they had set out to cripple and destroy Forrest, and now, with less than fourteen days to their credit as avengers and destroyers, they came, humiliated by reverses, scattered in fright, and with no signs of victory on their colors. Their leaders could make but little excuse for their ignominious failure, and the only chance to palliate or mitigate defeat was to magnify General Forrest's army that had at first stood them at bay and then, with pitiless pursuit, had driven them to the place from whence they had started with such dazzling dreams of glory and triumph.

This expedition disposed of, Forrest began at once to cut out new work. There were no furloughs for him. War in his mind was constant, ceaseless activity. The scarcity of horses and ammunition as well as clothing was a constant charge upon Forrest's energies. He could not get from the Confederate quartermaster or commissary what he most needed, and far out on the front he could not wait for transportation even if the Confederates had the essential things. In the Federal Army and outposts he always found an unfailing supply of those things his men must have to faithfully fight.

Three regiments of Kentuckians, about this period, were sent over to help General Forrest, and they were fully up to his high standard of fighters. They only numbered seven hundred men after the decimation of three years in infantry, but they proved a most valuable asset. None of his men were more dependable. Buford, Lyon, Faulkner, Hale, Thompson, Tyler and Crossland could always be counted on for gallant leadership, and the men under them were never averse to fighting at the closest range. These men needed clothing. The Government had given them poor mounts, some of them had rope bridles, with no saddles. They used blankets as a substitute and now and then rode for a while bareback, until they drew from the Federal commissary, by force, what they needed. Up in Kentucky, if any good horses were left after impressment from both sides, these Kentucky boys would surely find them. As for clothing, that would come in far greater quantities than would be desired, and sight of home faces and home places would make them stronger for the subsequent work at Bryce's Cross Roads, Harrisburg and Johnsonville, and other conflicts, where only highest courage could avail.

Then, too, the Tennesseans, who had come from the northwestern part of the State, also needed mounts and uniforms, and they longed to see what the sad ravages of war had done for their homes and kindred in that part of the South where the cauldron of pillage and bloodshed seemed ever to be seething.

General Forrest reorganized his command into four brigades, and on the 12th day of April Fort Pillow was taken. A year before this, General Forrest had penetrated a considerable distance into Kentucky and had captured a number of posts and looked askance at Fort Pillow. This was deemed a valuable possession, it was used not only for the defense of the river, but as a recruiting place for fugitive slaves. The story of Fort Pillow has been told so often that it need not be repeated here. The loss of Federals was supposed to be five hundred killed and an equal number captured. Forrest's loss was twenty killed and sixty wounded. Fort Pillow was considered remarkable among cavalry achievements. Forrest, with a few untrained soldiers, had accomplished and won this great victory and given his foes new reasons for animosity. Much, very much has been written and spoken about Fort Pillow. It became a name with which to conjure the colored troops, and through it abuse was so heaped upon General Forrest as to create the impression that he was a brutal, ferocious and merciless monster. The Federal Congress set afoot an investigation, but Forrest's defense from the calumnies heaped upon him satisfied his friends, if it did not convince his enemies.

The character and antecedents of the garrison had much to do with the events of the histories connected with its capture. Renegade Tennesseans and fugitive slaves comprised the larger part of its defenders. The white men there had perpetrated many wrongs and outrages upon the defenseless families of the Tennesseans under Forrest. Great numbers of his men had come from the regions where these hideous wrongs had been inflicted. Feeling was high on both sides. Human passions had been thoroughly aroused in Confederate and Federal hearts, and both sides were rejoiced at a chance to "have it out." Neither side went into the conflict looking for any signs of surrender, and had the Confederates changed places, they would have fared no better than those they defeated and captured. But the fall of the Fort was a great windfall to General Forrest, and while it increased the hate of his foes, it detracted nothing from his renown and fame amongst his own people.

Many Federal generals had tried their hand with Forrest only to meet failure. William Sooy Smith had lost, and General Stephen A. Hurlbut had also failed. General C. C. Washburn had taken his place and then Samuel D. Sturgis came and then Bryce's Cross Roads. Later followed the Confederate defeat at Harrisburg, which for awhile saddened Forrest's heart. Wounded shortly after this battle, General Forrest was forced to ride in a buggy with his torn foot lifted up so as to cause him the least pain. It was persistently rumored that he had died of lockjaw, and there would have been no tears among the Federals if this had turned out to be true. By the beginning of August, General Forrest had recovered from his wounds sufficiently to enable him to enter upon one of his greatest exploits. Riding into the heart of Memphis, he caused Generals Washburn, Buchland and Hurlbut to flee from their beds at night and seek safety in the forts around the city. General Washburn's uniform and effects were captured, but he managed to escape. General Washburn sought to lay the blame for this successful and marvelous feat upon General A. J. Smith. Under all the circumstances, Forrest's raid into Memphis was admittedly amongst the most brilliant and daring cavalry exploits of the war. That two thousand men should avoid the cities in which the Federal garrisons were quartered, pass them by, travel a hundred miles, and then rush into the city of Memphis, make good their escape with an embarrassing contingent of supplies and prisoners, up to that time had few if any parallels.

The tremendous power and efficacy of the methods of General Forrest had at last been realized, and the Government at Richmond resolved to turn Forrest loose upon Sherman, in connection with General Richard Taylor, who had command of the department of the Mississippi. General Taylor, sympathizing with Forrest in his style of fighting, on the 16th day of September, 1864, set him afloat for twenty-one days' operations on the rear of the enemy. Forrest's entry into Memphis had caused A. J. Smith's army to return to that city and had temporarily withdrawn a large and threatening force from Mississippi. Up to that time General Taylor had never seen Forrest. He described him as a tall, stalwart man with grayish hair, kindly countenance and slow of speech. Nature made General Forrest a great soldier. With opportunities for the development of his marvelous genius, there could have been no limit to his performances.

On the 16th day of September, Forrest started from Verona, Mississippi, with three thousand five hundred and forty-two effective men. He undertook to cross the Tennessee River at Newport, where boats had been provided. The artillery, ordnance and wagons were crossed at Newport, but Forrest waded the river at Colbert Shoals. Chalmers commanded one division and Buford the other. Reinforcements now joined Forrest, which made four thousand five hundred soldiers, four hundred of which, however, were dismounted and were following on foot with the expectation of capturing mounts during the raid. These hardy men were glad, by walking and many times running, to be allowed to join the expedition. A horse was the most desirable of all earthly possessions. They were hesitant at no fatigue and hardship which led them to a mount. Those who went with Forrest well knew they would at some point be sure of a captured beast. They all had some friend who would ride and tie with them. Here and there, on some short stretch of good road, they might when nobody was looking get a lift in an ammunition wagon. Then, too, they could escape the slush and mud in the bespattered road, and trotting alongside the fences or passway, they would find it no great task to keep even with the artillery and heavily loaded horses, unless when the haste of battle or the rush of pursuit quickened the pace of the advancing column. Life was worthless to a cavalryman under the great leaders of the Confederate troopers if he had no horse, and thus these nervy men for days followed the expedition, with unfailing faith that in a reasonable time General Forrest would at least give them a sufficient chance with their enemies to enable them to forage upon the Federal Government for the much needed steed. None who ever witnessed these dismounted battalions marching on foot to the scenes of devastation and battle could fail to be impressed with the power of the human will or the strenuosity of the human body under the impulse of war's hopes and calls.

At this time there was a railroad which ran from Nashville, Tennessee, to Decatur, Alabama, called the Alabama and Tennessee Railroad. This had been a feeder for Federal commissary and general supplies, and General Forrest undertook to destroy it. The Confederates had not been expected. Athens, Alabama, was the first Federal stronghold to fall. Forrest's presence had never been suspected until his troops were in sight of the place. It surrendered without contest. Nine hundred prisoners were captured at Athens. This invasion of Forrest stayed for a little while Sherman's great march to the sea. From Pulaski, Tennessee, General Forrest moved to the Nashville & Chattanooga Railroad. He reported that the enemy had concentrated at least ten thousand men on the 27th of September, and on the 28th he began to play havoc with the railroad at Fayetteville and Tullahoma. The Federal forces, under the direction of General Sherman, were concentrated in the hope of capturing Forrest. General Sherman telegraphed that he could take care of the line between Atlanta and Chattanooga, but the line from Nashville to Chattanooga must be protected by others. The rage of Forrest's enemies was evidence enough to convince the men of the South that he had done his work well. At that time General Sherman telegraphed to General Grant on the 29th of September, in which he said, speaking of Forrest, "His cavalry will travel 100 miles in less time than ours will travel 10." He also said, "I can whip his infantry, but his cavalry is to be feared." Again he telegraphed to General Elliott, chief of the cavalry department of the Cumberland, "Our cavalry must do more, for it is strange that Forrest and Wheeler should encircle around us thus. We should at least make 10 miles to his 100."

On the 1st of October, on this raid, Forrest reached Spring Hill, twenty-six miles from Nashville. So far no reverses. The time had come now for General Forrest to escape. On the 3rd of October, with all possible speed, to avoid the Federal columns, he marched south, reaching Florence, Alabama, where he had forded the river two weeks before, but now it was swollen and could no longer be passed. At this point, in what would be considered almost a crisis, Forrest was compelled to carry a thousand of his men out to an island in the Tennessee River, which was filled with an impenetrable growth of cane and timber of all kinds, and hide his boats behind the island, while the enemy was still watching to prevent his troops from crossing. General Forrest, in speaking of this wonderful expedition, said, "I captured 86 commissioned officers, 67 government employees, 1,274 non-commissioned officers and privates and 933 negroes, and killed and wounded 1,000 more, making an aggregate of 3,360, being an average of one to each man I had in the engagements." He further says, "I captured 800 horses, 7 pieces of artillery, 2,000 stands of small arms, several hundred saddles, 50 wagons and ambulances with a large amount of medical, commissary and quartermaster's stores, all of which have been distributed to the different commands."

Now a still greater victory and a new departure in military work was to mark the closing months of 1864, in which General Forrest acted with an independent command. Towards the end of the war, Memphis became a center of the most important operations. The Mississippi was always open and it gave entrance into the grain fields of the West and through the Ohio, the Missouri, the Wabash and the White Rivers, and put at the service of the Federal Army abundant supplies of food and raiment.

The Tennessee River, the fifth largest stream in the United States, like the New River, is one of the marvels of nature. Rising far up in the mountains, close to the Virginia line, it pushes its way southwardly through Tennessee, swinging around into Alabama, as if by some capricious fancy, it changes its direction and then turns north about four hundred and fifty miles to its mouth, where it mingles its waters with those of the Ohio, sixty miles above its union with the Mississippi. After leaving Alabama, pursuing its course within fifty miles of the Father of Waters, it appears to be reluctant to reinforce that stream with which it runs parallel for hundreds of miles. It would appear according to reason and nature that it should again have veered to the west and effected its connection with the Mississippi, but as if wishing to defy this mighty stream, it still moves onward and northward. It comes then within two miles of the Cumberland, which is fed by the waters from the mountains close to where the Tennessee River has its source, and then, as if running a race with the Cumberland, it flows along parallel with that stream and, at last, wearied by its tortuous journeys for nine hundred miles, at Paducah it mingles its waters with those of the Ohio, and these in turn pass westward and reach the Mississippi at Cairo.

About one hundred and fifty miles from Memphis, on the Tennessee River, was a little town called Johnsonville, and at that time it was at the head of the navigable part of the Tennessee River. To that point the larger boats could most always come and it was a great depot for supplies, and in an emergency these might be carried over to Nashville or Memphis, as either one or the other might require.

Forrest was beginning now fully to recover from the effects of the loss of the troops he trained in the earlier months of the war. Successful beyond all question in cavalry service, he had again gathered about him a corps of almost invincible men. His new recruits and such soldiers as were reimbued with patriotic impulses, after having left the army when it abandoned Tennessee, by Forrest's coming into West Tennessee, cheerfully returned to the post of duty and under the impulse of Forrest's success, and the love and courage with which he impressed all who once saw him enter battle. The ranks of depleted skeleton regiments were partially filled, and the commanders of these new organizations had now, under Forrest's eye and control, learned how he deemed it wisest to fight, and they were ready to do and dare all that his impetuous valor required, or his marvelous skill as a leader pointed out as the true way to carry on war under the conditions that then existed in his department.

He had now a division of more than four thousand men. He felt sure he could trust them in all emergencies, and he was eager and willing to put them to the highest test, and he undertook at this period what will always be considered as a remarkable cavalry foray, the expedition to Johnsonville, Tennessee.

Before undertaking this arduous work, Forrest had pleaded for a furlough. This had been promised, but an emergency arose which neither he nor General Taylor could foresee or control, and it became impossible for him to be absent even for a brief while; and so Chalmers and his division were directed to report to General Forrest at Jackson, Tennessee, on the 16th day of October.

General Forrest and General Dick Taylor were kindred spirits. Their relations were most happy and pleasant. They were men who fought the same way and thought the same way, and Taylor recognized the greatness of Forrest and fully understood that he did best when left to his own devices.

On October 12th, 1864, Forrest telegraphed Chalmers, commander of one division, "Fetch your wagons and the batteries with you. I will supply you with artillery ammunition at Jackson." Buford was ordered to take up his line of march for Lexington, a short distance from the Tennessee River, where Forrest had crossed in his December, 1862, expedition. Gun boats and transports were being moved along the Tennessee River. These could go a little south of Chattanooga, and the line of communication had been protected and held open from the river to General Sherman and his men. Forrest had resolved to destroy some of these gunboats and capture some of the transports. He needed some new guns, the clothing, shoes, arms and ammunition of his troopers needed replenishment and, too, he had a conviction that he could enact such scenes on the Tennessee as would disquiet Sherman at Atlanta and by imperiling the river transportation, and destroying the railroads north of Chattanooga, he could bring Sherman, by sheer starvation, out of Georgia. It was a splendid conception, and could the Confederacy have sent Forrest on one line and General Wheeler on the other, it would have stopped or delayed the march to the sea, and prolonged the war another year. Optimists said, it might bring final victory to the banners of the Southland.

On this Johnsonville raid, as often before, he marched with such tremendous rapidity and covered his movements so thoroughly that the enemy knew nothing of either his plans or his positions, until far up in Tennessee they felt the touch of his avenging powers. He had parked batteries at Paris Landing and Fort Heiman on the Tennessee River, and his men began to wait for the unsuspecting Federals before his foes had an inkling of what he really intended to do. He struck the river about forty miles above Johnsonville. The two batteries were five miles apart. He knew what all his enemies were doing, but they caught naught of where he had gone, or was going. Like a great beast of prey, he hid along the river banks in the cane and undergrowth, watching and waiting for his victims to cross his path, or to come his way. A vast majority of the people of West Tennessee were intensely loyal to the South, and it was only here and there that Federal persuasion could win from a native any facts about the movements of any Confederate force. News about Federal movements was always accessible to Forrest's scouts, who knew accurately every road and by-way of this entire region. It was one hundred and fifty miles to Memphis where a large Federal force was stationed, but none passed Forrest's line to carry tidings of his doings, and when Forrest's guns opened on the transports and gunboats on the river, north of Johnsonville, it was a most startling revelation to the Federals of the ubiquitous movements of the Confederate chieftain. The Federal generals knew he was loose somewhere, but they had no power of divining where he might break out to terrorize their garrisons and destroy their railroads or depots of supplies. Forrest, Wheeler, Hampton, Stuart and Morgan had the most efficient scouts that ever kept an army informed of an enemy's movements. Forrest's territory for operation was larger than that of any of these other leaders, and he never once failed, thanks to the courage, daring and intelligence of his scouts to know just how many they were and just where he would find his foes.

A grateful people will some day build a monument to these daring and successful purveyors of information, who deserve a very large share in the splendid victories and triumphs of the Confederate cavalry. The South may never know their names, but the world will some day fairly and justly measure what they were in the campaigns which will live forever amongst the most brilliant of military exploits.

Forrest was playing a great game. He had taken big risks and was figuring on tremendous stakes. In the night time he made all necessary dispositions. His scouts had told him that boats were coming and Forrest was glad, for he had come for boats. The Confederates had waited both patiently and impatiently all the night long. Patiently, because they felt sure of their prey; impatiently, for they anxiously desired to feed upon the good things the vessels contained, and also because they had made a long and trying march and, tiger-like, they were ready to spring upon the victim. It was chilly and raw. It had been raining heavily off and on during the past week. The river bottoms, or even the hill tops, were not comfortable places in October without fire, and these things, added to the excitement that preceded great actions, made the Confederate troopers long for the coming of the rising sun. There was something in the very surroundings that gave portent of great deeds and glorious triumphs on the morrow, when they should be sent forth on their mission, and it was difficult to repress, even amidst their depressing environments, the enthusiasm which they felt sure must break forth in the inevitable happenings of the next twenty-four hours.

Early in the morning of October 29th, the Mazeppa, a splendid steamboat, laden with freight, and two barges which she was towing to Johnsonville, came around the great bend of the Tennessee River. The sections of artillery had been posted some distance apart on the river. Passing the lower one, the boatmen discovered its presence only to find themselves between the two hostile batteries. Both were turned loose and in a few minutes the boat was crippled and the pilot headed for the shore. She was abandoned, and the crew in wild dismay found refuge in the woods along the banks. The immediate trouble was that the Confederates were on the opposite side from the stranded steamer. In this crisis, a valiant Confederate, Captain T. Gracy of the 3rd Kentucky, came to the rescue, and although the water was chilling and the current swift, he strapped his revolver around his neck, mounted on a piece of driftwood, and with a board for a paddle, propelled himself across the stream. Keeping true to the instincts of the sailor, the pilot refused to desert his care, and he surrendered to the naked captain who had so bravely crossed the stream. This was probably, in some respects, the richest capture that Forrest had ever made, and his soldiers began to unload the cargo and carry it away from the river bank to a place where it might be watched and preserved until it could be taken away.

The Federal gunboats got the range on the Mazeppa and opened such a heavy fire that its new captors were glad to consign the boat to the flames, while they energetically packed and hauled its precious contents to places so far inland that the guns of these sea fighters could not find the places of hiding.

A little while and another large steamer, the J. W. Cheeseman, approached the upper battery. It was allowed to pass in between the two Confederate positions. No sooner had she gone well into the trap than fire was opened upon her, both from the troops upon the shore, and from the artillery, and her officers were glad to hasten the surrender of this splendid steamer. The gunboat, Undine, had also gone in between the batteries, but the Confederate artillery were not afraid of gunboats, and so they pounded her so severely that she was disabled and driven to the shore, and her crew and officers hastily abandoned her and escaped through the woods, while she became a prize to Confederate daring and marksmanship. In a little while, the transport Venus moved up the river.

On this boat was a small detachment of Federal infantry. This boat was attacked by Colonel Kelley and his men, and so heavy was the iron hail upon her that she, too, was glad to surrender and with the gunboat was brought safely to the shore. Half the garrison were killed or wounded and all captured.

On this day it seemed to rain gunboats. Another one, the No. 29, had probably heard the firing, and, coming down the river, anchored within half a mile of the Confederate batteries and opened fire. This was too slow a game for the Confederates, so General Chalmers took the guns and his escort and a company of videttes, and going through the cane and brush got nearer to the gunboat and soon drove it away. The steamboat Cheeseman could no longer be serviceable, her stores were removed and flames lapped up what was left of her. The Venus and the Undine were slightly injured. The Undine was one of the largest gunboats that had been sent up the Tennessee river. She carried eight twenty-four pound guns, and when she became a victim to Confederate courage, her entire armament went with her. Her crew attempted to spike the guns, but in this they were unsuccessful. In all these captures the Confederate loss was one man severely wounded. Five or six Federals were killed on the Venus, three killed and four wounded on the Undine and one wounded on the Cheeseman.

General Forrest, ever resourceful, and whose capacity for all phases of war seemed unlimited, determined to begin a career as a naval officer, and from the cavalry a volunteer crew was made up; two twenty-four pounders were placed on the Venus, and Captain Gracy placed in command. Gracy had shown himself to be a great land fighter, but he was yet to make his reputation as a marine. The captured gunboat was also put into commission. The new commodore was directed to steam his boat up the river toward Johnsonville, a few miles away, while the troops marched along the road parallel to the river. The gunboats were put in charge of Colonel Dawson. He evidently did not want to secure Forrest's ill will, and so he made a covenant with him that if he lost his fleet, Forrest was not to "cuss" him. The boats got separated. The artillery were not skilled so well on water as they were on land, and so when a Federal commodore, with boats No. 32 and 29, got within range of the Venus, they soon damaged her so badly that she was of no service, and was run ashore and abandoned without even setting on fire. The Undine, seeing the disaster to her companion ship, sought safety on the river bank under the protection of the Confederate batteries. The Federal gunboat soon closed in upon the Undine, and it was necessary to abandon her, also, and set her on fire.

So far General Forrest had inflicted a great amount of damage upon the Federals. He had captured the Mazeppa with seven hundred tons of freight, two other steamboats, two other gunboats, the transports Venus and Cheeseman, and another steamer over at Clarksville on the Cumberland was also destroyed. It was not very far, something like twenty-five miles, across to the Cumberland, and Forrest undertook to operate upon both rivers. Johnsonville was on the east side of the river.

On the 3rd day of November, Forrest reached the scene of action with his chief of artillery, John W. Morton. Johnsonville, at this time, appeared as a sort of heavenly resort, or a Commissary Utopia, to the Confederates, and Forrest promptly undertook its destruction and all that was gathered in it. The landing was filled with transports and barges and gunboats. The great problem with the Confederates in the later periods of the war was something to eat, wear, shoot and ride, and the little town beside the Tennessee, with more supplies than these oftentimes hungry and illy clad horsemen had ever dreamed of, appeared to contain all the provisions in the world. On the banks were houses filled to overflowing with valuable supplies, and acres of army stores were piled around the warehouses. A new battery had come up during the following night, under Captain Thrall. This was placed just above the town, while the Morton and Hudson batteries were placed just opposite and below the town. At two o'clock Forrest opened with his artillery. He had kept his movements so well concealed that the Federals at Johnsonville were unaware of his presence until the Confederate guns announced the presence of an enemy. Morton promptly opened fire upon the forts and gunboats. For a little while the Federals had no apprehension that Forrest could effect very much, but Morton, always skillful, soon obtained the range and by cutting the fuses with precision, he put his shells into the midst of the supply station. Flame and smoke soon began to rise from many of the boats that lined the river, and from the goods along the wharf and the warehouses. By nightfall, the boats and the walls of the commissary were fired, and for three-quarters of a mile up and down, the river presented a great forest of flame. Flames illuminated the horizon for miles and huge volumes of smoke rose up towards the heavens in glorious signals of a great consuming fire. Some said that the Federal soldiers fired their own boats. Morton, Thrall, Bugg, Zaring, Brown and Hunter, the men who directed the artillery firing on this expedition, won splendid laurels by the accuracy of their aim. Colonel Rucker had an extended experience in artillery service in the Mississippi in the earlier stages of the war; while General Lyon, who before his resignation from the United States Army had served as an artillery officer, gave their assistance in the important work of destroying the Federal boats and supplies. The artillery were the chief instruments in this crowning act of destruction, and all others in the other corps were glad to give them due praise and plaudits for the splendid way in which they had performed their part in this magnificent victory.

Forrest had now accomplished all he had come to do. He had burned up millions' worth of property. The Federals said he had thirteen thousand men with twenty-six guns. Sherman, telegraphing General Grant, said, "That devil, Forrest, was down about Johnsonville, making havoc among the gunboats and transports."

The roads had become well-nigh impassable, and the return march to Corinth was slow and toilsome. On November 10th, however, he arrived at Corinth in reasonably good order. He had been absent a little more than two weeks. He had captured and destroyed four gunboats, fourteen transports, twenty barges, twenty-six pieces of artillery, and six million seven hundred thousand dollars' worth of property. One thing that particularly pleased the Confederates was the capture of nine thousand pairs of shoes and one thousand blankets, and strange to say, in all these operations and fourteen days' fighting of the Confederates, two were killed and nine wounded.

Forrest always was able to mystify his enemies. He had left enough troops in the neighborhood of Memphis to keep the commanders there busy and to fear an attack on the place. General Smith reported from Memphis, on the 16th of October, that the houses had been loop-holed for sharpshooters, and an inner line of cotton defenses constructed, and told his commander that Forrest was at Grenada on the Friday night before. Halleck, in Washington, wired Thomas that Forrest was threatening Memphis. General Sherman was so alarmed by this destruction of Johnsonville that he telegraphed to General Grant, saying, "Sherman estimates that Forrest has 26,000 men mounted and menacing his communications." The 23rd Corps was despatched to Johnsonville, and up at Columbus, Kentucky, Sherman had given orders that guns must be defended to death and the town should be burned rather than that Forrest should get a pound of provisions. The Federals seemed to be doing more telegraphing than fighting and marching. While they were comforting each other or alarming each other, Forrest's soldiers, well dressed, well mounted, thoroughly equipped, were pulling through the mud, trying to get out of Tennessee. The mud and slush became such a menace that General Forrest was required to use sixteen oxen to pull one gun. The teams were doubled to carry the cannon, sixteen horses were hitched to a single piece. The oxen would haul the guns ten or fifteen miles and then were turned back to their owners, who were allowed to drive them home.

On the 15th day of November, Forrest reached Iuka, and then by rail from Cherokee Station, Forrest and his men were transferred to Florence, Alabama. On this trip, horseshoes and nails became very scarce. Many times Forrest was compelled to take the tires from the farm wagons along the route and have these forged into shoes and nails for the use of the horses.

This marvelous expedition was to close the really great destructive career of General Forrest. The ink was hardly dry upon his letter to General Dick Taylor, detailing a portion of the work under his command, until orders were given for General Forrest to proceed at once to Florence and there take command of the cavalry of the Army of the Tennessee, under General Hood.

It was a sad mistake when the Confederate Government at Richmond had failed, a year before, to invest General Forrest with command of the cavalry of the Army of the Tennessee. He was not braver than General Wheeler; he was not more patriotic than General Wheeler; but without any reflection, it may be confidently said that from the same number of men, General Forrest would get more fighting than any officer of the Confederate Army, General Lee not excepted. When damage to his enemies was to be calculated Forrest had no superior in the world. He captured and destroyed more Federal military property than any other officer of the war.

Forrest, like Wheeler, always went to the front. Both seemed destined by miraculous interposition to be preserved from death. Many times all those about them went down before the enemy's fire. Both Forrest and Wheeler were several times injured, but never very seriously. No two men were more reckless or courageous on the battlefield, and no two men with the means at their command ever did more for any cause than Forrest and Wheeler. Of these two men many thousands of pages might be written, and yet much would be left unsaid that ought to be said in recounting their wonderful campaigns. With charmed lives, with brave spirits, with courageous souls and intrepid hearts, they seemed immune from death.

Chapter XIII

CAVALRY EXPEDITION OF THE TEXANS
INTO NEW MEXICO, WINTER, 1861-62

Only three rivers escape from the American Desert—the Columbia, Colorado and Rio Grande. The last of these, the Rio Grande, rises far up amid the mountains of Colorado, close to the Montana line. It was named by the Spaniards Rio Grande del Norte, or Grand River of the North, because of its great length. It was sometimes called Rio Bravo del Norte, "Brave River of the North." Fighting its way amid mountain gorges, through canyons, cutting channels deep down into rocky defiles, it forces a passage over nature's fiercest obstacles and drives its currents through New Mexico and Colorado for seven hundred miles. Then turning southwardly, it seeks a resting place in the waters of the Gulf of Mexico. For more than eleven hundred miles it is the boundary between Mexico and the United States.

Moved by love of conquest, or desire to spread the gospel, the Spaniards followed the meandering course of the stream for hundreds of miles, overcoming the barriers which nature had placed in the pathway of those who sought to conquer the arid and inhospitable wilderness, through which this great stream passed to its union with the far off sea. Navigable for only four hundred and fifty miles from the ocean, it held out no hope to those who might seek an easy way to its source. The great trail which led from the settlements on the Atlantic to the new-found lands on the Pacific required the travelers to pass the Rio Grande near Santa Fe. There was no chance to start at El Paso and travel northward by the Rio Grande to the heart of New Mexico and thence find an outlet to the Pacific Ocean. The men who pushed from the East to the Golden Gate preferred to mark out a line from the Missouri River, overland from Missouri, Kansas and Colorado, the Indian Territory and New Mexico. A southern trail might have been shorter, but mountains intervened and nature forced men to make their highway for wagon trains by Santa Fe from the East. The pioneer spirit was strongest in the Missouri Valley, and the population on the Mississippi was content to let those farther north pursue the passage to the Pacific by the northern route. A thin line of settlements had been established along the trail, but no large population was willing then to endure the hardships which surrounded those who lived in those isolated regions; and the white men refused to pass southward by the Rio Grande or the Mexican border, for the country was so inhospitable that it held out no inducements to emigration, commerce or settlement.

When the war between the states began to stir the hearts of the people of the South, after a brief delay, Texas, that great empire with more than two hundred and sixty-six thousand square miles, but thinly populated area, caught the patriotic spirit of the hour, and cast herself, body and soul, into the struggle of the Southland for liberty and independence.

In February, 1861, an ordinance of secession was passed, and nine years later Texas was re-admitted to the Union. General H. H. Sibley, a native of Louisiana, resigned from the United States Army and entered the service of the Confederate States. Familiar with the geography of New Mexico, he visited Richmond, Virginia, was commissioned brigadier general and returned to Texas with authority to lead a brigade up the Rio Grande to Santa Fe. Few believed, at that early date, that war would last a year, and one of the reasons impelling this expedition was to possess as much territory as possible, so that when hostilities ceased, the territories of the Confederacy would cover the largest possible space. General Sibley reached San Antonio, where the troops raised to compose his command were being mustered in. A statement of his plans aroused the zeal and enthusiasm of those who were to engage in the adventure.

The conquest of New Mexico appeared feasible and important. It would cut in twain the land route between the Atlantic and Pacific coasts, and by reason of its supposed strategic importance, prove of tremendous value to the Confederate states.

The project was bold, daring, but illy considered, and in the end, while sustained by heroism and courage that certainly has no superior in the great story of Southern manhood, yet proved a most unfortunate and distressing failure. From El Paso, on the extreme western boundary of Texas, to Santa Fe, by the route along the Rio Grande, was something like six hundred miles. The Santa Fe railroad of later days has rendered this journey easy and pleasant, but in 1861-62, the route was a vast wilderness, not producing enough food to sustain the sparse number of people who had settled along this trail. Venomous reptiles hid themselves in the recesses of the sandy and rocky ways, or laid in wait for their victims amidst the numerous crevices that marked every mile. The very shrubbery seemed to defy the advance of civilization, and the thorns and thistles that stood out on every bush appeared to enter fierce protests against habitation by man or beast.

In the earlier days of the war, before experience had made men deliberate, and to sit down and count the cost ere entering upon any great military enterprise, it was only necessary for someone to cry "Forward!" and chivalrous patriots were ready to follow wherever any leader might bid them go. The 4th, 5th and 7th Texas mounted regiments were mustered into the Confederate service for three years, or during the Civil War. This enlistment took place October, 1861. Colonel James Riley commanded the 4th. Later, at the head of his regiment, he met a soldier's death in Louisiana. Thomas Green became colonel of the 5th, and William Steele, colonel of the 7th Regiment. These formed a brigade under the command of Brigadier General H. H. Sibley. Steele did not go with his regiment, which was led by Lieutenant Colonel J. S. Sutton, who died heroically while leading his men at the Battle of Val Verde near Fort Craig. Later, General Thomas Green was promoted to the rank of brigadier general. These regiments reorganized, then became known as Green's Brigade. When the true story of the war shall be fitly told, the world will realize that no men who marched under the stars and bars did more to win the admiration and applause of the entire Southland than those who composed this wonderful organization.

At this early period of the war, arms were scarce. The fruits of victory had not then given Federal equipments to Texas, and these soldiers were supplied with shotguns and hunting rifles of varying calibre and necessitating the preparation of each man's ammunition by himself. Many of these volunteers had mingled with the Mexicans and heard their stories of the fiery charges of the Mexican Lancers and of the deadly execution which they made with their shafted spears, and following, unwisely, the suggestions of General Sibley, two companies of the 5th Regiment were induced to exchange their guns for that medieval arm, the Mexican lance.

The troops were enlisted and sworn in at San Antonio, and before beginning the most difficult part of their journey up the Rio Grande, marched from San Antonio to El Paso, seven hundred miles, in broken detachments. At this point, the government had accumulated a small supply of commissary stores. Between San Antonio and Santa Fe, there was not a town or village which could have furnished, from its own storage, a full day's supply of rations and forage for the command. The settlements were not only few in number, but very far apart, and with small populations. It thus came about that the troops were compelled to carry rations for the whole march. These were very meagre, and were transported in wagons drawn by small Mexican mules. Meat was provided through beeves that were driven on foot. No forage of any kind was to be had other than the grass which grew upon the plains. As if to make the journey still more difficult, water was extremely scarce; and many parts of the journey, both men and beasts were compelled to go on as long as thirty-six hours before relieving their thirst. The men carried a day's supply in their canteens, but the poor beasts had no provision for quenching the burning of their fevered throats. There was not then living in the entire territory from El Paso to Santa Fe as many as three hundred sincere Southern sympathizers. The great majority of the population were poor, illiterate Mexicans, who had a traditional hatred of all Texans. The secession of Texas from Mexico in 1835, the Santa Fe expedition in 1841 and the war between the United States and Mexico in 1846, had planted in the minds of these rude frontiersmen bitter memories of the Texans.

Almost everywhere, without exception, this brigade, when leaving El Paso and ascending the great river, found itself in a hostile country, a country so devoid of food that it was hardly able to maintain its own people from want, and which with great difficulty supplied them with the bare necessities of life. To make this journey still more difficult for the Confederates, General Canby, then and later on, showing himself to be a wise and sagacious officer, had already, by force or purchase, secured for the support of the Federal troops whatever the needs of these poor people could spare.

Most of the great marches of the war, made by cavalry, were through countries that could at least supply food for a few hours for man and beast. None of them undertook to haul their commissary stores six hundred miles or to rely upon beef driven afoot to satisfy their hunger. The great passion of the brigade was to be led forward. They had gone too far to return without a fight and were anxious to find somebody to engage in conflict. Practically no preparations had been made to arrange for the wants of the soldiers. No foresight had provided stores where food might be garnered, nor wells dug, from which water, that greatest essential of long marches, might be supplied. The brigade finally composing this expedition consisted of the 4th and 5th and part of the 7th Texas mounted infantry, five companies of Baylor's Regiment, Tool's light battery and Coopwood's independent company, aggregating twenty-five hundred men. One-sixth of all these men were required for the protection of the supply train and herd of beeves, and therefore could not be relied upon in case of battle.

General Canby, through couriers, had full notice of the coming expedition and its purpose, and he was not slow to avail himself of the topographical as well as the physical condition of the country in preparing for the emergency. About a hundred and fifty miles north of El Paso, on the river, Fort Craig had been constructed, years before, by the United States Government. The fortification was situated on the west bank of the stream and within musket range of the only road leading from El Paso to Santa Fe. Here General Canby had concentrated over four thousand troops, regulars and volunteers, including infantry, artillery and cavalry, with supplies of every kind in abundance. As the Confederates could travel only one road, the Federal general had only to sit down and wait and prepare for their coming and had ample time to obstruct the narrow pathway along which they must reach Santa Fe. This march was undertaken in the midst of winter. Those who led and those who followed seemed to feel that an hour's time was of the most tremendous importance, and neither want of preparation or danger could deter them from pushing on to some point where they might meet a foe. Zeal and haste to fight was universal with the southern soldiers in the earlier days of the struggle. Without any disparagement of their splendid courage under all conditions, it may be safely said that a few months' experience greatly lessened the intensity of this feeling.

Beyond Santa Fe, in the northeastern part of the territory, another fortification, called Fort Union, had been built before the war. This Post had been reconstructed and manned, and here again were established large depots of supplies. Troops had come down from Colorado, and the United States regulars had been hurried hither, and still farther, from the West, the war-trumpets had called volunteers from California who were hastening en route to the scene of hostilities.

A march so carelessly considered and so inadequately provided for, with weather becoming cold, demanded most strenuous sacrifices from the devoted Texans who were engaged in this hazardous task.

The Confederates had no tents, their clothing supply was confined to the uniforms that each wore, there was no covering at night except their saddle blankets, and yet, while the fierceness of the climate and the illy provided commissary spread disease and death among them, these gallant Confederates went pushing forward with what would seem to thinking men but little hope, yet without fear. It was not long until disease began to grapple with its gaunt fingers numbers of these chivalrous men. Pneumonia attacked many of the advancing heroes, and under such conditions rarely allowed any of its victims to escape with life.

By the 10th of February, 1862, the command came in sight of Fort Craig. Surveys and reconnaissance soon convinced even the inexperienced that the capture of the Fort by direct assault would be practically impossible, and that it would be equally impossible to follow the road which the Fort commanded, and to run such a gauntlet simply meant great decimation, if not destruction of the entire command. A council of war determined that the wise thing was to turn the Fort by crossing to the east bank of the Rio Grande and to march by it to a point called Val Verde (Green Valley), some nine miles above Fort Craig. To carry out this plan required a tremendous amount of courage and endurance, for there was no road nor even a broken trail, and this way was almost impassable for wagons. It had never been traveled, but lay across deep and wide gulleys and over steep sand hills. There was not a single foot of made highway and men and animals, beset by poisonous thorns, which infested well-nigh every vegetable growth, and tramping over loose stones which rendered almost every resting place for their feet insecure, struggled, stumbled and toiled over the arduous way that the exigencies of the hour forced them to follow. After such laborious, depressing and dangerous effort, two days later, on the evening of the 20th, the command had reached a point nearly opposite Fort Craig, only seven miles from their starting place on the 19th. Here the weary troopers, wearier mules and the thirsty cattle were encamped for the night. The beasts had no water; the men only such as their canteens contained. The conditions were enough to cower the hearts of any soldiers and to dampen the ardor of any patriot, but everybody realized that the very desperate conditions must be met by supreme valor.

Long before the sun had risen above the mountain tops to illuminate and brighten the plains with its cheering beams, the march was begun, so as to reach, at the earliest moment possible, the river, at some point above Fort Craig, and begin the advance again upon the traveled highway, which, while rough, was delightful in comparison to the two days' march along the inhospitable ground over which these brave soldiers had, with uncomplaining fortitude, forced their way during the past forty-eight hours. The Federal commander did not sit still in the fort. Thoroughly advised of this movement on the part of the Confederates, he pushed his forces north along the road and when the advance guard of the Confederates reached the river, their enemy was there to dispute its passage. To provide against loss of the cattle driven on foot, upon which they depended for meat, and for the protection of the commissary train, a considerable portion of the Confederate force was detailed. The very desperation of the situation stirred the hearts of the Confederates with the noblest courage. Only about two thousand fighting men were left available, after details were provided for the protection of the cattle and the train. These had been left behind at the camp from which they had marched out in the morning to force the battle. There was nothing for the Confederates to do but to win. The Federals were not averse to fighting, and so they crossed the river with thirty-eight hundred men, including a battery of six-pounders and two twenty-pounders. A force sufficiently large to protect Fort Craig against the assault had been left within its walls. These two thousand Confederates, hungry and thirsty, were to oppose, in a position chosen by the Federal commander, a force nearly twice as large as their own. With a fierceness born of difficulty and of courage quickened by the unpropitious surroundings, the conflict was short, sharp and decisive. The Federals were driven back into the fort, with considerable loss of officers and men, and their six-gun battery was captured by the Confederates. The casualties on the Confederate side in this Battle of Val Verde were less than those of the Federals, but it included in the list several of the most promising and prominent officers, who, at this time, were sorely needed. Colonel Green, who commanded the 5th Regiment, owing to the illness of General Sibley, was in immediate charge of the forces. He was a cheerful and experienced soldier, and was later to demonstrate such great genius as a commander, that when he died in April, 1864, at Blair's Landing, La., it was said of him by the Federal generals that the ablest man west of the Mississippi had been lost to the Southern cause.

While the battle had been won and the enemy driven back to the fort, it was not decisive; the Federals were safe in the fort, and the Confederates, with their small number of fighting men, were not sufficiently strong, nor did they have the necessary ammunition to carry the fort by assault. The little Confederate army was not in condition to sit down and hesitate and argue or even to delay action, and a council of war determined that the wisest thing to do was to push on to Santa Fe, in the hope of inducing the enemy at Fort Craig to follow along the trail, come out into the open and risk the issue of another contact.

The desperate condition of the Confederates was apparent to any well-informed military man, and General Canby, with an army at Fort Craig twice as large as that of the Confederates, with a still larger force at Fort Union, northeast from Santa Fe, all well supplied with food and ammunition, decided that he had only to bide his time and wait. He perfectly understood the character of the country, the antagonism of the people to the Confederate cause, and the limited resources for providing maintenance for man or beast. He knew the exact number of the Confederate command. He understood they would be unable to carry out the Confederate plan and closely calculated the difficulties which awaited these brave men, who seemingly violating the laws of prudence and ignoring caution, were pushing themselves forward without support, apparently indifferent to consequences.

In possession of Fort Craig, south of Santa Fe, and Fort Union, north of Santa Fe, defending the well-known and traveled north and south roads, which were the only passable exits from the territory, with troops which largely outnumbered his foes, half of whom were regulars, tried, well equipped and exceeding Confederates four thousand in numbers, the Federal commander foresaw that the end could not be very far off and that waiting was the wise and sagacious course to pursue. No one needed to tell him that the Confederates could have no hope of reinforcements. His spies had already assured him of their meager supplies, the vast number of sick and of the many graves along the road of the Confederate march. These told him that disease and hunger would be efficient allies, and that only a few weeks could possibly intervene before the Confederates would be compelled to abandon the territory, and most probably be forced by want and starvation to surrender as prisoners of war. With a force twice as large as their own behind them and with a force twice as large in front of them, with only one traveled route along which they could pass, and that totally inadequate for the supply of food for the invading Confederates, the condition of these brave men became almost desperate. Though the conditions were so discouraging, General Sibley and his subordinates advanced to Albuquerque and Santa Fe and took possession of the immediate towns and villages.

On the 20th day of March, about sixteen miles north of Santa Fe, a second battle occurred in Glorietta Canyon. Here the worn Confederates came in contact with Federal troops which had been sent forward from Fort Union. The Confederates held possession of the field of battle, but something worse than loss of men had occurred. On account of the smallness of the force, a sufficient rear guard had not been detailed for the protection of the wagon train, and their entire supplies had been captured by an attack of the Federal forces. While the Federal soldiers had been defeated and fell back to Fort Union, and the Confederates returned to Santa Fe, hunger was now staring these brave invaders in the face. They were not afraid of their enemies, but lack of food, ammunition and other necessities, oftentimes more terrible than bullets, rarely fails to strike terror into the hearts of the bravest soldiers.

The situation had been thoroughly tried out, the Confederates had now been reduced to less than two thousand men. They were practically destitute of provisions and ammunition. One regiment had been dismounted, its horses were reduced, not only in flesh but in number, and so, some walking and some riding, but all still stout at heart, these Confederates now prepared to abandon the territory for which they had risked and suffered so much. In a few days, the retreat to El Paso was begun. Leaving strong forces at Fort Union and Craig to protect them from any possible force the Confederates could bring to their assault, all available Union soldiers were rushed forward to contest the retreat of General Sibley and his men, and to cut off every avenue of escape. The only thing General Canby failed to fully comprehend was the supreme courage and valor of his foes, the intrepidity and skill of their leaders, and the capacity of men and officers for fatigue and their readiness, if needs be, to die, rather than surrender as prisoners of war to their enemies.

Officers and men all understood the gravity of the situation. They realized that safety lay not only in retreat, but to escape at all necessitated the co-operation and courage of every survivor of the depleted command.

At Peralto, a small town on the Rio Grande, below Albuquerque, the Confederates occupied the town, but before them in battle array were six thousand Federals, well armed, and this was the numerical problem that faced the tired, half-clad and brave men of the South. There was not the slightest disposition to yield or run away, and so all day long the

Confederates, with their ill-equipped forces, calmly awaited the attack of the Federals. But there was something the men who were following the stars and bars feared more than the men in blue—starvation. This was now their most dreaded enemy, and this, accompanied by the weather conditions, made a combination that would strike terror into the heart of any ordinary man.

Along the Rio Grande River, the temperature arises during the day to a hundred degrees and then by midnight, it has dropped sixty degrees, alternating between summer's heat and winter's frost. These climatic changes shatter even the rocks that so greatly abound in this dreary region and accompanied by lack of warm and necessary clothing, depleted the energies of the Confederates, but at the same time it stirred them to renewed activities.

There was only one feasible route open to the retreating invaders. This was down the Rio Grande, and across this single path was a Union army numbering more than three times those who essayed to escape. The Confederates forded from the east bank to the west side of the river, and for several days, both forces, Union and Confederate, marched southward along the stream on opposite sides. Now and then they exchanged shots. It was soon discovered that to avoid an engagement, which the Confederates were not prepared to risk, something must be done to escape the presence of the enemy, so superior in numbers, food and equipments. The thought of capture aroused the hearts of all the men to heroic resolve to do and dare all that was possible to avoid the humiliation and misfortune of a surrender.

From out of the conflict one thing had been brought, and these brave men were desirous of bearing this back to Texas so that the great march should not be without one trophy, and like grim death they hung to the six-gun battery of twelve-pounders that they had captured at Val Verde, a short while before. They were to haul these cannon over the wilds safety had forced them to traverse. They were to push and pull them to the crest of hills to find that they could only be lowered with ropes to the depths below, and each hour of suffering and companionship with the mute and inanimate guns would add renewed purpose to save them, if their saving was to be compassed by human determination and indomitable will.

In this campaign Joseph D. Sayers came to the front. He was destined to play a distinguished part in the war, and later in the history of Texas.

When the battery was captured at Val Verde, young Sayers was not twenty-one years of age. His cheerfulness under trial, his valor and dauntless courage attracted the attention of the leaders, and he was designated by common consent captain of the battery which held so dear a place in the hearts of all who survived this expedition. He had enjoyed a brief season at a military school, but he was a born soldier. He was authorized to select the members for the battery and with them he clung to the guns with bulldog tenacity, and brought them safely through the dangers that ever loomed up on the homeward march.

Captain Sayers, while in command of the battery, was severely wounded at Bisland, Louisiana; and also at Mansfield, Louisiana, while serving on General Green's staff with the rank of major. At General Green's death the young officer crossed the Mississippi River with General Dick Taylor, upon whose staff he served until his surrender in Mississippi in April, 1865.

On every field and in every sphere he met the highest calls of a patriotic service and when paroled had won the commendation and admiration of those who fought with him. His war experiences fitted him for a splendid civil career. He became lieutenant governor, and later governor of Texas. He served fourteen years in Congress, and when he voluntarily retired, his associates in the House of Representatives passed a resolution declaring that his leaving Congress was a national rather than a party calamity. Amongst Confederates, his career in the trans-Mississippi, and later in the cis-Mississippi armies, gave him universal respect, and the good opinion of the great state of Texas was manifested in the bestowal of every honor to which he aspired.

He still lives, in 1914, at Austin, and there is no one who loves the South but that hopes for lengthened years to the hero of Val Verde.

Councils of war were called, and it was resolved to leave the river, march inland, over mountains and canyons and through forests that had never been trodden by civilized man. The Spaniard, whether stirred by religion or love of gold or gain, had never ventured to traverse the country through which General Green and his men now undertook to march. Half-clad, nearly starved, footsore, with both nature and men rising up to oppose their escape, without water sometimes for two days, except what was carried in their canteens, they hazarded this perilous journey. Trees and vines and shrubbery with poisonous thorns stood in their pathway. With axes and knives, they hewed them down, and boldly and fearlessly plunged into the wilderness to escape their pursuing and aggressive foes. Over this rough, thorny road they traveled for one hundred and fifty miles; and then, guided largely by the sun, moon and stars, and nature's landmarks, they reached the river highway along which they had marched in the early winter and struck the Rio Grande, some distance below Fort Craig. With exuberant joy, they realized that they had left their enemies behind. Nine long and dreary days had been consumed in this horrible journey. Man and beast alike had suffered to the very extreme of endurance. The average distance for each twenty-four hours was sixteen and two-thirds miles. Where the intrepid and exhausted column would emerge, even the experienced and stout-hearted guide, Major Coopwood, did not know. West, south, east, the gallant band must search for a path, and down canyons, over precipitous cliffs, where the eye of white men had never penetrated, these gallant Texans, half starved and consumed for many hours with the fierce and debilitating burnings of thirst, hunted for a path which would enable them to leave their enemies behind and miles below emerge into the Rio Grande Valley, at a point from which they could, unmolested, pursue their march to El Paso.

One-fifth of their number had died in battle or from wounds and sickness, and three-fourths of the survivors marched into San Antonio on foot. Eight months had passed since the journey was begun. More than three men each day, from either wounds or on the battle field or through disease, had gone down to death, and along the march of twelve hundred miles, on an average of every four miles beside this devious and suffering road, was the grave of some comrade, to tell of the ravages and sorrows of war.

Barring the battery which had been captured in the earlier periods of the expedition, the brigade came back empty handed, but the men who composed it brought with them a spirit of courage, a quickened patriotism, a self-reliance, a steadiness of purpose, and a conception of war that was to make them one of the most distinguished and successful organizations of the world's greatest war; and trained for future services and succeeding triumphs and victories that would endear them not only to the hearts of the people of Texas, but to all who loved or fought for the independence of the South.

After a few months of rest, remounted and recruited, this splendid command entered upon a new career of active service, and through the campaigns of 1863 and 1864, they were to make honorable records for themselves; at Bisland, Fordocho, Bortrich Bay, Lafourche, Fort Butler,

Donaldsville, Bourbeau; Opelousas, Mansfield, Pleasant Hill, Blair's Landing and Yellow Bayou. At Blair's Landing, General Green met the fate of a chivalrous, patriotic commander, dying as he had fought, with his face to the foe. He and his command were second to no horsemen who were enlisted on the Southern side. The sad and unfortunate experiences of the march into New Mexico proved a great education for these valiant and gallant soldiers. They have been less fortunate than the cavalry commands east of the Mississippi in having chroniclers to exploit their heroism, yet in their splendid career they were never surpassed in the best elements of the cavalry soldier, by any of those whose fame as champions of the Southland and defenders of its glory and its honor has gone out into the whole world.

Chapter XIV

GENERAL J. E. B. STUART'S RIDE AROUND McCLELLAN'S ARMY—CHICKAHOMINY RAID, JUNE 12-15, 1863

General J. E. B. Stuart was born on the 16th of February, 1833. At the commencement of the war he had just passed his twenty-eighth year. His father had been an officer in the War of 1812. He was born in Patrick County, Virginia, a few miles away from the North Carolina line. In his veins there was the richest mingling of Virginia's best blood. In 1850 he was appointed a cadet at West Point, and graduated thirteenth in a class of forty-six. At West Point he was not a very great scholar, but an extremely good soldier. He had a splendid physique, and was popular wherever he went. In his early youth he had hesitated between the law and war, and finally concluded to remain in the army. He was commissioned as second lieutenant in 1854 and served in Texas. He saw a great deal of active service in Indian warfare and in the early part of 1861 was at Fort Lyon. On the 7th of May, 1861, he reached Wytheville, Virginia. His resignation was accepted by the War Department on that day and he offered his sword to his native state. On the 10th of May he was made lieutenant colonel of infantry and directed to report to Colonel T. J. Jackson. His commission was from the State of Virginia. Sixty days later he was commissioned a colonel of Confederate cavalry, and on the 24th of September was made brigadier general, and on July 25th, 1862, major general.

General Stuart, in the summer and fall of 1861, was busy on outpost duty, harassing the enemy and continually active. His operations were not on any extended scale.

General Joseph E. Johnston had a very high opinion of General Stuart. As early as August 10th, 1861, he had written to President Davis: "He—Stuart—is a rare man, wonderfully endowed by nature with the qualities necessary for light cavalry. If you had a brigade of cavalry in this army, you could find no better brigadier general to command."

He took an important part in the Williamsburg campaign, at the Battle of Williamsburg in May, 1862, and at Seven Pines on the 31st of May and June 1st. It was impossible at the last engagement to use cavalry, but Stuart, always anxious and ready for a fight, was only too happy to go to the front, and became General Longstreet's aide.

In March, 1862, McClellan had brought his Army of the Potomac up to two hundred and twenty-two thousand men, and with these undertook to capture Richmond. He concluded it was wisest to take Richmond from the rear and recommended that his forces should be transferred to Fortress Monroe and he should proceed from there in a northwesterly direction.

The forces under General Joseph E. Johnson and later under General Lee were widely scattered. Some of them were a hundred miles apart.

From the valleys of Virginia, and from Norfolk down through Fredericksburg, great armies were advancing with Richmond as the converging point. Stonewall Jackson had played havoc with McClellan's forces in the Shenandoah Valley, and had inaugurated and won a campaign which brought him world-wide fame. In three months Jackson had fought three battles and marched five hundred miles, a feat which was almost unsurpassed in the history of military movements. He held a large Federal force over in the Valley. This was at that period the most important factor in the preservation of the armies of Joseph E. Johnston.

On the 16th of May, advancing from Fortress Monroe, McClellan had taken possession of Whitehouse, on the Pamunky River, and here established his army and reached out to Seven Pines, within eight miles of Richmond. It appeared now as if, with the large forces at his command, McClellan would crush Johnston and reach the coveted capital of the Confederacy. Camped east and northeast of Richmond, in a position chosen by himself, and to the acquisition of which the Confederates made little resistance, McClellan sat down to wait for the forty thousand men McDowell was to bring through Fredericksburg and unite with him in his present camp. The Confederates were roughly handled by the Federals at Hanover Court House on the 27th of May, and General Joseph E. Johnston looked anxiously toward McDowell at Fredericksburg, only fifty-two miles away. He resolved, if possible, to crush McClellan before McDowell could come to his assistance. On the 31st of May the Battle of Seven Pines was fought. Brilliantly designed by Johnston, he claimed that he only failed to destroy McClellan by the neglect of his subordinates to march as directed. General Johnston was wounded on the 31st of May and was succeeded by General Gustavus W. Smith, who commanded for a few hours. At two o'clock on the 1st of June, President Davis rode out upon the field with General Robert E. Lee and turned over to him the command of the Army of Northern Virginia, which he was to hold until the shadows of national death overtook and overwhelmed Lee and his army at Appomattox, on May 9th, 1865.

A large part of McClellan's army was now south of the Chickahominy River. It was extremely important to know the situation of his forces. He was getting so near to Richmond that the situation had become intensely critical.

General Lee sent for General Stuart and in a private interview explained that he desired to have full information about the exact location of McClellan's army. On the 12th of June he despatched Stuart, with twelve hundred of the best cavalry that the Army of Northern Virginia could furnish, to ride round McClellan's camps and get full facts concerning their several locations and movements. His ride on this errand is known as the "Chickahominy Raid."

Stuart did not wait a moment but instantly undertook this perilous task. Prior to this time no great cavalry raids had been made. Wheeler had not been developed, and Morgan and Forrest had only short forays to their credit. At this period Mosby had not appeared in the Virginia campaigns which he was later to brighten with many wonderful performances, but rode with Stuart as his chief scout, guide and adviser, and no general ever had abler aid. Stuart and Mosby were the same age, were men of like courage and dash, between them was mutual admiration and affection, and each believed implicitly in the genius of the other.

Stuart had been vigilant on outpost duty, but no one had conceived so bold a move as to ride in the rear of a great army of more than a hundred and twenty-five thousand men at a time when the rivers crossing the road were filled with the June rise. Figuratively taking his life in his hand he cut loose from all communication with his allies, and began the circuit of the opposing army, which then stood north and east of Richmond. It was a great work, requiring masterful genius, superb skill, highest courage and transcendent faith in his destiny. He was to make history in cavalry service, set new standards and a new pace for horsemen in war. The original letter which General Lee wrote to General Stuart is still in existence. General Lee informed General Stuart that his purpose was to get exact intelligence of the enemy's forces and fortifications, to capture his forage parties and commissary depots and as many guns and cattle as it was possible to bring away with him, and to destroy, harass and intimidate the wagon trains which were then supplying McClellan's army.

General Lee was not as full of confidence in Stuart's ability then as he was later. He cautioned Stuart about going too far, staying too long, attempting too much. He looked deeper into the situation than Stuart possibly could. Twenty-six years more of life and his lengthened military experience made him cautious where Stuart would be reckless. It was well for Stuart that he was only twenty-nine years old. Had he been fifty, he would have hesitated long before undertaking such hazardous work. Faced by such desperate odds, the youthful blood coursing with unstinted forces through his veins, and his ambition to wrest early from fame its highest rewards, subordinated prudence and caution to the promptings of glory and success, had faith that no odds could defeat his plans and that misfortune was impossible where he should go, with the chivalrous horsemen who would follow in his lead.

It was easy to see that the primal object in General Lee's sending Stuart was to definitely locate the right wing of McClellan's army, to know how far it extended east, and whether Jackson could be brought in strong pressure upon it.

Justly Stuart was allowed to pick out his command. He had a section of artillery. This was under Lieutenant James Breathed. Wisely concluding that if you do not want anybody to know your plans, you had better not communicate them, Stuart told few of his associate commanders his destination. The general outlines of his expedition he communicated to Fitzhugh Lee, W. H. F. Lee and W. T. Martin.

The first day's march was not a heavy one, twenty-two miles due north brought General Stuart to Taylorsville. Having demonstrated that McClellan's right had not been extended east of a line north of Richmond, General Stuart now turned due east and in a short while marched southeast. He was singularly blessed with scouts who had a full and complete knowledge of the whole country. These had been despatched in various directions. It was beyond all things essential for him to have accurate information regarding the roads he was to travel. He began his movements at early dawn. He had a great work before him; he was to take a march of forty miles, the safety of which depended upon the absolute watchfulness and the unfailing vigilance of his troopers. The eye of every soldier scanned the horizon. None knew aught of what was ahead. Any instant might develop a cavalry or infantry force across their pathway which would bar their progress. No baggage delayed their speed. Stale rations prepared before leaving would stay hunger until they could pounce down upon a Federal wagon train and take from their enemies the food necessary to sustain them upon their strenuous ride. The best horses had been provided for the artillery, so that it could keep pace with the rapidly moving horsemen. A rider was mounted on each of the animals attached to the guns. It was necessary to move with extreme rapidity, and all the preparations were made so that nothing should delay or hinder the march.

A force of Federal cavalry was found near Hanover Court House. Failure to attack would indicate fear, and so General Stuart ordered a charge. Fitzhugh Lee had been sent south to intercept their retreat toward McClellan's army. The enemy moved south of the Tunstall Station road, and Stuart concluded that if they would let him alone he would let them alone. A captured sergeant from the 6th United States Cavalry showed that this force had been in position at Hanover Court House. He had no time to pursue those who did not pursue him, and taking a southeast course, almost parallel with the Pamunky River, he spurred his column to the highest possible speed. A Federal force had been stationed at Old Church, which was on the line of the road Stuart had determined to follow. Moving with such great rapidity and with his presence not expected, Stuart had no reason to believe that the enemy would be able to know his purpose, his plans and his place. A couple of squadrons of the 5th United States Cavalry were stationed at Old Church. A part of the duty of this command was to scout north towards Hanover Court House. Observing Stuart's force, the lieutenant in command of one of these companies saw the Confederate cavalry at eleven o'clock. As he had only one company he estimated that the Confederates had with them two squadrons of cavalry; he concluded that he was not able to fight Stuart and so he withdrew and avoided a conflict. Reporting his observation to his superior officers, he was directed to fall back upon the main body at Old Church. Stuart was now ten miles north of the rear of McClellan's infantry. Numerous detachments of cavalry were scattered about. It would not take long for couriers to tell the story of Stuart's presence and to estimate his forces. Lieutenant Lee, who was in command of the 5th United States Cavalry, had now fallen back toward the bridge at Totopotomy Creek, and he had resolved, even though his command was small, to give Stuart battle and test out the strength of the invader. The bridge across the creek was intact. There was nothing to do but fight. Captain Royal, who was in command of the squadron, aligned his forces to receive Stuart's attack. Two of the companies of the 9th Virginia were sent to drive these Federals out of the way. The onset was quick and furious. Captain Latane, of Company F, of the 9th Virginia, rode to the charge. Royal was severely wounded by Latane's sabre, and Latane was killed by Royal's revolver. The Federal line was broken and fell back. Discipline, however, asserted itself, and although fleeing, they wheeled into line to receive the second assault, and then Captain Royal left the field to the Confederates. Quite a number of the 5th Cavalry were captured, and there Fitzhugh Lee met many acquaintances, pleased to come in contact with an officer under whom they had served, even if he now wore the gray. These men conversed freely with General Lee, who was anxious to capture as many of the regiment as possible. He received permission to follow the enemy to Old Church and, if he could do so, make the entire squadron prisoners. He captured the camp, but the soldiers had fled.

At this time Stuart might have retraced his steps. There was nothing to prevent his returning by the road over which he had passed. Anxious to get the most out of the expedition that was in it, although he had told Fitzhugh Lee to follow the enemy back up the road over which he had advanced, Lee now saw Stuart turn and face southward. A less brave man would have hesitated. Dangers awaited him upon every mile. He was traveling southward and with this line perils increased with every step of his trotting squadrons. For a moment uncertainty filled his mind, but it was only a moment, and then without an expression of fear on his face or the feeling of a doubt in his heart, he bade the column quicken its pace and into the uncertainty of immeasurable and incalculable hazard of a dangerous, unknown path, he hurled his little army.

Stuart now knew that the right wing of McClellan's army had not extended as far west as General Robert E. Lee thought it had. It was important that General Lee should have this information at the earliest possible moment. One and a half days had been consumed in coming. Should he go back, or should he make the circuit of the Federal army, and endeavor to reach General Lee south of the Chickahominy River? The rivers in front and to the east were unfordable. He must go north to find an easy way to escape and he knew that the Federal infantry, south of him, was within five miles of the road along which he must operate to reach his starting point at Richmond. He must, in the nature of the case, take the long road. His attack on the 5th United States Cavalry had aroused the enemy and his presence would be communicated quickly to the Federals. These could hardly believe that such a small force could be so far from home. The daring of such a movement was incredible at this period of the war. Later, many horsemen on both sides would be glad—even anxious—to engage in such an expedition. To General Stuart with any considerable Confederate force belongs the credit of the inaugurating such enterprises. Twenty-one days later General John H. Morgan conceived and executed his first raid into Kentucky and with twelve hundred men marched a thousand miles in territory occupied by his foes. The example of these two brilliant and successful commanders would soon find many to follow their lead, but to them belongs the credit of having successfully demonstrated that possibility of such campaigns and the practical safety of a cavalry force in such expeditions.

A Federal lieutenant reported that he had seen infantry along with the cavalry, that he thought he had counted as many as five regiments. Some put it as high as seven regiments. The rumored presence of infantry in their rear alarmed the Federals, who were afraid that a large force had reached in behind them, and so certain were the Federals of the presence of infantry that General Porter directed General Cooke not to attack the cavalry. This indecision on the part of the Federals gave Stuart the advantage of several hours. If he could pass Tunstall Station, twelve miles away, he would have a wide territory in which to operate, and in which the Federals would find it difficult to ride him down. Fortune was extremely generous and propitious. Numerous wagon trains were coming along the road to Tunstall Station, carrying supplies to McClellan's army. The Pamunky River was the base from which supplies were transported to McClellan. It was navigable for quite a distance from the Bay. Many trains were destroyed, two large transports at Putney's Ferry on the Pamunky River were burned. The railroad from the Pamunky River to the Chickahominy, under McClellan's forces, had been repaired. At White House, on the Pamunky, tremendous quantities of supplies had been collected. This was only four miles from Tunstall Station. Some gunboats and six hundred cavalry protected this depot. Stuart was now only five or six miles from McClellan's camp, and the cavalry and infantry might be despatched at any time to close the path he had chosen for a return to Richmond. The idea suggested itself to Stuart that he capture White House. He could have done this, even with the small force under him, but General Lee had told him he must not do all that he might desire to do, and he refrained from attempting this brilliant achievement. Cars, teams, sutlers' stores, rations were destroyed, telegraph lines were torn down, and from four o'clock in the evening until darkness came on them, Stuart's men were engaged in the grim work of destruction. A company from New Kent County composed part of the 3d Cavalry, and Stuart had the advantage of having numbers of men in his command who knew every path and by-way of the country through which they must later pass. This fact gave him great faith to ride away in safety should Federal pressure become too tense. Detachments were sent out in all directions to destroy as many wagons as possible. The Chickahominy was full, but it had fords. Eleven o'clock at night, and the last of Stuart's men had not left Tunstall Station. The Federal infantry in large numbers began to arrive, and some Pennsylvania cavalry as well. General Stuart had calculated that he would cross at a ford near Forge Bridge. This was ten miles from Tunstall's. A young lieutenant, who had most accurate knowledge of the country, was confident the ford of which General Stuart spoke would give a safe and easy passage over the river. Alas, when the river was reached, new perplexities arose and new dangers angrily stood out to thwart Stuart's plans. The rains had been more copious than the guides had predicted or believed. The waters, with pitiless currents rushing oceanwards, seemed to forbid the passage of the Chickahominy. The storms, which had raged two days before higher up the stream, had widened the volumes of water, and to the imagination of the wearied horsemen, these increased in width every moment they stood upon its banks.

Colonel W. H. F. Lee was unwilling to surrender the possibility of passing the stream at this point. Boldly entering the water and swimming his horse he reached the other side. The waters were so deep that the horses' feet became entangled in the roots of trees and prevented a landing. These difficulties raised new doubts and gave warning that some other ford must be found, or means other than swimming must be discovered for reaching the south bank. In this dire extremity there was no hesitation or alarm and all the gallant squadrons felt sure that fate, hitherto gracious and helpful, would, in the crisis, come to their rescue. Only heroes could be calm and cheerful under these dispiriting conditions. Axes were hunted up and trees were cut down in the hope that

221

a temporary bridge might be made, but the swift current, catching up the trees, swept them down the stream like playthings and made the labor of the horsemen a useless waste of energy and time. In these moments, for a moment now appeared hours, everybody seemed anxious except General Stuart. It was important for General Lee to know what Stuart had found out, and calling upon one of his most trusted followers, he repeated in detail to him what he had learned and bade him ride with all haste and tell General Lee the story, and ask that an advance be made on Charles City, to relieve his command of the difficulties with which they were surrounded.

Every mind was now moved to the most vigorous action. The imminence of danger quickened thought, and to think must be to act. Someone under the pressure of extreme peril remembered that an old bridge one mile below had not been entirely destroyed. Hope of escape quickened every step and with unreined and highest speed, the troopers galloped to the site of the ruined structure. Bents, stripped of girders, stood out above the angry, muddy waters, but even they in their desolation and isolation gave but scant promise of escape. Warehouses close by, with the long planks that enclosed their sides, were stripped of their covering. Laid from bent to bent, they made a passway over the stream, but they held out no means of crossing to the weary steeds or offered no prospect to avoid a plunge into the water. The tired beasts were unsaddled and lashed and driven down the banks. Their masters, bearing their equipments on their own backs, with loosened bridle reins, walked along the narrow plankway, while the horses, with their feet beating the water, struggled in its turgid currents in their efforts to cross to the opposite side.

While one part in ever-quickening haste thus convoyed their mounts across, the other with renewed energies strengthened the floors of the tottering bridge and added braces to the timbers, which, under the pressure, trembled and swayed and bade the men beware lest they make too great calls upon the weakened bents. Time, more time, was now the call. If money could have enlarged minutes, every soldier would have given all his possessions to win from Providence another hour of freedom from pursuing foes. Stuart was not willing to abandon his artillery. He had saved his cavalry, but he did not want to give up his guns. Orders for tearing more planks from the warehouse and hunting longer and heavier lumber were sternly and earnestly issued. Officers pleaded with the men to rush, as they had never rushed before. They took hold themselves. No rank stayed the exercise of every man's energies. With one-half of the command on the south side and the other half on the north side, anxious eyes, reinforced by brave yet questioning hearts, watched with intensest eagerness the roads upon which pursuing Federals might come. Attack now meant capture or disaster. There was no escape, east or west. The remnant on the north side might, if assailed, ride through and over the attacking lines, but the artillery could have no chance to run away, and scattered troops, with their lines broken, would have but slender opportunities of escape should they essay to ride back along the roads they had so successfully and rapidly traversed the two days before. Couriers, wires and scouts would hunt out and reveal the lines of retreat and their presence. Even the bravest hearts could evolve naught but disaster, if the Federal cavalry should now, when they were divided, force them to give battle. Those on the south side had forty miles between them and Richmond. To reach this goal they must pass within a few miles of large numbers of McClellan's army. Whether the troops were on one side or the other of the Chickahominy, the moment was full of forebodings and presented difficulties calculated to make even the bravest of men fearful of what even an instant might bring forth. Sharp eyes scanned the roads along which the enemy might come. The crossway was quickly patched and completed, and by one o'clock the artillery was sent over. Strong, vigilant rear guards had been stationed some distance away from the bridge. Two or three times the enemy made their appearance, but unwilling to show the least sign of hesitation or doubt, these Federal forces were vigorously attacked.

When the difficulties of the Chickahominy had been surmounted, Stuart recognized that great tasks were yet before him. He was forty miles from Richmond, two-thirds of the distance lay within Federal lines. He must follow the course of the James. His enemies were between the James and the Chickahominy. There was no other route for Stuart to travel. His courage and his orders had brought him into the extremities of the situation. A small force of infantry, properly disposed, could cut off his escape, and he knew nothing of what his enemies were doing to thwart his plans and encompass his ruin. If he calculated the dangers or doubted his courage and skill to meet all emergencies, he would be overwhelmed with fear and misgivings. Great legions of difficulties rose up before his vision to disturb the quietude of his valiant soul. With a wave of his hand and with a peaceful smile upon his compressed lips, he bade fear begone.

He answered doubts and quieted them with the response that the men who followed him never wavered at duty's call, and forward he moved, calm, serene, and with not a shadow of distrust or misgiving hovering in his heart.

Having used the bridge themselves, the torch was applied with willing hands by the grateful troopers. They might not abuse the bridge that had carried them over, but they joyfully burned it lest it might bear relentless enemies over to the side to which they had so fortunately come by reason of its succor and help in the hour of desperation and uncertainty. In the gloaming of the evening, turned into flames, the blazing timbers, so lately a rescue, rose up as a great beacon light, which lit up the surrounding country. If the Federals saw these flames, they understood that the daring raider with his tireless followers had escaped from Federal toils and was temporarily safe from their assaults. A fordless stream now rolled between them and the men they were pursuing.

From the highest point which he touched on Newfound River to the lowest point touched on Queen's Creek, a tributary of the James River, was forty miles, and from Richmond to the farthest point east, a short distance from Tunstall Station, was only twenty miles. From Richmond to the main force of McClellan's army was eight miles, and from the Chickahominy to the Pamunky at Tunstall Station was twelve miles. South of the Chickahominy, five miles, was the largest force of the Federal army; north of it, at Cold Harbor, was another strong division and then five miles east at Ellyson's Mill was another large infantry Federal force.

At Ellyson's Mill, down the Chickahominy, to Cold Harbor, at Fair Oaks, McClellan had infantry forces practically covering the entire territory which Stuart must pass. He traveled around the Federal army one hundred and thirty miles, and at no point of his whole journey was he removed from some Federal force as much as five miles. With his small command, at several places he was less than eight miles from large infantry commands. The inexperience of the Federal cavalry was one of Stuart's chiefest aids in carrying out his splendid conception of this brilliant march. Two years later it would have been impossible even for Stuart, with his seasoned and trained soldiers, to have made such a movement. Stuart had knowledge of the men who would oppose him, and particularly of the cavalrymen who would pursue him, and this made him calmer and more confident than he would otherwise have been. No enemy came. The artillery was saved. United on the south side of the stream, their delivery from such imminent danger gave them renewed and enlarged confidence. They did not know what was ahead. The past was a sure guarantee of the future. Hitherto they had come in safety, and they confidently believed that fate would still be kind and helpful. The very uncertainty of what might at any moment appear to prevent their escape or impede their progress made them brave and cheerful. They rode swiftly along the road which might at any moment prove to be thronged with vigilant foes. The close call at the river, their triumph over apparently unsurmountable difficulties, made them complacent and contented. They pitied their weary and hungry beasts, and took little account of what privations they themselves had endured, or from what great danger they had so fortunately been delivered. General Stuart might now breathe easier, but he could not yet breathe freely. On the James River, along the banks of which he must pass on his route to Richmond, were Federal gunboats; and Hooker, from White Oak Swamps, five miles from the only course that Stuart could follow, could within a couple of hours, under forced marches, place infantry in the front. There was no time for rest or food; a splendid exploit, a magnificent expedition, was now nearing completion, and no appeal of tired nature could find response in the heart of the gallant leader. With marvelous genius he had brought his men out of difficulties that seemed unsurmountable, and so riding and riding and riding through the long hours of the night and the day, with ever-watchful eyes and ever-increasing vigilance, he pursued his journey to reach the place from which, four days before, he had set out upon what was then the greatest cavalry expedition of the war. He had lost one soldier, but he was a soldier worthy of any cause. Captain Latane's burial by lovely Southern women, with the assistance of a faithful slave, has become one of the most pathetic incidents of the war. Aided only by the faithful negro, to whom freedom had no charms when associated with the abandonment of those he had served and loved, they dug a grave, folded his pale, brave hands over his stilled heart, and alone and without the protection of the men they loved, they read the burial service for the dead and committed the dust of the young patriot to the care of the God they truly and sincerely worshipped.

The Burial of Captain Latane

A brother bore his body from the field
And gave it unto strangers' hands, that closed
The calm blue eyes on earth forever closed,

And tenderly the slender limbs composed.
Strangers, yet sisters, who, with Mary's love,
Sat by the open tomb, and weeping, looked above.
A little child strewed roses on his bier,
Pale roses, not more stainless than his soul,
Nor yet more fragrant than his life sincere,
That blossomed with good actions, brief but whole.
The aged matron and the faithful slave
Approached with reverent feet the hero's lonely grave.
No man of God might say the burial rite
Above the rebel, thus declared the foe
That blanched before him in the deadly fight.
But woman's voice, with accents soft and low,
Trembling with pity, touched with pathos—read
Over his hallowed dust the ritual of the dead.
"'Tis sown in weakness. It is raised in power."
Softly the promise floated on the air,
While the low breathings of the sunset hour
Came back, responsive to the mourners' prayer.
Gently they laid him underneath the sod
And left him with his fame, his country and his God.

Stuart had left behind him, even when pressed by his enemies, but one artillery limber. From sunset until eleven o'clock at night these fierce raiders and their harried steeds slept. Awakened at midnight, by dawn they reached Richmond. General Stuart turned over the command of the brigade to Colonel Fitzhugh Lee, near Charles City, at sunset on the night of the 14th, and taking with him one courier and a guide, he hastily rode to report to General Lee the result of his expedition. Once during the night the wiry trooper stopped to refresh himself with a cup of coffee. For twenty miles of his journey he was liable at any turn in the road to meet Federal scouts. The hours of the night were long. Stuart both in body and mind had borne tremendous burdens on his great march, but he felt more than repaid for all he had suffered and endured when, as the sun rose over General Lee's headquarters, with his two faithful companions he dismounted to tell the great chieftain what he and his men had accomplished. He had captured one hundred and sixty-five prisoners and brought them out with him. He had captured two hundred and sixty horses and mules, which he was enabled to turn over to the quartermaster's department. He had destroyed not less than seventy-five wagons, two schooners and great quantities of forage, and to the Federals more trains were lost than were in the possession of the brigade quartermaster, at the front, with McClellan's great army.

This exploit gave General Stuart a leading place among Confederate cavalry leaders, which he ably and fully sustained until the end so sadly came to him at Yellow Tavern, almost to an hour, two years later, in his desperate defense of Richmond from the approach of Sheridan and his raiders. He deserved all the world said and thought about him. His genius, his daring, his unfaltering courage, his cheerfulness and calmness in danger stamped him as a military prodigy and gave him a renown that would increase and brighten, as, month by month, fate was yet to open for him the paths of true greatness.

Chapter XV

BATTLE AND CAMPAIGN OF TREVILIAN STATION, JUNE 11th AND 12th, 1864

General Meade, notwithstanding his splendid service to the Federal Army at Gettysburg, did not receive the promotion to which he and many of his associates and friends felt that he was entitled. In the fall of 1863 and in the early part of 1864 the failure of Meade to meet public expectation induced President Lincoln to bring General Grant from the West to direct the military movements around Washington and Richmond. There had been so many disappointments under the impetus of the cry, "On to Richmond," that General Grant determined, as he said, "to make Lee's army my only objective point. Wherever Lee goes we will go and we will hammer him continuously until by mere attrition, if nothing else, there shall be nothing left him but submission." General Grant had many successes to his credit, but he had never faced General Lee, and he had not yet fully comprehended the character of the foe he was to encounter in the new field to which he had come. He had before him a gigantic task. It required several great battles to awake General Grant fully to the burdens he must carry in the mission he had, with some degree of both egotism and optimism, assumed.

These pronunciamentos of victory sounded well in orders and reports to his superiors. The rulers and overseers in Washington were gladdened by these expressions of confidence and assurance. True, many here and there had thus spoken, but these had no such history as General Grant, and could give no such reasons as he for the hope that was within him.

During the first week of May, 1864, the roads and conditions were such that an advance could be safely made by the Federal forces. On the 2d of May General Lee ascended a high mountain in the midst of his army and with a glass took in the situation. Around and about him were scenes which his genius had made illustrious and which the men of his army, by their valor, had rendered immortal. Longstreet had come back from Tennessee and Georgia and the Army of Northern Virginia had

228

been recruited as far as possible, so as to prepare for the onslaught which the springtime would surely bring, and which the military conditions rendered speedy and certain.

Grant's forces were well down in Virginia near Culpepper Court House, forty-five miles from Washington. He had one hundred and fifty thousand men under his command. This large army demanded vast trains for supplies, and one-seventh of General Grant's army was required to take care of his wagon train. Grant had two hundred and seventy-five cannon of the most improved kind, and he had Sheridan, then in the zenith of his fame, as his cavalry leader. There were thirteen thousand cavalrymen to look out for the advance and take care of the flanks of this great array. It is calculated that if Grant's supply train had marched in single file, it would have covered a distance of one hundred miles; and one of General Grant's well-informed subordinates said to him, "You have the best clothed and the best fed army that ever marched on any field."

About the first of May General Lee had sixty-two thousand men ready for battle. He had two hundred and twenty-five guns; five thousand artillerymen and eight thousand five hundred cavalrymen under the renowned "Jeb" Stuart. Each of the great leaders realized, although they gave no outward expression of their conclusion, that the month of May would witness a mighty death grapple, the fiercest and most destructive that the war had seen. Neither the men in gray nor the men in blue would possibly have fought so vigorously had they known what the days from May 4th to June 4th had in store for the legions now ready to face and destroy each other. Day by day the calls of an astounding mortality would be met. Day by day each would accept the demands that duty made, with a fortitude that was worthy of American soldiers, but only General Lee fully realized what these days would bring forth. Not until twenty days later did General Grant grasp the true extent of what this advance meant to the soldiers he had been called to lead.

It was clear from General Grant's telegrams that he had not expected the sort of campaign that General Lee put up against him in this march to Richmond. On the 4th of May, after he had crossed the Rapidan, he wired to his superiors at Washington that "forty-eight hours would demonstrate whether Lee intends to give battle before receding to Richmond." General Lee was in no hurry to throw down the gage. He could afford to take his own time. He had met many Federal generals before and he had out-generaled them all. His army was at Orange Court House. Later, to

229

protect his flank, it turned eastward to Spottsylvania County. Gradually Lee was nestling his army between Fredericksburg and the Pamunky River. Richmond was almost due south of Washington, but the Potomac drove Grant westward and in sight of Fredericksburg, where in days gone by Burnside had been crushed. Grant had resolved to go to Richmond, but between him and Richmond was General Lee with his matchless fighters, and hitherto these had proved an unsurmountable barrier to all who undertook to travel this road.

By the morning of the 5th the lines had been formed on the Wilderness Road and it became apparent that every step that General Grant would take on his southern advance was to be skillfully and savagely contested.

On the 5th of May, when the first day of the battle was passed, General Lee had suffered no reverse, and he telegraphed to Richmond: "By the blessing of God we maintained our position against every effort, until night, when the contest closed." By five o'clock on the morning of the 6th the armies were engaged again. In the midst of a crisis at the front, long expected reinforcements came on the field; General Lee advanced to meet them. The turning point was at hand. The men of Texas were the first to reach the scene of action. Hitherto General Lee had never lost his equipoise, and, riding in the midst of the Texans, did what he rarely ever did before—gave an immediate command on the battlefield. He exclaimed to the Texans: "Charge! Charge! Charge, boys! Charge!" He was rushing amongst them to the front where the storm of lead and iron was heavy and momentarily increasing. When these devoted soldiers saw their great commander exposed to the fire, with one accord they cried out: "Go back, General Lee! Go back! Go back!" The brave artillerymen under Poague shouted, "Come back, General Lee! Come back! Come back!" Oblivious of these tender expressions of their solicitude, lifting himself high up in his stirrups, on "Traveler," and waving his hat he headed the charge. Up to this moment there had been no firing from the Confederate soldiers. From one end of the line to the other there arose over the battlefield the cry, "Lee to the rear! Lee to the rear!" The roar of artillery and the sharper crackling of musketry could not drown this outburst of solicitude along the Confederate ranks. No danger could quell this agony of his followers or still their fear for his safety. His life was to them above all other considerations, and their concern for him even in the midst of greatest danger was an absorbing passion and consuming desire. A brawny Texas sergeant sprang from the ranks and seized the bridle of

"Traveler" and turned him about. The Confederate column refused to move until General Lee retired from the scene of danger. The love and devotion of his followers forced him to go. No commander could, or dare, resist such an appeal.

On the morning of the 10th of May General Grant felt that Washington would like to know what had happened down in the Virginia hills, and so out of the smoke and gloom of the firing line and the burning summer sun he said: "We were engaged with the enemy all day both on the 5th and 6th.... Had there been daylight, the enemy could have injured us very much in the confusion that prevailed." He confessed that his loss in this battle had been twelve thousand. He quieted the alarms at Washington by saying that the mortality of the Confederates no doubt exceeded his, but he admitted, that was only a guess based on the fact that they had attacked and were repulsed. He added: "At present we can claim no victory over the enemy, neither have they gained a single advantage." General Grant had now discovered that General Lee would give him battle "this side of Richmond," and it had cost him seventeen thousand men to reach this conclusion.

By the 8th of May General Grant began to take General Lee more seriously, for he wired: "It is not demonstrated what the enemy will do, but the best of feeling prevails in this army and I feel at present no apprehension for the result." He now resolved to go east of the route he had chosen and so he despatched the following to his superiors: "My exact route to the James River I have not yet definitely marked out." It was evident that General Lee had changed General Grant's plans.

General Grant now set his cavalry to raid General Lee's trains. Sheridan swung to the right and struck the highway to Richmond. The contending forces had now reached Spottsylvania Court House. It had been a slow march, and it was a death march. By the 10th General Grant became still more uncertain, and he wired: "The enemy hold out front in very strong force and evince a very strong determination to interpose between us and Richmond.... I shall take no backward steps but may be compelled to send back for further supplies. We can maintain ourselves and in the end beat Lee's army, I believe."

On the 11th General Grant had still further reason to revise his opinions. He wired General Halleck: "We have now ended the 6th day of very heavy fighting. The result to this time is in our favor, but our losses have been heavy as well as those of the enemy. We have lost to this time eleven

... general officers killed, wounded and missing, and probably twenty thousand men. I propose to fight it out on this line if it takes all summer."

Not sufficiently protected, twenty-eight hundred of General Lee's men had been captured. Artillery had not been ordered to their support promptly enough, and twenty cannon were the prize of Hancock's valiant followers. General Lee heard the sounds of a fierce conflict and rode to the scene of danger and advanced into a line of heavy fire. He found himself in the midst of General John B. Gordon's men. General Gordon, with that voice that thrilled men in war and peace, wherever it was heard, shouted: "General Lee to the rear!" and flaming with courage and enthusiasm he rode to the Confederate chieftain and exclaimed, "General Lee, these men are Georgians and Virginians; they have never failed you. They will not fail you now." A soldier, moved by the spirit of the moment, rushed from the ranks and seizing "Traveler" by the bridle turned his head to the rear and led him away, and up and down the line came a mighty cry, "Lee to the rear!" With a wild rush Gordon drove the enemy from his front, but not a step did the soldiers advance until General Lee had obeyed their peremptory order to find a place of safety.

General Lee, remaining close to the position where Gordon had left him, attempted to lead the Mississippians under Harris. These again took up the great heart cry of the Confederate hosts, and shouted, "Lee to the rear! Lee to the rear!" The conflict became appalling. Men from opposite sides of breastworks climbed to their tops and fired into the face of their opponents. They grappled with each other and drew each other across the breastworks. The trenches were filled with blood, and nature sent a cold and dreary rain to chill the life currents of the wounded men that lay on the field. It was said by those who listened to the sound of musketry and the crash of artillery at Spottsylvania and elsewhere, that it was the steadiest and most continuous and deafening that the war witnessed.

By the 13th twenty-eight hundred of Lee's men had been captured under General Bushrod Johnson, but he had only lost eighteen per cent of his army. Sixteen thousand of General Grant's had been killed and wounded. To this loss must be added the twenty thousand who had already fallen bravely before the men of the Army of Northern Virginia.

By the 12th General Grant had telegraphed: "The 8th day of battle closed. The enemy obstinate. They seem to have found the last ditch." On the morning of the 13th General Grant's subordinate again telegraphed: "The proportion of severely wounded is greater than either of the previous day's fighting." He further said in the afternoon: "The impression that Lee had started on his retreat which prevailed at the date of my despatch this morning is not confirmed.... Of course, we cannot determine without a battle whether the whole army is still here, and nothing has been done today to provoke one. It has been necessary to rest the men, and accordingly we have everywhere stood upon the defensive."

It was on the evening of May 11th that along the wires came to General Lee the startling and shocking intelligence that General J. E. B. Stuart had fallen. For seven days Lee declined to give any official announcement of this tragedy. He carried the depressing secret in his bosom. A year before, Stonewall Jackson, at Chancellorsville, had been stricken down in the midst of another gigantic conflict. General Lee was unwilling to let his fighters know that death had called the illustrious cavalry chieftain at the moment when they most needed the inspiration of every Confederate leader.

Grant sat down to wait five days and in the meantime he added twenty thousand fresh troops to his legions.

The hammering process had not proved such a wonderful success after all, and so Grant had ordered Sigel down the Shenandoah Valley to break Lee's communication. In the meantime General John C. Breckinridge came up from Southwestern Virginia and brought with him some infantry and some cavalry, and on the 15th of May, while General Grant was waiting, Breckinridge had crushed Sigel and captured six of his guns as well as one-sixth of his men. On the 17th of May, Halleck wired General Grant: "Sigel is in full retreat on Strasburg. He will do nothing but run—never did anything else"; and there came also to General Grant on this eventful day the news that Beauregard over at Petersburg had driven General Butler back and bottled him up on the James River.

On the 20th of May, Grant moved still further eastward at Spottsylvania Court House. Since crossing the Rapidan on May 4th, sixteen days before, he had suffered a loss of thirty-seven thousand men. This was thirty per cent of all the fighting men that he had led out from Culpepper Court House.

Grant was still moving eastward and Dana telegraphed: "Now for the first time Lee prevented his southward march." He seemed to have forgotten what had been happening since the 4th of May.

Sigel disposed of, Breckinridge came to join in the conflict at Cold Harbor. By the 26th of May General Grant had withdrawn from Lee's front, and pressing eastward and southwardly, attempted to find another road to Richmond. He telegraphed to Washington: "I may be mistaken, but I feel that our success over Lee's army is already insured," but yet he directed that his supplies be brought up the Pamunky River to the White House. He was looking for a base and he was going to find the path that McClellan followed when he met defeat from General Lee two years before.

By May 30th General Grant had again changed his views about General Lee and so he despatched to General Halleck: "I wish you would bring all the pontoon bridging you can to City Point to have it ready in case it is wanted." He found out that Lee might fight outside of Richmond—and anywhere else in its defense.

The two armies were swinging around now to Cold Harbor. This place was already known in history. The armies now facing each other had met there before, in June, 1862. The results then to the Federals were not encouraging. This time they were to prove far more disastrous and exceedingly horrible.

On the morning of June 3d, 1864, at half past four o'clock, General Grant opened a great battle—Cold Harbor—the greatest battle of this campaign and the only battle he afterwards said that he ever regretted having fought. Persisting in his policy of forcing his way south to Richmond, he was unwilling to confess failure. Confident of the power of the "hammering process," committed by his boast to fight it out on this line if it took all summer, he was too proud to admit that he was mistaken. He hoped and believed that fate, hitherto so propitious, would now come to his rescue and relief in the extremity of the situation into which war's surprises had brought him. Between four and nine o'clock in the morning, assault after assault was made and the whole front of Grant's line was so decimated that his men drew back from the scenes of conflict. At nine o'clock it became so dreadful that even as brave men as Hancock refused to transmit General Grant's peremptory orders to his subordinates to renew the attack. Each time it was transmitted, each time the men on the line refused to obey the order, and officers who had never before quailed, and who were strangers to fear, stood still and allowed their men to stand still in the face of peremptory orders to advance. Ten thousand men on the 1st and 3d of June were wounded and killed, and then General Grant moved away from Lee's front. It was impregnable, and General Grant realized that the Army of Northern Virginia, although only half as numerous as his own, would not be driven away from their places. It cost thousands of dead and wounded, but it was demonstrated to be a verity, and General Grant, with all his hitherto indomitable will and with his tremendous pride of opinion, yielded to the inevitable—that General Lee's genius and the courage of his followers had forced into his mind and set up in his path.

Seventeen thousand killed, wounded or sent away by reason of sickness, were the tidings that came from this ensanguined field to Washington, where thirty days before every heart was so full of hope. General Grant had permitted his dead and wounded between the lines to lie uncared for until the 5th of June, and then humanity with fearful protest forced him at least officially to admit that he was vanquished. He at last sought the right to succor the wounded and bury the dead.

With the Army of Northern Virginia behind the breastworks, with their courage and dogged determination to defend their capital, there was no force of men and no legion however brave or intrepid that could move these men in gray. The men under the Stars and Bars had sufficient ammunition to keep their guns in use, and so long as it was possible to fire these guns, no earthly foeman could break their lines. True, for an instant, at one angle the line had been forced, but quickly it was retaken and the Confederate front restored.

Grant had lost approximately seventy thousand men, killed or wounded. General Lee had suffered a loss of twenty thousand, making a total on both sides of ninety thousand, and from Culpepper to Cold Harbor, covering a period of thirty days, the world had never seen such a trail of blood. The life currents of valiant soldiers flowed almost in a stream. These armies had traveled fifty miles. They had been battling and killing all the way. This road was two hundred and sixty-four thousand feet in length. Every three feet had witnessed the sacrifice of a life or the infliction of a wound. Men looked aghast at this loss of life and limb.

On the 11th of May, General Stuart had fallen at Yellow Tavern. He died on the 12th. Universal sorrow filled every heart. A year before Stonewall Jackson had died, and now came the death of Stuart, as a sort of final stroke to the Confederate hopes. When Stuart died, on May 12th, General Wade Hampton, as senior major general of cavalry in the Army of Northern Virginia, took his place. Sheridan had gone down to the west of Richmond and made the attack which resulted in Stuart's death, and after a repulse rode back to the shelter of General Grant's infantry.

Sheridan had reached the gates of Richmond, but there his course was stayed and his raid ended and he turned about and came to the west of Grant's army and resumed his place with it on the 25th of May. He had not suffered a very great loss, six hundred and twenty-five men, but the Confederates had lost Stuart, and now Hampton was to come to the front. He was forty-six years of age; he had passed through three years of vigorous warfare and a wide experience. Under him now were some of the best cavalry leaders the country had known. He had M. C. Butler, with his South Carolinians; he had P. M. B. Young, with his Georgians; he had Rosser, with his Virginians; he had Wickham and Lomax, with their Virginians, under Fitzhugh Lee. He had James B. Gordon, with the North Carolinians, and Chambliss, with his Virginians, under W. H. F. Lee, son of Robert E. Lee. Dismounts, wounds and casualties had reduced his forces to the point where they could only do the necessary cavalry work for General Lee's army.

The Federal cavalry, at this time, was commanded by General Sheridan. He had three divisions under Torbert, Gregg and Wilson, and these had between them fifteen thousand eight hundred and twenty-five serviceable horses and men. For every horseman of Hampton, Sheridan had two. A little while before there had come into use among the Federals the Spencer & Hall magazine rifles. Each man not only had one of these magazine rifles, but he had a revolver and a sabre. The horses were always fed and they could be changed whenever the exigencies of war demanded. After the experiences at Fleetwood Hill, General Hampton realized that the methods of fighting must be altered. He had read of what Morgan and Forrest and Wheeler had done with dismounted men. He did not yield his mounted drill, but he expanded and developed his dismounted drill.

General Grant had failed to break General Lee's lines. He must now resort to flank movements. General Hampton never for a moment hesitated at the tremendous responsibilities which now rested upon the cavalry. He was conscious of his power and the efficiency of his followers, and was ready to do the best he could. He was the successor of one of the most distinguished, brave and dashing cavalry leaders of the war. It required genius and courage to rise to the situation, but General Hampton, with calmness and intrepidity, was willing to meet every call and face every emergency.

Over at Hawes' Shop, on the 28th of May, Sheridan was trying to find out the position of the Confederate infantry, and Hampton was trying to find out the position of the Federal infantry. They fought seven hours.

Some of Hampton's men had never heard the battle sound before. They had been sandwiched in with the veterans, and they made good soldiers even in their first conflict.

Custer and other Federal officers said that the fight at Hawes' Shop was the severest cavalry fighting in the war. Colonel Alger of the 5th Michigan says it was a hand-to-hand battle. The South Carolinians bore the brunt of it, and they won new laurels. When the result of the fighting at Hawes' Shop was made known none doubted that Stuart's mantle had fallen upon a worthy successor. It was immediately preceding the death of General Stuart that General Sheridan said either to Grant or some of his commanders that he "could whip hell out of Stuart"; to which General Grant laconically replied, "Why in hell didn't he go and do it?" He went, but he came back without making good his boast, and he was now to take a turn with General Hampton.

Next came Atlee Station, with its close, sharp contest and with its victory.

After the Battle of Cold Harbor, on the 4th day of June, Grant began to fortify and swing around to the east and north. Later he crossed the James River and sat down for the siege of Petersburg. He had not at first recognized General Lee's true greatness. Here he was to realize the stern, unyielding courage of the Army of Northern Virginia. He had found it would do no good to "fight it out on that line, if it took all summer," and to save his army from annihilation he must change his plan of campaign. At the Battle of Cold Harbor, the ratio of loss had been for fifteen Federals, one Confederate. Nothing had happened like this before. No man could deny the valor and persistency of the Federal soldiers under Grant. They did not flinch when the test came. They bared their breast to the awful storm, and it swept more than seventy thousand either into the grave or the hospital. We know now all that passed. The wonderful book published by the Federal government, entitled "War of the Rebellion, Official Record," tells the whole story, and the reader can see by the daily records and despatches of the actors on both sides, in these days of tremendous conflict, what these two armies did in the gigantic struggle for the possession of the Confederate capital.

On the morning of June 8th, General Hampton with his forces was out near Atlee Station, eight miles north of Richmond. In the early hours of that morning Sheridan marched away with a cavalry force of nine thousand men. He had been ordered by Grant to march northwest, to capture and destroy Gordonsville and Charlottesville, and then to move down the valley and help Hunter, who was then on his way to Lynchburg.

All the fury and storm of war now seemed to be turned loose on General Lee's army. Hunter had penetrated the valley and was setting his face toward Lynchburg. The torch, with the horrors of hell behind it, was reducing the beautiful and happy homes of Virginia to heaps of ruins; piles of ashes and chimneys standing stark and lone were the memorial to the savagery of the invasion of this once hospitable and cultured country. Now Sheridan, later the "Scourge of God" in the Shenandoah Valley, was to add new atrocities at Charlottesville to war's devastation and brutality.

The signal stations told the story of General Sheridan's departure. General Hampton divined where he was going. He conferred with General Lee, and asked to follow Sheridan's path and attempt the defense of the valley. As greatly as General Lee needed men, he could not allow Sheridan to march unmolested and destroy lines which were so essential to the maintenance of the Confederate position in and around Richmond.

Rations were light in these days. Quickly, three days' food was cooked and with a few ears of corn tied round with strings and fastened to the saddles became the commissary equipment of Hampton's forces, which were to engage in one of the important cavalry campaigns of the war. The cavalry under Hampton and Sheridan was to be removed fifty miles from the infantry supports and the cavalry alone was to fight out the issues of this campaign. Like mighty wrestlers repairing to some desert to try out their skill alone, these two cavalry forces marched away where none could see them in their struggle, and where none could come to the rescue of the vanquished.

Hampton could not take more than forty-seven hundred men. These were all that Lee could spare. He had twelve pieces of artillery.

Sheridan had two divisions. They numbered nine thousand men. They carried twenty-four pieces of artillery, and were the best the army of the Potomac could send. Sheridan had the 1st, 2d and 5th United States Regulars and there were no better trained cavalry than these. He had Custer's brigade, who had imbibed the dash and courage of their leader, and he had New York, New Jersey and Maine regiments that had won renown not only at Fleetwood Hill, but on many other fields. These horsemen had witnessed the terrors of the march from Culpepper to Cold Harbor. Its wrecks and its losses stood out before their minds in sharpest lines. The horsemen had fared well, and the infantry had borne the burden of the thirty-seven days' decimation, and with the instincts of brave men they were rather glad to be sent to take a hand in any movement which should either avenge or compensate for the defense of that terrifying campaign.

Few people knew of Sheridan's going. He had marched away first towards Washington, but he could not march out of sight of the skill or the watchful eyes of General Hampton's scouts. Hope beat high in the breast of Sheridan. He had felt chagrined that he had failed in his attack on Richmond a few days before and now he hoped to destroy Gordonsville and Charlottesville and march down the valley to Lynchburg and take Richmond from the rear, come in behind Petersburg, and bring wreck and ruin to General Lee. It was a great plan of campaign, laid out along broad lines. He had hoped to keep away from his wily antagonist, but Hampton divined whither he was going, and it turned out when Sheridan had reached the first objective point of his campaign, he was to face a tired but vigorous and dauntless pursuer, and one who never quailed or doubted even when nature was almost pitilessly resistant.

Sheridan marched in three days sixty-five miles. It was hot, dusty and water was scarce. He marched leisurely, because he felt that his antagonist knew naught of his plans, and he was confident that Hampton could not reach him where he was going. He was sure that he had gotten away unobserved, and that he would have nothing to do but burn, waste and destroy from Gordonsville to Lynchburg. He could see in his mind's eye the flames licking up the buildings that stood by the path he was to march. A feeling of profound satisfaction filled his heart, and on the terribleness of his work he felt sure he could found a new reputation for victory and success.

On the night of the 10th Sheridan and his soldiers slept calmly in the summer air. They did not know where Hampton was, but they felt sure he was not where they were, and no dreams of danger or battle disturbed the tranquility and quiet of their rest.

On the morning after Sheridan started north and then turned west, Hampton set his forces in motion. He was sure that he knew where Sheridan was going. He was staking his all on the correctness of his instincts. He was confident he could march more rapidly than Sheridan; he knew the road and he had the short line; but yet he must march under tremendous difficulties. The temperature was torrid, the dust was so thick that it almost could be cut with a knife. After breathing it a few hours, the nostrils and eyes of the men became inflamed, and the moisture of the body combining with the dust made an oozy, slimy substance that half blinded their vision. Water was scarce and food was scarce, but courage was still abundant.

By the night of June 10th Hampton had traveled something like fifty miles. Sheridan had gone sixty-five miles, and as darkness came on, Hampton's forces reached Green Spring Valley, a few miles away from Trevilian Station, an insignificant railway stop, from which the battle on the morrow was to take its name. The two Confederate divisions were a few miles apart. This hard marching, the cooked rations, the corn upon the saddles, told the intelligent men that constituted Hampton's forces that they were after somebody and it did not take them long to figure out that this somebody was Sheridan. With their parched throats and swollen eyes, and suffering with inflamed nostrils, they laid down to sleep, not worrying about the morrow. Careless as to what it would bring for them, they were ready to answer every call of duty, wherever that should lead them in the day to come. As the streaks of light began to come over the mountain sides from the east, every man in the Confederate line was up and at his post, ready for action. The last of the corn that was brought on their weary backs from Atlee Station was fed to the hungry brutes, and the last of the soggy bread, which had been cooked for the men before they had set out on this march, was eaten. General Hampton knew that now he must be close to the Federal lines. The night before his scouts had brought him back information that Sheridan was near by. Some of these had looked into his camps, and the Federals, unconscious of the presence of Hampton's legions, had been sounding their bugles and were quietly and leisurely making their morning's meal. They felt there was no need for haste. As there was no hostile force near, they believed they might in safety enjoy a brief repose, which they had fully earned by hardest service.

Hampton's scouts knew the topography. They had described Sheridan's location. He formed his plans accordingly, and they were plans which involved savage work. General Forrest's quaint saying, "Get the bulge on them," had traveled to the east and fallen on Hampton's ears. With an inferior force he well understood that strategy and skill would stand him well in hand, and that he must take fullest advantage of all that chance might send his way. It was worth some hundreds of men to get the drop on Sheridan. The first lick is oftentimes of great value, and General

240

Hampton was resolved if it was possible to strike an unexpected blow. He hoped in this way to equalize the disparity of numbers. He began his work early and he set about the business of the day furiously. His orders were to assail the enemy wherever and whenever found and not for a single moment to stay the tide of battle.

The country had not been denuded of its wood. This would help to hide from the enemy the full strength and position of the Confederates, and at the same time it would make more effective the slower, steadier and more accurate firing of the men in gray. The Federals had sarcastically referred to General Hampton as a "woods fighter"; in other words, he was afraid to come out in the open, but when he had forty-seven hundred to nine thousand, he had a right to take advantage of all that the surrounding conditions would give him in the conflict.

Hampton had undertaken to intercept Sheridan's march. He had out-marched him. He had done in two days that which had taken Sheridan three, and his men were as fresh and bright as those of Sheridan. The journey had told on man and beast, but they had both become used to the severest toil, and were willing and ready for any fray that would pass that way.

Some picket firing was heard, but the Federals, not yet realizing that Hampton was in their front and on their flank, supposed that the desultory shots were from the guns of raw militia who had pressed forward with more vigor than discretion.

Sheridan and his most dashing lieutenant, General Custer, no sooner heard heavy firing than they comprehended the real situation. They understood that the Confederates had followed them in heavy force, that the clash would be serious, and that hard fighting was at hand, and that if they were to continue their march down the valley, they must discomfit the men who were now assailing their lines and drive them out of their path. The Federals began to fight back with spirit. It did not take them long to get ready for the grave task that was forced upon them. While the Confederates were charging, the men in blue were charging, too, and by good luck and by boldness Custer passed between Fitzhugh Lee and Hampton's two divisions and was at the Confederate rear before anybody caught on to this serious condition. When General Hampton, guided by the sound of firing, rushed to the spot, he found that Custer was vigorously assailing his rear. Custer had taken many of his caissons and wagons and led horses, and he felt that victory was already within his grasp. In this emergency, Rosser, who could always be depended upon for a fierce, impetuous charge, was ordered to attack Custer. In a few moments the crash of charging horses, the roll of revolver firing, and the cuts of sabres demonstrated to Custer's men that the people they were fighting were not militia, but foemen worthy of their steel. Nearly all that Custer had captured was retaken, and an entire regiment made prisoners. Rosser fell wounded. The enemy, finding the opportunity, pressed hard upon Butler's and Young's brigades. The result of the battle hung in the balance. A mistake on either side would be fatal. Hampton's presence was always an inspiration, and he rode from place to place on every part of the field. Outnumbered, Hampton's division under Lee was sorely pressed, and General Fitzhugh Lee's division was cut off and became so thoroughly separated that it could be of no help or support for twenty-four hours.

Sheridan's forces were now turned with severe impact upon Hampton's division, and gradually it was forced back toward Gordonsville, but still protected that place and Charlottesville. Hampton quickly took advantage of a railroad embankment, dismounted his men and put them behind it, and against this, Sheridan, all during the afternoon of the 10th, in vain hurled his forces. When the sun rose on the morning of the 11th, Hampton, his men, his artillery and his horses were still in position. Sheridan, strangely enough, waited until three o'clock in the afternoon. By this he lost his chance to win. Had he rushed the Confederate line with a real impetuous assault he would have broken it. He waited without a good reason. Fitzhugh Lee, with two-fifths of Hampton's men, was marching to avoid Federal interruption, and when he came, Hampton's heart was gladdened and his hopes lifted high. Fitzhugh Lee coming once more united the Confederates, and now all of Hampton's men faced all of Sheridan's men with Hampton protected by the railroad embankment. When this barrier, as the battle front was lengthened, failed, fence rails were pressed into service and such earth as the men could throw up with their hands and plates and cups reinforced the rails. So far little had been done or accomplished, and Sheridan moved up his men close to the Confederate lines. They had plenty of ammunition, and the roar from the constant discharge of the magazine rifles made a terrific din. Again and again Sheridan's men with supreme courage assailed the Confederate breastworks, but each time they left their dead and wounded and fell back from the scenes of slaughter. Chew and Hart, with their artillery, poured deadliest discharges into the Federal columns. At one time General M. C. Butler's men exhausted their ammunition. It looked as if all was lost. When despair seemed to fill every heart in this brave command, an ammunition wagon, with the horses lashed to a gallop, came dashing by, and the occupants of the wagon flung out from its sides loose handfuls of cartridges, and these the men joyously seized and returned to the fray. Seven times Sheridan's men advanced to the charge, and seven times they recoiled from the tremendous fire that greeted them from the Confederate lines. At the moment of the last assault a Confederate shell exploded a Federal caisson. Somebody realized that this was the psychological moment, and from over the breastworks the Confederates, moved by instinct and valor, charged with the speed of racers upon the Federal line. The rebel yell was heard from end to end, and the Federal forces, disheartened by their many failures, were swept away by the unexpected and impetuous advance of Hampton's soldiers. The turning point had come. The Confederates seized their opportunity and the battle was won.

From three o'clock in the afternoon until ten o'clock at night the contest had raged, and the record showed that it was a fierce contest. Both sides had dismounted. On the ground they were assailing each other with greatest energy and persistence. The Confederates had the best of position, but the Federals had the most of men. All through the afternoon and in the darkness of night neither side was willing to give up the struggle. The stars came out with feeble light to relieve the gloom and shadows that overspread the wreck and suffering of the battlefield. Naught could stay the surging tide of war, and in the darkness, as in the light, these soldiers continued to wage the contest. There was no time to bear away the dead or relieve the wounded. Orders had been given by General Hampton to Fitzhugh Lee for rapid and fierce pursuit, and to intervene between Sheridan and Carpenter's Ford on the North Anna River, at which he had crossed the day before; but the orders failed or were not executed and Sheridan marched away, leaving the unfortunate wounded behind, and returned by the same road over which he had come. He left in the hands of the men of the South six hundred and ninety-five prisoners and one hundred and twenty-five wounded. Again was demonstrated the power of the single-firing guns. The Federals claim to have carried away more than five hundred wounded, but they abandoned their dead and a hundred and twenty-five wounded were left with Hampton.

Little time was allowed for expressions of humanity. The Confederates, with the possession of the battlefield, assumed thereby responsibility for the care of those whose misfortunes left them suffering and helpless in the fields and woods that had witnessed the harvest of death on the two days of the struggle. When the storm of battle had passed, Federal and Confederate wounded were placed in improvised hospitals constructed of flat cars, thence conveyed to some convenient hospital further south. The few people that were left in this war-stricken country brought such food as they could spare to feed Hampton and his men; but these, rising to the highest calls of humanity, hungry and thirsty themselves, willingly made an equal division of what had been brought with their wounded and captured foes. This was a splendid demonstration of the noble and generous instincts that ever dwell in the hearts of brave men and which quicken and expand under the influence of opportunity. The bitterness of a fratricidal war could not stay the exercise of benignity and mercy.

General Sheridan endeavored to mitigate the unfortunate results of this expedition upon which he had started with high and boastful hopes. He had promised so much and accomplished so little that it required no small genius and much of rhetorical skill to satisfy those who had sent him on so important a mission. He had his own choice of troopers. Those he took with him had shown that in any contest they were ready to give a good account of themselves. Equipped, armed and provided with all that money could bring, and brought to a high degree of discipline, and already fully proved as able to cope with their foes, General Sheridan had either to exaggerate the number of men under Hampton, magnify the difficulties he encountered or admit a complete defeat. He chose the former. He claimed that he had attacked the Confederates in fortifications. He reported that Hampton had been reinforced by infantry on the second day of the fight, when in fact there was no infantry closer than General Lee's camps, eight miles from Richmond. The barren results of this expedition temporarily shook General Grant's faith in General Sheridan's capacity and fighting qualities, and this was only restored, when later, in the Valley and around Petersburg, General Sheridan repaired his shattered reputation, and with the experiences of another four months demonstrated that he was both a brilliant and aggressive cavalry leader.

He had hoped to do great damage to the railroad at Gordonsville and south to Staunton, and yet he only disturbed two hundred feet. General Torbert reported that the Confederates had a large brigade of mounted infantry armed with rifle muskets. A Federal prisoner had written in

244

his diary on the last day of the fight—"Sunday, June 12th, ... fought on same ground and got whipped like the devil...." Anyhow, whatever may have been the results as figured in General Sheridan's imagination, he made a night ride, crossed the North Anna River, and marched back to Cold Harbor, from whence he had come. For eight days Hampton was on one side of the river and Sheridan on the other. If Sheridan wanted to fight he had pontoon bridges and he had only to lay them and cross over. For at least a portion of the time the two cavalry commands were within sight of each other and now and then they exchanged shots. After fifteen days General Sheridan had gotten back to where he left Grant's army, from whence he started out with such flattering hopes and alluring expectations. He now found that Grant had determined to abandon his summer line, cross the Chickahominy, ferry over the James River, and take up a position on its south bank, from whence the long siege of Petersburg would begin, and proceed by inches until it would culminate in the overthrow of the Confederacy.

General Hampton had a second chance at General Gregg at Nance's Shop on the 24th of June, eleven days after the cessation of hostilities at Trevilian. He came close to making a complete rout of General Gregg's forces. Attacking in the afternoon he harried his lines,—pursued him until eleven o'clock at night, and a short distance from Charles City Court House captured one hundred and fifty-seven prisoners. So sorely was General Gregg's division handled in this affair that it required some time to recruit and mend up.

General Sheridan, in making his report, was bound by his backward march to express his regret at his inability to carry out his instructions. It was with much humiliation that he admitted failure. In the campaign Sheridan lost, according to Federal reports, more than fifteen hundred killed, wounded and taken prisoner, while General Hampton's forces lost less than eight hundred. This Trevilian expedition was another test out of the spirit and power of Federal and Confederate cavalry of the armies in Northern Virginia. It demonstrated anew that the Confederate cavalry under Hampton was just as enterprising, as valiant, as enthusiastic and as brave and dauntless as when it fought under Stuart. Down to the very end the horsemen of the Army of Northern Virginia maintained their proud spirit and their indomitable will, and when the last call was made, when the lines at Petersburg had been broken, and when General Lee, in the vain hope of effecting a union with Johnston in Georgia, had turned his face west and reached Appomattox, there to be met with sad and appalling disaster, the cavalry was still ready and willing to fight and give valiant response to the last call that their country could make upon their fealty and their courage. Many of them marched into North Carolina and Georgia to make one more stand under the Stars and Bars, and once more offer their lives to win life for the Confederate Nation.

Chapter XVI

MORGAN'S RIDE AROUND CINCINNATI,
ON "THE OHIO RAID," JULY, 1863

In June, 1863, General Banks was hammering Port Hudson, Louisiana, where General Gardner, the commander of the Confederate forces, made such gallant and fierce resistance. The fall of Vicksburg on July 4th did not affect the valor of Gardner and his command. He fought until his men from mere exhaustion could fight no longer. Without rest, in constant battle for six weeks, flesh and blood could resist no more. He inflicted tremendous loss upon his assailants, and he yielded only when further resistance was physically impossible. These were very dark days for the people of the Southland.

After the Battle of Murfreesboro at Stone River, December 31, 1862—January 1, 1863, General Rosecrans remained inactive for five months. The mortality in this struggle measurably paralyzed the energies of both Confederates and Federals. Each general sat down to rest, renew hopes, recuperate and plead for reinforcements.

While Rosecrans had behind him almost unlimited resources, an ample fighting force of trained men and abundant supplies, the experience at Murfreesboro rendered him uncertain about grappling again with General Bragg, and the latter, with the awful memory of that struggle, was glad to wait for the other side to move.

That, in June, 1863, Bragg's troops were at Shelbyville, Tennessee, about twenty miles away from Murfreesboro, was convincing evidence that Rosecrans was not eager for battle. The clamors of those in authority at Washington indicated that Rosecrans must advance. It was necessary for him either to go forward or resign, and in June he undertook to force Bragg still farther south.

Fifty miles from Nashville, at Shelbyville, General Bragg decided again to try the fortunes of war, but Rosecrans, with a larger army than Bragg, was able to turn his flanks. On the 27th of June General Bragg concentrated his army at Tullahoma, which was twenty miles from

Shelbyville. He had at first determined there again to risk a battle. At this time, General Bragg was in extremely poor health. With friction among his generals and with enemies in front, he had suffered both mental and physical depletion, and General Hardee had said of him that he "was not able to take command in the field." His corps commanders advised him to recede and retreat to Chattanooga, where with his army he arrived on the 7th of July, 1863. The spirit and courage of his men had suffered no depreciation. He had lost no guns and no supplies, and the rank and file had no sympathy in the movements which surrendered so much of Tennessee to Federal occupation. A third of Bragg's army were Tennesseeans, and they looked upon a retreat to Chattanooga as little short of treason. Left to these men thus expatriated by military necessities, they would gladly have fought a battle every week.

Determined upon another trial of strength with Rosecrans, General Bragg undertook, through General John H. Morgan, to threaten and destroy the Federal lines of communication, to force the withdrawal of men to defend wagon trains, railroad bridges and trestles. Morgan was directed to enter Kentucky at or near Burksville on the Cumberland River, proceed northward to the Ohio River, and then retreat out of the state by the route which the exigencies of the moment should suggest as the most feasible road for a return to the army in Tennessee. For some days previous General Morgan's division had been concentrating in Wayne County, Kentucky, in and around Monticello, its county seat, and he gradually worked his way towards Burksville. Across the Cumberland, Federal cavalry were guarding the paths into Central Kentucky and keeping a sharp lookout for Morgan and his followers. They had stringent orders to be vigilant and under no stress to allow the Confederate raider to steal by and start havoc and ruin on the Louisville & Nashville Railroad, then essential for feeding Rosecrans' advancing legions.

Here, waiting for the moment which would be most critical in General Bragg's southward retreat, on the morning of July 2d, 1863, General Morgan's division, twenty-six hundred strong, crossed the Cumberland River at Burksville and at Turkey Neck Bend, a few miles west of the town. Nine-tenths of the men composing this division were Kentuckians and all very young men. A thrill of joy stirred every heart and quickened every body, when the order came which turned their faces homeward. The men of Missouri, Maryland and Kentucky were the orphans of the Confederacy, and to them home-going in army days gave a touch of highest bliss. The First Brigade, under General Duke, crossed a short distance above Burksville, while the Second Brigade, under General Adam R. Johnson, crossed at Turkey Neck Bend, a few miles below Burksville, some five or six miles apart. The First Brigade had some flat boats, and the Second had one leaky flatboat and a couple of canoes. All the horses and some of the men of the Second Brigade must swim. There was no organized resistance to the crossing of the stream, which was full from bank to bank and its currents running at tremendous speed. The Federal watchers thought the great flood in the Cumberland River would temporarily stop Morgan, and with the water on their side, they did not believe it possible for the Confederates to pass over with their artillery and ammunition and get lodgment on the north side of the stream. They could not learn exactly where he would try to ferry; they knew he could not ford, and so, trusting to luck and high water, they securely waited in their camp for what the morrow would bring forth.

In the Second Brigade the saddles, guns, ammunition, cannon and clothing were placed in the ferryboat, and regiments one at a time were brought down to the river. The horses with their bridles and halters were driven into the stream and forced to take their chances, not only with the rapid current, but with the driftwood, which was very abundant and large. At some places it covered almost the entire surface. The stream was five-eighths of a mile wide. Many of the men clung to the ferryboat and thus swam across. Some held to the canoes and floated by their side, while others swam with their horses, holding to their manes or tails to prevent being swept down stream by its fierce tides. As the first detachment crossed over, the Federal pickets undertook to resist the landing. The part of the Confederates who were in the ferryboat and canoe with their clothes on, rushed into line, while those who swam, unwilling to be laggard, not halting to dress, seized their cartridge boxes and guns and rushed upon the enemy. The strange sight of naked men engaging in combat for a moment amazed the enemy. They had never seen soldiers before clad only in nature's garb; they concluded that warriors, fully grown and armed, just born into the world, were the men they must fight. Amid such scenes as this was begun the thousand mile march which constituted Morgan's Ohio Raid. The animals were quickly corralled and saddled, lines promptly formed, and the onslaught upon the Federals begun. It did not take long for Morgan's men to discover that their presence was not only unwelcome, but was expected. In a little while dead troopers, dead steeds, abandoned clothing, lost haversacks and wrecked wagons along the highway gave mute but convincing proof of war's terrors and war's exactions. The Southern raiders thus early learned that the campaign would not be completed without much of conflict and loss. It did not take long to drive Woolford's Federal cavalry out of Columbia. Nothing could stay the impetuous rush of these riders towards the Bluegrass. The resistance was feeble, but it was enough to show that enemies were abundant and alert. A few dead and wounded were left by both sides in Columbia, but these were remitted to the ministrations and care of non-combatants, while the fighters rode forward to new conflicts. The enthusiasm of homecoming lent renewed courage and ever-increasing vehemence to the Kentuckians, and they were ready to ride over anything that obstructed the way that pointed toward their friends farther up the state.

At Green River Stockade was stationed the 25th Michigan Infantry, commanded by Colonel O. B. Moore. The position of the stockade had been selected with great skill and protected by an impassable line, consisting of trees and rifle pits and sharpened pieces of wood with some wires and fencing. Against this a couple of regiments were hurled, but in vain. When surrender had been demanded of Colonel Moore, the Federal commander, he returned the laconic answer that "the Fourth of July was no day for me to entertain such a proposition." He was a brave, gallant and fearless foe, and his patriotic response won the respect of his enemies. The tone of his reply foreboded trouble. The Confederates were not long in finding out that he was prepared in action to back up his words of eloquent defiance. General Morgan was compelled in a little while to do what his judgment now told him he should have done in the outset, that is to leave the stockade and the infantry alone. They were really not in his way, could do him no damage if left unmolested, and could join in no pursuit when once he had passed them by. In thirty minutes' fighting more than forty men were killed and forty-five wounded. Of the enemy, nine were killed and twenty-six wounded. Colonel Chenault of the 11th Kentucky, Major Brent of the 5th, Lieutenant Cowan of the 3d, Lieutenants Holloway and Ferguson of the 5th were among the valiant and gallant officers who laid down their lives on that day for their country.

In any protracted war, all commands which extensively participate have their dark days, and in some respects, outside the disaster at Buffington Island, fifteen days later, the darkest day that ever came to General

Morgan's division was this sad 4th of July. For a little while it checked the enthusiasm and stilled the quickened heartbeats of the returning exiles. On the morrow at Lebanon there would be other sorrowful experiences and the hope of home-going would temporarily vanish when at Lebanon the head of the column turned west instead of continuing east.

On that grim day at Green River Stockade the 11th under Chenault and the 5th under Colonel Smith were asked to do the impossible. They stood until standing was no longer wise, or even brave. The Federal commander reported that the fighting lasted three hours, but the real fighting lasted less than three-quarters of an hour, and with something less than six hundred men engaged, about forty-five were killed and the same number wounded. This was a distressing percentage of mortality under the circumstances of the battle.

Chenault, impetuous, gallant, died close up to the enemy with his face to the foe. Major Brent, of the 5th Kentucky, so full of promise, was killed as he rode up to salute Colonel James B. McCreary, who succeeded Chenault in command of the 11th. Captain Treble, of Christmas raid fame, was among the men who gave their lives on this field for the Southland. As he rose to salute the colonel, who had become such by the death of Chenault, and waved his hand to let him know that he would be ready when the order came, he fell, struck by a bullet that crushed through his brain.

None of those who saw these dead brought out under the flag of truce, and the wounded carried in blankets from out of the woods and from the ravines and laid along the turnpike road from Columbia to Lebanon, will ever forget the harrowing scene. When they looked upon the dead, with their pallid faces turned heavenward, and their pale hands folded across their stilled breasts, poignant grief filled every heart. It did not take long to bury or arrange for burial of the dead. Humanity would care for the wounded, and war's demands bade the remaining soldiers press forward, and by midnight the division camped a few miles out from Lebanon to rest for the conflict on the morrow.

Colonel Charles Hanson, who commanded the 20th Kentucky Federal Infantry, had prepared to make the best defense possible at Lebanon. He placed his men in the brick depot and in the houses surrounding it. General Morgan disliked to leave anything behind, and so he resolved to capture this force. It was captured, but the cost did not justify the losses. It was there that we saw General Morgan's youngest brother, "Tom," as

251

they familiarly called him, go down in the storm. He was a first lieutenant in the 2d Kentucky and was then serving on General Duke's staff. With the fiery courage of youth, backed by a fearless heart, in the excitement of battle he exposed his person and was struck down by a shot from the depot. War allows no time for partings. It permits no preparation for the great beyond. Standing close to his brother, he could only exclaim, "Brother, I am killed. I am killed," and then fell into the grief-stricken brother's arms. He was a mere lad, but he died like a hero.

The taking of a brick depot with several hundred men inside, in war, is not an easy job. It was to cost ten killed and thirty wounded. Here I witnessed what appeared to be one of the bravest things I have ever observed. The 8th Kentucky—Cluke's—with which I was connected, was ordered to charge the front of the depot. The men were advancing through a field where the weeds were waist-high. It was difficult marching. The thermometer stood over a hundred in the shade, and the foliage of the weeds made the heat still more intense. It was this regiment's fortune to face the larger door of the depot. It was said that somebody had blundered, but the charge was ordered and the men enthusiastically and bravely obeyed. When within a few hundred feet of the door, the order was passed along to "lie down." The time in which the "lying down" was done seemed many hours. The regiment was subject to the stinging fire of the Federals in the depot. A number of the men were hit by shots which struck the front of the body and ranged downward through the limbs of the soldiers. Such wounds produced excruciating tortures.

A man by my side was shot in the shoulder this way. He was a brave, uneducated, but faithful mountain soldier. He came from around Somerset and had been a cattle drover before he went away to war. Why he had ever volunteered I never could fully fathom. He had no property, he had no relatives in the Confederacy. He had made a few casual acquaintances in his journeyings as a drover, but these could hardly have influenced him to risk his life for the Southland. He was not a man to seek war for the glory or excitement of campaigning.

Men of his calling are rarely communicative or confidential. Finally one night, on a lonely scout through the mountains, he unburdened his soul and told me why he had gone to war. There was something in the isolation of our surroundings, the constant presence of danger, the depressing shadows of the trees which shut out even the starlight, that made the heavy-hearted man long for human sympathy, and in sad, sad tones he told me his life's tragedy. He was thirty-two years of age and had fallen desperately in love with a young girl he had met while driving stock along the Wilderness Road, having stopped one night at her father's house. At the end of each journey he had purchased souvenirs for his sweetheart, small mirrors, plain rings, garnet breastpins and plated bracelets and an occasional dress of many colors, the equal of Joseph's coat, and these conveyed in the most delicate way to the young lady the great love that was being enkindled in the heart of the silent, undemonstrative drover. He could speak no words, but in deferential courtesy, through these simple tokens, he endeavored to declare the turmoil raging in his bosom.

He had never the courage to tell her of his affection. He had worshipped in this patient style at the shrine of her beauty and forecast in his mind a happy, happy time when in a log cabin on the mountain side he should claim her for his bride and set up his household gods in a humble abode. He had in the past loved nobody else, and he had persuaded himself that in the future he would never love again, and at the end of each trip he carried back these homely offerings, showing how, in his humble way, he worshipped her ruddy face, her bright eyes and wavy hair, and dreamed as only lovers can dream of the exquisite joy and happiness that would overshadow his life if he might but make her his own.

Upon returning from one of his long drives, he found that she had married another. He uttered no word of complaint, he gave expression to no outcry of grief. He realized that his case was hopeless, that the brightest dream of his life had been shattered, that he had lost his first and only love. He nursed in the depths of his soul the disappointment and sorrow that overwhelmed his joyous anticipations of a blissful future. He could not bear to pass her home any more. He had naught of this world's goods but a few dollars in coin, a saddle, bridle and an old bob-tailed black horse which had become his when style and symmetry had put him below the more exacting standards of the Bluegrass, and condemned him to spend the last years of his horse life amongst the less fastidious fanciers of the mountains. He called his steed "Bob-Tail." He had been nicked in his youth, and now that age had dignified his demeanor and slowed his speed, he made a hardy and reliable mount for his steady-going owner, who loved him for his kindly disposition and for his cheerful performance of every duty, however severe. They seemed to have a common sympathy and fellowship in that both had lost out in the struggle of life.

He gave up driving, and one day when Morgan rode through Somerset, he mounted his old black steed, waved a kindly adieu to his few acquaintances, and rode away to war, little caring whether he lived or died.

He was always cheerful, brave, patient and well up at the front. He insisted upon doing for me all possible services, caring for my horse, keeping my saddle, bridle and arms in good shape. There was no sacrifice he would not have made for me, and he had won my heart. He clung to me because I knew his heart's tragedy and because he must love somebody now that his life was a ruin and blank.

The Enfield ball passed almost through his entire body and the suffering was so horrible that his groans were agonizing. He begged somebody to bear him off the field. The order had been issued to shoot any man who arose. This was done to prevent the Federals from getting the exact range of the regiment which was now lying down with their heads toward the depot. While in this position, I observed what was to me the bravest thing I had ever seen in the war. I always thought it was the 5th Kentucky, but General Duke says it was the 2d. The men from this regiment charged on the south side of the depot with their pistols and guns and marched up to the windows and put their weapons in through the openings and fired into the mass of Federals inside. It required almost superhuman courage to undertake this act, yet it was done with a calmness that would thrill every observer, and those of us who were lying on the ground and watching this splendid move and realized what it meant for our relief, cheered and cheered the courage of these valiant warriors. The groans of my wounded friend became so distressing and harassing that finally I received permission to rise and take him on my back and bear him from the field, where the bullets were still whizzing. Wounded and suffering as he was, I had only time to commend him to the surgeons and bid him good-bye. He took my hand and pressed it to his now bloodless lips, and his great black eyes filled with tears when he looked up at me and said that he would see my face no more. After my return to Louisville in 1868, succeeding a three years' exile, I observed in Cave Hill Cemetery the grave of my wounded friend, Vincent Eastham. The stone which comrades had erected to his memory was marked "5th Kentucky Cavalry," but I pointed out the mistake and put the proper endorsement on his marker, "Company B, 8th Kentucky Cavalry." Each Decoration Day, with those near to me, we carry armfuls of flowers to make beautiful the mound where he sleeps, and my children and my children's children have been asked to keep green the spot where my mountain friend so calmly rests amongst his Confederate comrades in Louisville's beautiful "City of the Dead."

The next ten days were full of intensest excitement and harassing marching. This marching was done in the midst of stifling dust, intense heat and almost constant battle. On the 8th day of July the command crossed the Ohio River at Brandenburg, capturing a couple of steamboats and fighting off gunboats, until at last, on the evening of that day, General Morgan and his division camped on northern soil.

No courtesies were expected, and certainly none were received from the people of the "Hoosier State." They harassed and distressed Morgan's march all they could. If they worried Morgan, he was more than even with them. Absurd stories of the Confederate and his followers had gone on before the line of his march, and fear and dismay filled all hearts when they saw the dust clouds or heard the shots that proclaimed his presence. These reports with each telling became more gruesome and horrible and when they stole from behind trees, or out of the thickets, for a sight of his riders, they refused to believe that these men in gray were not real, sure enough devils, horns, hoofs and all. Even rhyme was put under conscription to help tell how awful they were, and words like these were carried by speedy couriers in their dashes along the roads to prepare the country folk for the dreadful catastrophe that was breaking upon the innocent people of Southern Indiana:

"I'm sent to warn the neighbors, he's only a mile behind.
He's sweeping up the horses, every horse that he can find.
Morgan, Morgan, the raider, and Morgan's terrible men,
With bowie knives and pistols are galloping up the glen."

Each day was full of strenuous work, night marching, incessant fighting, guerrilla firing, obstructions of roads, and on the night of the 12th of July, General Morgan and his men were sixty miles north of the Ohio River and far up into the State of Indiana. The average march for all these days was forty miles, counting detours, under difficulties that sorely taxed human powers.

On the 12th of July the command made thirty-eight miles, although this was the eleventh day in the saddle.

Scattered along the fence corners for four miles, at a little town called Milam on the line of the Ohio & Michigan Railroad, Morgan and his command caught a few hours' rest. Some subtle and mysterious instinct came to them that the morrow would demand heroic work. They seemed to breathe in the very air that something great was expected of them. The beasts laid down in slumber and rest beside the tired bodies of their persistent riders. Voices of unseen bodies seemed to whisper to them that on the morrow they would attempt the longest continued cavalry march ever said to have been made by twenty-five hundred men in column. Stuart, when he started from Chambersburg, was rested. For twelve hours he had slept. Forrest, when in pursuit of Streight, had briefly halted at Courtland, Alabama, but these Morgan's men had been marching and fighting for ten days and yet fate was to put up to them the task of excelling human records. Two and a half miles away were twenty-five hundred Federal troops. Although humanity would suggest that the saddles should be stripped from the backs of the tired horses, the calls of the hour were such that mercy could make no response and every man slept with his bridle rein over his arm, and in his weary hand he held his trusted gun.

They were now over four hundred miles from the place where they began their march, in territory held by the enemy. They were beset on every side with forces sent for their capture. Guides were unfaithful, and sometimes the main roads were blockaded and ambuscades frequent. The column was three miles long and already there was a number of sick and wounded in buggies and wagons. Under all these conditions, men might well ask, "Can this great task be accomplished?"

Morgan felt that the men riding with him were thoroughbreds. They were the grandsons of the pioneers given by Virginia, Maryland, Carolina, in the savage work of wresting Kentucky from the Indians, and the pioneers had given Kentucky men a name and fame wherever the English tongue had been spoken. They were sons, or grandsons, of the men who had fought the Battles of Blue Lick, Maumee, Fort Stevenson, the Thames, of the Raisin, Tippecanoe, New Orleans, Cerro Gordo, Buena Vista, and their great leader, with the knowledge of what they had done and faith in what they could accomplish, already in his own mind was asking, "Can this thing be done?"

These troopers had never failed him either in the march or on the field. If it were possible for men to do it, he knew it would be done. He knew that they would try, and if they failed it would be only because the accomplishment of such a task was humanly impossible.

The command to mount was his answer to these curious questionings which forced themselves into his brain, as in the dim light of the early dawn he looked over their sleeping forms and found it hard in his heart to rouse them from their death-like slumber.

Out into the dusty roads before the rays of the scorching July sun should be felt, he bade them wake and ride.

By twelve o'clock thirty-two miles were done. Across the White River into Harrison, Ohio, they rode. The torch was applied to the great bridge that crossed White River and as the blazes lifted hissing tongues high in the air, and while they watched the timbers crumble under the conquering hand of fire, the advance guard of the Federals exchanged shots over the stream with the rear guard of the Confederates.

The men could manage a few hours without food. They had fared well along the line in the plenteous and forsaken kitchens and dining rooms of the frightened inhabitants, who, upon the advance of the Confederates, left their tables loaded with well-prepared food and fled into the woods and fields to escape the terrors of what they called Morgan's "murderers and horse thieves."

The well-filled cribs and stables of the people of Harrison supplied the tired horses with a good feed. This was the last stop they were to make until they should end the march, and so the General allowed a brief rest and time to satisfy appetites, quickened by the long and tedious ride of the morning.

An hour was consumed in marching and counter-marching so as to mislead General Burnside and his thirty thousand soldiers at Cincinnati, only thirty-two miles away. These men at Cincinnati were planning to create a wall of infantry which it would be impossible for Morgan to pass.

Haste, haste, haste, was the watchword of the hour, and down the valley toward the Big Miami River the Confederate column moved. At dusk the long, wooden bridge across the Big Miami was struck. Bridges and railroads were dangerous enemies to leave in the rear, and the torch was called into requisition. As the red flames, created by the great burning timbers, rose skyward, they illumined the entire valley; and in the flickering shadows which they cast for several miles around, in the gloaming of the evening, among the trees and fences and buildings, huge, weird forms, born, it is true, of the imagination, filled the minds and hearts of the invading horsemen for the moment with apprehensive awe and depressing forebodings.

At midnight fifty-five miles had been marched by the ceaseless tramp of the wearied steeds. A hundred and forty-four thousand steps they had already taken, and still more than a hundred thousand were to be required before they could rest their tired limbs, and well might they inquire as their riders still spurred them onward, "Masters, masters, be ye men or devils which exact from your beasts such unseemly toil and fearful sufferings?" With the darkness of the night the fears seemed to subside, if fears there were. The wearied bodies called for sleep, sleep, yet there could be no staying for "tired nature's sweet restorer." The early hours of the night were filled with suffering, but as the intense darkness which preceded the coming dawn enveloped the column, the strain became still more terrible. Horses, unwilling and unable to go further forward, sank down in death with their riders astride still urging them onward, and under the dreadful physical burdens, strong men fell from their beasts as if smitten with sudden death. Hundreds of the men lashed themselves to their saddles while fighting the assaults of sleep. Riders losing consciousness failed to close up, and by the time the rear of the columns was reached, this closing up kept a large portion of the column much of the time in a gallop. Once it became necessary with lighted candles to crawl upon hands and knees and by the tracks determine which road the vanguard had ridden. Comrades, dismounted by the breaking down of their weakened steeds, walked beside the line, keeping pace with the horses, while others, where possible, sprang up behind their companions until a convenient stable by the roadside would provide a new mount.

A common sense of danger told even the most careless rider that the passage around Cincinnati was the moment of extreme danger, and as the column came nearer and nearer to that line, the thought that the supreme moment was at hand gave renewed strength and wakefulness to the majority of the men now attempting an unprecedented march.

Three times during the night General Morgan changed guides, and each time it was necessary by either open or covert threat to force an enemy to lead the column. Guides were informed that the compass would tell the story of their treachery and that death would be the sure consequence of their bad faith.

There was no direct line along which the command could march, and the change of direction did much to confuse the column. The crawl of the artillery and a large number of buggies bearing sick and wounded comrades over a hilly and woody country amidst almost absolute darkness, with here and there an unfriendly shot, made an ordeal which rarely if at all had come into soldier life.

By two o'clock in the morning the dead line at Glendale was passed. The Federal commander, deceived by Morgan's marching and counter-marching, had carried a large body of troops too far north and Morgan had slipped through at this neglected point, and his strategy had foiled the Federal commander's chances and efforts to check the invader. This line was crossed at a high rate of speed. If the passage of the troops had been obstructed, there was nothing to do but to ride over those who attempted to stay the march, and so every man rose in his stirrups, grasped his bridle reins with firmer hold, unswung his gun from his shoulder and carried it on the pommel of his saddle, and felt to be sure that his trusted revolvers were in their appointed places in his belt at his side. If foe appeared, woe be unto that foe unless he could present himself in such vast numbers as to stay the charge of twenty-five hundred troopers upon whose courage at this moment depended the escape of the division. The calls of the hour were met with a cheerful response. Every man carried in his bosom a firm resolve to sweep any foe from the appointed path and to cut his way through any ranks that might oppose his going. The intense emergencies of the moment made them almost hope that somebody would get in their way. There came into their minds a desire to fight rather than ride through, and a touch of pride made them anxious for some sort of contest to show that after all the wear and tear of the past twelve days they were quite as brave and virile as when in the flush of the beginning they had forced a passage of the Cumberland River. Fear seemed to vanish and prudence fled away, as these night riders saw the people of Glendale rush out into the streets, or from raised windows, with dreading apprehension, watch the strange procession gallop through the streets. In the enthusiasm of the moment, the dust-stained Confederates cheered for Jefferson Davis and the Southern Confederacy and bade the alarmed onlookers tell General Burnside and his bluecoats that Morgan and his men had come and gone. Mind rose superior to the pain and weariness of body, and in these words of good-natured badinage was a new evidence of the valor and spirit of these bold raiders.

Though the line was passed, safety was not yet assured. The larger bodies of infantry were close at hand. A great task had been accomplished, and still there were thirty-eight miles ahead, and this distance, now every moment growing longer and longer, the weary horsemen knew must be covered before solid rest was attainable. In a little while the sunshine came to brighten the earth and to cheer as it always does cheer struggling humanity, but the record was yet unbroken. Every mile seemed to grow into a dozen miles. Each step brought increasing suffering. Skirmishes and contact with the militia would arouse the men for a brief while, but with the cessation of the excitement, nature would again lift its cry for mercy and plead for sleep for man and beast.

And so on and on and on until the sun was about to hide its face behind the western slopes, and at four o'clock in the afternoon, on the 14th, the column, now struggling and oppressed with both hunger and weariness, reached Williamsburg, Ohio, and camped for the night, and the greatest single cavalry march of the world, composed of as large a force as twenty-five hundred men, was ended.

Ninety-five and a quarter miles in thirty-two hours of marching! Surely such work was not unworthy of what the Confederacy asked of its sons.

As these hard riders dismounted they stood for a moment helpless with fatigue. Leaning against a horse or a fence they would sleep standing, and in taking food to recuperate their wearied bodies, would sink into slumber. It was a great triumph for Confederate cavalry, and amid all its terrors and horrors it was worth something to realize that the record of human endurance had been lifted several degrees higher. The future had yet in store for some of these men much of hardship and much of renown—imprisonment in the Ohio penitentiary, at Camp Chase, Camp Douglass, Johnson's Island, Fort Delaware, for many, death under the chafings, starvation and cruelties of Northern prisons; but out of these there would come a remnant who should, when others had capitulated, ride as an escort for Jefferson Davis when Richmond and Columbia would be in ruins and all hope for the nation's life had fled.

There would yet come a time when to these still hoping men, hope would fail, when the Confederate Armies would be shattered and scattered, when Lee had surrendered and Johnson capitulated, when the western army and the Army of Northern Virginia, its veterans paroled, would turn their tear-stained faces toward their desolated homes and take up anew the burdens of life; when all the mighty legions west of the Mississippi, which had maintained for four years the mightiest conflict of the ages, would stack their guns, sheath their swords, and accept war's decrees for surrender.

They were yet to see a time when the President of the Confederacy should go forth from the seat of government, and in sadness and gloom ride away from the Confederate capital to seek refuge south of Virginia.

There were some of these men who were here at this hour destined and appointed still to cling to Jefferson Davis' fortunes and defend his person in the period of surpassing disaster and sadness, when with a broken heart he would realize that his nation was dead and he was without a country. There would come a time when a pitying Providence should provide out of these soldiers for the first and only Confederate President a depleted bodyguard, who would go with him in his reverses and humiliation, and who were to stand guard over him and his cabinet, to beat off pursuing foes at a time when every man's hand would be against him and them, when fate would hide its face and give him over to a cruel, brutal mocking and an imprisonment which would shock the world's sense of mercy and justice. There were men now closing this great ride who would be present when the wretchedness of death would hover over and around the Southern cause, and would look upon the last council of war. When the greatness of the South should end in desolation and ruin, some of these riders were, in the closing hours of the Confederacy, to offer anew their lives and their all to the cause which they loved to the end, and for which they had sacrificed their fortunes; and yet in the blackness of death and the final agonies of their nation would again cheerfully tender their all, to prolong even for an hour its hopes and its existence. They were yet by their exalted courage to glorify that cause for which the South had endured untold and immeasurable suffering, and would by a crowning act of constancy take a deserved place on the brightest pages of human annals that record patriotic fortitude and valor.

A few hundred of these men now closing this wonderful march would accompany Jefferson Davis in his last effort to avoid capture, and would only leave him and those he loved, when he should plead that their presence would only endanger his escape. They would only depart when he commanded them to go, and urged them by their loyalty and devotion to him to listen to his appeal—that they leave him alone in the supreme hour of his political grief and distress.

Some of these men would also be present when the last sun that ever shone on the Confederate States, as a nation, was lengthening its rays on its western course, and sending forth a fading glow on the sad scenes of national dissolution which would, if it were possible, with nature's shadings, make glorious and immortal the faces of the heroes who, in anguish and awe, looked upon its death throes, a nation that in its brief days of four eventful years was to make a history that would win the

261

admiration and love of all the people of succeeding ages, who read the story of their suffering, their valor, their loyalty and their devotion to principle and country.

Some of these riders were to be faithful unto death, and have a full share of that glorious crown of immortality which fate would hereafter decree to the men of the South as a compensation for a victory, which, though deserved, should be denied.

Chapter XVII

RICHARDS WITH MOSBY'S MEN IN THE FIGHT AT MT. CARMEL CHURCH, FEBRUARY 19, 1864

In all military history, Colonel John S. Mosby and his command had neither a counterpart nor a parallel. Man for man, Mosby and his men did more, proportionately, to damage, to harass, to delay and to disturb the Federal forces than any equal number of soldiers who wore the gray.

John Singleton Mosby was born in Powhatan County, Virginia, in December, 1833, fifty miles south of the scenes of his wonderful military exploits. He came from refined, cultured and well-to-do people, and as was the custom in those days amongst the better class in that State, he was educated at the University of Virginia. His courage early developed itself. Some trouble with a fellow-student suspended his career in the University. He prepared himself for the practice of law, and when the war broke out, he was engaged in his profession at Bristol. He was among the very first men to offer for the Confederate service for twelve months. War, especially partisan war, had peculiar fascinations for this young lawyer. He had read and re-read the history of Sumter and Marion, and he longed for opportunity and occasion to engage in similar work. He knew every detail of the things they had done in the struggle of the colonies for liberty. While his eyes scanned the lines of Blackstone and Story, dreams of military glory flitted before his vision. The excitement, din, rush and fury of war appealed to his nature and he sighed for a chance to see and know what real war was. He shirked no duty, sought every possible opportunity for inflicting loss upon his country's enemies. Enlisted for twelve months, he refused the furlough accorded men who served that length of time, and he re-enlisted for the war. His enterprise and his daring won him promotion, and by February, 1862, he was the adjutant of his regiment. He resigned because of some misunderstanding between Colonel William E. Jones and General Stuart, but the latter was quick to note men of Mosby's ability and military aptitude and he put him on his staff as a scout and adviser. He held this position and rode with Stuart on his Chickahominy raid in June, 1862. He was almost the same age as his commander. He was quieter, but none the less brave. He took service more seriously than General Stuart; war with him was a passion, not a pastime. He loved war for the excitement and experience it brought, for the opportunities it offered to his genius for development, and devoid of fear, he was glad when chance brought his way the legal right to fight.

It was only a brief period until his marvelous efficiency and his masterful sagacity, as well as his extraordinary courage, caused General Stuart to give him a small independent command. He used this so effectively that his forces were quickly increased and the area of his operations enlarged. He had men in his battalion from almost all parts of the world, but the majority was composed of young soldiers who came from Virginia and Maryland. There was so much that was fascinating and attractive in the service in which Mosby was engaged that there was no difficulty in finding recruits who were the impersonation, not only of valor, but of dash. He enjoyed in the highest degree the confidence not only of General Stuart, but of General Lee, and the only criticism which General Lee ever passed on Mosby was his ability to catch bullets and win wounds.

In 1863 he engaged in a successful exploit, which largely added to his fame. With twenty-nine men, he penetrated the Federal lines and captured General Stoughton in his headquarters in the midst of his division, at Fairfax Court House, Virginia. This secured promotion for Mosby. Nothing in the war was more skillfully or recklessly done than this capture of General Stoughton. There are no mathematic quantities by which the damage that Mosby inflicted upon the Federals can be calculated. For every one man under his command, he kept one hundred Federals from the front. Had Colonel Mosby enjoyed the opportunities of other Confederate cavalry leaders, he would have won a fame and rank equal to either Forrest or Wheeler or Morgan or Stuart or Hampton. Had he gone to West Point and entered the war with the experience and prestige which came to men who had enjoyed military education, there would have been few officers in the Confederate Army who would have surpassed him in military achievement. At the period when Mosby first began his partisan career, there was no other man in the armies of the South who, with the means at hand, could have inflicted such damage on the enemy, or have accomplished such great results for his country.

A number of books have been written about Mosby and his men, and yet they can only touch a few of the wonderful things done by this wonderful man with his wonderful followers. He had no equipment of any kind. His men knew nothing about tents, and they had substantially no commissary and no quartermaster. They lived largely off their enemies and when not pursuing these, passed the time with their friends.

Mosby operated in four Virginia counties. This country became known as "Mosby's Confederacy," and the "Debatable Land." However often the Federals invaded it they never could feel that their title was secure. This "Debatable Land" was not more than sixty miles long by forty miles wide, and yet in this limited area Mosby and his men subsisted, fought and disquieted the Federal army, in a way that demoralized its trains and kept its soldiers in a state of constant dread and apprehension. While the organization consisted of several companies, never at any one time did Colonel Mosby have more than four hundred men, and most of the time far less. These four hundred men, or whatever their number may have been, destroyed more Federal property than any other equal number of men in the Confederacy; and it is truly said of them that they gave the Federal troops more trouble than any five thousand men of any other command. Most of their work was in the rear of their foes. In a fight, General Forrest said one man in the rear was equal to three in the front, but in Mosby's operations, one man behind the Federal lines counted more than twenty in front.

Mosby was cool, calm, fearless, dauntless. He inspired his men with his own confidence, faith and hope. They all respected him—most of them feared him—and all were glad to follow him. There was something in his personality that created in the minds of his followers absolute trust. They believed in him and they knew that he could be relied upon in all emergencies and that whether in the storm of battle, in the haste of retreat, or in the rush of the charge, Mosby was always at himself, and he was sure to do the wisest and the most sagacious thing under any contingency that might arise.

In Mosby's command there was no room for cowardice and no place for cowards. The men who went with him took their lives in their hands. They knew that following him meant constant danger, ceaseless activity, incessant watchfulness and reckless service, and they were willing in exchange for the glory which they might gain, to assume all the risks that were incident to the daily life of the adherents of this silent, bold and fearless man.

Mosby's operations were largely confined to Fauquier and Loudoun

County, Virginia. Occasionally he crossed the line into Prince William County, and sometimes operated in Culpepper, but Fauquier County was the chief scene of his operations. In the later months of the war he was practically always within the enemy's lines. He never had a camp, except for a small number of his men, and then only for a brief while. There was no place for Mosby to hide himself except among those who loved the Cause in these counties. In cabins and barns and in the forest and among the hills, his command found their home. Rarely more than two or three of them ever remained together. They scattered, as has been said, like the mist when the sun rose. When the Federals undertook to pursue them, the pursuit became like the chase after a phantom. If followed, they dispersed through the country into the crossroads and by-ways and among their friends and sympathizers. The exploits of Marion and Sumter become as a fading light when compared with the glamour and splendor of the work of Mosby and his men for the Confederacy. When they met, it was by preconcerted arrangement, or in answer to the calls of couriers. Much of their work was done at night. For the three years in which Mosby was engaged in active operations, there was rarely a single day that some of his men were not operating somewhere on the enemy's line and on the enemy's forces. In the activity of his campaigning the death rate was high, but there was always an abundance of daring spirits that were ready to take the places of those who had fallen in this desperate game of war.

Mosby taught his men to eschew sabres, to use no guns, but to rely upon the pistol alone. This meant fighting at close range, hand to hand combat. He and his men seemed to be everywhere; they were ever the terror and dread of the Federal Army. The men who guarded the wagon trains heard always with tremor the name of Mosby. With the exception of General Forrest, Colonel Mosby was the most feared and hated of all Confederate leaders. The writer of a history of his command says: "He kept in a defensive attitude, according to their own admission, thirty-five thousand of their troops which would otherwise have been employed in the active theatre of war. But this was not all. More than once, with his band, he compelled the invading army to relinquish actual and projected lines of communication, to fall back from advance positions, and, if we may credit the assertion of the Federal Secretary of War, occasioned a loss of an important battle."

The things done by Mosby and his men were so out of the ordinary that they simply challenge belief and surpass comprehension. In the capture of General Stoughton, two of his staff officers and thirty other prisoners, in the midst of the Federal division, and removing them and their equipment and fifty-eight horses into Confederate lines without the loss of a man, appears impossible.

With a small body of men, he passed the rear of Sheridan's army in the valley of Virginia, and after a brisk skirmish, captured and brought away General Duffie of the Federal Army. With less than one hundred men he made a forced march into the enemy's lines at night, captured many prisoners, derailed a train, destroyed it, and secured as his prey two paymasters, who had in their possession one hundred and sixty-eight thousand dollars in United States currency. Refusing to take anything himself, he divided this money amongst his followers and each one with him on this expedition received twenty-one hundred dollars.

With three hundred men he rode to the rear of Sheridan's army in the valley of Virginia and attacked in broad daylight a brigade of infantry and two hundred and fifty cavalrymen, guarding a wagon train. He burned one hundred wagons, captured two hundred and eight prisoners and brought away five hundred mules and horses and two hundred head of cattle.

When all these amazing things have been told they would make any one man great, but Mosby had to his credit dozens of other feats almost equally as remarkable.

Colonel Mosby was wounded several times, and in December, 1864, he was desperately injured and was compelled to take a long furlough.

In 1863 there came to Colonel Mosby's command a young Virginian, A. E. Richards. Beginning as a private, by his soldierly qualities he rose to be major. Christened Adolphus Edward Richards, he became known among Mosby's followers as "Dolly." When he succeeded Mosby he was just twenty years of age, and no man in the Confederacy, twenty years old, accomplished more or exhibited a nobler courage or more remarkable skill and enterprise.

From December, 1864, until April, 1865, was one of the most strenuous periods of Mosby's command. The Federal Army was then engaged around Richmond, and this left a hundred miles' space for the operation of these aggressive cavaliers. For months, while Mosby was off, wounded, Major Richards not only took up but efficiently carried on his work. Two of the fights in which he commanded were used by Colonel George Taylor Denison, of Canada, in his work on "Modern

Cavalry," published in 1868, to illustrate the superiority of the revolver as a weapon for cavalry.

Just at this time, Colonel Harry Gilmor, who enjoyed a wide reputation as a partisan leader in Northern Virginia and Maryland, had been surprised and made prisoner. The Federals, encouraged by this success, undertook to capture Major Richards and scatter Mosby's men.

General Merritt, then in charge of the Federal cavalry operating in "Mosby's Confederacy," sent the same detail which had caught Gilmor to hunt down Richards and his followers. The party comprising this force numbered two hundred and fifty men and was in charge of Major Thomas Gibson of the 14th Pennsylvania Cavalry. This officer, in the past, had shown that he was not only brave but resourceful, and his superiors hoped as well as expected that he would do great things on this expedition. If he could catch Major Richards and a part of his command, it meant peace in the Federal rear, and the release of many thousands of men for action at the front. Promotion was sure to follow success, and the Federal leader dreamed of becoming a brigadier and winning a renown that would make him famous.

Attracted by the adventurous nature of the expedition and also lured by the hope of success in the work, two of Merritt's staff officers, Captain Martindale and Lieutenant Baker, volunteered to aid in this scout. This command crossed the Shenandoah River at night. A few miles away from the river, at Paris, in Fauquier County, the force was divided. Major Gibson took with him the men of his own regiment, which comprised one-half of the command, and placed the other half, from the 1st New York Cavalry, in charge of Captain Snow. These forces separated with the understanding that they would make wide circuits through the country, would gather prisoners and seize horses, and meet at Upperville at daylight, six miles from Paris. A couple of deserters from the 12th Virginia regiment acted as guides for the two detachments. Through the report of a spy, Captain Snow learned that Major Richards had come that night to his father's house, near Upperville, and the captain felt it would be a great feather in his cap if he could make the leader of Mosby's command a prisoner. This was what Major Gibson had been chiefly sent to do, and the Federal captain calculated if he could do this, he would win the applause and gratitude of his countrymen. They reached "Green Garden," the Richards' ancestral home, at one o'clock in the morning. Without warning or signal of any kind the Federal soldiers surrounded the house and the leader knocked for admittance at the front door. Hearing was very acute in those days where Mosby's men slept, and the knock, although at first not very heavy, awoke Major Richards, Captain Walker and Private Hipkins, who were together spending the night under the hospitable roof. The moon was shining with brilliance; not a cloud obscured its brightness. The ground was covered with snow. When the Confederates looked through the blinds, they saw the yard filled with Federal soldiers. On other occasions, when the odds were not so great, Major Richards and some of his companions had shot their way out, but he dared not try this experiment this time, for it meant almost certain death. To meet such emergencies, the Richards family had provided a trap door in the floor of the family room. Major Richards had only time to seize his pistols and his field glasses, and his companions hastily caught up their arms, and all went scurrying down through the trap door into the space under the sills. This trap door was in the lower floor and covered with an oil carpet, over which a bed was rolled. The Federals remained silent for a few moments, knocked again with more fury, and upon forcing themselves into the house, the men in blue found Major Richards' uniform, his boots with the spurs attached, his white hat with its black ostrich plume, and they chuckled and said to themselves, "We have caught him at last." Forcing the father of Major Richards to furnish them candles they searched the house over and over again. They went from cellar to garret and from garret to cellar. One officer suggested that in order to make sure of their game they burn the house, but another, with nobler instincts and better impulses, protested so vigorously that this plan was abandoned. For two hours they scrutinized every portion of the house, the outbuildings, the stables, the cabins, but all in vain, and they finally concluded that by some strange sport of chance their victims had escaped; and they mounted their horses and rode away to Upperville.

The hours of this search were moments of sore trial to the three Confederates under the floor. A sneeze, a cough, would betray their hiding place. Discovery meant prison—maybe death—and certainly retirement from the work in which they delighted and which gave them the consciousness of service to the country to which they had offered their fortunes and their lives. Minutes lengthened into days. The tread of the searching Federals echoed ominously into the silence and darkness of their place of refuge. Their hearts beat strong and fast—so furiously that they feared they might reveal their presence to their enemies. Huddled close together, with a trusty pistol in each hand, they waited for what fate might bring. They reviewed over and over again in their minds what they should do, if found. Should they open fire and sell their lives as dearly as possible, or by sudden rush seek to run the gauntlet of their foes, and thus bring ruin and the torch upon their family and friends, or accept a long and baneful imprisonment. In the gloom and dread of their prison, they could hear every word that was spoken. The curses and threats to the father and mother cut deep into their hearts, and they longed for a chance to resent the insults that were heaped upon the inmates of the home. Only an inch of wood separated them from their pursuers, and thus through two long hours they listened, watched—even prayed—that they might not be found. The torture of body and mind became almost unbearable, and they questioned if they should not rise up, push the trap door ajar, open fire, and rush away in the din and confusion such an attack was sure to bring. Each moment that passed they realized added new chances for escape, and though moments seemed years, with hearts for every lot, they bided the end.

Captain Snow and his men rode to the place of rendezvous. There, fortunately or unfortunately, the Federals found a barrel of apple brandy. It was a bitter cold night, and after taking a little brandy they all took some more and a large number of the men became intoxicated. Captain Snow decided that the best thing for him to do was to hurry back through Paris and cross the Shenandoah, lest when the sun rose, Mosby's men might turn out in large numbers and destroy him, with his force weakened by their potations.

Suspecting a ruse, the Richards family looked well in every direction to see that all the Federals had gone, and that none were lurking in the shadows of the farm structures. They waited, and then waited some more, to be sure that there was no mistake about their departure, and then the bed was rolled back, the trap door raised, and Major Richards and his two companions, called by those above, hastily emerged from their hiding place. Though their uniforms were carried away by their enemies as a trophy, they felt that they were not without some compensation. Their horses, which had been turned loose in a distant pasture, had neither been seen or captured.

They greeted their steeds with affectionate pats on their noses and sincerely congratulated themselves that these had been spared them in the very close call which had passed their way. The Confederate commander immediately sent Captain Walker and Private Hipkins in different directions with urgent orders to all the men to follow in the track of the enemy. This they could easily do by the moonlight. All three rode at highest speed in different directions to tell the news. The steeds were not spared. Haste was the watchword of the call to comrades once found. Each was urged to spread the news in the plain and on the mountain sides, and to let nothing stay them in the ride for vengeance and retribution. The Federals had left a well-marked trail, and this made pursuit sure and rapid. Those following were told that it was the plan to strike the enemy before they could recross the Shenandoah, and that they must ride fiercely, halt not, and be prepared for onslaught, pursuit and battle.

Captain Snow rode hard and fast, and he got across the river before the sun was up. Major Gibson was not so fortunate. With one hundred and thirty-six men, when the Confederates under the urgent call of the couriers that were sent in every direction began to get together, Gibson was still on the turnpike leading through Ashby's Gap across the Blue Ridge Mountains. They had not gotten down to the foot of the mountains and were just ahead of Major Richards and the men that he and his companions had so quickly summoned. There was no time to count or figure the odds. This incursion must be resented and few or many, Richards resolved to attack wherever he found the foe. He had fought as great odds before, and the extraordinary experience of the night had quickened his taste for battle and blood. When he came in touch with the Federals, he had only twenty-eight men. Five to one had no terrors for these galloping cavaliers, and Major Richards determined to make an attack, be the consequences what they would. In the meantime, ten others came up, and now he had one to four.

The turnpike at Ashby's Gap winds its way up the mountain side by a succession of short curves. Major Richards arranged his men to press an attack on the enemy while they were passing around these curves, so that his real strength would be concealed. The Federal officer, uncertain what might happen in this country, but sure that dangers were lurking in every quarter, had increased his rear guard to forty men, under the command of Captain Duff of the 14th Pennsylvania. A sight of the bluecoats aroused every Mosby man to impetuous and furious action. They longed to resent some rough handling that had been given their comrades a few days before and they bitterly remembered with indignation the treatment accorded their associates, and above all they desired to serve notice on their invaders that it was a risky business to hunt Mosby's men in their chosen haunts. The Confederates rode down in a furious, headlong charge around the bend of the road and received a volley from the Federal rear guard. This did no damage, but the Federals broke into a gallop; with disordered ranks and shattered files they all scrambled away for safety, and undertook to reach the main force. The Confederates, spurring and whooping and yelling, dashed in among these retreating Federals and used their six shooters with tremendous effect. The Federals could not fire their longer guns. There was no chance to turn, and the rear files felt the pitiless onslaught of the Confederate column, which was riding so furiously and bent on destroying their fleeing foes. The shooting was almost altogether on the side of the Confederates.

At the top of the mountains was Mt. Carmel Church. Here the Baptists of the neighborhood hitherto were accustomed to come and worship long before the war. Its peaceful surroundings and its memories of God's service were not in harmony with the rude and savage war scenes enacted about it on this wintry morn. The men who rode at that hour with Richards were not thinking of the dead, who in the quiet and peace of the country churchyard were waiting Heaven's call for the resurrection. They were now dealing only with the living, and those living who had invaded their country, ravaged their homes, and sought to destroy their liberty. Courage nerved every arm, valor moved every heart. They thought only of punishing their foes and bringing ruin and destruction on these men who had oftentimes, with ruthless barbarity, inflicted grievous wrongs upon their kinsmen and countrymen.

The turnpike passed in front of the church. Upon the road Major Gibson drew up his men in column. When they heard the firing and saw the galloping cavalrymen, they did not at first understand the situation, but as the surging crowd came closer they observed the Federals and Confederates in undistinguishable confusion. As the Confederates were riding toward the rear guard and these were in a gallop, the latter could not use their carbines. At the gait they were going it was impossible to aim and fire with the least assurance of hitting anybody.

The pursuit was rapid and fierce. The fleeing enemy were helpless. The Confederates were moved to savage onslaught and resolved to kill and slay with all the abandon that war creates. There were few of the Confederate riders that did not have some wrong to avenge, and to these there was no better time than the present. There were at first no calls for surrender. There was no chance for parley. War meant fighting, and fighting meant killing those who opposed. The Federals had no chance to turn and ask for their lives. The time in this battle had not yet come for this cry. The Confederates rode into the files of the Federals with their pistols in hand; they shot as they rode, and they made no distinction among their foes. When one file of the Confederates exhausted their shots another took their place. There was no let up in punishing the fleeing Federals. When the loads were all used, they reversed their revolvers and knocked their foes from their steeds with the butt end of their weapons. The hotly pursued rear guard, under Captain Duff, had no time to tell Major Gibson of what had happened. The turnpike went down the mountain, and that was open. If they turned aside they knew not what might come, and when they saw Major Gibson's men drawn up in line ready for the fray, it came into their minds that he was better prepared than they were to deal with these men in gray who were riding and firing with devilish vehemence, so the rear guard galloped on by.

It was a perplexing sight to see these men of opposite sides thus mingling in combat, and the soldiers in Major Gibson's line looked with amazement at the confusion, pursuit and flight.

The men of the rear guard had no time to inform Major Gibson of the situation; the men with Major Richards were not disposed to pass them by, and the thirty-eight Confederates responded to the command to turn and attack the column waiting by the roadside. The men with Richards veered to the right and galloped into the midst of Gibson's men, pushed their revolvers into the faces of the surprised Federals and opened a furious and murderous attack.

The assault was so unexpected and so savage that it disorganized Major Gibson's line. Richards' men broke through the column and severed it in twain, and then a panic struck the Federal force. Its men, demoralized, quickly followed the madly fleeing Federal rear guard down the mountain side. Another chance was now opened up. It was seven miles to the Shenandoah River, and the Federals, unless they re-formed, could expect no respite or safety until this stream was passed. It would require an hour for the Federals, in this race for life, to reach the ford, and until then there was little hope of escape from danger, capture and death.

The Federals could not use their carbines with one hand, while the Confederates could hold their bridles with their left hands and fire their revolvers with their right. Part of Major Gibson's men were shot down before they could even offer resistance or turn in flight. In an instant, the Federals began to give way and started down the side of the mountain, along which only two men could ride abreast. The moment the retreat was begun it became headlong. Again and again brave officers in blue attempted to stay the flight. A few men would halt by the wayside, but the feeling of the hour with the Federals was to escape, and it was impossible to get enough Federals together to stop the stampede.

As the Confederate advance guard fired their revolvers into the backs of the retreating foe, they would either drop back and reload their weapon, or else those behind them who had full cylinders would ride up and continue the fire into the fleeing enemy. In the wild chase of the Federals the Confederates observed one on a dun horse. He was brave and was fighting desperately to protect the rear of his men, and urging them to halt and face their foe. When Major Richards observed that the efforts of this Federal soldier were having some effect upon his comrades, he called to two of his soldiers, Sidney Ferguson and Charles Dear, to "kill the man on the dun horse." This person had not bargained for this singling out of himself as a target for Confederate shots. When these ominous words fell upon his ears, he put spurs to his horse and in a reckless frenzy forged his way past his comrades and was not afterwards seen in the rout. The two Confederates who were endeavoring to capture or kill the man on the dun horse, at this point made Lieutenant Baker of General Merritt's staff a prisoner. This rapid and relentless following was continued for seven miles down the narrow road, and it only ended on the banks of the Shenandoah River. Scattered along the highway were wounded and dead animals. Thirteen Federal troopers were still in death on the roadside. Sixty-four prisoners were taken and more than ninety horses captured. Captain Duff, the commander of the rear guard, was among the wounded prisoners. Among the revolvers captured was one with Colonel Harry Gilmor's name carved upon the guard. Reading this inscription, Major Richards asked Lieutenant Baker, his prisoner, how the Federals happened to have this pistol, and he was then informed for the first time that Colonel Gilmor had been captured.

Major Gibson, the Federal commandant, was among the few who escaped. He reported his misfortune to General Merritt. It is published in Series 1, Volume 46, Part 1, Page 463, of the Records of the Rebellion. He said:

"I placed Captain Duff in charge of the rear guard, which consisted of forty men. I made the rear guard so strong, in proportion to the size of my command, owing to the enemy's repeated and vigorous attacks on it. I was at the head of the column, and turned around in order to observe the condition of the column, and looking to the rear, I observed several men hold up their hands and make gestures which I supposed were intended to inform me that the rear was attacked. I immediately ordered the command, 'right into line.'

"No sooner had I issued these commands than I saw Captain Duff and his party at the rear of the small party who marched in the rear of the led horses. Captain Duff's command was coming at a run. I saw rebels among and in the rear of his party, charging. I ordered the command forward, fired a volley and ordered a charge, which the men did not complete. Captain Duff in the meantime was trying to rally his men in the rear of my line. Before his men had reloaded their pieces, I had fired another volley and ordered another charge.... The charge was met by one from the enemy and the command was broken. The men had no weapons but their carbines, and these were extremely difficult to load, and inefficient in the melee that ensued. I made every effort, as did Captain Duff and Captain Martindale and Lieutenant Baker, of the corps staff, to re-form the men, but our efforts were fruitless. The rebels had very few sabres, but were well supplied with revolvers, and rode up to our men and shot them down, without meeting more resistance than men could make with carbines. There was a small ridge overlooking both parties, through which the path led. I rode up to the side of this and formed the advance guard, which had returned to aid me. The enemy were amidst the men, and both parties were so mixed up that it was impossible to get the men in line. As fast as the men could force their horses into the path, where many of the men were crowded together, they broke for the river. I waited until I was surrounded, and only a half a dozen men left around; the balance had retreated toward the river, or were killed, wounded or captured. Captain Martindale, as he left, said to me: 'It is useless to attempt to rally the men here; we'll try it farther on.' I tried to ride to the front. Men were crowded into the path by twos and threes where there was really only room for one to ride. Men were being thrown and being crushed as they lay on the ground, by others; they were falling from their horses from the enemy's fire in front and rear of me. I rode past about twenty of the men and again tried to rally the men, but all my efforts were fruitless.

"... I was ordered to surrender, two of the enemy in advance endeavoring

275

to beat me off my horse with their pistols.... I reached the river; my horse fell several times in it, but at last I got across. Captain Martindale forced most of the men across to halt and form here, and cover the crossing of the few who had reached the river. Captain Martindale, myself, two scouts and twelve men were saved. We waited to see if more would come, but none came; eight had crossed and arrived at camp before us."

Major Gibson, in accounting for his disaster, says that his men being armed with carbines alone were "unable to engage in a melee successfully with an enemy armed with at least two revolvers to the man; also, I didn't know of the attack until I observed the rear guard coming in at full flight, mixed up with and pursued by the enemy." He concluded his report by asking for a "court of inquiry at the earliest practicable moment."

Colonel George Taylor Denison, who long held a leading commission as a Canadian Cavalry officer, in his book on "Modern Cavalry," describes the results of this battle as one of the most remarkable in the history of cavalry warfare. He asserts the fight of Mosby's men at Mt. Carmel Church demonstrated the superiority of the pistol and revolver above all other weapons in cavalry combat, when these are in the hands of men who know how to use them.

The Confederates pursued the fleeing foe right up to the Shenandoah River. With his limited force Major Richards deemed it unwise to cross that stream. He marched back with his followers over the Blue Ridge Mountains to Paris, a little town in the northernmost part of Fauquier County. In this immediate neighborhood, and about Upperville, there had been many engagements between cavalry on both sides. Some of the severest cavalry fighting of the war occurred in this vicinity a few days after the Battle of Fleetwood Hill. Stuart and Pleasanton were for three days in contact about Upperville, Middleburg and Aldie, but none of these, considering the number engaged, were so brilliant as this conflict between Major Gibson and Major Richards. Only two Confederates were wounded and none killed. This gallant fight was complimented by General Lee in a dispatch to the War Department.

As the Federals left the home of Major Richards' father, they took with them his uniform and his other trappings. When he emerged from the trap door there was nothing left for him to wear. The Federal soldiers had taken everything that they could lay their hands upon, hoping thereby to make the Major ride thereafter with a limited wardrobe. They wished also to exhibit them as a trophy won from Mosby's men.

Searching around, Major Richards found an old-fashioned, high top, black felt hat, badly worn and with many holes around the brim. He managed to secure a suit of brown Kentucky jeans and a pair of laborer's boots which had been discarded by some farm hand. Lacking an overcoat, his mother pinned her woolen shawl about his shoulders. It was not a very attractive garb. It might have served in a pinch for an infantryman, but it did not sit well upon a dashing cavalryman.

When Richards' command reached Paris the Federal prisoners had been corralled in an old blacksmith shop. While resting there the Confederate commander was informed that one of the prisoners desired to speak with him. When Major Richards arrived at the blacksmith shop, the courier indicated a handsomely dressed young officer as the one who had sent the message seeking an interview. The Confederate commander asked why he had been sent for. The Federal officer, surprised at the appearance of the Confederate, not then twenty-one years of age, said to Major Richards: "I desire to speak to the commanding officer." Major Richards, in his pride of achievement, forgot the sorry appearance he was making in the cast-off clothing of the farm hand, and calmly looking the Federal in the eye, he said to him: "I am the commanding officer." The lieutenant, amazed, gazed carefully at the stripling, so grotesquely clad. He was too astounded to be able to speak. Waiting a brief time, Major Richards, in order to relieve the embarrassment, said, "Well, what is it you want?" The Federal lieutenant then informed the major that there was a captain among the prisoners who was severely wounded, and he wished to know if he could not be properly cared for. The solicitude of the wounded man's comrade appealed to the finer sentiments of the Confederate. Learning the name of the Federal captain, he directed him to be paroled and removed to the village hotel and placed under the care of the neighborhood physician, and directed that the bills for medical attention and board be sent to him for payment.

After this preliminary had been arranged, Major Richards turned to the lieutenant and said, "I notice you are wearing a staff officer's uniform;" to which response was made: "Yes, I am a lieutenant on General Merritt's staff." Then the Confederate commander asked, "How did you happen to be in this command?" The Federal replied that he had been sent with the orders under which Major Gibson was to make this raid, and he asked General Merritt to permit him to go along just for the fun of it; to which the Confederate replied: "I hope, Lieutenant, you have enjoyed it more than your surroundings seem to indicate."

The wounded officer was Captain Duff, who had commanded the rear guard. He speedily recovered and was permitted to return to his home. In later years when statements were made that Mosby had mistreated his prisoners, the grateful captain made a vigorous defense of Mosby and his men, and extolled both their humanity and their mercy.

Chapter XVIII

MORGAN'S CHRISTMAS RAID, DECEMBER 22, 1862, TO JANUARY 2, 1863

The distance between Nashville and Murfreesboro is thirty miles. For sixty days after assuming command of the Federal forces at Nashville, General Rosecrans was making his preparations to advance south. The Confederate Army was at Murfreesboro. The center, under General Leonidas Polk, around the town; the right wing, under General McCown, at Readyville, ten miles east of Murfreesboro; and the left wing at Triune and Eaglesville, under General W. J. Hardee, ten miles west of Murfreesboro. These comprised the entire Confederate Army called the "Army of Tennessee." It was in front of the Federal forces, styled the "Army of the Cumberland," and covered the lines around Murfreesboro.

General Rosecrans took with him out of Nashville forty-seven thousand men. He had seventy-five hundred at Nashville, thirty-five hundred at Gallatin and four thousand at Bowling Green, Kentucky, and Clarksville, Tennessee. General Bragg, all counted, had thirty-eight thousand men to resist the Federal advance.

Between Murfreesboro and Nashville there was a macadam road. Along this, Rosecrans advanced, and it took him four days to get close enough to Murfreesboro to justify an attack on the part of the Confederates. The outlook to the Federals was flattering. On the afternoon of the 30th, General Palmer, who was commanding the Union vanguard, telegraphed that he was "in sight of Murfreesboro and the enemy was running." On the next day, he discovered that this was a great mistake, and when he felt the impact of the Confederates on the 31st, he realized that if "the men in gray were running," they had suddenly changed their mind and their ways. The four days consumed by Rosecrans in making this twenty miles were full of intense activities. Generals Wheeler and Wharton of the Confederate cavalry were the potent factors in delaying and embarrassing the Federal movements.

No one in the Confederate service knew better than General Wheeler

279

how to obstruct an advancing foe. On the 26th, 27th, 28th and 29th, he harassed and assailed the Federals at every opportunity and made them hesitant and extremely cautious.

At midnight, on the 29th of December, General Wheeler was ordered by General Bragg to ride around the Federal Army. It was only a thirty-five mile dash, but it had much of excitement, danger and difficulty. On the morning of the 30th, Wheeler reported that he had captured a brigade train and fifty prisoners. At Lavergne, a few hours later, he took seven hundred prisoners and destroyed an immense train. This carried with it a loss to the Federals in supplies and munitions of many hundreds of thousands of dollars. Nearby, at Rock Springs, he caught another train. At Nolensville he captured still another and three hundred prisoners, and then without any disturbance from his foes, he proceeded to take his place on the left wing of the Confederate Army. In these brief hours he had swung the circle and deeply impressed on his opponents that they might expect trouble at every step of their way.

At dawn of the day following, General McCown opened the Battle of Murfreesboro. General Wheeler, with his cavalry, joined in the attack on the Federals and aided in driving them two miles. General Wharton, with the other portion of the Southern cavalry, was ordered also to ride to the rear of the enemy. He captured hundreds of prisoners, and as if defying all rules of safety, he turned the head of his column due north, in the direction of Nashville. He destroyed many wagons and made numerous prisoners. A large majority of those he safely delivered within the Confederate lines. The Federals had good guns; Wharton, inferior ones. He immediately provided his two thousand riders with the improved arms which had been taken from the Federals, and then returned to the rear of the enemy, passing entirely around the Federal forces. These successes inspired every man in Bragg's army with courage and hope. The example of these bold horsemen was contagious, and the infantry were anxious to try their luck with the invading columns.

Not satisfied with these adventures, on the 1st day of January, General Wheeler with his own and Wharton's cavalry, decided to return to the rear of the Federal Army, where there was such rich reward for his labors. Revisiting Lavergne, he attacked the garrison, burned many wagons and captured a number of infantry and a splendid piece of artillery. Fate was so propitious in all these expeditions and the field for destruction so wide, the same night he again went to Rosecrans' rear, capturing a large number of wagons and horses and prisoners, and by two o'clock the next morning was on the left flank of the army. At nine o'clock on the night of the 1st, he made his last expedition to the Federal rear, and, as before, found his foes easily demoralized and ready to flee or surrender when vigorously and promptly assailed. On the 4th of January, after these adventurous and successful operations, he emerged from his Federal surroundings to find that General Bragg had fallen back. No cavalry in any great battle of the war played a more distinguished part than Wheeler's and Wharton's men at Murfreesboro. Their audacity was only equalled by their success, and it is difficult to comprehend how even the greatest of leaders, with only twenty-nine hundred horsemen, could make such havoc with foes, or move with such ease, celerity and with freedom from disaster, in the rear of an opposing army, when rarely was he at any time more than ten miles from the tents of its commanders. A few hundreds of Federal cavalry properly led and disposed, with such numbers of infantry close by, ought not only to have obstructed Generals Wheeler and Wharton in their marches, but should have forced or driven them discomfited within their own lines. In the battle the Federal losses in killed and wounded was eight thousand, seven hundred and seventy-eight and three thousand six hundred and seventy-three captured, making a total of twelve thousand four hundred and fifty-one. Rosecrans also lost twenty-eight pieces of artillery. Bragg, with thirty-eight thousand men, had a loss of ten thousand, two hundred and sixty-six, of which nine thousand were killed and wounded, and about twelve hundred of them were left in the hospitals at Murfreesboro, which later were taken possession of by the Federal Army.

A third of the forces in this battle were from Tennessee. They fought desperately on their native soil, contesting for their homes and firesides, and they suffered a terrific decimation. Cheatham's division, composed entirely of Tennesseeans, had thirty-six per cent wounded or killed. Cleburne's division suffered a like mortality, and Johnson's and Palmer's Tennessee brigades sustained a loss of twenty-nine and a half per cent.

In order to prevent reinforcements at Clarksville, Nashville and Bowling Green from coming to the assistance of Rosecrans, General John H. Morgan was directed by General Bragg on the 22d of December, 1862, to make a raid along the Louisville and Nashville railroad into Kentucky, and, as far as possible, destroy it, so as to break the Federal communications.

Alexandria, in Wilson County, Tennessee, was forty miles east of Nashville. The Federals did not spread out very far from Nashville in this direction, and there was a neutral zone in and around Lebanon, the county seat of Wilson County, to which the Federals and Confederates each now and then came. It was necessary to protect this line in order to prevent danger to Knoxville. It was still in the nominal possession of the Confederacy. South and west of Nashville, Wheeler, Wharton and Forrest were campaigning. Forrest's December raid into West Tennessee had not only demonstrated that he was one of the most ferocious fighters in the Confederate service, but also the tremendous power of cavalry when skillfully handled. He had largely recruited his skeleton regiments, and when he came out, although he had seen hard service, he numbered several hundred more men than when he was ordered, against his judgment, by General Bragg to make the raid, in the face of most inclement weather and with an ill-equipped force. His personal pride had been subordinated to his patriotism, and he was ready to give and do his best for the work now before Bragg.

Morgan was now to be given a chance to try his hand in Kentucky. For some months there had been no material interruption of the Louisville and Nashville railroad, and Rosecrans was using it and the Cumberland River to supply his army at Nashville. General Bragg was perfectly familiar with the preparations that Rosecrans was making for the advance of his army southward, and he knew that a decisive battle could not be long delayed.

General Morgan's name was now on every tongue. His July raid from Knoxville into Kentucky, where he had marched a thousand miles, destroyed millions of dollars worth of property, and terrorized a district three hundred miles long and sixty miles wide, his services during the invasion of Kentucky by General Bragg, and his splendid exhibition of genius demonstrated in covering General Bragg's retreat from Kentucky in October, and the Battle of Hartsville had given him not only a well-deserved but wide reputation. The things he had done were along new lines and everywhere created wonder and admiration. The Battle of Hartsville, one of the most brilliant exploits in the history of the Confederacy, resulted in Morgan's being advanced to brigadier general. Seven days after the Hartsville expedition, General Morgan was married to Miss Ready, of Murfreesboro, among the most brilliant, charming and attractive women of the Southland. There were those at the time

282

who predicted that this marriage, under the circumstances surrounding Morgan's military career, would affect his success. Be this as it may, this splendid woman enthusiastically entered into the military hopes and ambitions of her now greatly distinguished husband, and moved and inspired with the loyalty and courage that filled the hearts of the women of the South, urged rather than restrained the enterprise and activity of her companion.

Morgan always did best when he was allowed to act independently. When operating his own way and managing his campaigns, he was one of the most successful, dangerous and destructive of Confederate cavalry leaders. Full of resource, glorying in adventure, he imbued his men with his marvelous fervor and passionate ardor. Within a few days after his promotion to brigadier general, his forces were materially strengthened. Colonels W. C. P. Breckinridge and Robert G. Stoner each recruited battalions in Kentucky in the fall of 1862. These were now consolidated and thereafter known as the 9th Kentucky Cavalry, with Breckinridge as colonel and Stoner as lieutenant colonel. Toward the end of September Colonel Adam R. Johnson reached Murfreesboro with a regiment which he had recruited in Western Kentucky, of about four hundred men. It had been battered by service, and received rough handling in the Federal lines, but had a splendid organization. Its lieutenant colonel, Robert M. Martin, was confessedly one of the most daring and dashing of the men who wore the Confederate uniform. The brigade was now thirty-nine hundred strong. The misfortunes of war had dismounted some of the troops, and part of them were not fully armed, but all knew that the next raid would remedy these deficiencies. Morgan divided his regiments into two brigades, the first under command of General Basil W. Duke, Colonel of the 2d Kentucky, and the second under command of Colonel W. C. P. Breckinridge, of the 9th Kentucky. Colonel A. R. Johnson was at this time considered the ranking colonel, and when offered by General Morgan the command of the second brigade, declined it, preferring to act as colonel of the 10th Kentucky. Later, however, he accepted promotion to a brigadier.

Then, many believed that Colonel Roy S. Cluke, of the 8th Kentucky, should have been made brigadier general, and it is said that his raid into Kentucky, which followed in February and March, 1863, was projected in order to equalize things on account of Colonel Cluke being ranked at this time by Colonels Breckinridge and Johnson. Both Cluke and

Johnson hesitating, Morgan appointed Breckinridge to command the second brigade. The first was composed of the 2d Kentucky, Duke's, the 3d Kentucky, Gano's, the 8th Kentucky, Cluke's, with Palmer's battery of four pieces. The second was composed of the 9th Kentucky, Breckinridge's, the 10th Kentucky, Johnson's, the 11th, Chenault's, and the 14th Tennessee under Colonel Bennett. These had a Parrott gun and two mountain howitzers. By November, 1862, Morgan's forces had reached in equipment and numbers a very high grade of efficiency. True, there were some unmounted and unarmed men, but these could be used as horse holders, and as out of every four men, one must hold horses, when four thousand cavalrymen should go into battle, one thousand of them would have to remain at the rear with the animals while the other three-fourths dismounted to fight.

For a few days preceding the 21st, the farriers were busy shoeing the horses. Equipments were inspected with minutest scrutiny. Ammunition was counted out, the mounts were carefully examined, as only soldiers and horses that could stand a strenuous and long drawn out expedition were to be taken. These men and beasts were to be subjected to the rigors of storms, travel and cold that would try out the highest resistance of flesh and blood to nature's warfare. These preparations the rank and file knew portended immediate and intense activity. The division then comprised a remarkable body of young men. It represented a full share of the chivalry and flower of the states of Kentucky and Tennessee. Lawyers, physicians, farmers, clerks, and here and there clergymen were either officers or in the ranks. A large proportion of these were liberally educated. Intelligent and patriotic and full of the spirit of adventure and romance which attached to cavalry, they were ready for any service and always would go without fear where duty called. They were proud, and that made them brave. The vast majority of the men were under twenty-five years of age, and youth always makes the best soldiers if the material and leadership are good.

On the morning of December 22d, in and around the little town of Alexandria, the lines of the divisions were formed. The Kentuckians sat astride their horses most anxiously, longing for the command to move. They looked and acted like men who understood that work was cut out for them.

In a brief while a general order from their leader was read. There was no longer any reason for concealment. In a few moments they knew they were going into Kentucky, and the hope and promise of home-going caused the blood to tingle in their veins and their hearts to beat with quickened rapture and joy. These boys could guess the path they would follow, and the confidence of their commander added new courage to their hearts. He told them candidly where they were going; he reminded them who they were, and he impressed upon them what was expected of them. Prolonged and vociferous cheering was heard when the order was read, and the hills and the woods were filled with the glad shouts of these exiled youths who were now to turn their faces homeward. With wild hurrahs they expressed their delight, and with exultant outcries gave dauntless response to the call of their chieftain. The one Tennessee regiment felt the spirit of the hour. Though going from home, they caught the delirium of joy that thrilled these horsemen, now commencing one of the great marches of a great war.

From Alexandria for some distance there was a good road. In a little over two hours the column had covered eight miles. Suddenly the stillness of the march was disturbed. The men far up in front heard, away to the rear, triumphant yells and tremendous cheering. They knew what this meant. Morgan was coming. Alongside the column, with a splendid staff, magnificently mounted, superbly dressed, riding like a centaur, bare-headed, with plumed hat in his right hand, waving salutations to his applauding followers, the general came galloping by. Pride and happiness were radiated from every feature of his joyous face. He was now a brigadier general, and new opportunity was opened to add to his already superb fame. He had just been married to one of the most beautiful and gracious women of the South. As he released himself from her tender embrace and felt the touch of her lovely lips upon his own and saw the tear-drops trickle down her cheek, painted by the delicate touch of nature with most exquisite colors, he caught an inspiration that lifted him up to the sublimest heights of human heroism, and imbued him with a valor that stirred every fibre of his soul, and made him feel that with him there must be victory or death. He had with him four thousand Kentucky boys, well armed, for so large a force well mounted, and there spread out before his enraptured fancy scenes of conquest and glory that filled his mind with ecstasy and delight. There was in such an hour of splendor no omen of the gloom and darkness of the future, and no signal came to warn of the time when, a few months later, by war's harsh and cruel edict, his hopes would be shattered, when his dead body would be

285

mutilated by his vengeful foes and the weeping wife and an unborn babe would feel forever the rude shock of the awful bereavement.

No time was now to be wasted. Every moment must count. To do the work that he had undertaken and to do it well meant that he must ride like the whirlwind and march like the storm. Biting cold, drenching rains, chilling sleet, were not to be considered. Rapid night rides, days without food, sleepless watchings, ceaseless vigils, constant battle, fording or swimming rivers, and defiance of nature's protest and barriers, held out no terrors for these high-spirited riders. All believed that leaders and men were invincible and that a generous fate would protect and guard them in whatever dangers and difficulties the fortunes of war would bring, on the campaign to which their country and Cause had bid them come.

By the night of the 22d, the first brigade had forded the Cumberland River at Sand Shoal, and at dawn the second had crossed the stream. There were not enough rations to require long delays for feeding. The horses ravenously munched the meagre supply of corn and fodder that had been impressed to satisfy their hunger. By sundown the column had covered thirty miles. There was heavy work ahead. They would meet and attack Federal garrisons who were in stockades and forts. This made it necessary to have the artillery; but the guns, however important, slowed down the speed of the march.

By the 6th of May, 1862, Andrew Johnson had spoken savagely of Morgan and his men. In writing to Horace Maynard, Member of Congress, he said: "Morgan's marauding gang should not be admitted to the rules of civilised warfare, and the portion of his forces taken at Lebanon should not be held as prisoners of war. I hope you will call attention of Secretary Stanton to the fact of their being a mere band of freebooters." The seven months that had transpired since this utterance had not increased the good opinion of the Federals concerning Morgan's brigades. The Union forces were so much afraid of General Morgan and talked so much of his exploits and his expeditions that they created in the minds of the public, who did not sympathize with the South, a most exaggerated and ridiculous idea of him and his men. They were singing and talking of "Morgan, Morgan and his terrible men."

By the 24th of December Morgan had reached up into Barren County, five miles from Glasgow and ninety miles from the place where he had started. Two companies were sent forward to secure information of conditions at Glasgow. One of these was commanded by Captain William

E. Jones of the 9th Kentucky Cavalry. About this time the advance guard of a battalion of the 2d Michigan Cavalry entered the place upon the opposite side from that which Jones had come in. As both parties were looking for trouble, it did not take long to bring on a fight, and they met about the center of the town. Jones was mortally wounded, and William Webb, of Breckinridge's regiment, one of the best men in Kentucky, fell in the conflict. In the melee Lieutenant Samuel O. Peyton, of the 2d Kentucky, was wounded, having been shot in the arm and hip. His foes, gathering around him, demanded his surrender. He fired his revolver, killing one of his assailants, grappled with the second, threw him to the ground and stabbed him to death with his knife. The Federals were not expecting such a reception or such resistance, and so within a very few minutes, they were driven away. Twenty-two prisoners, including a captain, were captured and paroled. The gage of battle had been thrown down and conflict must be expected at any moment. The command was in a territory where both garrisons and obstructing and opposing forces would be vigilant and aggressive, and where every energy of the Federal authorities was put under stern requisition to harass and delay or destroy this Confederate force, which on mischief and devastation bent, in the face of winter's defiance, and far from supports, was offering battle's wage to those who stood in their pathway of ruin and destruction.

The roads had now become better. There was a turnpike leading from Glasgow toward Louisville. Mysteriously Morgan's coming had been known to the citizens. The entire length of the Louisville & Nashville Railroad was thickly studded with stockades, and every bridge of any importance had a full guard, and towns like Elizabethtown and Munfordsville, Bowling Green and Shepherdsville were all protected by strong garrisons. The great importance of the Louisville & Nashville Railroad as a means of feeding and supplying the Federal Army at Nashville and below, demanded that it should be fully and thoroughly defended, and no small force could hope to avail against this thorough preparation on the part of the Federals for the guarding of this essential highway.

Captain Quirk, in command of the advance guard and the scouts, had not gone very far until he found a battery across the road and supports on either side. An impetuous attack was the answer to this challenge, and it did not require very long to brush this obstruction out of the Confederate path. Johnson's regiment had been sent in the direction of Munfordsville to threaten that place, but General Morgan turned his forces south and east of the Green River, which was not forded without much difficulty. The banks were steep and muddy and the water high enough to give great inconvenience. As there was a long railroad bridge at Munfordsville, a strong Federal garrison had been gathered at that point to defend it. His force was not large enough to assault the earthworks protecting this structure. General Morgan had determined to destroy the trestles at Muldraugh Hill, six miles north of Elizabethtown. The damage there would more than equal any he could inflict at Munfordsville. It was of importance that he should create upon the minds of the Federals the impression that he would assail the garrison at Munfordsville and force them to concentrate there, when his men should reach the Louisville & Nashville Railroad between Munfordsville and Elizabethtown, and bridges and culverts torn up, there need not be any particular worry about the Federal forces in the rear. Infantry would have to be moved along the railroad and they would stand a slight chance to catch Morgan and his horsemen on lines removed from the thoroughfare. Little sleep was allowed that night. On the morrow General Morgan had mapped out great work. He intended to take the stockades at Bacon's Creek and Nolin River and destroy the bridges there. During the night a tremendous rain had fallen, and all day it still kept coming down in torrents. The cannon and caissons in the mud and slush made slow progress and prevented very rapid movement. A regiment had been despatched to Bacon's Creek bridge, and at eleven o'clock the cannonading there was distinctly heard. It was necessary to reduce the stockade and capture the Federal garrison at that point in order to prevent the Federals from sending new troops to Nashville.

The force sent thither not returning delayed the march, and it was three o'clock before it got under way. General Morgan took the reinforcements that had arrived from the feint toward Munfordsville, and he went over with these to learn what was the cause of the detention at Bacon's Creek. Upon his arrival, peremptory demand was made by him for surrender, and the Federal forces under Captain James of the 19th Illinois promptly complied. The stockade was immediately burned and the torch applied to the trestle. The garrison at Nolin was less disposed to fight than those at Bacon's Creek, and these laid down their arms without resistance. The stockade and bridge were consigned to the flames. Great fires were built along the tracks of the Louisville & Nashville for several miles, the iron rails, torn from the ties, were placed upon these and were warped and bent so as to be unfit for use until carried to a rolling mill.

On the morning of December 27th General Morgan learned of the presence of a considerable force at Elizabethtown, and moved over to that place. When within a short distance of the town a most ludicrous communication was sent out under a flag of truce. It ran somewhat like this: "Elizabethtown, Kentucky, December 27th, 1862. To the commander of the Confederate forces: I have you surrounded and will compel you to surrender. I am, sir, your obedient servant, H. S. Smith, Commander United States Forces." General Morgan smiled and chuckled. He informed the bearer of this extraordinary despatch that he trusted he would convey the impression to his commander that the positions were reversed, that it was the Federal forces that were to surrender and not the Confederates, and he requested their immediate capitulation, to which he received the rather unique reply that "it was the business of a United States officer to fight and not to surrender." As nothing but a fight would satisfy the six hundred and seventy men under command of Colonel Smith, General Morgan prepared to give him what he wanted. Surrounding the town, skirmishers were thrown forward and the position of the enemy developed. He had taken position in brick houses on the outside of the town and resolved to have a street fight. The Federals had no artillery, and the Confederates had seven pieces. It was a very unequal contest. The Confederates marched boldly in. They had seen street fighting before. Colonel Cluke and Lieutenant Colonel Stoner, who later at Mount Sterling in February and March were to win additional fame, entered the town at the head of their men. A few well-directed shells convinced the Federals of the folly of resistance. The gallant Federal colonel still refused to surrender, but his men, rushing out, displayed the white flag, and left him to his fate. Six hundred and fifty-two prisoners, including twenty-five officers, were the result of this fight.

The great prize for which the Confederates were contending was yet six miles away. Two mighty trestles, one nine hundred and one a thousand feet long and ninety feet high, were the means by which the Louisville & Nashville Railroad climbed Muldraugh's Hill and debauched on the Elizabethtown side of that small mountain range. The bridges and trestles heretofore destroyed were small in comparison to these two immense structures. Both of these trestles were defended by garrisons, and both were well fortified. These troops had been especially ordered to fight to the last ditch. Seven hundred men had been placed to guard these giant viaducts. They were the highest and most valuable on the

Louisville & Nashville Railroad, and the Confederates had never been able to reach them before. Full stores had been collected at this point. On this expedition Captains Palmer and Corbett handled the artillery with consummate skill and bravery. Their well-directed shots in a brief while brought both garrisons to terms. The flames ascending high into the air told the story of the victory and triumph of the Confederate forces, and the columns of smoke lifting their shadows up toward the heavens proclaimed to the pursuers that the dreaded calamity had overtaken the all-important trestles which meant so much to the railway, and that they had gone down before the avenging hand of enemies. Small forces were sent out a few miles north toward Shepherdsville and destroyed some unimportant structures. General Morgan had wrecked the road now for something like fifty miles. Nothing inflammable had escaped the touch of his destructive torch. Having accomplished all they had intended to do, with Federal forces south and southeast and others in the path in every direction, he now faced the problem of safely escaping from these foes which beleaguered and beset him on every side. He had now reached one hundred and seventy miles into the enemy's territory. He had destroyed twenty-three hundred feet of bridging and put the railroad out of commission for many weeks.

In cavalry experiences it is sometimes easier to get in than to get out. The whole country south and east of Morgan was aroused. The Federal commanders at Washington and Nashville were beginning to question with vehement pertinacity how Morgan had been allowed to ride so far and do so much damage without serious interruption. It was true that the defenders at Bacon's Creek were not very numerous, that those at Nolin were less so, and that those at Elizabethtown and the Muldraugh trestles had no chance against the well-directed artillery of the Confederates, backed by thirty-five hundred cavalry; but up in Louisville, at Nashville, at Washington, Morgan seemed to be going where he pleased and doing what he pleased. At these centers, so far removed from the scene of his action, it appeared that those who were opposing him, or following, were neither diligent nor brave. The men at Washington, Louisville, or Nashville were not marching in the cold, or riding through the mud and the rain. They could not take in the surroundings of the men who were at work on the spot, and so they became both inquisitive and critical. General Morgan, however, was not underrating the efforts of his foes to minimize the damage he might do or to prevent his escape. Great soldier as he was, he foresaw what he must face and overcome when he turned his face southward and undertook to break through the cordon his enemies were establishing around him. He had before him for outlet a territory sixty miles wide, filled with numerous highways. Nearly all these were merely country roads, which when cut by his artillery and churned by the sixteen thousand feet of the horses his men were riding, would be only streams of mire.

Mud and slush would face him along any line he should march except one, and that was through Bardstown and Springfield, Lebanon and Campbellsville. Lebanon was on the railroad and it could be promptly and largely reinforced. The Confederate chieftain was too great a leader to be trapped. He realized that he must go higher up the Cumberland in the first place, and find another crossing, and in the second place to get out of the line of those who were bent on his destruction. The Federal leaders did not seem to be in a very great hurry. He turned southeast and on the night of the 28th of December camped on the Rolling Fork, a tributary of Salt River. This was a deep and ordinarily a sluggish stream, with high banks. The rain, a few days before, had filled its bed with angry currents and good fords were infrequent, and particularly fords that would let artillery over. There was a peculiar pride in part of the artillery that made the command ready to fight savagely for them. One of the pieces was a Parrott gun, a trophy of their valor at Hartsville. It was called "Long Tom" because of its extreme length. Closely associated with the victory at Hartsville, it became a great pet of the division, and was treasured as a mascot.

In the midst of the exciting surroundings of the campaign, a court martial had been sitting at intervals, as a little leisure could be spared, upon Lieutenant Colonel Huffman, in command of Gano's regiment. General Morgan had given generous terms to those who surrendered at Bacon's Creek, and he was displeased with Colonel Huffman's apparent violation of these terms, and five regimental commanders, Duke, Breckinridge, Cluke, Hutchinson and Stoner, comprised this court. Marching all day and some nights, with an average of forty miles every twenty-four hours, with an occasional diversion of a fight, it was rather difficult for these judges to apportion exact justice to the offending officer. An hour would be taken at night and a little while during the rest of the day, but on this particular morning a full session was held and Huffman was acquitted. As the court martial was writing its finding, couriers came scurrying from the rear with the information that a large Federal force of infantry and cavalry was close at hand and had opened fire. The firing of the pickets and skirmishers was already audible. Some of the troops had crossed the Rolling Fork, but the others were on the same side with the Federals. Cluke's regiment under Major Bullock had been sent to burn a railroad bridge, and to hold the enemy in check, but the enemy did not seem willing to be checked and they vigorously pressed his rear guard. If the fording of the Rolling Fork had been practicable at every point, it would be easy enough for those now defending it to ride across, but when Cluke's men got down to the stream it was found there to be impassable. The fields and roads were full of bluecoats, and they were coming where Morgan's men were. They were not advancing very eagerly, but all the same they were coming. The skirmishers along the fences and in the woods were delaying their progress as much as possible, but formalities seemed to be waived, and the Federals were pressing down upon the men on their side of the stream in large force. The Federal artillery, well managed, got the range of the ford where the Confederates were crossing and was throwing shells with accuracy and rapidity, which was splashing the water along the line where the men in gray must pass. About seven hundred men, including several companies of Cluke's regiment, were on the west side of Rolling Fork. The Federal Army, composed of infantry and cavalry, was closing in upon them. With an enemy in front and the river behind them it looked especially gloomy for the men under Cluke. This 8th Kentucky Cavalry in camp, with a high type of soldierly pride, styled themselves "Cluke's War Dogs," and it looked now as if the "war dogs" were to get all the war that they could possibly desire.

At this moment General Duke was struck on the side of the head by a fragment of a shell and rendered unconscious. A brave and agile soldier sprang behind him and held him on his horse and carried him over the stream. The skirmishers were plugging away at each other at close range. One of the enemy's batteries was proving especially destructive, and Captain Virgil Pendleton of the 8th Kentucky was ordered to charge this battery. He killed the cannoneers or drove them from their guns, and this silenced these destructive agents for a quarter of an hour. This brave captain was struck by an exploding shell from other guns of the enemy and seriously and dangerously wounded. Ninety days later he was killed while charging through the streets of Mount Sterling.

Colonel W. C. P. Breckinridge assumed command of the Confederates on the side with the Federals, and with great skill and gallantry helped bring them out of the perils that were thick around them.

Seconds were lengthened into minutes. The strain was intense. It was a critical moment for the Confederates not yet over the stream. Another assault by the Federals meant capture or death or a plunge into the deep, icy waters of Rolling Fork. At this juncture the Federals suddenly retreated. No one has ever been able to explain this let-up at this opportune time for the advancing hosts, nor been able to guess why the men in blue failed to attack and scatter their foes when victory was so easy and only needed the closing in to insure its certainty.

Hope appeared to be departing, and when it looked darkest, some of Cluke's men, by riding into the stream, had found a possible but difficult ford. This had been experimentally discovered. The emergencies forced the men to ride out into the water. They had no guides, and fortunately someone had found by testing that there was a way of escape, and in the lull the rearguard of the Confederates hurried across the stream. The bulk of the casualties fell to Cluke's regiment. They had sustained their reputation as "war dogs." They were proud that the enterprise of their leaders, their luck, and their courage had brought them safely through.

General Morgan now turned detachments loose upon the bridges upon the Lebanon Branch; some of these were destroyed. This would prevent reinforcements from rapidly reaching Lebanon. The stockade at Boston and other small structures were burned. On the night of the 30th the division camped at Bardstown, and by three o'clock next day it bivouacked at Springfield, nine miles from Lebanon. The fierce cold, the long ride, the severe strain, physical and nervous, demanded a brief halt. The leader realized that Morgan's men were human. He apprehended the seriousness of the situation. Over at Lebanon, stretched far away along the pike up towards Campbellsville and Muldraugh's Hill, the Federals were waiting to contest the only good road by which he could reach the Cumberland River. If he could get around Lebanon to Campbellsville, he calculated that over the pike from Campbellsville to Columbia he could make a forced march that would enable him to outride the Federals, who were taking a short cut from Glasgow and surrounding towns, to head him off from Burksville on the Cumberland River.

The Federals had been massing forces at Lebanon. The glare of the camp fires could be seen from Springfield, where Morgan was resting for the great spurt. Enemies were there in such numbers that General

Morgan dared not attack the town. They were reported eight thousand. Harlan, who had crossed swords with him at Rolling Fork, was in his rear. Colonels Halisy and Hoskins and their eight thousand men were in his front. The night was intensely dark, and the thermometer was below zero. The turnpike between Springfield and Lebanon was full of Federal pickets, backed up by infantry, that were double Morgan's numbers.

Early in the night Colonel A. R. Johnson of the 10th drove in the pickets on the Lebanon road and attacked them with such fierceness that a cavalry regiment which was stationed six miles from Lebanon, on the Campbellsville road, was called in to help defend the town. The withdrawal of this cavalry regiment opened up a possible way of escape for Morgan without a fight. At Springfield there were many friends and sympathizers. They were honest and safe advisers. Had Morgan's men been fresh and his horses not wearied, the situation would have been less perplexing to the dauntless general. From every direction enemies were fast approaching and, stirred deeply by the criticisms of superiors, were closing in to destroy the Confederate leader.

The hour had now come for Morgan again to demonstrate the force of his genius and the extent of his resources. He saw that the best way of escape was the longest way; that he could not whip the eight thousand Federals at Lebanon and he must manage to get around them. He determined to make a detour to the right of Lebanon, pass the Federal Army there, then swing back on to the road which led from Lebanon to Campbellsville and rush to the latter place with all possible speed. He calculated that by outwitting the enemy and by a forced march, he would reach Campbellsville before his escape would be discovered and before the Federals could get in his front to seriously interfere with his going.

An appalling night's experiences were now to face the bold raider and his hardy followers. They were without even hope of succor or support. Here Morgan could rely only upon himself and those who were with him to rid his path of the dangers, which, if he doubted or hesitated, would be unsurmountable.

As the Federals at Lebanon did not come after him he decided to remain at Springfield until eleven o'clock at night. This would give time for sleep for the men and opportunity to rest and feed the beasts. By the hospitable firesides of sympathizers, the Confederates warmed their benumbed limbs and the patient brutes were allowed to feed and munch to their fill. To multiply troubles, the temperature, already cold, had become colder. Sharp, penetrating winds whistled through the naked trees and whirled around the corners of the houses, warning the wise to seek and keep shelter. Wintry blasts notified the soldiers of what might be expected if they dared defy their suggestion. The mercury in the thermometer nestled several degrees below zero and hid far down in the tube as if afraid to expose itself to the cold. Morgan's enemies had not learned exactly where he was, but they knew he was about and they knew that they were in his front.

General Boyle, commander of the Kentucky Department, telegraphed Abraham Lincoln in Washington: "Morgan is fleeing precipitately. He has paid dearly for what he has done." The wires were kept busy by the Federals, prophesying what would happen to the bold raiders. Superiors were assured that disaster was bound to overtake Morgan within a few hours. Fate had decreed that these prophecies were not to be verified.

Everybody knew that really great work had been cut out for the night. No order was required to tell the men of this. The long rest at Springfield of eight hours was a sure augury that a furious night march was in store. The men prepared themselves as best they could. At the hospitable little town of Springfield, in cavalry parlance, "square meals" were available. This meant that one could eat enough at a sitting to tide over forty-eight to seventy-two hours without hunger's interference. A common sense of danger filled the minds of all the soldiers at this resting place. They knew that heavy work was expected, certainly a night's ride, facing the winds that cut to the marrow and cold that struck into the joints, and maybe a battle or attack in the darkness. They had wrapped blankets about their bodies and covered their feet with strips of cloth. The strain was too great for a few, and here and there a man or so had succumbed to the terrific pressure of the elements and had fallen out of line; but in thirty-nine hundred men that such a small number were unable to meet these difficulties was a great tribute to both the physical and mental vigor of these horsemen. They warmed themselves and satisfied their appetites to the limit, and with the bravado of true cavaliers, they bade care flee away and fears begone as they mounted into their saddles. They were not afraid to face any emergency, even all that the dreadful night ahead had in store for man and beast.

The aid of the best available guides was secured. These bundled themselves up as if they were in Lapland. At eleven o'clock on the night of the 30th, General Morgan set out on his journey around his enemies.

He counted darkness as his best ally. It was nine miles from Springfield to Lebanon and nine miles from Lebanon to St. Mary's, where he must pass the Federal trocha, and then it was fifteen miles from St. Mary's to the point where General Morgan could hope in safety to strike the turnpike from Lebanon to Campbellsville. This meant a loss of fifteen miles, with jaded horses and tired men. Before General Morgan left Springfield he had a strong line of skirmishers drive in the Federal pickets. These stacked rails for a mile through the fields and then fired them. The reflection of the flames on the sky caught the eyes of the Federal pickets. The Union commanders came to the conclusion that no men would dare march through the wind and cold of such a night and Morgan was where the flames were blazing, and that on the morrow, to get by, he must engage them in combat. The mud roads which the Confederates must follow to St. Mary's and to Newmarket were uneven, frozen, ragged. The cold was so intense that it partially stupefied the beasts. The men were compelled to dismount to keep themselves from being frost bitten, and walk beside their stumbling steeds. It seemed as if humanity could not stand the dreadful punishment that nature was inflicting upon these intrepid men. The game was too fierce for a few, and these by sheer exhaustion fell by the wayside. The horses in sympathy with their masters hung their heads low. Icicles gathered on their manes and breasts, covered their bridles and halters, and dangled from their nostrils. Ice coated the beards and moustaches of the men. Half the time they walked by their steeds, stamping their feet, swinging their hands and beating their bodies to drive away the stupor which extreme cold imposes upon flesh and blood. There was no loud word spoken. Commands, if given, were uttered in soft tones, and all were directed to ride, walk or march in absolute silence. These things added much to the hardships of the night's work. If they could have jollied each other, or cheered or enlivened the hours with badinage, it would have somewhat relieved the oppressiveness of the continually lengthening miles. The men obeyed the orders in patient submission to the severe calls of the moment, and uncomplainingly bore the burdens that patriotism exacted of them in the dire emergency that war's fortunes had decreed they must endure. Man and beast seemed to be well-nigh overwhelmed with the chilling air. It was a long, long night, and one that no man who had undergone its terrors would ever forget. Morgan's men had suffered many hardships and were yet to know many more, but with one voice they declared that this march around Lebanon to St. Mary's and back to the Campbellsville Pike was the most fearful experience they had ever suffered, except, when ninety days later, they rode the sixty miles from Saylersville to Mount Sterling with Cluke, on March 20th, 1863.

At half past six o'clock day began to dawn. The guides were bewildered or indifferent and had lost their bearings. When the light enabled them to take in the surroundings, it came out that the command had only made something like two miles an hour, and instead of being well on the road towards Campbellsville, they were only two and a half miles from Lebanon. The Federals in camp had laid upon their arms all night. They could sleep and cover up their heads and rest with some degree of comfort in their tents, but they were not astir very early, and they had no accurate knowledge whither Morgan had gone. It was a glad moment when light lifted the burdens from the weary marchers. The sun riding from the east through the clouds assured these nervy horsemen that the terrors of darkness no longer overshadowed them. Once again on the macadam highway, the horses seemed glad and quickened their pace. Increasing speed, with its accelerated motion, brought warmth to their bodies and cheer to their masters' hearts. At nightfall the command was safe at Campbellsville. They pondered over the terribleness of the past night's experiences, but the enemy was behind, and this repaid them for the sufferings and agony they had endured.

On the march up the long hill where the turnpike, by constant but easy and tortuous gradients, reaches the tablelands around Campbellsville, the county seat of Taylor County, occurred one of the real tragedies of the war. Colonel Dennis J. Halisy commanded the 6th Kentucky Federal Cavalry. He had charge of the advance in pursuit of Morgan. He was a bred fighter, young, ambitious, game to the core, and as adventurous as he was game. Halisy was following Morgan's rear guard with the Federal horsemen, picking up the stragglers, if any could be found, and pushing the Confederates as strongly as prudence would allow. Captain Alex. Treble and Lieutenant George B. Eastin were both officers of the 2d Kentucky Confederate Cavalry. These lagged behind the rear guard in search of adventure, anxious to show that nobody retreating was afraid, and not unwilling for a fight, if favorable opportunities came their way.

The top of Muldraugh's Hill, which overlooked the plain below, where Lebanon, St. Mary's and Springfield had been passed, was reached a brief while after midday. Treble and Eastin were superbly mounted. Both were over six feet tall, wiry, vigorous men, whose nerves and muscles had been hardened by the exposure and training of severest military experiences. Coming along an open stretch, a thousand feet away, these two young soldiers observed Colonel Halisy and three officers quite far advanced ahead of the Federal column. They were both proud, born brave and dauntless, and they resented the idea that two Kentucky Confederate cavalrymen would run away from a fight with four Federals. Placing themselves behind a sudden turn in the road, they waited for the pursuers to appear. Both skilled revolver shots, they were confident that by a sudden onslaught they would kill two of those following and then grapple with the remaining couple and win out. If they had reasoned they would have, hesitated, but in that period of the war, the courage and pride amongst the Kentucky boys who went south did not consume time reasoning nor making many figures in calculating the hazards and dangers of rencontres, and so they resolved to stake their lives, or at least their liberties, on the issue with these foes, who appeared equally indifferent to peril.

Curiously, as Halisy and his lieutenant came close upon Treble and Eastin, their two companions fell back to the head of the column and thus left the battle two and two.

Swinging out into the road as Colonel Halisy and his aide approached, the two officers in gray fired at their opponents. They were greatly surprised and disgusted that neither shot took effect. Four men, too brave and too intrepid to run away from a foe, grappled on their horses. They pulled each other from their mounts and fell, side by side, to the ground. Treble seized his foe and pushed his head into a pool or stream of water, from whence, half drowned, he asked quarter. Eastin had Halisy underneath him, and with his pistol at his head, forced him to surrender. The Federal colonel yielded but still held his pistol in his hand. As he arose from the earth, quickly cocking his revolver, he fired at his captor, but the bullet only grazed the cheek of the Confederate, who in turn instantly fired his weapon and killed Halisy. The conflict, the struggles, the shots, attracted the attention of the advancing Federals, who rushed to the rescue of their leader and comrade. Hastily taking the colonel's sword and the pistols of the two men, Treble and Eastin galloped off to join the Confederate rear guard, which was now nearly out of sight. The Federals claimed that Colonel Halisy had been shot without provocation after he surrendered, but subsequent investigation showed that such a charge was totally unfounded and that Eastin was fully justified in the course he pursued. Just six months later, Captain Treble, having been transferred to Chenault's regiment, was killed at Green River Stockade on July 4th, 1863, on the road between Campbellsville and Columbia, twenty-two miles from the scene of this conflict, as Morgan was commencing the Ohio Raid. In the assault on the Federal fortification Colonel Chenault was killed, and Major James B. McCreary, now governor of Kentucky, assumed command of the regiment. He rode down the line to notify Captain Treble that he was to act as lieutenant colonel, and in case he—McCreary—fell, to take charge of the regiment. As Treble rose from the line and waved his hand to salute his superior, to let him know the order was understood, he was struck by a shot from a Federal sharpshooter and fell dead at McCreary's feet. Strangely enough, when Major Brent of the 5th Regiment, sent by General Morgan to get information as to how things were going, rode forward, as he lifted his hand to salute Colonel McCreary, he was shot through the brain and fell dead at his side.

Eastin, after a brilliant and highly adventurous war experience, became a learned and distinguished lawyer in Louisville, a member of the Kentucky Court of Appeals, and after a long and splendid career, died in Louisville in 1896. He was beloved and honored wherever he was known. He was courteous, gentle, brave and loyal in all phases of life and was universally mourned when he died at the early age of fifty-four.

The Federals, fortunately, had laid by large supplies of commissary stores at Campbellsville, and in these captured goods there was enough to satisfy, clothe and feed man and beast. Strong pickets were ordered out on every road so that there could be no possible surprise. The wear and tear of the day previous had been so dreadful that General Morgan resolved to give his horses and men time to recuperate. True, it was a risk, but the voice of humanity as well as necessity appealed for a brief respite to those men who so uncomplainingly had borne up under a physical strain that, in all the great war, where cavalry had done what no other cavalry ever did, had rarely been equalled and never surpassed. It was twenty-two miles to Columbia. The artillery had good roads and fresh horses, and they could keep any pace the cavalry might set. Caution spoke of a night march, but mercy protested, and mercy prevailed, and for eight hours riders and beasts slept as only the weary and cold could sleep. The day had not broken when the call of the bugles bid the sleepers rise and prepare for another struggle against nature and its adverse forces. There were enemies who were bravely and vigorously marching to thwart their escape from the state, and hem them in on their homeward ride.

When the command ascended a hill on the Columbia Road, heavy cannonading was heard. It was the sounds which were coming from the far-off battlefield of Murfreesboro, Tennessee, ninety miles away, and it fell like a pall upon the minds and hearts of these men far up in the Kentucky mountains. These dull, rumbling tones proclaimed that Bragg and Rosecrans on Stone River were grappling with each other in gigantic conflict.

When at three p. m. the division rode into Columbia, the marchers breathed more freely, as the first danger post was passed. Only a couple of hours was given for rest and food. The Cumberland River, the real line of safety, was thirty miles away. General Morgan, not sure that his foes might not yet intercept him, bade the men get ready for another all night ride. It was still bitter cold, the road to be traveled was rough and broken, but the voice of safety was whispering that over the Cumberland alone could absolute security be found. The leader loved his men. He realized how loyal, brave and patient they had been in the ten days since they had ridden out of Alexandria. It was a hard order to issue, but everything was at stake; he dare not, with all his love for his brave riders, compromise his duty to the Cause he and they loved so well, and for which they were placing their lives in constant jeopardy.

At night, in the darkness and bitter cold, the division rode into Burksville on the Cumberland River. No enemy appeared. The spirits of the men returned. Even the beasts seemed to catch the hopefulness of the hour, and by the night of the 2d of January the Cumberland River was crossed. The raid was ended. The expedition had been successful and the command was safe. The pursuit was not resumed, and so, leisurely marching down through Livingstone, they reached Smithville, Tennessee, on the morning of January 5th. Here they rested for several days to allow the men and horses to build up and to forget the dreadful experiences of the terrific march. They had been absent seventeen days. They had ridden five hundred miles, captured eighteen hundred and seventy-seven prisoners and stores indescribable, and of tremendous value. Twenty-six had been killed and sixty-four were wounded and missing. A few had fallen out of the line of march around Lebanon and been captured, but less than two and a half in every hundred were lacking when, on the south bank of the Cumberland, an inventory was taken and a roll call made. These thirty-nine hundred horsemen had been roughly handled and battered both by their foes and by the fierce elements, but they had borne it all with heroic fortitude and were not only ready but anxious at the earliest moment to try another issue with the enemies of their country.

Chapter XIX

FORREST'S PURSUIT AND CAPTURE OF
STREIGHT, APRIL 28-MAY 3, 1863

The Battle of Murfreesboro closed on January 2d, 1863. The Army of the Cumberland under Rosecrans and the Army of the Tennessee under Bragg made no important moves or advances until late in the spring. Both armies had suffered a tremendous shock and great decimation, and it took them some time to recover from the effects of that frightful conflict.

Among the most enterprising Federal officers in the Army of the Cumberland was Colonel Abel D. Streight. Born in Wheeling, New York, in 1829, he was at this time just thirty-four years of age. He had recruited the 51st Regiment of Indiana Infantry, and his regiment had been a part of the Army of the Cumberland for some months. The story of success of the Confederate raids of Wheeler and Forrest and Morgan and Stuart had kindled the desire among some of the Federals to carry out similar operations.

During the time that Rosecrans and Bragg were waiting to get ready for another great battle, Streight conceived the brilliant plan of moving a cavalry brigade up the Tennessee River by boats to a point near Tuscumbia, Alabama, and there disembarking, march a little south of east to Rome, Georgia, a distance of a hundred and sixty miles. Although an infantryman, he had pondered the marvelous raids of the western cavalry and he longed to imitate the example of the horsemen. He calculated that along the route of his march, both coming and going, he could play havoc, and destroy at will all manufactories and other property which could be, directly or indirectly, used for the maintenance of the war. It required a man of great genius and transcendent courage at that period of the war, who had no more experience than Streight, to organize and carry out such a scheme. He argued if Forrest in Mississippi, Wheeler in Tennessee, Alabama and Georgia, and Morgan in Tennessee and Kentucky, could successfully win out in their raids, he also might hope for equally good fortune. It was as bold if not a bolder feat than any Confederate

302

cavalryman up to this time had undertaken. Streight deserved in this expedition more than fate accorded him. There had been some Federal companies recruited in the northern part of Alabama. Quite a portion of the people in that part of the state were disloyal to the Confederate cause. Frequent invasions of the Federals had developed this spirit of resistance to the authorities of the Confederacy and also promoted enlistments.

Streight had come in contact with these companies of cavalry which had been recruited while refugeeing from Alabama. They would be thoroughly familiar with the route Streight intended to travel. Without the assistance of guides like these, such an expedition would be impossible. He had heard of the disloyalty of these people, and he was sure they would be glad to welcome his coming into their midst, and would in considerable numbers flock to his standard.

In a little while, Colonel Streight, who in sleep or waking pondered his plans, had so far worked out his project that he put it on paper and submitted it to his superior officers. They were delighted with the possibility of such an expedition, capable of doing such tremendous damage to the Confederacy, and his superiors concluded if Streight was willing to risk his life and his reputation, the Federal government could afford to risk a couple of thousand troops, as many mules and a cannon or two. His associates encouraged him in every way possible, commended and applauded him, and told him the government was ready to place at his disposal all the resources necessary to conduct such a campaign.

He was regarded by his superiors as the most daring and enterprising man of the hour, and not a word of caution was sounded in his ears. No echo of possible failure, or faintest warning escaped the lips of those with whom he counseled. If they questioned, naught of their doubts came to him.

In order that Streight's command might start fresh and be prepared to make a great spurt, his brigade was organized at Nashville and it was proposed to transport it from there on eight or ten large steamers, down the Cumberland River to the Ohio, thence to the mouth of the Tennessee River and up the Tennessee for several hundred miles to Eastport, Mississippi, and from this point to enter upon the real work of the expedition. The fact was emphasized that under this system of transportation, men and horses would start on the campaign absolutely fresh and ready for a headlong rush of ten days. It was calculated that possibly even more time could be consumed in the daring work which had been assigned for this adventurous command. In these days, on both sides men were prepared to take boundless risks. Their hopes and not their fears were their guides. It was decided that Streight might choose his own troops. He selected his own, the 51st Indiana Regiment. He felt that it was reliable. To this he added the 73d Indiana, under Colonel Gilbert Hathaway, hardly less brave and resourceful than Streight, the 3d Ohio and the 80th Illinois, and two companies of Alabama cavalry, with a small battery. They made up a force of two thousand men. Nobody ever seemed to think it was necessary to advise with cavalry officers. Streight wanted to make the raid and he felt that he could accomplish what he had proposed and he consulted only with infantrymen. These officers, who had had no cavalry experience, decided that mules would be more reliable than horses, that they could do better service in the mountainous country through which the expedition would pass, in that they could live on less and were hardier. When they came to this conclusion, they made their great mistake. It was strange that men with the experience and judgment of the Federal officers who were advising Colonel Streight would permit him to start out with untrained animals. At Nashville, they gave him a few hundred mules, some two years old, many unbroken, and a number of them in the throes of distemper. As the expedition was to be one of spoliation, the impressment of horses was to be an essential for success. The troops and such mules as could be spared were placed on steamers and brought down the Cumberland River, to a landing called Palmyra, and there they marched through to Fort Henry on the Tennessee River. This march ought to have been done in a few hours, but it required four days. Streight's men were sent out in every direction in squads and singly to scour the whole country and impress every mule that could be found. They spared nothing that could walk or which could be saddled, and they took everything of the horse or mule kind that was attainable in the territory through which they forayed. With all this diligence and impressment they were still short of mounts. They had saddles and bridles, but they had no animals on which their equipment could be placed. After re-embarking at Fort Henry, with a convoy of a brigade of marines, and several gunboats, Streight reached East Port, Mississippi, where he put his men ashore and dismissed the boats.

General Granville M. Dodge, in command of the Federals in that locality, had been directed to give Streight every possible assistance. Dodge was twelve miles away from where Streight landed, but the leader of the expedition immediately rode over to where Dodge was. The Federals numbered some seven thousand or eight thousand men. Colonel P. D. Roddy, with a small brigade of Confederate cavalry, intercepted the advance of Dodge's troops. It was the plan that Dodge should make a feint for a few miles into Alabama. This would protect Streight until he got started on his march, and would also terrorize the Confederates by threats of an invasion by a larger force.

At Eastport, the troubles of Colonel Streight began. Mules when broken are patient workers, but they are very uncertain performers, and when thirteen hundred had been corraled they all set up a loud braying. For a while this puzzled and disturbed the Confederates, but in those days Confederate cavalrymen were very quick-witted and they took in the situation and stole across the picket lines covering Streight's men and mules, crawling in amongst them, and began hooting and yelling and firing their pistols and guns. This was a new experience for these long-eared military appliances; they immediately stampeded, and at daybreak Streight found four hundred of his best mules gone. This was precious time wasted. He spent thirty-six hours in recovering his lost property, but more than half of the mules never came back. They had been picked up by Roddy's scouts, who thanked God for this addition to their mounts.

Roddy and Colonel William A. Johnson, with three small Alabama regiments, were plugging away at Dodge's advance, and so thorough were their efforts that it took practically four days to reach Tuscumbia. Here Streight brought up his own men and mules, and Dodge gave him six hundred mules and some horses, together with ten thousand rations of bread and six wagons. The Federal leader realized the tremendous task that he had undertaken. He looked over all those who were to go with him, and saw to it that the faint-hearted and the physically ailing dropped out of his column.

Colonel Streight, with all his courage, was afraid of one man. That man was General Nathan Bedford Forrest. Dodge told Streight that Forrest had crossed the Tennessee River, and Streight knew well that if this was so, it meant trouble. The most precious hours of Streight's life were the 24th, 25th and 26th of April. The delays made on those days were his undoing. The Confederates had not yet apprehended the Federal purposes. They knew where Dodge was, and they brought some cavalry down to impede his march, but they did not know that Streight was behind Dodge and that in a few hours, like a meteor, he was to be hurled down into their territory under orders to make a raid of more than one hundred and fifty miles into the very heart of the Confederacy, to destroy there what no money could replace, and which was absolutely vital to the maintenance of the Confederate armies at the front.

It was passing strange that the Federal government, with men wise in so many military ways, and so many West Point men—like Sherman, Halleck and Grant—would permit Streight's enthusiasm to induce authority to enter upon such an expedition without the most complete preparation. Under the most favorable conditions, the odds were at least even, and the Federal soldiers were certainly entitled, in view of the risk they assumed, to the very best their government could give. Instead, Streight got the worst. He started short of horses and mules, and, although brave, intrepid and ambitious, he could not make a raid without reasonably good mounts. Streight was anxious to go. He felt that if he succeeded, he would become renowned, and forge at once to the front as the greatest of Federal cavalry leaders.

Still lacking animals, it was decided that Streight should move out in front of Dodge's forces and pounce upon the unsuspecting planters and farmers in contiguous territory. Several hundred of his men were still unmounted. Russellville was the county seat of Franklin County, Alabama—eighteen miles south of Tuscumbia. By swinging down these eighteen miles, it would permit the scouts from his command to penetrate ten miles farther, and impressment was driven to the extremest limits. Some animals escaped, but many were taken. Turning directly east, Streight moved up to Moulton—twenty miles distant. This gave him still more territory for impressment and confiscation, so that when he reached Moulton he had only a few men who had not some sort of a beast to ride. Upon the day following, Streight left Moulton, and on the morning of the 29th of April, Forrest was just sixteen miles away at Courtland. By this time, Forrest had thoroughly divined Streight's plan. He hurried in behind him and resolved to make escape impossible. Streight had left Moulton in the night, and by the time Forrest reached Moulton his trail was a little cold. Forrest told his soldiers that whatever else got wet, the cartridges were to be kept dry. As he rode out of Courtland, a cold, drizzling rain set in, but there was nothing could dampen the ardor and enthusiasm of the pursuers. They were man-hunting, and that always makes the drive furious. With hard riding, Streight had reached Sand Mountain. He had bravely struggled to get on, but bad roads, bad weather, inferior mounts, and the wagons and artillery held him up. He was not sure that Forrest was behind. He earnestly hoped he was not. Streight rested all night, while Forrest was riding most of the night. He had only twelve hundred men and Streight sixteen hundred. There was never a time when Forrest needed more faith in his men. He had that faith, and he knew that if he could put his followers to the test, they would be found always dependable. Nobody thought about leadership or suggested anything to Forrest. The men who rode with him believed that he knew everything, and all they asked was to be allowed to follow where he led. Forrest, rushing his men all the night of the 29th and the morning of the 30th, came close upon Streight's command without their knowledge. Both men had started just at the dawn of day, and both were dreadfully in earnest. Streight's men were already marching up the tortuous road to the crest of Sand Mountain. As the head of the column reached the summit, the bursting of a shell at the bottom and the driving in of the pickets told Streight that the man he feared was at his heels and had already begun to harass and harry. No sooner had the sound of the guns been heard than Streight, with the instincts of a soldier and the courage of a warrior, rushed back to the rear. He wanted to be where the danger was greatest and the conflict keenest. General Dodge had promised Streight to hold Forrest in check; and, if he got away, to pursue and nag him. He failed to keep his pledge.

In the beginning, Forrest underestimated both the courage and resources of his antagonists. Up to this period in his career, he had never struck anything that was so game and so wary as this intrepid brigade of Streight's. He had not then realized that they were dauntless soldiers—led by a man as brave as the bravest. His first idea that they would become a lot of fugitives who had neither skill nor courage was soon dissipated. Captain William Forrest, brother of General Nathan Bedford Forrest, was in command of the advance guards and scouts. With a valor born of unlimited courage, he rushed up to the fleeing Federals, now climbing the sides of the mountain. He manifested neither fear nor discretion. He had absorbed his brother's genius for quick and fierce assault. In a little while he ran into an ambuscade skillfully designed by Streight, who had left Colonel Sheets of the 51st Indiana in the rear. A minie ball broke Captain Forrest's hip, and he fell in the midst of his enemies. Forrest had been accustomed to reckless use of his artillery. It was not often that his enemies disturbed him, but on this occasion he lost two of his pieces, and, right or wrong, he felt that the young lieutenant in charge of these pieces had not exactly measured up to his standard of determination. He requested later that this young officer be assigned to some other command. This brought about an altercation; the young officer attacked Forrest and shot him—as was supposed to be—mortally. Forrest, ferociously pursuing his antagonist, killed him. In death they were reconciled: the patriotic young officer expressing joy that his shot had failed of its purpose, that Forrest was to live and he to die.

Fighting, fleeing, feinting, ambuscading, hammering was now the order of the day. With his military experience and from fragmentary statements of his captives, Forrest knew that Rome was the destination of Streight. He understood what its destruction would mean to his people and to his country, and he resolved first, that Streight should never reach Rome, and second that he should never escape from the Confederate lines into which he had so boldly and fearlessly moved. At and about Rome, the Confederacy had unlimited treasures—there were foundries and manufactories of arms and munitions of war.

To his famous and gallant brother, Forrest gave only one command. He assumed that he and his forty scouts would need no sleep—at least they could have no rest—and so he told his brother to keep right on down the road and get up close to see what the enemy was doing. Streight made the mistake of ever taking any wagons at all. Climbing these narrow mountain roads with these impediments, his speed was greatly hindered. He had not gotten two miles from the top of Sand Mountain when he saw he must fight. Forrest's order to "shoot at everything blue and keep up the scare" was driving his men with the courage of demons to attack every blue coat, wherever it was found. He had only one thousand men. He advanced them fearlessly and recklessly. Streight's men fought vigorously and viciously. For a few moments they threw a considerable portion of Forrest's forces into disorder, and with a gallant and splendid charge, scattered the advance guard of the Confederates. When Forrest was told that his guns were lost, he was beside himself with rage. He had too few men to use horse holders. He directed his men to tie their horses in the forest, and then ordered every soldier to the front. The effect of the loss of his guns upon his men he felt might destroy their morale, and he assembled his entire force and led them in a charge on the Federal rear. While Forrest was making these preparations to retake his guns, Streight's men were all ready to remount their mules and ride in haste along the Blountsville Road. Streight had heard much of Forrest, and he was pleased with this repulse and the capture of Forrest's guns. He congratulated himself that he could make a good showing even if he faced Forrest's veterans.

Something like fifty of Streight's men had been killed or wounded, and he left his own lieutenant, Colonel James W. Sheets of the 51st Indiana, mortally wounded on the field. There was no time for burial services, regrets, tears or ceremonies. While Sheets was mortally wounded, Forrest's brother was desperately wounded. The Indiana colonel was left in the hands of his captors, and his lifeless body was consigned to a coffinless tomb. He died as brave men wish to die—at the front, with his face to his foes.

Forrest had sent two of his regiments by gaps parallel with Day's Gap, to attempt to head off the Federals. In this, they failed because of the long detours they were compelled to make. Forrest now detached a portion of his command to ride parallel with Streight and west of him, and to be sure that he would not be permitted to retrace his steps toward Dodge's protecting forces at Tuscumbia. It was well into the day before Forrest and his escort and his two regiments were able to overtake Streight again. He was once more repulsed. They fought and battled with unstinted fury until ten o'clock at night, and then Streight silently stole away. The Federals held their ground with unflinching courage and far into the night, when their only guide was the flash of their guns. Forrest had one horse killed and two others wounded under him in this encounter. A flank movement impressed upon Streight the danger of his position, and he hurried away, leaving his dead and wounded in possession of his foes, and Forrest retook his guns. They had been dismounted, spiked and the carriages destroyed; but he had them, and, though useless, he had regained them from his foes.

Streight had a great helper with him, a man who had not so much experience, but he had as much courage. This was Colonel Gilbert Hathaway, of LaPorte, Indiana. In August, 1862, he had recruited a regiment which was mustered in at South Bend. He and his command had been at Stone River, and there paid very heavy toll. His soldiers were well drilled and seasoned. Colonel Sheets had gone down at the front with the 51st, and since he fell, Streight laid heaviest burden upon Colonel Hathaway. Streight had now behind him a man who knew neither faintness nor fear, and when he rode away, Forrest and his men rode savagely behind him. Two or three hours had elapsed, when the impact in the rear was so fierce that Streight decided to use another ambuscade to stop, if possible, until daylight, the impetuosity of the pursuers.

With the obscurity of the night, Streight had used great skill and genius. Forrest called for volunteers to ride into the Federal lines and develop their fire, so that he might fix the position of his foe. Lots of men volunteered, but three were selected. They rode in knowingly to the death trap that had been arranged with such care and cunning. All three came out of a storm of shot and shell untouched. No sooner had the scouts informed General Forrest of the position of the enemy, than he ordered forward a piece of artillery, filled almost to the mouth with canister. Noiselessly, the artillery was pushed up to the Federal position, and then by the moonlight, the inclination of the gun was fixed so as to reach where Forrest had been told the Federals were. It was three o'clock in the morning, an hour that tries men's nerves. A second piece of artillery was brought into requisition. This disturbed Streight and his men, and they were called in and hurried on to Blountsville. From Day's Gap to Blountsville was forty-three miles. It had been a march of fighting and ambuscading, marked on both sides with noblest courage. At Blountsville, there was yet hope for Streight. If he drove due north, he was only thirty miles away from Guntersville, on the Tennessee River. There he might be safe; but Streight had started out to go to Rome, and to Rome he resolved to go at all hazards. Forrest felt that the troops he had despatched from Sand Mountain to head Streight off would meet him, if he veered from the line to Rome. Streight, true to his plans and promises, kept on the road he had mapped out to follow. Forrest had now been riding forty out of forty-eight hours, and for more than a third of the time he had been fighting. Seeing that Streight had now resolved to keep upon the direct course toward Rome, Forrest did the wisest thing that any cavalry officer could do. He concluded to rest his animals, and give his men two hours' sleep. The horses were unsaddled and fed the last shelled corn that they had packed on their weary backs from Courtland.

Streight gave his men no rest, and at ten o'clock, upon the morning of the first of May, he rode into Blountsville. Strange scenes were enacted in that little town on that May Day. People from the surrounding country had come into the village to enjoy the festivities of such a holiday. They had driven or ridden their best horses and mules. There was food enough in town for Streight's men to eat and enough fresh animals to assure every man in blue a mount. The pleasures of the picnic were rudely shattered; robbed by hungry Federals of baskets or lunches, they scattered like bird coveys, and from the homes of friends, hidden behind fences, or peering from the bushes with grief, rage and indignation, they witnessed their family steeds unhitched or unsaddled, harnessed with cavalry equipments, forced into the Federal column, and galloped away with the hated soldiers on their back. Girls, with tears raining down their cheeks, saw their pet saddle horses fade into the dim distance. The older men groaned in spirit, and the young men writhed in anguish to realize that the mounts which had long been their chiefest pride were thus ruthlessly taken from their possession. This first of May was the dreariest and saddest that ever came into the lives of Blountsville folk.

Refreshed with food and a momentary rest, the Federal leader realized that all impedimenta must be thrown away; that to escape Forrest, he must march with quicker gait and move with longer strides. Rations and ammunition were counted out to the men. A portion of the contents of the wagons were packed upon mules. He parked his wagons and set them afire. They had hardly begun to burn when the 4th Tennessee Regiment, under Starnes, charged into the village and drove out Streight's rear guard. Streight had rested two hours, but he had rested the wrong two hours. Forrest's men were fresh from their two hours' sleep. Streight's rear guard was constantly and vigorously pursued and attacked. Federals concealed in the bushes fired into the advancing column. Here and there a man fell wounded, maybe dead, and dying or disabled horses were the markers that were revealing to the pursued and the pursuers the savageness of war, but none of these stayed the men who were harrying the Federal rear guard.

Blountsville was ten miles from the Black Warrior River. The road had become wider and smoother, but Forrest's pursuit became still more aggressive. Protecting the crossing by heavy lines of skirmishers on each side of the river and pointing his two howitzers westwardly, a spirited resistance was made by Streight, but Forrest's men, seemingly never tiring, charging again and again, finally broke the line. It was five o'clock in the afternoon of May 1st when the last Federal forded the Black Warrior River. Men sleeping on their horses, here and there dropping from their steeds by either fatigue or sleep, reminded General Forrest that he had about reached the limit of human endurance, that there were some things even his trained riders could not do. Reserving one hundred men for pursuit, he now permitted his soldiers to go into camp for three hours. Scant forage furnished his horses a small ration, but his men preferred sleep to food, and they laid down to profoundest slumber. This gave Streight surcease from battle until nine o'clock next morning, but unwisely he drove his men every moment of the night. He reached Black Creek, four miles from Gadsden, but he reached it with his men fearfully worn and depressed. Forrest, true to his instincts and his knowledge of the powers of human resistance, let every man he could spare from picket duty enjoy a brief undisturbed repose. He calculated that he could release some from aggressive assault and sent one of his regiments to the rear and told them to sleep. Streight had marched during all the night. Forrest had rested three hours, and he was thereby enabled to begin pursuit with increased vigor. Riding at the head of his men, he spurred them on to supremest effort, to reach Black Creek and save the bridge. He hoped to push Streight so hard that he would not find time to wreck or burn the structure spanning that stream.

At Blount's Farm, ten miles from Gadsden, one of the dismal tragedies of the expedition was enacted. On the first day of May, at 4 p. m., Colonel Streight reached Blount's Plantation. There were only fifteen miles between him and Gadsden. This plantation furnished abundant forage for his horses. While the horses fed, the soldiers ate; a portion standing attentive in line ready to obstruct the advance of the Confederates. This rear guard was again vigorously attacked by Forrest. In resisting this advance, Colonel Gilbert Hathaway was mortally wounded. Forrest had become wary of ambuscades, and was so cautiously watching for them that Streight declined to waste his time in further preparing them. The rear guard was under the direction of Hathaway. This soldier Streight was now cherishing as his best helper. This Federal hero, leading his men in a charge, fell with his face to the foe, crying out, "If we die, let us die at the front," and there he went down, covered with the glory and honor which fame always accords to the brave. There was only time for comrades to request a decent burial for the brave Indiana colonel who had died so far away from home, and had been cut down in the full pride of his splendid career. These officers had known different experiences from the Confederates. They had been accustomed, when men of rank were killed, to handsome coffins and the consoling ornaments and trappings which robbed death on the battlefield of some of its terrors. The owner of the plantation was asked to provide a metallic case for the remains of the dead soldier. He mournfully said, "There are no metallic cases in this country." "Then give him a plain pine coffin," pleaded the Federal officer, now exposed to and endangered by the fire of the advancing Confederates. "We have no coffins," replied the man, sadly shaking his head. "Then take some planks and make a box and bury him and mark his grave." "You have burned all my planks," replied the man, "and I have nothing with which to make even a box." "Then," he pleaded once again, with the bullets whistling around his head and with the Confederates immediately in sight, "wrap his body in an oil cloth and bury him, for God's sake, where he may be found,"—and this the magnanimous planter agreed to do. He faithfully kept his pledge, and in the Alabama garden he gave sepulture to the gallant soldier. The Federal officer, with his enemies at his heels, and with the Confederate bullets buzzing about his person, waved the dust of his comrade a last sad adieu, and putting spurs to his horse galloped away and left the dead hero with his enemies to make and guard his tomb.

Far down in Walton County in Southwestern Georgia, a plain, hard-working farmer of Scotch-Irish descent, known among his neighbors as Macajah Sansom, lived at a little town called Social Circle. He heard of richer land in Alabama bottoms and decided to migrate. The youngest child in the family was Emma Sansom, born in 1847.

The change was not propitious for the father, and in 1859, seven years after his change of home, he died, leaving a son and two daughters to the care of his widow. In 1861, the lad, Rufus, the oldest of the family, heard the call of his country and went away as a member of the 19th Alabama Infantry, to defend its rights. The little farm was left to the oversight of the mother and her two daughters. War's ravages had not reached where they lived. The son and protector had been away twenty months, and all this desolate family knew of war was what Rufus had written of his campaigning and the narratives brought back by an occasional furloughed neighbor, or some who in battle had lost a leg or an arm, and returned disabled, bearing in their persons memorials of how terrible was real war.

The father had settled on Black Creek, four miles west of Gadsden, on the highway from Blountsville to Gadsden. On one side of his farm was an uncovered wooden bridge, plain and unsightly, but saved the passers-by from fording the deep, sluggish stream that essayed to halt man and beast on their travels across this new and thinly settled country. The dead father had built a small doubled, one-storied frame house from lumber sawed out of the pine trees that grew in luxuriance on the hills, a short distance back from the Creek. These two girls and their mother had but little of this world's goods. Some cows, chickens, a few pigs and a horse constituted all their possessions. They loved their country, and they gloried in the courage of the young man who was so faithfully and bravely fighting at the front. Joseph Wheeler was the first colonel of the 19th. This regiment had been at Mobile and later at Shiloh, where two hundred and nineteen of its members had been killed and wounded. It had marched with Bragg into Kentucky and down through Mississippi, and later in the valley of Stone River, at the Battle of Murfreesboro, where one hundred and fifty-one of its members were killed or received wounds. In his simple, guileless, homely way, he had written the awful experiences through which he and the neighbor boys had passed, and the mother and sisters were proud of him and loved him for the dangers through which he had come, and what he had done made them zealous for the cause for which they had sent him away to endure and dare so much. Each mail day—for mails did not come often into this isolated territory— they watched and waited for the letter to tell what the brother was doing at the far-off front. A fifth of the neighbors and friends who made up the Gadsden company were filling soldier's graves in Tennessee, Kentucky, Mississippi and Alabama, and these defenseless women were afraid to open the letters that were post-marked from the army lest there should come tidings of the death of the one they so dearly loved.

By the afternoon of May 2d, the pressure of Streight and his men by Forrest was at its fiercest tension. Guided by his two companies of Alabama refugee horsemen, Streight had been told if he could only cross Black Creek and burn the bridge, that he might hope for a few hours' respite, and if he could not feed his weary men and wearier beasts, he could at least let them sleep enough to restore a part of their wasted energy, and from a few hours' repose get new strength for the struggles and trials that yet faced them in this perilous campaign upon which they had so courageously come.

The rear guard was the front of the fighting, and there the plucky and indomitable Federal leader was pleading with his soldiers to stand firm and beat off the pitiless onslaught of the relentless Confederates, who seemed devilish in their vehement and impetuous charges. He had chosen men of valor for this work, and they nobly responded to his every call.

Sitting in their cottage, mayhap talking of the soldier brother, there fell upon the ears of these defenseless home-keepers strange sounds: the galloping of horses, the clanging of swords, frequent shots, sharp, quick commands. They wondered what all this clamor could mean, and rushing to the porch, they saw companies of men clad in blue, all riding in hot haste toward the bridge over the creek. They were beating and spurring their brutes, who seemed weary under their human burdens, and in their dumb way resenting the cruel and harsh measures used to drive them to greater and more strenuous effort. The passers-by jeered the women, asked them how they liked the "Yanks," and told them they had come to thrash the rebels and run Bragg and his men out of the country. They said "Old Forrest" was behind them, but they had licked him once and would do it again.

The well in the yard tempted them to slake their thirst, and dismounting, they crowded about the bucket and pulled from its depths draughts to freshen their bodies and allay the fever that burned in their tired throats. They asked if they had any brothers in the army; and not to be outdone, the women said they had six, and all gone to fight the Yankees. Two cannon went rumbling by. The men on their horses were belaboring them with great hickory wythes, and were driving at a mad pace to get over the wooden bridge. Some of the blue-coated men came in and searched the house for guns, pistols, and opened and pried through the drawers of the wooden bureau, and looked in the closets and presses and under the beds; but they found nothing but a side saddle; and one, more malignant than the others, drew his knife from a sheath dangling by his side, and slashed and cut its skirts into small pieces and threw them upon the floor at the feet of the helpless women.

The line grew thinner. In double and single file some stragglers were all that was left of the men in blue, and then the rear guard came, and over the creek the women saw the cannon on the banks, the horses unhitched, and the little Federal Army dismounted, scattered out among the trees and bushes and standing with guns in their hands, waiting for somebody else to come. They saw the men tear the rail fence down, pile the rails on the bridge, and then one started into the house; and, seizing a piece of blazing coal from the chimney place, ran in haste to the bridge and set fire to the brush and rails, and the flames spring high into the air. They looked down the road and wished that some men in gray would come and drive away these rude soldiers who had disturbed the peace of their home, ungallantly destroying their property, and cutting into fragments their saddle which had come as a gift from the dead father whose grave was out in the woods near the garden gate. As they looked down the road, they saw one single blue-uniformed man riding at highest speed, rushing along the highway as if mad, waving his hands and beating his tired mount with his sword. Just behind him, at full speed, came other men, shooting at the fleeing Federals. In front of the humble home, the single horseman suddenly stopped and threw up his hands, and cried, "I surrender. I surrender." Then up to his side rode with rapid stride a soldier in gray. He had some stars on his collar and a wreath about them, and he said to the women, "I am a Confederate general. I am trying to capture and kill the Yankee soldiers across the creek yonder."

Standing on the front porch of the house, these women watched these startling and surprising proceedings. The leader who was pursuing this single soldier in blue sat on his panting steed at the gate. The young girls knew that the gray uniform meant friends, rescue, kindness, chivalry. They walked to the fence and outside the gate touched the bridle of their deliverer's steed and patted his foam-covered neck, and looked up into the face of the stern soldier, without fear or dread.

With tones as tender as those of a woman, the officer who had captured the Federal vidette said, "Do not be alarmed. I am General Forrest, and I will protect you." Other men in gray came riding in great haste and speedily dismounting left their horses and scattered out into the forest on either side of the road. The youngest girl told the Confederate general that the Yankees were amongst the trees on the other side of the creek, and they would kill him if he went down toward the bridge. She did not realize how little the man in gray feared the shooting. Now the flames from the burning rails and bridge timbers began to hiss and the crackling wood told that the bridge was going into smoke and ashes and no human power could save it from ruin and destruction.

The leader said, "I must get across. I must catch these raiders. Can we ford the creek, or are there any other bridges near?" "There is no bridge you can cross," the younger girl replied, "but you and your men can get across down there in the woods. If you will saddle me a horse I'll go and show you where it is: I have seen the cows wade there and I am sure you, too, can cross it." "Little girl," the general exclaimed, "there's no time for saddling horses. Get up behind me"; and, seeing a low bank, he pointed her there. She sprang with the agility of an athlete upon the bank, and then with a quick leap seated herself behind the grim horseman, catching onto his waist with her hands. The soldier pushed his spurs into the flanks of the doubly burdened horse and started in a gallop through the woods, by the father's grave, along the path indicated by his youthful guide.

The mother cried out in alarm, and with ill-concealed fear bade her child dismount. General Forrest quietly said, "Don't be alarmed; I'll take good care of her and bring her safely back. She's only going to show me the ford where I can cross the creek and catch the Yankees over yonder before they can get to Rome." There was something in the look of the warrior that stilled fear for her child, and with eager gaze, half-way consenting, she watched them as they galloped across the corn field. They were soon lost to sight in the timbered ravine through which the soldier man and the maiden so firmly seated behind him now passed out of view. Following the branch a short distance, General Forrest found that it entered Black Creek three-fourths of a mile above the bridge. Through the trees and underbrush, as she saw the muddy waters of the stream, she warned her companion that they were where they could be seen by the enemy, and they had better get down from the horse. Without waiting for the assistance of her escort, she unloosed her hold from his waist and sprang to the earth.

The soldier, throwing his bridle rein over a sapling, followed the child, who was now creeping on her hands and knees along the ground over the leaves and through the thicket. The enemy saw the two forms crouching on the soil and began to fire at the moving figures in the bushes. Fearing that she might be struck, the soldier said, "You can be my guide; but you can't be my breastwork," and, rising, he placed himself in front of the heroic child, who was fearlessly helping him in his effort to pursue her country's foes. Standing up in full view of the Federals, she pointed where he must enter and where emerge from the water. Her mission was ended. The secret of the lost ford was revealed. Streight's doom was sealed. The child had saved Forrest in his savage ride, ten miles and three hours' time, and now he felt sure that Rome was safe and that Streight and his men would soon be captives in his hands. As they emerged into an open space, the rain of bullets increased; and the girl, not familiar with the sound of shot and shell, stood out in full view and untying her calico sunbonnet, waved it defiantly at the men in blue across the creek. The firing in an instant ceased. They recognized the child's heroic defiance. Maybe they recalled the face of a sister or sweetheart away across the Ohio River in Indiana or Ohio. They were brave, gallant men, the fierceness of no battle

317

could remove the chivalrous emotions of manly warriors. Moved with admiration and chivalrous appreciation of courage, they withdrew their guns from their shoulders and broke into hurrahs for the girlish heroine who was as brave as they, and whose heart, like theirs, rose in the tumult of battle higher than any fear.

Forrest turned back toward his horse, which was ravenously eating the leaves and twigs from the bush where he had been tied. The bullets began whistling about the retreating forms. She heard the thuds and zipping of the balls; and, with childish curiosity, asked the big soldier what these sounds meant. "These are bullets, my little girl," he said, "and you must get in front of me. One might hit you and kill you." Two or three went tearing through her skirt. General Forrest was greatly alarmed for the safety of his protege. He covered her more closely and placed his own body as a bulwark to defend her from shot or shell. He trembled lest he might be compelled to carry her back dead in his arms to her mother and sister, and he groaned in spirit and thought what could he say to the stricken mother if her child were killed. Death for himself had no terrors. He had faced it too often to experience even a tremor, but the strong, brave man shuddered lest harm should come to the child who had, with so stout a heart, served him and his country. Riding with quickening speed, he galloped back to the house. He tenderly placed his hand upon the red cheeks of the girl, now glorified in his eyes by her wonderful courage. He bowed to the mother and sister. He requested the daring lass for a lock of her hair, and gave orders to instantly engage the foe. He sent aids to direct the artillery to the newly-found ford, and while they were moving with all haste into position, he drew from his pocket a sheet of unruled paper and wrote on it:

Headquarters in Saddle,

May 2d, 1863.

My highest regards to Miss Ema Sansom for her gallant conduct while my forse was skirmishing with the Federals across "Black Creek" near Gadisden, Allabama.

N. B. Forrest,

Brig. Gen. Com'd'g N. Ala.

In half an hour this simple-hearted, untutored country child had won enduring renown. She had risen to the sublimest heights of womanly courage—written her name on fame's scroll in most brilliant letterings, and taken company with the world's noblest heroines. The opportunity came her way, she took advantage of all it brought, and reaped a harvest of immortality—the most generous award that fate could bestow.

Emma Sansom married October 29th, 1864, C. B. Johnson, a private in the 10th Alabama Infantry. She, with her husband, moved twelve years later to Calloway County, Texas. Her husband died in 1887, leaving her to care for five girls and two boys. She died in 1890 and sleeps in the Lone Star State.

The Gadsden Chapter of the United Daughters of the Confederacy erected a monument to her memory, which was dedicated in 1906. It rests on a stone base, with a statue of General Forrest with Emma Sansom riding behind. It was built on the banks of the Coosa River in the city park and has carved on the base, these words:

In memory of the Gadsden, Alabama, girl heroine, Emma Sansom, who, when the bridge across Black Creek had been burned by the enemy, mounted behind General Forrest and showed him a ford where his command crossed. He pursued and captured that enemy and saved the city of Rome, Georgia. A grateful people took the girl into their love and admiration, nor will this marble outlast the love and pride that her deed inspired.

The Sansom farm is now the site of Alabama City—a hustling, vigorous cotton town. Gadsden has grown to be a flourishing city, the result of the development of the Alabama iron and cotton trade, and an electric line connects the two places. The Sansom house still remains. The family have been widely scattered. A mill worker rents the old home. The father's grave, with its stone monument which was erected to his memory, is in a cottage yard nearby; but these sad changes cannot dim the glory of Emma Sansom's fame, or depreciate the love and admiration of the men and women of the Southland for the patriotic courage of the mountain lass.

Within less than thirty minutes after the time that Forrest had saluted Emma Sansom, his artillery was in place, and the Federals on the east side of Black Creek were driven away. It was short work to cross the stream. The guns, with ropes tied to the tongues, were hauled down to the bank of the stream; the ropes were carried over and hitched to two artillery horses; and, through the rough ford, the cannon were pulled across.

These were covered with water; but that did not hurt the guns. The ammunition was taken out of the caissons, handed to the soldiers who rode across carrying it in their arms, and, when on the other side, it was quickly replaced. No sooner was a portion of the advance guard across than they took up a furious gait, pursuing the Federals into Gadsden.

No time was given for Streight and his men to do damage there. It was now well toward noon of May 2d. Forrest had kept well in touch with the troops which were traveling parallel with Streight. They were not up, but they were in reach. His escort, by wounds, fatigue and death, had been reduced one-half. The brave Tennesseans, under Biffle and Starnes, melted away until there were but five hundred left. Some had fallen in fatigue and sleep from their steeds. Others were wounded and died by the roadside. Streight now realized that there was no escape for him to the west: he must go to Rome. He hoped still to outride his relentless pursuers.

Gadsden, on May 2d, 1863, produced both a heroine and a hero— Emma Sansom and John H. Wisdom.

The Federals reached Gadsden about twelve o'clock, m. They came into the town on the main Blountsville Road, and they came with much haste. The author had passed through the town five months before, when on sick leave. It was an insignificant village and had little to tempt an enemy or to feed a friend. He rode by the Sansom home, stopped for a meal, a drink at the well, talked to the mother and two daughters—little dreaming that the younger would, in less than half a year, spring into a world-wide prominence.

The failure to stay Forrest and his followers at Black Creek had disspirited some of Streight's officers and men. These had lost something of their buoyancy of march, and dark forebodings loomed up in their minds. They rode as fast as their wearied mounts would allow, the three and a half miles from the Creek to Gadsden. Emma Sansom, by revealing the lost ford—the track the family's cows so long had used—saved Forrest much of time and ride. Hardly had the men in blue dismounted in Gadsden before, a mile out, they heard the clatter of Enfields and the shouts of conflict. They had long hoped for a brief rest. They were confident Forrest would be delayed at least three hours at Black Creek. They were now to learn that Forrest's delays were most uncertain quantities.

A small stock of provender for beasts and food for man had been collected from the surrounding country by the Confederate commissaries; but the country was illy provisioned and there was but little to either impress or buy. The vigorous onslaught of the Confederate vanguard soon drove the Federals out of the town and the new-comers promptly extinguished the fires that Streight's men had kindled.

General Forrest, always well up to the front, rode rapidly into the village. He divined that Streight might push on a detachment towards Rome and mayhap do savage work there before he and Streight might reach the river. He called for volunteers to ride to Rome, cover the sixty miles' space intervening between Gadsden and Rome, and prepare the people there for the coming raid. The younger men had long since gone to the front. The astute Confederate general was no mean judge of human endurance. Amongst his wearied men and jaded steeds he doubted if there was one who would cover the sixty miles in time to save the town; but to Rome a messenger must go with all speed.

The weight of evidence seems to show that Forrest sent a messenger of his own. There is no account of the route he traveled, and no report ever came back to tell whether he reached Rome. There were men other than Forrest who loved their country and who would nobly respond to its call.

John H. Wisdom, familiarly known in that country as "Deacon Wisdom," because of his connection with the Baptist Church, owned the ferry across the Coosa River at Gadsden. Here the river runs north and south, and two roads lead to Rome—one on either side of the stream. Streight chose the one on the west. The ferryman had gone out into the country in his buggy early in the morning, and when he returned at three o'clock in the afternoon, he proceeded to hunt for his boat, which had disappeared. He could find no trace of this, and finally, two neighbors shouted across the stream, telling him that the Yankee raiders had come into Gadsden and turned his boat loose and sunk it, and that they were headed for Rome.

The deacon had heard of the large foundries and manufactories at Rome. He had never been there, but he knew their value to his country was beyond count, and in an instant he caught the burden of a great mission. He bade his neighbors tell his wife and children good-bye and to say that he had gone to Rome.

He had read the story of Paul Revere's Ride. "Now something greater than that," he said, "is passing my way. Revere rode eighteen miles, I must ride sixty-seven and a half miles, and two-thirds of the distance along roads of which I know nothing. I hear voices speaking. They tell me it is my time now—that fate is beckoning me," said the bronzed, wiry ferryman. "I must show myself a real man." With the simple faith of a child of God, he turned his eyes heavenward. He had heard what David has said of Jehovah, and he prayed thus: "Now, God of Israel! Thou Who dost neither slumber nor sleep, in the darkness of the coming night, keep me and help me do this thing for my country and my people." The humble ferryman in an instant had been transformed into a hero.

He sprang into his buggy, and his horse, hitherto used to kindly and gentle treatment, felt the cruel lash upon his sides, as with relentless fury his master forced him along the rough highway.

Wisdom calculated that it would take twenty hours for Streight to reach Rome. He believed that he could do it in half the time. He knew the road for twenty-two miles. Beyond that he must trust to the signboards, to the stars and to the neighbors. The darkness had no terrors for his brave heart. There were no telegraph wires, no telephones, and horses were the only means of rapid transportation. Upon his steed, and such as he might borrow by the way, he must now rely to save his nation from irreparable ruin. There was no time to feed the beast that had already traveled twenty miles. He led him to the river and let him drink. Moments were too precious for more. The weather was propitious and the panting of the weary animal in the wild dash showed how intent was the master in his purpose to thwart his people's foes. This steed had probably come from Kentucky, where speed and endurance were part of a horse's make-up, and now he must demonstrate that blood will tell. Wisdom measured the powers of his animal and exacted from him all that safety and prudence would admit. There were not many houses on the wayside, but wherever the hurrying messenger saw a man or a woman or a child, he cried out— "The Yankees are coming, and they are on the way to Rome!" Some were incredulous. Many took his warning words to heart and hid their horses and mules in the forest and buried their treasures in the earth. The messenger had no time for roadside talk. He felt that he was on the King's business and must tarry not by the way. His answer to inquiries was a wave of his hand, then lashing his reeking steed, and, madman-like, hurrying on.

By five forty-five he had covered just one-third of the distance. He had made twenty-two and one-half miles. The detours he felt impelled by safety to make had increased the distance. He had gone about ten miles an hour. If he could find two horses as good as his own, he could reach Rome before dawn. He looked at the sun and wished that, like Joshua of old, he might bid it stand still.

At the little village of Gnatville, he endeavored to secure a change of steeds. The best he could find was a lame pony belonging to the widow

Hanks. He unhitched his weary, foam-covered, panting horse and led him into the stable. The buggy spindles were burning hot and it must be abandoned. He must now ride if he would save Rome. Borrowing a saddle and mounting the lame pony, he listened to the many appeals from the widowed owner to go slow. He then started toward Cave Spring. When out of sight of the pony's mistress, he stirred him to greater effort. Night was now coming on, and the way was exceedingly lonely. He watched every crossroad, and now and then a fear passed his mind that he might miss the way. In these days, in Northern Alabama, there were few who traveled by the stars. Five miles of vigorous riding and whipping brought the horseman with his limping mount to Goshen, a little past sundown. Here he found a farmer and his son returning from their daily toil with two plough horses. The deacon pleaded with him for a horse, and the father finally saddled the two and told the messenger he could ride one, but his boy would go with him and bring them back. Darkness now overshadowed the way. The boy looked upon the forced ride with distrust and counseled a slower gait, but the more the lad protested, the fiercer Deacon Wisdom rode. In the stillness and silence of the night, they dashed along in a swift gallop for eleven miles. The riders exchanged but few words. The jolting of the fierce gait allowed no waste of breath. Here the messenger bargained with Preacher Weems for a fresh horse. If he was to ride nine and one-third miles an hour, no animal that could be picked up by the way would last very long. The boy returned with the led horse, but he had an idea that his companion of the long ride was an escaped lunatic.

Wisdom cared little for what those he passed thought of him. He had a message and a vision. All else was now shut out of his mind. He rode on to John Baker's—eleven miles further—and here he got another mount. No sooner was the messenger out of sight of the owner of the horse than he rushed into a swifter gait, and going down hill at a gallop, the horse stumbled and Wisdom was thrown violently over his head, landing in the middle of the road. He lay for a few moments unconscious, while the beast stood near, munching the bushes in the fence corner. Thought came back, and, half dazed, he pleaded with God to let him continue his journey. The thought that he might now fail burdened his soul with profound grief. He rubbed his limbs, pressed his temples, relaxed his hands, reached down and drew up his feet. In a few minutes complete consciousness and motion returned. Crawling, he reached the horse, and with his hand on the stirrup, he pulled himself half way up and finally after much effort he managed to get into the saddle again. Once again mounted, he held the reins with firmer grip, but still relentlessly drove his steed.

Twelve miles more brought him within six miles of Rome. It was now half past eleven o'clock at night. He told his errand and asked for another horse. The farmer gladly granted his request, and whipping into a gallop, Wisdom soon saw the lights of Rome. He anxiously peered through the darkness to see if the great wooden bridge over the Oostenaula was still standing. He could distinguish no flames or beacon lights of destruction along Streight's pathway, and he knew then that he was the first to Rome. A great joy welled up in his heart. He had not spared himself, and he had saved his country.

He had started late, but he started fresh. He had, as Forrest would say, "gotten the bulge on the blue coats," and had beaten them in the game of war.

From three-thirty in the afternoon until twelve o'clock was eight and one-half hours. He calculated that he had lost, in changing horses and by his fall in the road, an hour and thirty minutes. That gave him seven hours' actual driving and riding time. He had made an average of over nine and a third miles in every hour he had been in the buggy and in the saddle. He had been faithful to his country's call.

There were no citizens to receive him. He trotted through the deserted streets of Rome to the leading hotel, kept by G. S. Black, and in impetuous, fiery tones made known the cause and reason of his coming. He pleaded with the landlord that there was no time for delay, that everybody must awake and get busy and drive back the Yankees. The inn-keeper told him to ride up and down the streets and tell the startling news. It was a strange sight and strange sound as this weary horseman shouted in the highways of Rome, "The Yankees are coming! The Yankee raiders are coming to burn up the town." Some believed, some doubted, but still the tired man cried out and with shrill calls he yelled, "Wake up! Wake up! The Yankees are coming!" Rome was not as big then as it is now. Half dressed, scurrying hither and thither, old men and boys came rushing out on the sidewalk to inquire the details of the startling story of the Federal invaders. The women and children, slower of movement, soon joined the excited throngs, and with speechless wonderment hung with breathless interest upon every word that fell from Deacon Wisdom's lips. The court house and church bells rung out with dismal warnings. These sounds terrified even brave hearts, but to the mothers and their clinging offspring, they appeared as omens of woe and disaster. Rome was stirred as never before, and for the moment there was dismay and direful dread.

There were some in this appalling hour who knew what to do. One-armed and one-legged soldiers and convalescents were there, and in a moment they became the recognized leaders. Squirrel rifles, shotguns and old muskets—such as were left—were pressed into use and a little railroad from Rome to Kingston made rapid trips, bringing in all who were willing to help defend the town.

A little way out from Rome was the bridge across the Oostenaula River. It was the only gateway from the west into the city. Negro teamsters were awakened, horses and mules were harnessed and hitched to wagons, the warehouses were broken open and everybody began to haul out cotton bales and pile them along the highway by which Streight must ride to reach the bridge or the town. The sides of the bridge were filled with straw, and great stacks were piled on the roof. The straw was saturated with turpentine, so that when the test moment came, if the soldiers could not beat back the assailants, a flaming bridge would bar the way of the blue-coated invaders into the city. At least, it would stay their coming until the implacable Forrest, in their rear, might reach the scene of action.

Captain Russell, the Federal vanguard leader, had ridden as hard as he could ride with his weary men and his tired steeds. A little after sun-up, he approached the stream west of Rome, and when he looked he saw cotton breastworks and soldiers with guns behind them. On the hill outside the town he met an old negro woman and inquired if there were any soldiers in Rome, and she answered, "Yes, Massa, de town am full of sogers," and then he knew that he had lost and that the day ride and the long night ride, with all their suffering, had been without avail; that, though he had done all that he and his followers could do, fate had decreed that Rome should be saved. The defenders began to exchange shots with the invaders. The men at the bridge fired the cannon. The Federals answered with their carbines, but the casualties were few. Russell, with his two hundred followers, had done all men could do. They had come as fast as they could march; they had acquitted themselves as intrepid heroes; but John H. Wisdom, the brave, hardy Baptist deacon, in the language of Forrest, had "gotten there first," had beat them to the town and told them of their coming. Fate had decreed that Streight must fail, and Russell, with a heart full of sorrow and disappointment, faced about and rode

325

back to meet his chief. While Russell looked over the river at Rome, Streight was fighting at the Black Creek Bridge. The people of Rome presented Deacon Wisdom with a silver service, still preserved by his descendants as a priceless treasure, and they sent to widow Hanks, the owner of the lame pony, a purse of $400.

Darkness, Streight's best friend, began to hover over his weary and depleted brigade. He had directed Russell to ride over all barriers and to let nothing deflect him on the road to Rome. If he failed, he hoped Russell would succeed. Russell, through the long, long hours of the night, faithful to his orders, rode and rode and rode. After six hours of tireless effort, Russell reached the Chatooga River. He found a small ferryboat and managed to get his men over; but he forgot a most important thing. He failed to leave a guard to protect the little craft so that his comrades could find some means of crossing when they arrived. The citizens calculated the value of the craft and poling it down the stream, hid it where Streight's men, in the dark, would never discover its whereabouts.

Streight rode all night and struck the Chatooga River where Russell had crossed some hours before. He realized that he must go higher to get over. He found a bridge above; but it cost him a weary, dreary night's march. Several times his detachments lost each other, and it was not until daylight in the morning of the 3d of May that he got his last man across the river. He burned the bridge. He made no halts. He had marched twenty-eight miles from Gadsden under appalling difficulties. Most men would have stopped and either surrendered or died in the last ditch; but Streight had started to Rome, and to Rome he was bound to go. In this last effort, he reached Lawrence. A little way off, near the Georgia line, he ordered his men to halt; but there was no use for an order to halt. Nature, the greatest of captains, issued its command; and, while their ears were open, they heard and heeded no voices, but sank down on the ground—unconscious and powerless in sleep.

Streight had found some provender: his horses were as weary as his men. Still brave and hopeful, with a few of his iron-hearted and almost iron-bodied officers, he rode through the camp, picking out here and there a man, who with a stronger physique than his comrades had stood the pressure of the tremendous ride and incessant fighting. These he directed to feed the horses of their less vigorous companions. A little while before going into camp, Streight passed another ordeal. A squad of his returning soldiers told him the story of Captain Russell's failure. There were no foes in front of Russell. Streight was between him and the pursuers. He had hoped great things from this vanguard, and when he learned that Russell had turned back, even his brave soul began to question whether, after all he had dared and suffered, he must at last fail.

The scouts told him that Russell had seen Rome, but as an ancient negro said, "Dat Rome is plum full of sogers and dem big guns is a p'intin' down all de roads."

Russell had lost out, and his mission, upon which he had gone with high hopes and bright expectations, had failed, and with a heart burdened with disappointment and chagrin, Streight's messenger had turned his face back to the west.

He understood how Russell might have ridden through to East Tennessee, or marched north to the Tennessee River, but Streight was glad he had not deserted his commander and had come back to face with courage any disaster or ruin that the end might bring.

No thought of yielding came into Streight's mind. If he had chosen to map out the future, rather than surrender, he would have preferred death on the field amid the carnage and storm of conflict. No call of patriotism, no appeal of duty, no echo of glory could reach the ears of his men, now dull with sleep, or bodies overwhelmed with weariness. In the midst of these sad and harassing surroundings, with two-thirds of his command asleep on the ground, his persistent enemies again appeared on the scene. They looked to him to be tireless, vindictive, and with a strength more than human. Streight, still game, fearless, called upon his men to respond to the rifle shots which came whizzing from the guns of the Confederate advance. No order or pleading could move the men, now unconscious with sleep. With a touch of mercy in this supreme hour, when they were put into the line of battle, they had been told to lie down with their faces to the foe. When the foe came, they were reposing prone upon the earth, with their guns in their hands, cocked; but the motionless fingers had no will power behind them to pull the triggers; and thus, ready for battle; ready, if awake, to die—but unconscious and silent, they lay immovable and helpless. Streight walked through the ranks of his once valiant soldiers; and, pleading with tears in his eyes, begged them once more to rise and defend themselves from the foe—men, who, like mad devils, had relentlessly pursued them for one hundred and twenty hours.

In the midst of this direful extremity, Forrest appeared at the head of his vanguard a few hundred feet away. He was surprised that only a few shots were fired by the enemy, and that of those he was fighting and pursuing, there rose up only here and there an isolated form. He sent forward a flag of truce, demanding surrender. This Streight refused; but consented to imparl with the Confederate chieftain. These two brave men met between their lines. Forrest told Streight he had him surrounded, and that therefore resistance was useless; that it could only result in loss of life, and that, in view of the experiences of the past few days, it might be that no prisoners would be taken. Streight inquired how many men he had with him, to which Forrest replied, "More than enough to whip you, and I have more coming." Fortunately, Forrest's artillery appeared upon the scene. They came slowly, lashing and slashing the exhausted beasts as they dragged the heavy guns through the sand. Streight requested that they should not come nearer; but out in the road they made the appearance of more guns than Forrest really had. Streight, disturbed and still defiant, but not despairing, rode back and called a council of war. In saddened tones, rendered even sadder by fatigue and exhaustion, his officers advised surrender. They were as brave as Streight, but they had less to lose. They took a more rational view of the desperateness of the surroundings, and without a dissenting voice advised a capitulation. Fearlessly and dauntless of spirit, Streight still urged a last conflict. He pled with them for one more fight, telling them that Forrest's men were as tired as they were and they ought not to yield with fourteen hundred soldiers in line; but the burdens of wearied nature depressed their brave spirits and they said, "We had better yield."

With a calmness and courage born of a spirit that knew not fear and with grief depicted on every lineament, if not with tears streaming down his cheek, he told his comrades that he yielded to their judgment; but he would never vote to give up the fight. Forrest was glad enough to get the surrender. He granted most honorable terms, retention of side arms and personal property. The sleepers were awakened and marched out into an open field and stacked their guns, and Forrest's weary, tired men, marched between them and their only hope. Disarmed, there was nothing to do but accept the sad fortune of a defeat. Defeat it was; but these men were glorious even in defeat. Streight had only one request to make—that his men might give three cheers for the Union, and this was done with lusty shouts and enthusiasm in the Alabama forest. These brave men, valiant and loyal even in defeat, flung into the faces of their triumphant foes hurrahs for their cause and their country.

Streight says, "Nature was exhausted. A large portion of my best troops actually went to sleep while lying in the line of battle under a heavy skirmish fire."

Confederates and Federals were marched into Rome. To the Confederates, it was the greatest triumphal march of the western war. Brave men pitied the misfortune of the Federal raiders. They deserved, though they had not achieved, success.

War's wrecks were yet to be collected: there were Federal and Confederate wounded along the line of this remarkable march who were witnesses to war's savageness. The surgeons had hastily dressed wounds and amputated limbs; but somebody must now go back and gather up and care for these ghastly evidences of the horribleness of battle; and, with these, ended one of the most remarkable of all the experiences in cavalry service on either side from 1861 to 1865.

Streight was carried to Richmond and confined in Libby prison, and with one hundred other officers escaped through a tunnel in February, 1864. Hid by friends for a week, he finally reached the Federal lines; and, undaunted, returned to his regiment. He was offered command of Chattanooga; but, still brave and active, he declined the post and asked to be assigned to active service in the field. He was yet to see more of war. He was at Dalton when it was besieged by Wheeler. He was at the Battle of Nashville in the winter of 1864, and commanded a brigade in that memorable conflict. He was mustered out of the service in 1865, returned to Indianapolis, Indiana, and opened a furniture manufactory, and afterwards developed a wholesale lumber business. A man of such tremendous energy and physical endurance was bound to be successful. Elected State Senator from Marion County, of which Indianapolis is the county seat, he introduced a bill for the erection of the magnificent capitol since constructed at Indianapolis. In 1880 he was candidate for governor; but was defeated by Albert G. Porter. He died at his home near Indianapolis in 1892, in the 63d year of his age. He was never fully appreciated by his countrymen; and, when the story of his raid shall be fully and fairly told, he will take a high rank among Federal heroes.

General Joseph E. Johnson once said of Forrest that if he had received a military education, he would have been the greatest figure of the war. General Sherman declared Forrest was the greatest cavalry genius in the world's history. It was his judgment that if Forrest had been educated at West Point, it would have spoiled him; that he was greater as an untutored military genius than if he had received the benefits of the most thorough martial education.

North and South, the story of Streight's pursuit filled the people with wonder. In the South, to wonder was added an admiration which became almost idolatry. The men and women of the Confederacy might well adore this marvelous soldier. They placed him on the highest pedestal. He was so great and so brave that they saw none of the defects of his character, and nothing could make them believe but that he was all that was good and true and patriotic and grand. They looked upon him as a fierce, intrepid, determined, successful cavalry soldier, who was ever courageous of heart, in whose bosom fear never found place, and before whom difficulties melted away whenever the touch of his transcendent power passed their way.

Chapter XX

BATTLE OF FLEETWOOD HILL, JUNE 9th, 1863

The Battle of Chancellorsville was fought on the 3d of May, 1863. It stands in military history as one of the remarkable battles of the world. It was a great victory in one sense for the Confederate Army, but on that fatal field died Stonewall Jackson, one of the wonderful soldiers of the ages.

Amidst the gloom of an unsuccessful campaign, and when defeat was apparently impending about his hosts, a brave European general gathered around him his several commanders and asked of them a detailed enumeration of the forces that could be depended upon in the approaching conflict. Conscious of the inferiority of numbers, the reports were made, with countenances and words showing the profound fear of misfortune on the coming day. Distressed by this despondence, the unterrified leader rose and striking the table with his hands, vehemently cried out: "How many do you count me?" Instantly the scene changed. His courage restored the waning valor of his followers. In all battles the Confederate soldiers in Northern Virginia, who came in contact with General Jackson, counted him alone a mighty host.

In May and June, 1863, hope was still radiant in the hearts and minds of the defenders of Southern independence. The superb defense of Vicksburg, as well as Port Hudson, indicated that the possession of the Mississippi was yet a debatable proposition, and that the division of the Confederacy by the capture of that mighty stream would be long delayed. The crushing of Hooker at Chancellorsville demonstrated that none of the efficiency and power of the Army of Northern Virginia was gone. Beyond the Mississippi, the position of the army there made it certain that many months would come and go before the Union forces would be able to get very far south of the Arkansas River.

Soldiers as brave and self-reliant as the men of the Army of Northern Virginia had grounds of hope that ordinary soldiers could not feel. They were made of the best metal and fashioned in the finest mold, and thus could hope when others might despair.

The first sting of the death of Stonewall Jackson had abated. General Stuart had won honor when Jackson had fallen, and there were many, many great soldiers in this army of Northern Virginia who felt the uplift of faith in God, and these could but believe that in the end, some way, another leader would be developed to help General Lee in the future, and be to him what Jackson had been in the earlier campaigns of that loved commander.

The Battle of Fleetwood Hill, sometimes called "Brandy Station," was almost entirely a cavalry contest. It was fought on the 9th of June, 1863. Some of the most important as well as desperate scenes of the battle were on what was known as "Fleetwood Hill." This was the center of a once beautiful estate. War had despoiled some of its grandeur, but even in its ruin it was magnificent. The storm of conflict raged from dawn to late in the afternoon, with unabating fury. Men on both sides seemed immune to fatigue or fear, and for fourteen hours, as if endued with supernatural energy and power, struggled amidst dust, smoke, starvation and wounds and death with unflagging fury, in the maddening work of ruin and destruction. This hill was adorned by a colonial mansion. The ground about it rose with gradual ascent until it reached the top of the eminence, from which point there fell upon the gaze of the beholder one of the most beautiful views in Virginia. This country had hitherto been rendered famous by some of the greatest of military achievements known to men. Later it would add new titles to historic greatness with the names of Second Manassas, Spottsylvania and Cold Harbor, but on this day it was to crown the cavalry of both the Army of Northern Virginia and the Army of the Potomac with a glow that would never dim.

Culpepper Court House was the county seat of Culpepper County, and within the limits of this county was situated Fleetwood Hill. It was fifty miles from Washington, and Brandy Station was five miles south of the north fork of the Rappahannock River. From Kelley's Ford on the Rappahannock River to Brandy Station was five and a half miles; from Kelley's Ford to Stevensburg was seven miles; from Brandy Station to St. James Church was one mile and a half; and from Brandy Station to Beverly's Ford on the Rappahannock River was four miles. From Fleetwood Hill to St. James Church was one mile, and from Kelley's Ford to Beverly's Ford, three miles.

GENERAL ALFRED PLEASANTON

The Federal forces were commanded by General Alfred Pleasanton, who was born in Washington City, June 7th, 1824. In 1844 he graduated from the United States Military Academy and became second lieutenant in the First Dragoons. He was at Palo Alto and at Resaca de La Palma. He was in the Seminole war and in operations in Washington Territory, Oregon and Kansas. In February, 1861, he became major of the Second United States Cavalry and marched with his regiment from Utah to Washington. He was in the Peninsula Campaign of 1862 and in July of that year was appointed brigadier general of volunteers. By September he was a division commander. He was at Sharpsburg, Fredericksburg and at Chancellorsville. His friends claimed that he stayed the advance of Stonewall Jackson on May 2d, 1863. He was at Gettysburg and subsequently transferred to Missouri. He was made a brigadier general in the regular army in 1865, for meritorious conduct, and mustered out in 1866. He was a vigorous and daring leader and won a splendid reputation by hard fighting. Later in the struggle he was transferred to the West and won some signal victories in Missouri, and was at one time offered the command of the Army of the Potomac.

JOHN BUFORD

General Pleasanton had with him as second in command John Buford, who was born in Kentucky in 1825. He was graduated from the Military Academy at West Point in 1848, and became second lieutenant in the First Dragoons. He was in the Sioux expedition in 1855, in Kansas in 1856 and '57, and in the Utah expedition in 1857 and '58. In 1861 he was promoted to be a major and was designated inspector general of a corps in November, 1861. He was on General Polk's staff in 1862. On the 27th day of July he was made brigadier-general and given command of a cavalry brigade composed of some of the very best of Federal cavalry, the 1st Michigan, the 5th New York, 1st Vermont and 1st West Virginia. He was wounded at the Second Manassas. In the Maryland campaign he was acting chief of cavalry of the Army of the Potomac. He was also at Antietam. Upon the organization of the cavalry of the Army of the Potomac, General Stoneman became the ranking officer, and Buford commanded the reserve cavalry. He was at Fredericksburg, December 3d, 1862, in Stoneman's raid on Richmond in May, 1863, at Beverly Ford, June, 1863. He was at Gettysburg and his associates felt that he did wonderful service there. At Fleetwood Hill, he did some of the best fighting. He was not afraid of any sort of clash with his enemies. He died in November, 1863, and a statue at Gettysburg commemorates his work there.

GEORGE WESLEY MERRITT

General George Wesley Merritt was born in New York City, June 16th, 1836. He went to West Point in 1855, graduating in 1860, and was assigned at once to the cavalry service. By April 5th, 1862, he was captain of the 2d United States Cavalry. He served on the staff of General Phillips and St. George Cooke; later, under General Stoneman. By April 3d, 1863, he had attained to the command of the 2d United States Cavalry. He saw the fighting at Gettysburg. He was at Yellow Tavern, where Stuart received his fatal wound. By June 29th, 1863, he had become a brigadier general. He was with Sherman in the Shenandoah campaign and in 1864 was made major general. He was one of the three Federal commissioners to arrange the terms of surrender at Appomattox. In June, 1898, he was appointed military governor of the Philippine Islands, and with an army of eight thousand men arrived at Manila on June 25th. His active military career covered a period of nearly forty years, and he witnessed some of the most desperate and effective fighting of any soldier who served in the army to which his life was devoted.

BENJAMIN FRANKLIN DAVIS

With General Pleasanton also on that day was Benjamin Franklin Davis, who was born in Alabama in 1832, graduated from the United States Military Academy in 1854, and served with great credit in both infantry and cavalry in Mexico. In 1861 he sided against the state of his nativity. In 1862 he became colonel of the 8th New York Cavalry and was in command of a brigade of Federals in this engagement. With Wesley Merritt, D. McM. Gregg and Colonel A. N. Duffie, this made a splendid aggregation of cavalry experience and military genius.

General Pleasanton had under him ten thousand nine hundred and eighty soldiers. The best the Federal Army had in cavalry at that time was at Fleetwood. The generals in command were brave, able and experienced. They had been prodded about what Stuart had been doing. Their pride and courage were involved and aroused, and they were longing for an opportunity, which had now come, to have a real test of the spirit and grit of the Confederate cavalry.

The horsemen of the Union armies had now been taught both how to ride and how to shoot. They were well mounted and well armed, and their training made them formidable foes. The war had now been in progress for two years and the Federal cavalry drill and training had been brought to a very high standard. The Federal troopers had become apt scholars. They were anxious to demonstrate their valor, their discipline and their power.

On the Confederate side were nine thousand five hundred and thirty-six men, and these constituted the best horsemen the Army of Northern Virginia could send into battle—in fact, about all it could offer. Stuart himself had long since established a reputation as one of the most enterprising and successful of cavalry leaders, and he had with him lieutenants who were as brave and as able as any who could be found. The generals and men under him were superb horsemen and accurate shots when the war began. To great pride they had added wide experience in campaigning. Well educated, highly bred, and intensely patriotic, they were foemen the most intrepid men might justly fear.

WILLIAM HENRY FITZHUGH LEE

Major General William Henry Fitzhugh Lee was a son of Robert E. Lee and was born on May 21st, 1837. Graduating at Harvard when he was twenty years of age, he was appointed second lieutenant in the 6th Infantry, and he served under Albert Sidney Johnson in Utah and California. In 1859 he resigned his commission to operate his farm, known as the "White House," on the Pamunky River, which became not only important as a strategic position, but famous in the history of the war. At the beginning of 1861, he organized a company of cavalry and later became a major in the new-made Confederate Army. In West Virginia he was chief of cavalry for General Loring. In the winter of 1861 and '62, he was commissioned lieutenant colonel of the 9th Virginia, and in less than two months became its colonel. His regiment constituted a part of the brigade of General J. E. B. Stuart. In the Chickahominy raid he was one of the three colonels with Stuart, and his troops defeated the Federal cavalry on June 13th in this expedition. He suffered rough treatment at Boonsboro. He was knocked from his horse and left unconscious by the roadside; but reached Sharpsburg in time for the fight. He rode with Stuart in the Chambersburg raid. His courage and intrepidity saved Stuart, by protecting the ford at which he must cross. In November Lee became brigadier general. He was prominent at Fredericksburg and Chancellorsville, and at Fleetwood he was captured after being severely wounded. He was carried to Fortress Monroe and subsequently to Fort LaFayette and was exchanged in March, 1864. At this time he was promoted to be a major general and commanded a division of Confederate cavalry in the Army of Northern Virginia. He was with General Lee, his father, to the end. After the war he returned to his plantation. He was a member of the Fiftieth, Fifty-first and Fifty-second Congresses from the Eighth Virginia District and died at Alexandria in 1901.

WILLIAM CARTER WICKHAM

Another prominent leader on the Confederate side was William Carter Wickham, who was born in Richmond, Virginia, in 1820. He graduated at the University of Virginia in 1842. He was bitterly opposed to the war and voted against the Ordinance of Secession. He recruited, however, the Hanover Dragoons, was in the first battle of Manassas, and in September, 1861, was made lieutenant colonel of the 4th Virginia Cavalry, and in August, 1862, became colonel of that regiment. He rendered valiant service at the Second Manassas, at Boonsboro and at Sharpsburg. At Upperville he was wounded the second time, and took part in the Battle of Fredericksburg, December 12th, 1862. Elected to Congress in 1863, he remained with his regiment until the fall of 1864. He helped to stop Kilpatrick's raid on Richmond and Custer's attack on Charlottesville. He was in the Battle of the Wilderness and at Spottsylvania Court House, and was with Stuart on May 11th, at Yellow Tavern. The last brigade order issued by General Stuart was to General Wickham to dismount his brigade and attack. Wickham was with Early in the valley. After the reverse at Fisher's Hill, he stayed the advance so as to allow the reorganization of Early's forces. On the 5th of October, 1864, he resigned his commission in the army, transferring his command to General Rosser, and took a seat in Congress. He died in Richmond,

Virginia, in 1888. The state of Virginia erected a statue to his memory on the capitol grounds in Richmond.

BEVERLY HOLCOMBE ROBERTSON

Brigadier General Beverly Holcombe Robertson was a graduate of the United States Military Academy in 1849, and became second lieutenant in the Second Dragoons. By hard service in the West he was promoted to first lieutenant in 1859, and was under Edgerton of the Second Dragoons in the Utah campaign. He severed his connection with the United States Army and became a colonel in the Virginia cavalry. He was sent to take command of Ashby's cavalry. In September, 1863, he was assigned to the command of the Department of North Carolina, and took charge of the organization and training of cavalry troops. Immediately preceding the battle at Fleetwood, he was sent to reinforce Stuart. He was at Gettysburg and in the raid through Maryland. After returning from Gettysburg, the regiments comprising his brigade were so reduced that he sought service in another field, and was given command of the Second Division of South Carolina. His cavalry forces were particularly prominent in the Battle of Charles City Cross Roads, and in the battles with Sherman's troops, on their march to the sea, he bore a valiant and distinguished part.

JOHN RANDOLPH CHAMBLISS

General John Randolph Chambliss was born in Greenville County, Virginia, in 1833, and graduated from the United States Military Academy in 1853. In July, 1861, he was commissioned colonel of the 13th Virginia Cavalry, and was under the orders of General D. H. Hill on the James River during the fall of that year. He was assigned to General W. H. F. Lee's cavalry brigade, and was regarded as one of the most determined and intrepid fighters. After General W. H. F. Lee's wound and the death of Colonel Sol Williams, Colonel Chambliss took command of the brigade. He was at Gettysburg and in the Bristoe skirmish. In December, 1864, he was commissioned brigadier general. In the cavalry battle at Charles City Cross Roads on the north side of the James River, he was killed on the 16th of August, 1864. His body was buried by his enemies, but was afterwards delivered to his friends. General Lee, in speaking of his death, said: "The loss sustained by the cavalry in the fall of General Chambliss will be felt throughout the army. By his courage, energy and skill, he had won for himself an honored name."

WILLIAM E. JONES

General William E. Jones, another of the Confederate leaders, was born in Washington County, Virginia, in May, 1824. He graduated from West Point in 1848. He did splendid service in the West. At the time of the passage of the Ordinance of Secession by Virginia, he had organized a company of cavalry known as the Washington Mounted Rifles. His company was part of General Stuart's command. He became colonel of the 1st Virginia Cavalry with Fitzhugh Lee as lieutenant colonel. In 1862 he was displaced by regimental election, and was assigned to the 7th Virginia regiment. He was at Sharpsburg and was promoted on November 8th to be brigadier general and was assigned to the command of the Laurel Brigade. In April and May, 1863, he conducted a daring and successful raid on the Baltimore & Ohio Railroad, west of Cumberland. From this expedition he joined Stuart, and at Brandy Station no leader acquitted himself more splendidly. At Boonsboro his command captured over six hundred Federal prisoners. In 1861 differences had begun between General Stuart and Colonel Jones. This became so intense that it was necessary to remove Colonel Jones, and he was sent to Southwestern Virginia. A man of splendid executive ability, he organized an excellent brigade and was with Longstreet in Tennessee. He prevented Averell from destroying the salt works in Southwestern Virginia. On May 23d, 1864, he was placed in command of the Department of Southwestern Virginia, while General Breckinridge was absent in the valley. In the fight at Piedmont, Virginia, he fell, leading his forces in the conflict, and his body was not recovered until after the battle.

THOMAS TAYLOR MUNFORD

Another officer of deserved distinction was General Thomas Taylor Munford, who was born in Richmond in 1831. He graduated from the Virginia Military Institute in 1852. At the outbreak of the war he was a planter. He became lieutenant colonel of the 30th Virginia Mounted Infantry, organized in 1861. This was the first mounted regiment organized in Virginia. It was subsequently designated as the 2d Regiment

338

of Cavalry, General Stuart's regiment being the 1st. In the re-organization under Stuart, Munford became colonel. He was in the first fighting and the last fighting of the Army of Northern Virginia. His career as a cavalry officer was brilliant and notable. The discharge of all duties committed to him were performed with absolute faithfulness. When General Ashby died, General Munford was recommended by General Robert E. Lee as his successor. He received two severe wounds at the Second Manassas. He was in the Maryland campaign, was at Sharpsburg and commanded a division of cavalry that confronted Hancock's troops. Later he became commander of Fitzhugh Lee's brigade. He was at Gettysburg and in the valley campaign with Early. In November, 1864, he was promoted to brigadier general. At Five Forks and at High Bridge he maintained the splendid reputation that he had won in the earlier days of the war. He was with Rosser at High Bridge, and, in the retreat from Richmond, bore both a prominent and valiant part. After Lee's surrender, he endeavored to collect the scattered Confederate forces and form a junction with Johnson's army. General Fitzhugh Lee commanded his excellent services as a division commander. With large agricultural interests in Virginia and Alabama, he still survives, full of honors and full of years, and occupies a most exalted place in the hearts of his Confederate comrades.

At no other place in the war were such a large number of cavalry engaged in a single conflict. It was practically forty per cent more men than were engaged in any one cavalry battle during hostilities, and in few battles were such a large proportion of the leaders West Point graduates.

On the 22d of May General Stuart reviewed the brigades of Fitzhugh Lee, W. H. F. Lee and Wade Hampton. He counted four thousand troopers. This review occurred between Brandy Station and Culpepper Court House, and a sense of pride and exaltation filled Stuart's heart as he looked over the chivalrous and intrepid legions. A few days later there came over from the valleys of Virginia General William E. Jones, who brought with him a brigade of fairly well mounted and armed men. They were of splendid material. There also came from North Carolina another brigade under General Beverly H. Robertson. Stuart's forces now numbered five brigades, constituting a magnificent array of cavalrymen. Always proud, he announced a great review for June 5th. He wanted himself and he wanted others to see in array this grand body of horsemen, in every respect the equal of any nine thousand men who ever aligned as cavalry. He asked General Robert E. Lee to be present and to impress these troops with a sight of his magnificent personality. These horsemen rode, and walked, trotted and galloped, and salvos of artillery magnified the splendor of the movements and thrilled the hearts of the riders. General Lee could not come, but General Stuart had all that the pomp and pageantry of war at that date in Virginia could present.

General Stuart, still anxious that General Lee should see his men and that the men should see him, announced another review and parade for the 8th day of June. Many of the horses were the worse for wear, the men's uniforms were worn, faded and many threadbare, but the sabres, guns and pistols were bright, and if their equipment showed the marks of heavy service, their hearts were true and loyal to their beloved country and they were ready to respond to its every call.

The mind of the Confederate commander was revolving the scheme of the invasion of Pennsylvania, which was to culminate three weeks later at Gettysburg. He was prone to look at things more quietly than General Stuart, and so he reviewed this important part of the army of Northern Virginia, but he forbade the discharge of artillery, and he only allowed them to pass by him at a walk and trot. He knew who and what they were and he knew that when the testing moment came they would be worthy of the Confederacy. Neither General Lee nor General Stuart had any foreshadowing of what the next day would bring forth, and General Lee returned to his headquarters in the midst of his infantry. Stuart's headquarters were at Fleetwood Hill. General Pleasanton's headquarters were across the Rappahannock River, eight miles away. Neither seemed to know just what the other was doing. Pleasanton had marched his men down the Rappahannock. He allowed no fires. He had been sent by General Hooker to find out just what General Lee was doing and where his army was encamped. Two fords were accessible, Beverly's Ford and Kelley's Ford. General Pleasanton had resolved to use both to force the fighting and to back up the cavalry with infantry, to drive anything out of his way that might cross his path. Stuart, unconscious of the large force of cavalry and infantry that was ready to cross the Rappahannock, had his men at and about St. James Church, over at Fleetwood Hill, and down at Beverly's Ford.

Pleasanton had with him some splendid artillery, especially the 6th New York Battery. At Chancellorsville, thirty-seven days before, it had written history, and on the morrow it was to write history again at Fleetwood.

With thirty men beginning the day, it would bring out unscathed only six; four-fifths were to go down in the storm.

New Jersey, New York, Maine, Pennsylvania and Rhode Island were getting ready with their troops to try out the question of the courage and endurance of the horsemen from Virginia, North Carolina, Mississippi, South Carolina and Georgia.

There was to be an all-day fight, and it was to be a hand-to-hand fight. It was to be a fight in which the sabre would be used. The ever-handy revolver was to be an incident. The highest type of courage was to play an important part. In this hard-fought contest cowards would have no place. If there was cowardice hovering around on that day it did not come to the surface. Valor oozed out from the pores of the actors. The very atmosphere was full of courageous inspiration. Death would lose its terrors on Fleetwood Hill, and fear would be relegated to the rear. Smoke and dust would obscure the sight but could not and would not affect the courage of those who participated. It might hide the vision and obstruct the breathing, but the men who were to fight at Fleetwood were to take no heed of weather or atmospheres. It was to be a complete triumph over all that nature could offer to impede, and a fight with an almost supernatural fierceness that was apparently to be something more than human.

With the dawn General Gregg, with Duffie, crossed at Kelley's Ford. Gregg traveled with Duffie to Stevensburg and then turned north toward Brandy Station. Duffie went on farther and passed by Stevensburg, and then turned north to Brandy Station; and Pleasanton crossed at Beverly's Ford, and he headed his columns toward Fleetwood Hill, around which were to be woven wreaths of glory for the men on both sides who here went to battle.

Stuart himself on the night of the 8th camped at Fleetwood Hill. This position commanded a view of the entire country with the exception of immediately westward, which was known as the Barbour place, which was a little higher than Fleetwood Hill.

Telepathy, which frequently pervades the movements of armies, spoke to the Confederates. Their slumbers were disquieted and they breathed in the air that something important was close at hand. Stuart and none of his men knew, for his scouts had not found it out, that less than four miles away, indeed, in some places less than one mile away, there were thousands of Federal cavalry ready to dispute the question of supremacy. General Stuart was himself a mile in the rear of his forces, which were at St. James Church, a third of the way between Fleetwood Hill and Beverly's Ford, on the road which ran from Beverly's Ford, and which led along the north bank to Duffin's Run.

Pleasanton had crossed the Rappahannock in the early morning and was starting on an expedition to break up Confederate communications and find out where all the Confederates were. With twenty thousand horsemen equally matched and in such close proximity, all on the alert, battle could not be long postponed. General Hooker had suspected a forward movement of General Lee's army. General Pleasanton had behind him Russell's and Ames' brigades of infantrymen, and with real military skill had managed to conceal his presence from his enemies, and the Confederates were surprised when, at the dawn of day, Colonel Davis of the 8th New York Cavalry passed the Rappahannock at Beverly's Ford. The Federals had begun operations very early, even before light. A company of the 6th Virginia Cavalry was ready to dispute the passage of the river and these Virginians, under command of Captain Gibson, persistently and skillfully delayed the advance of the Federal forces. The pickets contested every inch of ground, and for half a mile Davis' brigade was fighting its way—still pressing forward—and its men realized before the sun had gotten up that the day's work would be serious. After Davis and his New York regiment had traveled half a mile, Major Flournoy, who commanded the 6th Virginia Cavalry, collected one hundred men. It was barely light, but he went after the 8th New York with vigor. A third of the Confederates were either killed or wounded, but they were not without recompense. Colonel Davis was killed in the fight. Amongst those in the Confederate charge was Lieutenant R. O. Allen, of Company D, 6th Virginia Cavalry. In the movement under Flournoy, his horse was wounded and this induced him to remain in the woods. Observing a Federal officer in the road, about two hundred feet in front of his column, Lieutenant Allen advanced upon him. The Federal commander's attention was given to his men, and with his sword he was waving them forward. Allen was upon him before he realized the situation, and when Colonel Davis turned his head, he assaulted Allen with his sabre. The fearless Virginian had only one shot in his pistol; he was taking large risks. He reserved his single shot for the crucial moment, and swinging himself upon the side of his horse, he avoided the sword stroke of the Federal; and arising in his saddle, he fired the one shot which he had reserved for the emergency, and the Federal colonel fell dead.

Both Federals and Confederates advanced to the scene of this tragic conflict. Losses were suffered on both sides. The Confederate lieutenant hastily returned to his lines. The firing attracted the attention of General Jones, who promptly ordered up the 7th Virginia Cavalry. The men had been gathered in such haste that a number of them were coatless, and some of them had pressed forward with such impatience that they had not taken time to saddle their beasts. The 7th Virginia charged fiercely, but the Federals met the charge with such courage that the Virginians were forced back and they passed two guns, of Hart's Battery, stationed in the road.

Early in the morning the artillery on both sides had given a wonderful account of themselves. The 7th Virginia Cavalry, many without their saddles, had rushed to stay the tide of Federal advance from Beverly's Ford. These, by sheer force of numbers, were swept away, leaving the two guns of Hart's Confederate Battery unprotected. The Federals, animated by their success in scattering the cavalry, believed they would find these guns an easy prey, but the gunners were in no mood to yield their pieces or to run away from their speechless companions, who, with them, had so firmly stood in battle array for many months. They had learned to love the iron and steel, cold and emotionless though it was, and the thought of these long-time friends passing into the possession and use of their enemies gave them keenest pangs of regret. Supports or no supports, they resolved to fight out the right of ownership, and come what might, to stand or fall by their beloved guns. They saw the advancing foe. The vibration caused by the tramp of the rushing squadrons could be felt, and to escape from capture or death seemed hopeless. Once determined at all hazards to protect their cannon, all questions of escape were dismissed and all fears banished. With haste quickened by danger, they fired shot after shot into the advancing columns of the assailants. Shells were discarded and the deadlier canister pushed into the pieces, now warm by rapid firing, was sent crashing into the front ranks of the foe. These dauntless files went down before the withering currents of death that were starting every moment from the two guns, and when at last they reached the pieces, their ranks were shattered and their columns broken. Slowly the brave men by hand moved their guns to places of safety, and at length they found shelter behind the ranks of the forces disposed around the little country church, and about which for five hours the storm of battle had been raging with intense fierceness. The men who had stood for these

343

guns had risked much and dared everything without counting cost, and as they rolled their guns and caissons into the Confederate ranks, so gladly opened to receive them, their comrades greeted them with shouts of admiration and approval. They had accomplished more than they had even hoped. They had caught the contagion of intrepidity that was in the air on that day. The conduct of the men on both sides was such as to stir the hearts of brave people everywhere in the world and to win for the American volunteer soldier immortal acclaim.

At ten o'clock the din and turmoil had become appalling. Both sides had changed positions, but fought with a courage like to that born of despair. Wherever the men in gray found mounted or unmounted bluecoats they rode at them with furious savagery, and likewise the men in blue seemed to rise out of the earth fully armed and pressed on to unrelenting conflict.

Some Confederate guns near St. James Church were especially destructive and annoying to the 6th Pennsylvania Cavalry and a regiment of United States regulars. Their officers concluded that the quickest and most effective way to get rid of this battery was to ride it down. The cavalry was twenty-four hundred feet from the annoying artillery, and the way led across an open space. The bugles were sounded, the guidons were lifted and the order to charge stirred the souls of these brave soldiers. Aligning themselves, they burst into the open space like a devastating cyclone. The earth trembled beneath the tread of the galloping steeds. They were riding, many of them, to death, but death in the excitement of the moment lost all its terrors, and madly they rode forward. There was no organized force in front of this magnificent column to oppose the ride. The guns were to the front and stood out boldly in the perspective. The men at the guns knew well their duty and understood the call. Not a man flinched. The horses were behind, but the cannoneers had no use for horses now. Something like five minutes was necessary to reach the battery. Every man, with quickened movements, prepared to fight to the death and to drive, with promptness and despatch, grape and canister into the ranks of the approaching Federals. The men in blue looked ahead; they saw the gunners with nimble movements loading and ramming the missiles. These they knew must soon send havoc into their ranks, but not a man swayed from his place in the line where duty bade him ride. Starting with victorious cries, they galloped to the muzzles of the thundering guns. They rode over the pieces, they sabred the gunners who did not dodge under the wheels and limber chests. They could not stop. The gait was too rapid to rein up at the guns; they dashed around and over them. If a man in gray showed himself, the swish of a sabre drove him to cover. Now, beyond the guns, they saw moving, charging men. The Federals had cut in between Hampton's and Jones' brigades, and the moment of reparation had arrived. Hampton and Jones ordered an assault upon these intrepid assailants. Orders rang out shrill and clear. The gunners who for a moment had disappeared under the wheels and chests sprang up and began to push more grape and canister into the throats of their cannon. They hurled their guns about, stood at their appointed stations ready to turn the storm loose once more against these brave men in blue, who, though balked in their work, had no mind to give up the contest.

With the Federal lines a little scattered, Hampton and Jones rushed down with impetuous fury and the Federals were glad to ride away and escape from the onslaught of these numerous, new-found foes. The guns were saved, but as if by fire; and the artillery at Fleetwood had won, if it were possible, greater fame for the horse artillery of the Army of Northern Virginia.

The morning was well advanced when a single horseman from one of Robertson's North Carolina regiments, riding with the swiftness of the wind, advised General Stuart that the Federals were advancing from Kelley's Ford, that they were now at Brandy Station, and were immediately in the rear of the Confederate line. This looked like a bad mix-up all round. The Federals were in the rear of the Confederates and the Confederates were in the rear of the Federals, and nobody seemed to know exactly where the other body was.

When this startling announcement was made, which appeared so unreasonable to General Stuart, because he did not know the man personally, he directed the scout to return and satisfy himself by closest inspection if it could be possible that the troops in the rear were Federal forces. In five minutes the man returned and with confidence pointed General Stuart to the Federal lines, then within less than half a mile of Fleetwood Hill; and there, sure enough, General Stuart saw a long column of the enemy passing. They were the men that had gone under Gregg and Duffie, down by Stevensburg, and had changed their front. They had sought and found their foes. These Federals were facing toward Brandy Station. It was apparent that in a few minutes this place would be captured, and half a mile away was Fleetwood Hill, and this was the key to the situation.

General Stuart, great commander though he was, now faced difficult and perplexing problems that might have embarrassed a man less experienced and less great.

A single gun of Chew's Battery, because of its exhausted ammunition, had been abandoned on the side of the hill. Some imperfect shells and some shot had been left over in the limber chest and this one single gun was pulled up on the hill and was opened upon the advancing Federals. A courier in great haste was dispatched to General Stuart to tell him of the gravity of the situation. Only three Confederates were there, and they saw that if the Federals once gained Fleetwood Hill and were enabled to plant their artillery on its heights that it must be recovered or the day was lost. General Gregg and General Buford were advancing up the hill, and expected to take it without any fight. They were surprised to find artillery there. They had intended to attack General Stuart in the rear, where they believed there was no protection, and the stubborn defense with this gun amazed and puzzled the Federal commander. He did not know that on the hill there was only one gun and three men; one of these was Major McClellan, Stuart's adjutant general. It would not have taken long for a charging squad to have gotten control of this important post.

General Gregg, deceived by this stout resistance, prepared to meet artillery with artillery, and he lost some time in unlimbering the three guns he had with him, and as soon as possible they opened vigorously upon the gun and three men who were defending Fleetwood.

To the first courier General Stuart had been incredulous; when the second came, the sound of the Federal cannonading announced unmistakably that the report was true. The Confederates, had nothing closer to Fleetwood Hill than the 12th Virginia under Colonel Harman, and a few men under Colonel White. Major McClellan had done all he could to get orders carried to General Stuart. To get the orders delivered and have reinforcements returned seemed many hours to him and his two companions, now maintaining a place, the retaking of which was necessary to win the battle, and if retaken would cost many lives. Riding in hot haste, with lines broken, Colonel Harman was the first to reach the scene of danger. As he rode up, Major McClellan urged upon Colonel Harman the emergency of the situation. He gave him no time to form his regiment, but ordered him to go in pell mell. Harman was brave and enterprising and he obeyed his orders and rode at full speed to the top of the hill, as the brave cannoneers were retiring, after firing their last cartridge from the lone gun that was standing off Gregg and his men.

One hundred and fifty feet away the 1st New Jersey Cavalry, under Colonel Windom, was advancing in columns of squadrons, with banners flying and sabres drawn. Colonel Harman's followers of the 12th Virginia had reached the top of the hill at this critical moment, but in columns of fours it went north westwardly of the summit. The men behind their intrepid colonel rode hard to follow him and save the situation. Harman, realizing that instantaneous action was necessary, took the men he had and directed the artillery at the Federals. General Stuart, now alive to the exigencies of the situation, had ordered General Hampton and General Jones to leave the position at St. James Church and concentrate on Fleetwood Hill.

Hampton himself was a good soldier, and he had the perception of a sagacious leader, and when he heard firing he realized the danger and he had already commenced withdrawing his forces to meet the new situation.

The 12th Virginia under Harman, always gallant, at this time seemed to have failed by reason of their inability to get into line in time to make the charge. Harman notified Colonel M. C. Butler, of the South Carolina Legion, that he must look out for enemies that were in the rear, and now the Confederates set about the task of holding Fleetwood Hill, the center of this great cavalry fight. All the regiments of Jones' brigade and Hampton's brigade participated in charges and counter charges, and both sides had now reached the top of the eminence. The 1st New Jersey Cavalry had temporary possession of the hill. Harman and White had failed in the first attempt to prevent the 1st New Jersey from this movement. Harman now re-formed his regiment and went on furiously to avenge his former failure. Half way up the hill the gallant Confederate colonel was wounded in an encounter with the Federal commander. Colonel White re-formed his squadrons. He charged along the west side of the hill and attacked the three guns which General Gregg unlimbered and with which he had opened a fierce fire. He drove the Federal cavalry away from the guns, but the gunners of the 6th New York Battery, though the cavalry left them, were not disposed to give up their pieces. Of the thirty-six men, thirty were killed or wounded. All were killed or wounded beside their guns. The Confederates took possession of the pieces, but this was only after a resistance and valor that made this Federal battery famous for all time to come. The possession of these pieces, however, was not to remain long with the Confederates. The captors were quickly surrounded with superior numbers, and the Confederate commander was compelled to cut his way out with heavy loss. He was glad to get away with even a remnant of his brave followers.

Hampton, Jones, Robertson were all now converging upon Fleetwood Hill. No sooner had Flournoy, who had already been seriously battered, arrived with the 6th Virginia Cavalry than he was ordered by General Stuart to charge the Federals on the right flank, which was to the east and south of Fleetwood Hill. The decimation of the day had reduced Flournoy's regiment to two hundred men. Disparity of numbers had no terrors for these brave riders. They forced the lines of the enemy and attacked and captured their battery, but they were unable to hold it, as more than one thousand Federals attacked this regiment in the rear. But the scenes, like a kaleidoscope, were changing. Every turn of the wheel seemed to make new combinations. In the midst of this confusion and uncertainty General Wade Hampton appeared upon the scene. He entered upon their view at a gallop. As he approached Fleetwood Hill he saw the plateau covered with Federal cavalry. There was nothing to do but fight it out and so General Hampton ordered a charge of his columns.

This field was now to witness one of the most thrilling and stirring incidents of the entire war. By the commands on either side, two brigades of horsemen in column were to make an attempt to ride each other down. Such scenes with small numbers had occurred many times, but now it was to be tried out on a larger scale. Nearly evenly matched, the contest was to put to severest strain the valor and the grit of all who should enter the arena.

Neither dared await the shock that the charge of the other would bring. Motion, rapid motion alone would counteract the impact from either side. To stand still meant to be overwhelmed. To ride meant overturning, mayhap going down under a great crash, and possibly, if the sword and bullets should be escaped, then mangling or death beneath the bodies or hoofs of the maddened or injured horses.

The spirit of the hour was doing and daring. The leaders thought quickly and acted promptly. The day was well advanced when this event occurred.

Fifteen hundred horses would weigh one million, six hundred and fifty thousand pounds; fifteen hundred men would weigh two hundred and forty thousand pounds, an aggregate of one million, eight hundred and ninety thousand pounds.

One million, eight hundred and ninety thousand pounds of flesh and blood to rush at the rate of seven feet per second against a moving wall of like weight and material meant woe, ruin, desolation. It did not require long to cover the intervening space. Each side moved toward the other with grim determination, and two bodies thus in motion were to clash in a brief interval.

The men were enthused by the cries of "Charge! Charge! Charge!" and the excitement and exhilaration of battle and struggle made every heart fearless, defiant and reckless. They plunged their spurs into the sides of their steeds. Some drew their sabres, others their revolvers. The men spurring, shouting, yelling, by their enthusiasm, excited and aroused the dumb brutes, who seemed to feel the energy of combat. Racing at their highest speed, with mouths open and distended nostrils, madly and furiously they galloped to the onset.

Horses and men alike seemed to catch the animation of great deeds, and, as if in sympathy with each other, men and beasts together were willingly rushing onward to make destruction and wreck. Not a single man hesitated. Here and there a horse fell and his master went down to earth, but not one turned aside from the path of jeopardy and peril. The surging crowd, from both directions, was now, at highest speed, pushing relentlessly forward to overwhelm their foes. The beasts seemed almost human in the exhilaration and dash of the rapid charge, and appeared to apprehend the call that was being made upon their spirit and powers. Neither side took time to count the cost or figure the result. If either rode away or hesitated, they felt that the last state of that soldier would be worse than the first. There was nothing left but to fight out the issues that war at this moment had thus joined. Its terrors, if they reasoned, would overwhelm reason. Three minutes was all the time that was allowed to calculate before the awful shock would come. The crash would be bad enough, but on the eve of this, the deadly sabre loomed up before the eyes of the actors, the flash of the revolver and then the crush and down-going of stricken, maimed, dead brutes, and with them broken limbs and maimed bodies of the daring riders stood, if only for an instant, before the vision.

The fearful onset speedily came. Some horses passed their heads by, but this meant the lifting of the riders from their saddles to take their chances in the crush below. Horses' heads met horses' heads, and these sprang high into the air, and then fell in a heap on the ground. Others by the tremendous shock were killed and lay gasping in agony. Some swept by only to be turned about and anew to dash at their opposers. Of the men, some already pale in death lay beneath the bodies of their gasping steeds. Others, with glistening sabres, were cutting and slashing those who fell or lay by their side, or stood in their front. Again, others with their revolvers or carbines were firing at their foes and with savage determination fought without mercy or pity.

A dense cloud of dust rose from the spot where the struggling men and beasts had met. The smoke of firearms shut out the light of day. Amid these scenes of horror, darkness and suffering, men fought to the death. In a little while, from the dust and smoke, with blackened and stained faces the fighters began to rise. Those who had escaped returned to help those who had fallen. The passions of war seemed for a brief while satiated. The men in blue singly and in squads, glad to be relieved from the horrible surroundings, some walking and some riding, turned their faces from the fearful scenes of ruin and disaster that loomed up in ghastly horror before their eyes. They realized that the men in gray had vanquished them, and without a stain on their valor and courage, they marched away to cross the river they had forded at the coming of the dawn, with highest hopes and grandest expectations of victory.

Over toward the west was a part of the 1st New Jersey Cavalry. They had fought much during the day and they had fought well, but they were not dispirited and they were ready to fight some more. Young's charge had cut them off from their comrades. They examined the field and saw that they must either surrender or cut their way through the Confederate lines. The Confederate guns were on a narrow ridge. To gain their friends, these New Jersey men must pass through or over these batteries. These Federal horsemen were too brave to hesitate at any danger, however appalling. What was to be done must be done quickly. Delay only increased danger and risks. The coward dies a thousand deaths, the brave man dies but one, and animated by the loftiest impulses of courage, they resolved to take the one chance, and if need be to face the iron storm they well knew must burst upon them, if they made gallant attempt to ride down their foes. The bugle blast ended all questionings, and forward they galloped to meet whatever the moment should bring.

The artillerymen looked and saw a new danger looming up on the horizon. With the speed of the wind the men in blue were riding down upon them. The pieces were quickly changed to meet this advancing foe. At this critical moment there were no Confederate horsemen to help defend or support the guns. The brave artillerists, spurred to sublime valor by the exigencies of the supreme test, resolved to defend their holdings or die with their pieces.

The blue-clad assailants came dashing upon the flank of the batteries. In a moment the guns were turned and hurling defiance and destruction in the face of the foes. They unhorsed and destroyed some, but they could not destroy all, and a remnant rushed in upon the nervy gunners who awaited the crash. It was a hand-to-hand fight between the men on horseback and the men on the cannons and on the ground. The Federal colonel fell at the side of a caisson. Another gunner fired a pistol ball into the heart of the Federal major. These died gloriously, but they died in vain. The charge failed. The enemy retreated and glory crowned the brave artillerists with new laurels. They were alone, but their name was legion, and they fought with fury and with success. The Confederates held the coveted hill. Gregg had made a great fight. He and his men had lost, but they had won for Federal cavalry great honor and had shown a valor that was worthy of any cause, and which entitled them to the praise of their people and their country. From the south, toward Culpepper Court House, clouds of dust now rose on the horizon. Long lines of Confederate infantry were seen advancing. They had come to help their cavalry comrades, but their coming so long delayed was of no avail. The horsemen, without help, had driven back their foes and these were now recrossing the Rappahannock, over which at dawn they had passed with sure and expectant hopes of a speedy and great victory.

Two men, who fell on the Confederate side, proved a great loss. Colonel Sol Williams, of the 2d North Carolina Cavalry, active, brave and gallant, observing that his regiment was inactive for a brief while, volunteering to ride with the charging column, went down at the front. His death was a great loss to his country and to the cavalry service.

Colonel Frank Hampton, younger brother of General Wade Hampton, discerning an emergency, placed himself at the head of a small squad, and charged a Federal column to delay its advance until other troops could be brought to resist it. With hardly one to fifteen of the foe, he assaulted the Federal column with fiercest vigor. His small company responded to duty's call, but it was a forlorn hope. They died as brave men are ever ready to die for the cause they love. Colonel Hampton fell, mortally wounded, but he fell where all the Hamptons were wont to fall—at the front.

The Federal cavalry lost the field. They left some guns in possession of their foes, many banners, hundreds of prisoners and numerous dead. They hesitated long about leaving these things behind them, and a real grief filled their hearts at the thought that, after a day of so much daring and such brilliant achievement, they must recede before their foes and desert their wounded—remit them to the care and mercy of their enemies, and their dead to sepulture by the hands of those they had so valiantly fought.

These memories were depressing, but notwithstanding these sad recollections, they carried some splendid assurances from the field of carnage and ruin. They had met in an open field the best troopers the army of General Lee could send to conflict. Against these brave and experienced riders of the Confederates they had held their own, and for fourteen hours they had fought with a courage and an intrepidity that not even the Confederate legions could surpass. They had demonstrated that the Federal cavalry, when the conditions were equal, was not inferior to the men who rode with Stuart, and who had rendered his name and theirs illustrious. This new-found realization of power and courage gave Federal cavalry a pervading consciousness of their strength as warriors, and created in their minds and hearts a quickened courage that would bear them up and make them more fearless and efficient in the service their country would expect from them, in the twenty-two months that yet remained before the end would come, and Lee and his legions be compelled by the decrees of a pitiless fate to ground their arms and acknowledge Federal supremacy.

Chapter XXI

GENERAL J. E. B. STUART'S CHAMBERSBURG RAID, OCTOBER 9, 1862

On the 9th, 10th, 11th and 12th of October, 1862, General J. E. B. Stuart performed his most brilliant military feat in the raid on Chambersburg, Pennsylvania.

Fording the Potomac on the morning of the 10th, at early dawn, he proceeded to Mercersburg and thence to Chambersburg. The crossing of the river had been skilfully and bravely done, and the march of forty miles to Chambersburg was no mean task in the fifteen hours which had elapsed since morn. Fair weather marked the day's ride, and at 9 o'clock at night the brilliant cavalry soldier of the Army of Northern Virginia housed himself and men in the quiet and quaint old town, well up in the boundaries of the Quaker State.

It was a new experience for the loyal men of the North to find the hungry Confederate raiders in their very midst and feeding themselves in their pantries and their horses at their granaries.

But the romance of the raid was to end here.

The Potomac, never very sure in its movements, might rise, and Stuart must then return some other way than the one he came. The splashing of the rain, relentless and constant, during the night, and the pattering of great drops as they drove against the window panes, awakened in his bosom the most harassing uncertainty; and throughout the long and (to him) almost endless hours of darkness, came the harrowing thought that the streams fed by the torrents now falling would swell the Potomac and thus cut off all possibility of escape for his command.

His aides and guides, less troubled with responsibility, assured him that his fleet troopers would outride the currents that flowed toward the ocean; but the danger and the trials of the coming day and night rose up in the heart of the dashing commander and disturbed the quiet of his gay and chivalrous soul.

On the morning of the 11th he began his homeward march. Eighty miles from the boundary, where he might pass it, far into an unfriendly country, every resource of which was now placed under contribution to effect his capture or the destruction of his force, and with thousands of troops, both mounted and unmounted, converging to the points where he must pass, rendered his situation acutely desperate and such as to cause keenest apprehension and profoundest fear.

But with Stuart rode officers and men who never quailed. Hampton, Lee, Butler, Robertson, Jones and Pelham, and 1,800 men, the pick of Virginia, Maryland and the Carolinas, were in the saddle with him, and there was no foe they feared and none who could whip them except by brute force and superior numbers.

Forth from Chambersburg this splendid division began the march homeward. Twelve hundred horses, the fruits of impressment, made up a part of the train—for already the Confederacy felt the need of stable recruiting—no stragglers nor laggards. A great work was ahead of a great command, and no heart felt solicitude at any fate which awaited.

All day long the steady trot of the troopers was kept up, and when the sun began to hide its face behind the Alleghanies the cavalcade had been less than half the distance required of it for safety and rest. A few minutes' halt was all that could be allowed. The troopers dismount and shake themselves; the wearied horses munch a little feed, and the bugle-call again commands to saddle.

Thirty-one and a half miles since morn, and yet thirty-three and a half more before dawn.

The knightly Pelham, later to shed his blood, rode all through the night with the advance, and close behind the watchful commander and his escort.

A full day's work already done, but a fuller night's work yet to be done.

Peremptory orders are transmitted to ride over everything that opposes the march; and so, trot, trot, trot, through the long hours of darkness, and the wearied horsemen peer through the gloom, and in silent and anxious wonder gaze at the spectres—the creation of their fancy and imagination—which on parallel lines ride by their side; and they scan the horizon with anxious longing to catch the first appearance of the much-desired dawn, which might relieve the dismal and oppressive foreboding of the lengthened night.

Sixty-five miles in twenty-four hours. No halt. Still sixteen miles more.

Thousands of busy and eager enemies and uncalculated dangers beset them. The bodies of these hard riders begin to feel the trying effects of the rapid march, and nature raises a solemn protest against war's demands upon her children. But the order for the swinging trot abates not, and man and beast, brightened by the rising sun, are put under sterner tribute for stronger effort.

Wearied marchers: the crisis is now at hand.

Stuart and his riders had vanquished nature: Could they now vanquish man? If Stuart crossed the Potomac to reach Chambersburg, he must recross it to reach Virginia; and to prevent the latter, all the skill, energy and genius of the Federal commanders were called forth.

Pleasanton, who with Federal cavalry was hard behind the Confederate raiders, had marched seventy-eight miles in twenty-eight hours, but this wonderful gait still left him in Stuart's rear, and now that the point at which Stuart was to cross was revealed, every Federal soldier that could be reached was pressed forward to dispute the passage. Whit's Ford was guarded, but not sufficiently well to impede the rush of the Confederates, and the Federals at the crucial moment retired, and the way was opened for the escape and safety of the valiant Confederate corps.

Twenty-seven hours and eighty-one miles. No sleep. No rest.

Galloping, fighting, scouting and ready to assail any enemy, with human endurance tested to the greatest possible limit—what think you, reader, of the conduct of these riders, when, out of those three brigades, only two men, either by sleep, illness, hunger, weariness or straggling, were missing when, at noon, on the 12th of October, on Virginia's soil, Stuart called his roll to calculate losses?

Measured by any human formula for patience or endurance, courage, loyalty and chivalry, this service of Stuart and his command stands with but few parallels in military history. They did all men could do, and the Divine Judge himself requires nothing more than this at man's hands.

Chapter XXII

GENERAL JOHN B. MARMADUKE'S
"CAPE GIRARDEAU RAID," APRIL, 1863

General John B. Marmaduke was a thoroughly born and reared Southern man. Descended from Virginia ancestry, he first saw the light on March 14th, 1833, at Arrow Rock, Missouri. Possessed of a splendid physique, with a common school education, he entered Yale. He was there two years and one year at Harvard, and then he was appointed to the United States Military Academy from whence he graduated when twenty-two years of age. As a brevet second lieutenant he went with Albert Sidney Johnston and aided in putting down the Mormon revolt in 1858. He remained in the West for two years and at the opening of the Civil War was stationed in New Mexico. Fond of military life, it involved much sacrifice for him to resign his commission in the United States Army, but he did not hesitate an instant and on the 17th of April, 1861, he severed his connection with the regular army and at once raised a company of Missouri State Guards. His West Point education gave him prominence at once and he was made colonel of a Missouri military organization. Brave and proud-spirited, he disagreed with his uncle, Claiborne F. Jackson, then governor of Missouri, and left the service there and reported at Richmond, to the Confederate government. He had five brothers in the Confederate Army or Navy. His father, Meredith Miles Marmaduke, was governor of Missouri in 1844.

With General Hardee, in Southeast Missouri, he was made colonel of the 3d Confederate Infantry. Crossing the river to aid General Albert Sidney Johnston destroy Grant's army, he participated in the Battle of Shiloh, and was signally honored by his grateful government for his splendid service and was made a brigadier general while he was yet an inmate of the hospital from wounds received on that field. There was a great call at that time in the West for brave and experienced men, and four months after the Battle of Shiloh he was transferred to the trans-Mississippi Department, and from August, 1862, to January, 1863, he

356

commanded the Confederate cavalry in Arkansas and Missouri. Vigilant, active and enterprising, he made a number of raids into Missouri. He was a fierce fighter, and never hesitated to attack his enemy when prudence justified an assault. Ordered to break Federal communication between Springfield and Rolla, Missouri, he inflicted great loss upon his enemies, but after a most valiant attack, through the failure of some of his troops to come on time, he was compelled to withdraw and retreat. He held a conspicuous place in the attack upon Helena, Arkansas, in July, 1863, and was successful in capturing the Federal camps at Pine Bluff. In the defense of Little Rock he played a notable part and covered General Price's retreat after the evacuation of the capital of Arkansas.

He fought a duel with General Lucien M. Walker which shadowed his life. Under the terms arranged by the seconds, the two men were placed ten feet apart. The weapons were revolvers, and they were to advance and continue firing until the weapons were empty. Walker was mortally wounded at the second shot. Marmaduke was placed under arrest and relieved of his command. The exigencies of the hour made his services so important that he was permitted to resume his command during the pending operations. He was finally released by General Holmes. All through Missouri and Arkansas and Louisiana he was in many engagements, and for his magnificent service in 1864 in delaying Steele and preventing his union with General Banks, and for his valor in the Battle of Jenkins Ferry, he was made a major general. He was with Price in his ill-fated campaign in the fall of 1864. Dauntless and gallant in the protection of Price's rear, while making vigorous battle he was captured near Fort Scott, Kansas. He was carried to Fort Warren and remained there until August, 1865, and when released went abroad, but returned to engage in business in St. Louis. For two years he was active in journalism. He served as secretary of the Missouri Board of Agriculture, was railroad commissioner four years, elected governor of Missouri in 1884, in which office he died in his fifty-fourth year, in Jefferson City, on December 24th, 1887.

Brave, of great resource, intensely loyal, few men of the war had as many wide experiences. The South had no more loyal son. His three and a half years of military service were marked with incessant and constant activities, and he had no rest, unless while in the hospital recovering from wounds received in battle. Although connected with the cavalry, in an engagement where some Missouri infantry were falling back before

357

a sudden and terrific fire, General Marmaduke, with an aide-de-camp, William Price, rode in among the hesitating infantry, and violently taking from two standard bearers their colors, rushed into the midst of these troops and lifting the banners aloft pleaded with the men to stand firm. His noble example restored order to the line, and out of retreat they moved forward with conspicuous gallantry, and won victory.

In March, 1863, General Holmes was relieved of the command of the Trans-Mississippi Department, and General E. Kirby Smith, who had made such a brilliant reputation in the Kentucky campaign with the army of Tennessee, was assigned to the full charge of the territory. He established his headquarters at Shreveport, Louisiana, and General Holmes was placed in command of the district of Arkansas, which included Arkansas, Indian Territory and the state of Missouri.

Early in April, 1863, General Price returned after his service in the army of Tennessee and the Trans-Mississippi Department, and was assigned to the command of an infantry division. In the northern part of Arkansas there was nothing except Marmaduke's division of cavalry, and this was in and around Batesville. The Confederates were loth to abandon the portion of Arkansas above the Arkansas River, and endeavored to hold the enemy in check for eighty miles north of that stream. The Confederates were not unaware that a most determined effort would be made to capture Little Rock. By the aid of the forces from Memphis and up the Arkansas River and down through Missouri, combinations were made which it was believed would render it impossible for the Confederates to hold that post.

The only really organized force operating in the territory northwest of Arkansas was Marmaduke's cavalry division, composed of Shelby's and Greene's brigades. Anxious to do something to relieve the pressure upon Little Rock, General Marmaduke felt that if he should march northeastwardly to Cape Girardeau, Missouri, he might accomplish two things: first, he might recruit quite a large number of troops. Missouri was one of the best recruiting grounds for the Confederate states. There was no time when an organized force entered Missouri, when there was any sort of opportunity for the young men, or even the middle-aged men to enter the Confederate service that hundreds of them did not rush to the Confederate standard. Marmaduke, Shelby, Price and all those who invaded Missouri were not only gratified but astonished at the readiness with which recruits flocked to join them.

General Marmaduke believed that he might stay the approach of the Federals in their advance upon Little Rock. General Holmes was so pleased with Marmaduke's offer to do something that he not only approved but encouraged him, and ordered forward to his support Carter's brigade of Texas cavalry, which was the possessor of a four-gun battery and counted fifteen hundred men. The men of this brigade were not experienced, but they had grit, endurance and courage, and they were not long in measuring up to the standard of veterans. This gave General Marmaduke a force of nearly five thousand cavalry and eight pieces of artillery, but nearly one-fourth of them were unarmed and one-fifth dismounted. This was a formidable array to turn loose either in the rear or in the face of the enemy. It was more than Morgan ever had under his command; it was more than General Wheeler was ever able to take on a raid; and was greater than General Forrest had hitherto been able to pull together.

Marmaduke also learned that there was a Federal officer at Bloomfield, five miles south of Cape Girardeau, who had become infamous in the eyes of the Confederates, and of all the men in the Federal Army the Missouri troops would rather have captured General John McNeil. He was known amongst the men of the South as "the butcher." This came from his brutality to prisoners and citizens, and he was the most hated man in the Federal Armies west of the Mississippi River.

The season of the year was fairly propitious for cavalry marches. The country was denuded of corn and oats, but green stuff was abundant and the grasses which grew with such luxuriousness in that section furnished bountiful feed, such as it was, for the horses. The scarcity of grain made raiding difficult unless grass was growing. Colonel John F. Phillips, commanding a Federal Missouri cavalry regiment, on July 30th, 1863, wrote of this section: "There is nothing to eat in this country. It is the impersonation of poverty and desolation."

From Batesville, Arkansas, to Cape Girardeau was about one hundred and eighty miles. Marmaduke had learned that McNeil had been ordered to march northward from Bloomfield, Missouri, toward Pilot Knob. This would be a distance of seventy miles. Marmaduke reasoned correctly that McNeil would obey orders, and so he sent a force toward Bloomfield to stir up McNeil, hoping that he would follow the directions of his superiors and march toward Pilot Knob. Frederickstown was ten miles southeast of Pilot Knob, and here Marmaduke purposed to intercept McNeil, and with

Carter behind him and Shelby in front of him, it was calculated that short work would be made of McNeil's two thousand infantry.

In the beginning of the march there was warm work at Patterson, a small town fifty miles from the Arkansas line. At this point a Missouri Federal militia regiment, under Colonel Smart, and several Home Guard companies had been stationed for quite a while. One of the most offensive of these Home Guard companies was commanded by Captain Leper. Neither Leper nor Smart stood well with the Confederates. They had been aggressive, cruel and malignant, and General Marmaduke had particular reasons for capturing both Leper and Smart. The presence of the Confederates had not been known fully to Smart and his associates, and General Marmaduke had made disposition of his forces to surround Patterson and its garrison, which he intended to capture at any cost. With his eight pieces of artillery he felt sure that within a reasonable time he could batter down the fortifications. Shelby was ordered to swing to the east, and a Texas regiment was to move west; the Texas forces were to go east of the place and close in from that direction, while Shelby came from the other side. The Missourians caught all the pickets, and without alarm were ready to assault the garrison. The officers in charge of the Texas brigade were not familiar with the Missouri tactics. Instead of capturing the pickets, they undertook to fight them and used the artillery and opened a vigorous fire upon these isolated videttes. Colonel Smart had been insistent that there was nothing but a few militia in proximity to Patterson, but when he heard the sound of the artillery, he realized that heavy forces were about to encircle him, and he speedily and hastily fled. A small part of the garrison was captured. The men the Confederates wanted, Smart and Leper, escaped. These fired the houses containing the supplies, and a large part of the town was burned. Later this was charged to the Confederates, and after the war suits were brought against quite a number of Confederate officers to make them responsible for the destruction of the town. This was annoying, but it was not effective. The escape of the hated men quickened desire to bag General McNeil.

A short while after this campaign McNeil still further increased his reputation for bloodthirstiness. A Federal spy was captured and disappeared near Palmyra.

Major J. N. Edwards in his splendid work, "Shelby and his Men," gives the following account of this terrible incident:

Colonel Porter captured Palmyra late in the fall of 1863, and during his occupation of the town, one Andrew Allsman, an ex-soldier of the 3d Missouri Federal Cavalry, and a spy, informer, guide, traitor and scoundrel generally, was spirited away, no one ever knew how or where. McNeil re-entered Palmyra upon its evacuation by Colonel Porter, confined ten worthy and good men captured from Porter's command, issued a notice to Porter dated October 8th, informing him that unless Allsman was returned within ten days from the date thereof, the prisoners then in his possession should be executed. W. R. Strachan was the provost marshal, and was just as cruel and just as bloodthirsty as his master. Allsman was not returned—indeed, Porter never saw this notice until the men were shot—and even had it been placed before him, the rendition of Allsman was an impossibility, for he knew nothing whatever of the men required to be produced. Deaf to all petitions, steeled against every prayer for mercy, eager and swift to act, McNeil ordered the execution at the end of the appointed time. Ten brave, good men—Willis Baker, Thomas Humston, Morgan Bixler, John Y. McPheeters, Herbert Hudson, Captain Thomas A. Snider, Eleazer Lake and Hiram Smith—were led out for the death shots. Fearless, proud and noble in their bearing, these innocent and excellent soldiers were sacrificed to the whim of a butcher, and to satisfy the cravings of a foreign and brutal soldiery. They met death without a shudder, willing to yield upon their country's altar the lives that had been devoted to her service. A young Spartan—one of the abovementioned men—volunteered to take the place of an old man whose family was large and helpless, was accepted, and untouched by the heroism of the boy, and indifferent to one of the finest exhibitions of chivalry upon record, McNeil and Strachan ordered his execution with the rest, thus covering their names with everlasting infamy.

Colonel Carter, of Texas, commanding the brigade called by his name, ambitious for distinction, solicited the leadership of the force which was to attack McNeil, and drive him either to follow the line of his orders or force him to Cape Girardeau. He was specially directed under no circumstances to follow McNeil into Cape Girardeau. That post was strongly fortified and was considered a position of great value on the Mississippi River. Carter was given a force equal to that of McNeil, so that there would be no question of McNeil's discomfiture if he disputed Carter's right of way. The men who fought in Missouri and Arkansas never hesitated about results if it was man to man. McNeil's courage had been hampered by a knowledge of the fact that the Missouri troops had declared if he was ever taken they would put him to death. His persecutions and atrocities had rendered him so odious that nothing could stay the vengeful resolves which filled the hearts of the Missouri and Arkansas Confederates. Carter had orders if McNeil went to Cape Girardeau to rejoin Marmaduke. Marmaduke with Shelby's brigade and half of Greene's reached Frederickstown, and there waited for a sight of McNeil or for a report from Carter. Neither came. Quickly marching his command to Jackson, half way between Frederickstown and Cape Girardeau, General Marmaduke there learned that McNeil had hastened to Cape Girardeau; that Carter, pursuing him, had become so enthused that he had lost sight of his positive orders from Marmaduke and had followed McNeil up to and partially into the fortifications of Cape Girardeau. McNeil's reinforcing the garrison rendered the Federal forces at the Cape impregnable. McNeil was inside the fortification and Carter was outside and he was afraid to go away lest the Federals should rush out and destroy him. Shelby was immediately despatched to extricate Carter from his embarrassing situation. In order to do this, it was necessary to attack the fortification, which Shelby promptly did, and lost forty-five men, killed and wounded, among them some of the very best in his brigade. Some were so seriously wounded that it was impossible to remove them, and they were left in charge of a surgeon, amongst their enemies. In those days of intense bitterness and malignity, this was barely preferable to death.

These four days lost meant much to General Marmaduke. The exuberant zeal of one of Carter's colonels, coupled with his courage, had changed the Confederate plan and destroyed its successful accomplishment, and seriously affected the ultimate safety of Marmaduke's whole division. It was only thirty miles from Cairo to Bloomfield, and from New Madrid, Missouri, to Bloomfield, Marmaduke must almost of necessity pass this point, and this rendered the Confederate Army assailable both in its front and in its rear.

Marmaduke, north of Cape Girardeau, started his army south on the 27th of April. General Vandever was north of Marmaduke, and McNeil was south of him. McNeil, who had one day's start and the shortest road to travel, could easily have intercepted Marmaduke and blocked his way of escape. Marmaduke, of course, might have ridden around him, and doubtless would have attempted to do this, but this was hazardous. McNeil became intimidated by the fear that he might be captured, and that, he well understood, meant direful consequences, and instead of pursuing the shorter road, it was charged that he intentionally took the longer one and let Marmaduke pass the critical point unopposed. This put the entire Federal force behind the Confederates, where it had no chance either greatly to disturb or arrest their march, unless the swelling currents of the St. Francis River might hold them in check until the Federal pursuers could, through such barrier, reach and overwhelm them.

General Curtis, from St. Louis, sent reinforcements to Cape Girardeau, and he had ordered from Columbus, Kentucky, several regiments through New Madrid, Missouri, to prevent or embarrass the escape of Marmaduke.

McNeil, on the 26th of April, telegraphed from Cape Girardeau that he was attacked by eight thousand men under Marmaduke.

General William Vandever, on April 29th, 1863, six miles from Bloomfield, Missouri, speaking of Marmaduke, said: "I think we have run him harder than he has ever run before."

Of the men who went with Marmaduke, as before stated, twelve hundred were unmounted and nine hundred unarmed. Some of the men had Enfield rifles, some Mississippi and squirrel rifles. Practically no captures had been made, and the opportunities for securing mounts in this already war-cursed country were very slim. The unmounted men, with hope stirring their hearts, half running, half walking, kept up with their more fortunate comrades who had started with beasts that could at least go a part of the way. If any of these walking troopers picked up a mount, it was the occasion for special thanks to the God of war. In the beginning General Marmaduke divided his forces over large territory and scattered them, to create the impression that he was moving northwardly instead of northeastwardly. He trusted in this way to throw his enemies off their guard. This would enable him to surprise, if not destroy them. McNeil heard of Marmaduke's coming and retired to Cape Girardeau. He was not willing to meet the Confederates in the open field. The best that Marmaduke could count on for fighting was thirty-five hundred men, a majority of them inadequately armed. He was to face at Cape Girardeau and elsewhere more than ten thousand men. When the Federals started southwardly, after leaving sufficient men to garrison Cape Girardeau, they had forty-five hundred cavalry, forty-five hundred infantry and fifteen pieces of artillery to join in the pursuit.

On the night of the 21st of April Captain John M. Muse of the Missouri division had been ordered with ninety men to Farmington, Missouri, in order to attempt the destruction of the bridge of the St. Louis & Iron Mountain Railroad. This was to terrify St. Louis and hold in check the garrisons north of Frederickstown. He was to travel through the woods until he reached Farmington. Enterprising, as well as brave, Muse moved with the greatest celerity. The bridges were all well guarded, and while he destroyed one bridge, the task was performed under tremendous difficulties and with supreme danger. The experiences of this force for four days in the work assigned them was one of the most difficult as well as the most dangerous and heroic happenings of the whole war.

In those days it was easy enough to get into Missouri, but sometimes it was extremely difficult to get out. The Confederates were sorely pressed by two commands, each of them outnumbering their forces. Marmaduke and Shelby did not count the Federals real peril. They believed they could, if necessary, fight and rout these. They could not whip or outwit the elements, and these gave them deep concern. Heavy rains fell, and as there was nothing but mud roads through the territory it required but a few hundred cavalry to pass over one of these to render it thereafter almost impossible to travel. But there was something even worse than these rains and the roads. That was the necessity of crossing swollen streams. Generals can rely upon the fidelity and courage of their troops, but they cannot control the weather. The heavy rains at this period came most inopportunely for General Marmaduke. When he realized the necessity of retiring, he was miles north of Cape Girardeau. General Vandever was behind him, and McNeil over at Cape Girardeau had the shorter route, and with diligence and energy could put himself at any time across his front. The Federals were intensely aroused. They resented this invasion and used the Mississippi and the Ohio Rivers in the endeavor to put armies athwart the path that Marmaduke must travel. The situation was full of discouragement. One could not look ahead without seeing dangers, nor think without facing difficulties. The ownership of horses under the exigencies of such a raid was never seriously considered, and while each side would prefer to take from their enemies, they were not unwilling, under the calls of necessity, in the end to impress from their friends. Everything in the line of march that could carry a man or that was better than some man's horse in the column was quickly appropriated. The heavy marching, the muddy roads and the constant rain had impaired the vitality of a majority of the mounts of General Marmaduke's men. The horses sank to their knees in the mud, and to carry the soldiers and their equipment and be subject to so much that was injurious under foot not only seriously tried the horses, but it laid grievous burdens upon the men who marched in the rear. The Federal and Confederate artillery had moved over these roads; Federal supply wagons had cut them full of deep ruts, and jug holes and gullies had been washed out, making the movement of artillery tedious and difficult. Three miles an hour with such passways and surroundings would be rapid marching. Many sought to escape the burdens and difficulties of the main road and scattered along the woods or in the fields which lay alongside the line of travel. No sooner would a third of the command pass over any given part of the road than it was a lagoon of mud and slush. Spattered in every direction by the horses' feet, this disgusting mixture was plastered upon the backs and hips of the beasts and the bodies of the men. Their necks and their faces were encased with the horrible substance. The sides of the horses were covered half an inch deep with the mud, and the clothes of the men were so bespattered that they looked as if they had been drawn through the disgusting mixture. There were no farms, no stores, and few homes to supply any food other than that carried in their haversacks, and this, by the constant rains and the churning on the backs of the men, became so unpalatable that it required fiercest hunger to force the men to eat at all.

When once the question of return was presented and settled it became the paramount thought of the hour. It would have been a tremendous blow to the Confederacy to have had Marmaduke and his men captured. The idea of surrender never entered the minds of these raiders. The marching was to be rapid, and the tired and hungry beasts could not expect much rest from their labors. The most they could have was to browse upon the grass which during the spring season had grown up in the woods and fields and pastures along the roads. The closest point from Cape Girardeau at which Marmaduke could cross the St. Francis River would be fifty miles. The size of the division did much to lengthen the hours of the march. Few cavalry commands ever undertook to ride through any worse country or to travel more difficult roads. The highway was just broad enough for two soldiers to ride abreast, and forty-five hundred men riding two abreast with eight pieces of artillery makes a column from three to five miles. There was no parallel road General Marmaduke could use. It was necessary to keep the Confederates in supporting distance to each other. The men who were pursuing not only had the best mounts, but they had complete supplies of every kind for man and beast.

General Marmaduke dare not separate his forces lest he should be attacked in detail by the forty-five hundred cavalry who were following his train. It might, and probably would happen, that he would need every man he could summon. It required a beast far less time to eat a gallon of oats or corn than to satisfy its hunger by browsing in the woods or fields and thereby secure a sufficiency to meet its hunger and maintain its vitality. The Confederates' ammunition was now much impaired. The horses for the artillery and the ammunition wagons and the ambulance had been worn out by the march of two hundred and fifty miles. Marmaduke resolved under no circumstances to abandon his artillery. Among the cavalry, the horse artillery was always to be saved, and only extraordinary emergencies would justify any command in giving up its guns. The armies, East and West, looked askance at cavalry who abandoned or permitted the capture of their artillery. Only extremest reasons would excuse such results. Cannon suitable for the artillery in Marmaduke's Missouri department was not over-abundant, and many requisitions and a good many petitions had to be made before the meagre supply possessed by the Missouri, Texas and Arkansas cavalry could be obtained, and Marmaduke in conjunction with Shelby resolved that only a great peril and severe disaster would justify them in leaving or destroying their few guns.

No officer had a tent. All—of whatever rank—took pot-luck with the men on the ground. Here and there a deserted stable, or an outhouse, or an abandoned home might afford shelter for a small part of the command. All were placed on a common level, in-so-far as conveniences were concerned. No officer was willing to accept anything better than that which the men obtained. Some brush or evergreen limbs, or—if the ravages of war had spared them—a few rails, were laid upon the soaked earth. Over these a gum or other blanket was spread, and these constituted the couches upon which these brave and self-sacrificing soldiers would find even a few hours of rest.

From Frederickstown to the St. Francis River was seventy-five miles. Once the St. Francis was passed, safety was assured. Starting from Frederickstown, on the 27th of April, Shelby, Marmaduke and Carter, the last men to cross the St. Francis River, went over on the 1st of May. This ninety-six hours was used to cover seventy-five miles. This was an average of three-quarters of a mile per hour. There was no human energy that could move a division at a much greater rate of speed. Nature put every possible impediment in the way of these tired, patient Confederate cavalry. Hour by hour, the officers and the men watched the falling rain, and they all understood that these meant increasing difficulties and added danger, and greater labor. The bridges had all been destroyed. Either Federals or Confederates had burned them before. Those who passed these streams must ford them or provide temporary passways. Hours before, Marmaduke and Shelby had been revolving in their minds what might occur when they reached the St. Francis River. They needed no weather prophet to tell them what was going to happen from the incessant rains which had fallen for the last four or five days. The Confederates had no pontoon bridges and no pontoon tackle. They had some axes, a few spikes, and the pioneers a few augurs. With this limited equipment, they understood that they must take what they could find on the banks of the stream and construct something that would carry over the guns and caissons and at least permit the men to walk (even though the bridge be partly submerged) across the rapid currents. The pursuers well understood the thoughts that were passing through the minds of the retreating Confederates. If they were cornered, there could be no doubt that a ferocious resistance would meet the men in blue. If the worst came to the worst, Marmaduke and his men might ride through and over the cavalry that was pursuing them and they could sweep aside the infantry that, by easy stages, along the lands outside the traveled road, were seeking to overtake them or at least to furnish backing for the cavalry who were to do the aggressive and sharper work. There were many anxious hearts among the forty-eight hundred Confederate cavalry. The rank and file had supreme confidence in both Marmaduke and Shelby. They were leaders who never ran away without good reason, and few wished to run away on this expedition. There was no place where they could find even reasonable hope if scattered. It was necessary for them to hang together and to Shelby and his brigade was largely committed the defense of the rear. They had been tried in many difficult circumstances in the past and the three thousand Confederates in front knew that they would discharge well all the duties which might be committed to them in this hour of extremity.

A trembling, crazy bridge had been built across the St. Francis River. This was full from bank to bank. Marmaduke, uneasy, had sent an engineer forward to make provision for crossing his army when it should reach the turgid stream. Shelby had ordered Major Lawrence, his pioneer officer, to ride without let or hindrance and construct the bridge, but Marmaduke had pre-arranged this and when Shelby's engineer reached the river, the bridge was ready for use. It was a slow process to erect this structure. Only men could tread its swinging lines. These were compelled to cross in single file. The river was not cold enough to seriously chill the horses, and they took their chances in the rapid currents. The artillery was the real perplexity. Huge logs were cut down and fastened together, an unwieldy raft was constructed, while an improvised barge helped hold the mass in line, and a piece at a time was run upon the raft and with great effort ferried over. It was a weird scene that night on the banks of the raging stream. All horses can swim, they do not have to be taught as men. With them it is an instinct. Fires were kindled along the bank, and with some oaths and much belaboring the brutes, in the darkness, were forced into the water. Some turned back, but they were beaten over the head with brush and limbs, and then some bold horsemen would plunge in and turn their heads southward across the stream, and, like a long flock of wild geese, with a leader, the horses would paddle themselves across the river. Eight hours of the night were consumed in this dangerous undertaking. To cross four thousand men in single file, and get eight pieces of artillery and eight caissons on a square raft against a rapid current was no mean task.

Two miles back on the road from the river was another weird scene. There were no lights there. General Shelby and his brigade were posted on each side of the battery which occupied the highway, and then the word was passed along the line that come what might, not an inch of ground was to be yielded. These orders are always portentous, and yet they are not terrifying to brave men. A sense of duty comes to the rescue of the human soul under such conditions, and this calms fear and makes hearts unfaltering.

The spirits of the weary horsemen rose to the sublimest heights. There was not a minute in these eight hours that a foe was not expected. Far out on the roads, vigilant scouts were riding, and far back on the way, for several miles, videttes and squads were posted, so as to catch the first sound of an enemy's approach. These were all watching and waiting to bring the Confederate rearguard warning of the coming of a foe. They had ridden hard every hour of the day. There was neither corn nor hay nor oats to stay the pangs of hunger which were felt by the half-famished beasts. In sheer pity at first they were permitted, at the ends of the halter, to nibble the grass which even the blight and ravages of war could not destroy, but later this was denied. Their browsing might disturb the acuteness of hearing, and more than that, at any moment they might be called to bear their masters into a night charge. Hard as it looked, they were saddled and bridled, and stood with their owners in line, waiting and ready to fight any foe that might come.

There was no sleeping this night. It was a night of danger, a night of extremest peril. Officers and men stood around in groups, and attack was expected every instant. A sleeping picket, forgetful of duty, at this momentous instant, a forgetful scout, tired out it may be by lengthened and incessant marching, might imperil the safety of the entire command. Men were not left alone to pass the fateful hours and important labors of this crucial moment; they were placed two and two, so that the strengthening of companionship would help them bear the burdens and endure the hardships of the weary hours and heavy tasks of the long, long night. A foe filled with vengeful desire to capture and destroy Marmaduke and his men was behind, and the deep, seething river was in front. No eye could penetrate far into the forest through which the column reached. Horses were brought close up to the line of battle. Here and there a horseholder might steal a cat nap, or at some moment when he was not watched, might, beside a tree, or a stump, enjoy a brief sleep, but it was only for an instant, for everybody was on the lookout. A thousand men were to do an heroic act for three thousand down at the river bank. Those at the river bank might hear the sound of artillery and the rattle of musketry, horses might be pushed into the stream and the riders, stripped and holding to their manes and tails, might possibly cross over the river, but these men who had been placed on the outpost with orders to stand in the face of all attacks, if need be to die there, found no time for sleep.

Shelby and Shanks, and Gordon, and Carter, were all there. They understood and appreciated the importance of the work which had been given them to do. The call of the impending crisis sounded in their ears and filled their souls with sublime courage. The past of these soldiers was a glorious and magnificent record. This lifted them up into a frame of mind which nerved them, if need be, to despise death and cheerfully to perish at the post when duty called. They waited and waited and waited, and no foe came. A little while before the gray streaks of light came coursing in long lines from the east, they were still ready to do and die. A courier came to tell them that all but they had passed the stream. The guns were limbered, and the horses with the artillery in silence were turned toward the St. Francis River, and Shelby and his men, with such horses as had been retained for the use of the rearguard, slowly and complacently rode down to the spot where their comrades had spent the night in ferrying the stream. All did not come at once. The line was long extended, and when the vanguard and the artillery reached the stream, the needed preparations to cross had been made. Two trips put the artillery on the south bank. The horses must take their chances in the stream, and then the men in single file, with water to their knees, slowly waded along the swaying bridge that the currents moved to and fro and threatened to engulf those treading it at every step.

In this retreat and escape across the river, somebody had to be last, and that somebody must take not only the chances of capture, but also the risks of annihilation.

Upon Captain George Gordon, with one hundred and twenty Missourians, this burden was laid. He had been marching and fighting and starving for more than half a month. Shelby had told his men that, as the rearguard, they must all stand together and if need be, fall, and that he did not under any circumstances intend to allow his artillery to be destroyed or captured. Upon Captain George Gordon was laid the duty of holding the last outpost, and with his men constitute the forlorn hope in defense of this little army in its passage of the St. Francis River.

The artillery had been saved. The rearguard, mounted, was not yet over. The sun was just rising when the raft made its last trip and landed the last caisson on the southern bank of the stream. With the sun came the Federal pursuers. They had not believed the Confederates would be able in the night to cross the St. Francis, and so they slept and waited, feeling assured that on the morrow capture would be easy. The Federal sharp-shooters came pressing through the heavy timber. They opened a severe fire, and the thud of a minie ball, ploughing its way through the body of some member of the faithful little rearguard, served notice that trouble was abroad in the land. The pressure grew stronger and stronger. Only a hundred and twenty men in gray were on the north side. All others were safely over the unfordable stream. Federal cavalry riding in hot pursuit could be seen galloping down the highway, and between them and the raging river was only a small column of brave riders clad in gray. The Confederates safely on the south bank looked across the water and grieved at the fate of the one hundred and twenty comrades who stood and held the pursuers at bay until all the others were safely over. Their courage and their generosity appealed to the better instincts of the courageous soldiers. Some offered to swim back and help and rescue the gallant remnant who still remained on the north bank. Sharp-shooters climbed the high trees on the south bank. Some found cozy places on the hills close to the stream, and with deadly aim warned the intruders to caution and reserve.

The water was too deep and the currents too swift to attempt with saddles and bridles and guns to swim the weary beasts over, encumbered as they must be, either in carrying or pulling their riders. There were only three alternatives for these rearguardsmen. One was to surrender; one was to swim, with the chance that more than half would be drowned; and the other was to ride up the stream and seek a more favorable locality for passing the river.

The Federal cavalry were in close and fierce pursuit. Twice this gallant band attempted, when a shallower spot had been found, to cross, but the Federals, angered by the escape of the main army, felt that they were bound to take this rearguard, and so they pressed in upon them with much vigor and determination, resolving to capture them at all hazards.

At last a better swimming place was found, and the rearguard, resolving to die or drown rather than submit to capture, forced their horses into the water. A fusillade of shots was directed at them as they swam across, and the bullets came quick and fast. These spattered the water in the faces of the receding Confederates, and here and there a fatal shot took effect and the lifeless body of a Confederate floated a little way on the surface and then sank in the current. Only a few were killed or wounded. More than nine-tenths of these brave fighters reached the opposite bank.

Shaking the water from their soaked garments, the sharp-shooters turned and fired upon their pursuers, and with steady and accurate aim avenged the death and wounds of those who had suffered in this retreat.

Shelby and Colonel Gordon and Carter were the last men to cross the bridge. Unsightly, tottering, shaky, the bridge had served its purpose. It was not much of a bridge, but it had saved four thousand men and their equipment. Fastened with cables on the south side, when Shelby and Carter stepped upon the shore, a ready knife was drawn by one of his followers, the moorings were cut and the faithful bridge, no longer required, was turned loose down the stream. As it floated out upon the rapid currents, the Federals on the opposite side, in rage and disappointment, opened a fusillade across the water, but a few well-directed shots from the cannon drove them to cover, and Marmaduke, Shelby and Carter and their followers, saved now from pursuit, took up their journey to Jacksonport, sixty miles away. They had no need now to hasten, there was no foe to disturb, alarm and harass them. For four days they waded and rode through muddy, slimy swamps. The experience in these sloughs was horrible in the extreme.

The troopers, willing to rest their faithful steeds, dismounted and walked by their sides. Three times a day they were permitted to graze upon the rich herbage that lined the roads to Jacksonport. Separated along different highways, both men and horses were treated with the greatest consideration and given easy journeys to the camp at Jacksonport, where the wounded might mend, where the horses with scalded backs might recuperate and permit their scars to be covered, and the men might burnish their arms, repair their trappings, wash their soiled garments, and be ready for some other expedition at their country's call.

For four days they had something to face worse than enemies. They were compelled to wade and ride through the muddy, slimy swamps south of the St. Francis. These sloughs, generating miasma in every particle that composed their horrible mixture, rendered these ninety-six hours excruciatingly trying. There was no escape from the slightly elevated roads that had been cut through these forests and swamps. Only a small portion of the cavalry and artillery could pass along these roads until they became practically impassable. The cannons were mired and the horses were tramping in mud and slush above their knees. With the gait of a snail, Marmaduke's men walked and rode amidst these dreadful surroundings. Had they not been brave men, they would have preferred to have laid down and died rather than to have endured the horrors of this march. A common suffering made them generous and helpful to each other. Food was scarce for man, and there was practically none for the beasts, and all pulled and labored through these quagmires. Longing for the sight of higher ground, praying to escape from these hateful and depressing surroundings, the terribleness of the conditions prevented the men from dismounting to help their wasted and emaciated beasts. Here and there in the mud and slush, the poor brutes, unable to move further, laid down in the water and mud, and neither coaxing nor lashing could induce them to rise. They preferred death to further torment on this God-forsaken road, and all along the path through these swamps, the beholder would constantly see horses either dying under fatigue or so burdened as to be unwilling to rise. They simply died rather than take another step forward. The constant riding by day and by night, the meagre supply of food, the perils in conflict, the tremendous fatigue, the long, long journey, all tried out their souls and their patience, but the worst and hardest of all was the ninety-six hours consumed in covering the horrible roads through these dismal swamps and gloomy bayous.

Chapter XXIII

GENERAL WHEELER'S PURSUIT AND DEFEAT
OF GENERALS STONEMAN, GARRARD AND
McCOOK, JULY 27-AUGUST 5, 1864

By July, 1864, the storms were beating heavily and mercilessly upon the Confederacy. The power of numbers was beginning to tell. The resources of the South, month by month, were more and more impaired. Munitions of war and supplies of food became the controlling elements, and in these the Confederates fared most grievously. The arsenals and manufactories were worked to their utmost limit, and one of the most marvelous things connected with the Confederate war was the ability of its people to supply the necessities of the fighters. The disparity of fighting men was tremendous, and the difference in resources and supplies was to the South appalling. That the war lasted so long is a most magnificent tribute to the loyalty and the patience of the people of the Confederate states. Few nations ever continued so fierce a struggle with such inadequate resources for so lengthened a period. The closest scrutiny of the conditions under which the South made the contest only adds wonder to the spirit and valor of those who thus hampered by adversity and inadequate resources faced so resolutely the losses, privations and sacrifices of so many battles through such lengthened years.

Most of the adversities, as well as much of the severest fighting, marked the campaigns in Tennessee, Kentucky, Alabama, Mississippi and Georgia. These states covered a vast boundary and into their very heart flowed many navigable streams. The Mississippi, the Ohio, Cumberland, Barren, Tennessee and Yazoo Rivers penetrated or skirted the regions this army was required to defend, and rendered defense not only more difficult, but made the movements of the armies more hazardous.

No such disaster as at Fort Donelson or Vicksburg was possible save in the territory defended by the Army of Tennessee.

The Virginia campaigns were pressed into very narrow limits and comparatively few miles of navigable water affected its strategic movements. Indeed, the James River was the only stream up which to any great extent gunboats could float.

The Army of the Tennessee was to defend the line from Pound Gap to the Mississippi River, a distance of about five hundred miles. It was vulnerable at many points, and the Mississippi, Ohio, Tennessee and Cumberland not only brought legions of troops to important military positions in this boundary, but also gave strongholds from which operations at many points, for a thousand miles, might be inaugurated. It was a long distance from Paducah to Vicksburg. On the navigable streams that bounded the western lines of this army, forts and stations could be at various points successfully established, and Paducah, Nashville, Memphis, Chattanooga and Vicksburg were centers from which forays could be successfully made for nine months in the year. There was nothing but bad roads and the Confederate cavalry to defend this territory from invasion or occupation.

Atlanta was evacuated on the 1st of September, 1864. General Joseph E. Johnson had been relieved on the 17th day of July, 1864, and General Hood assumed command. The enemy were close to the coveted situation. Slowly, but surely, the cordon were closing around Atlanta; and, as the flanks of the Federal Army stretched far out, east and west of the doomed city, the Federals began to employ their cavalry in harassing the rear of the Confederates and in destroying railroads south of General Hood's position, rendering not only its occupancy difficult, but the feeding of his armies almost impossible.

The Federals never lacked for serviceable horses. True, they were not up to the standard which the Southern cavalry had taken into the war in 1861 and '62; but well-fed, they could carry their riders, at a moderate rate of speed, a long distance in the day. Month by month, the Federal cavalry began to be better disciplined and better drilled, and became a great force in destroying the Southern armies. It required months, many months, for the Federals to learn successfully the plans under which the Confederate cavalry operated and along which they had so often disturbed and destroyed their communications; and now, at least, when Hood was at bay in Atlanta, the Federals, using their experience and the experience of the Confederates to the best advantage, began their raids. General Johnston had turned over to General Hood, according to Johnston's statement, forty-one thousand infantry and ten thousand cavalry.

General Joseph Wheeler's marvelous courage and enterprise had greatly endeared him to all the soldiers of the army of Tennessee. There was no service he would not accept. There was no risk he would not assume. On July 26th, 1864, with his limited command, he had relieved Hardee's corps, and taken the place of the infantry in the breastworks. While thus occupied, General Wheeler was informed that large cavalry forces had started in the small hours of the night, with ten days' rations, marching eastwardly, westwardly, southwardly from the rear of Sherman's army. Sherman's front covered a space along the Chattahoochee for twenty-five miles. It became apparent to General Wheeler than an extremely formidable cavalry raid was being inaugurated, and one which had most important bearings on the maintenance of Hood's army about Atlanta. He chafed with the knowledge that his dismounted men were in the infantry breastworks, while the Federals were going out to forage and desolate the country south of Atlanta, and wreck the railroads upon which Atlanta relied alone for food.

On the morning of July 27th General Wheeler was directed to still hold the breastworks from which Hardee had been removed, and to send such force as he could spare in pursuit of the Federal cavalry raiders. He could only put into this service, immediately, fifteen hundred men, and he could only hope that they would be able to delay and harass and not destroy the enemy. The Federal raiders had begun their march at daybreak, on the 27th, and by nightfall had covered twenty-five miles to the south. All through July 27th, at two o'clock, at five o'clock and at six o'clock, Wheeler was interchanging despatches with General Hood. Wheeler was longing to go after the Federal raiders, but he was denied, by General Hood, this opportunity. At length the menace became so portentous that General Hood dare not ignore its consequences. Realizing that unless the Federal expedition was stayed, Atlanta must fall, with reluctance and many misgivings, he consented to turn General Wheeler loose, to try his hand upon the numerous, vigorous and aggressive foe. At nine o'clock at night came the order that General Wheeler himself might go in pursuit of the enemy. A great strategist himself, General Wheeler figured in his mind about where the Federals would strike the Macon railroad, which he foresaw and calculated would be either at Jonesboro, fifteen miles, or Lovejoy Station, twenty miles south of Atlanta.

General Sherman had passed the Chattahoochee River. Atlanta was eight miles south of this stream. Sherman had intrenched his forces east of Atlanta about nine miles. Near Peach Tree Creek, the Confederates had erected a strong line of fortification, and against this Sherman was day by day forcing his volunteers. At this time two railroads entered Atlanta from the south. The Georgia Railroad, toward Augusta, had already been occupied by Sherman and destroyed, so as to be useless even if the Confederates should drive him back across the Chattahoochee. For several miles south of Atlanta, the two railroads now operated ran into Atlanta over a common entrance. One of these railroads, running southwest, reached the Alabama line at West Point; the other ran due south, leading to Macon, eighty miles distant. The Chattahoochee River swung to the south as it passed west from Atlanta.

General Sherman determined to start three cavalry forces to break up these two railroads, upon which the Confederates in Atlanta relied for transportation of ammunition, food, supplies and troops. If these could be destroyed, Atlanta must be evacuated. So long as the Confederates could hold the fortifications around Atlanta, and these two railroads, Atlanta was invincible.

General Sherman directed his subordinates to start a cavalry force twelve miles due west of Atlanta, on the Chattahoochee River, crossing at a place called Campbellton. When over the river, this force, under General E. M. McCook, was to move southeastward, and strike the Macon Railroad at Jonesboro or at Lovejoy. Two other forces of cavalry, under Generals Stoneman and Garrard, were to leave General Sherman's lines east of Atlanta, at Decatur, to meet at Lithonia, nine miles southeast from Atlanta, and thence to tear up the railroad between Macon and Atlanta.

Up to this time, General Sherman had great faith in General George Stoneman. This officer was born in Chautaugua County, New York, in 1822. He graduated at West Point in 1846, and entered the First Dragoons. In 1855 he became a captain in the 25th United States Cavalry, and was in command of Fort Brown when the Civil War broke out. He refused to surrender Fort Brown to General Twiggs. In a little while he became chief cavalry commander of the Army of the Potomac. Transferred to infantry, he became conspicuous in many of the great battles of Virginia, and in 1863 became a leader of raids in Virginia. One of his chief ambitions was to release the Federal prisoners at Andersonville. He had been given authority, under certain conditions, by General Sherman, after destroying the railroad south of Atlanta, to march through to Andersonville. Stoneman, after the war, became colonel of the 21st Infantry of the United States Army. In 1871 he retired and returned to California. He was elected governor by the Democrats, in 1883, and held this office for four years. With his splendid record and his wide military experience, much was expected of him in this ably-planned onslaught that General Sherman had projected on the Confederate lines.

General Edward M. McCook, who was to figure so prominently in this expedition, was born in Steubenville, Ohio, in 1835. He came of a family known as the "fighting McCooks," and fully measured up to the family record. He was senior major of the 2d Indiana Cavalry at Shiloh; then colonel at the Battle of Perryville and Chickamauga. He commanded the cavalry of the Army of the Cumberland during the Atlanta campaign. Brave, self-reliant, with a lengthened service, with his many successes in the past, both Generals Grant and Sherman were confident that he would give a most excellent account of himself at this important juncture.

GENERAL KENNER GARRARD

General Kenner Garrard, the third man, was born in 1830 in Cincinnati, and was a great grandson of James Garrard, once governor of Kentucky. He graduated from the United States Military Academy in 1851, and entered the Dragoons. While on the Texas frontier, in April, 1861, he was captured and afterwards released on parole, but was not exchanged until 1862. During this period, he was commandant of cadets at West Point. After successful service in the Rappahannock and Pennsylvania campaigns, he was promoted to command a cavalry division of the Army of the Cumberland.

It was not unreasonable for General Sherman to expect much of these three dashing and brave commanders. With more than nine thousand cavalrymen, General Sherman believed that they could march into any part of the South, and that no force the Confederates could muster could even greatly delay and surely not defeat them.

General Wheeler had under him, in his defensive operations, men who had done much fighting, and, wherever tried, had never failed.

General Alfred Iverson was born in Clinton, Georgia, on February 14th, 1829. He graduated from a military school and served in the Mexican War when only seventeen years old. For distinguished service, he was made first lieutenant of the United States Cavalry. He was in Kansas during the troubles in 1856, and was with the expedition against the Mormons, and also in that against the Comanches and the Kiowas, in which he made much reputation. He resigned when Georgia seceded, and went to Wilmington, North Carolina. Later, he became colonel of the 20th North Carolina Infantry. He won distinction at Gaines Mill, and was wounded during a seven days' fight around Richmond, and added to his laurels at South Mountain and Sharpsburg. He was made brigadier general in 1862. At Chancellorsville and Gettysburg, he acquitted himself with great credit, and later he was sent to Rome, Georgia to command the state forces, and became brigadier general of the Georgia Cavalry. He was attached to Martin's division, under General Wheeler.

GENERAL WILLIAM WIRT ALLEN

General William Allen was born at Montgomery, Alabama. He was made a captain of the 1st Alabama Cavalry, and then its colonel. He was in the Kentucky campaigns, and was wounded at Perryville in 1864. He was made colonel of the 6th Alabama Cavalry Regiment, then commissioned a brigadier general. In the closing days of the war, in Georgia, North and South Carolina, he evidenced great skill as a leader. Always cheerful, patient and brave, he did much to inspirit his men, when, to his foreseeing mind, it was a hopeless fight against heaviest odds.

GENERAL ROBERT H. ANDERSON

General Robert H. Anderson, who also took a prominent part in these stirring campaigns, was born at Savannah, Georgia, in 1835. He graduated from West Point in 1857. He was on the frontier from 1857 to 1861, and was with the Georgia troops at Fort McAllister. His pluck and courage won him the command of the 5th Georgia Cavalry. After a little while, he proved himself so competent that he was advanced to a brigade commander; and, in the dark hours—from November, 1864, to April, 1865—in the closing scenes and in front of Sherman in his march to the sea, he bore a most conspicuous and valorous part.

GENERAL JOHN H. KELLEY

General John H. Kelley was born in Pickens County, Alabama, in 1840. At the age of seventeen, he entered West Point. Within a few months of his graduation, Alabama seceded, and he went to Montgomery, enlisted in the government service and became second lieutenant in the regular army. He was sent to Fort Morgan; and, in October, 1861, became aide to General Hardee, with the rank of captain and assistant adjutant general. Later, he was made major, in command of an Arkansas battalion. Fearless, enterprising and courageous, he was promoted to colonel of the 8th Arkansas Regiment. He was then just twenty-two years of age. Conspicuous at Perryville, Murfreesboro and at the Battle of Chickamauga, he became commander of a brigade of infantry, under General Buckner. At Chickamauga, his brigade suffered a loss of three hundred men out of eight hundred and seventy-six. His great merit was recognized; and, on the 16th of November, 1863, he was made brigadier general, when only twenty-three and one-half years old. Almost immediately, he was assigned to the duties of major general. At the beginning of the Georgia campaign, he became one of the division commanders, under General Wheeler. His division was composed of Allen's, Dibrell's and Hannon's brigades. He was doomed to die just one month after this raid, at Franklin, Tennessee,—a spot three months afterward consecrated by the sublime heroism of the Army of the Tennessee, in its last great call to duty, where it met practical annihilation.

GENERAL LAWRENCE SULLIVAN ROSS

General Lawrence Sullivan Ross was Iowa born. His father moved to Texas during his early life. He entered a college at Florence, Alabama, but engaged in the Indian war and was wounded at the Battle of Wichita. In this battle, he rescued a white girl who had been with the Indians eight years, adopted her as his own child, giving her the name of Lizzie Ross. His courage was so pronounced and his skill so evident, that General Van Dorn and General Scott urged him for a place in the army. Not of age, he went back to the University and graduated, when he returned to Texas and enlisted as a private in the 6th Regiment. He became its colonel in 1862. At Corinth, he played the part of a hero—acting as a forlorn hope—he held the Federals at bay until the balance of the army escaped. For this great service, General Joseph E. Johnson recommended his promotion as brigadier general, and this came to him in December, 1863. He was always at the front, and had five horses shot under him. He became governor of Texas in 1886 and again in 1888, and was elected by one of the largest majorities ever given any man—a hundred and fifty thousand.

Colonel W. C. P. Breckinridge, on account of the illness of General John S. Williams, was assigned the command of the Kentucky brigade. In these days of depletion, brigades were not very strong in numbers. They very frequently had as few as five hundred men. This little brigade, however, was well seasoned, and though two-thirds of its original members were dead or disabled, the small remnant had lost none of that courage and valor which was regarded as the unfailing inheritance of men who left Kentucky to fight for Southern independence. A sketch of Colonel Breckinridge will be found in another part of this volume.

These were the leaders who, in this momentous hour, were to stand for the Confederate and Federal operations. Rarely, during the war, did so many West Pointers come into collision, or men so trained and so resourceful meet in battle or engage in maneuvering, when a mistake would mean so much to contending forces.

The Chattahoochee River was to play an important part in this historic cavalry movement. Rising in the Appalachian Mountains of Northern Georgia, it flows west, passing within eight miles of Atlanta; then, traversing almost the entire state of Georgia, it strikes the Alabama boundary at West Point. For one hundred miles, it becomes the boundary between Alabama and Georgia, and at the Florida line unites with the Flint River and forms the Appalachicola River, which empties into the Gulf of Mexico.

The expedition was worthy of General Sherman's splendid military genius. It was thoroughly discussed, wisely planned and ably conceived, and the men that he assigned were not only the best officers, but they had also under them the best regiments then in the three divisions of the army that he was directing against Atlanta.

General Kelley was designated by General Wheeler, with his brigade, to follow General Garrard, whose division was the first of the Federal forces to concentrate at Jonesboro and Lovejoy. Garrard seems to have failed in his part of the undertaking. He got as far as Flat Rock, and there he waited for General Stoneman; but Stoneman seemed to have forgotten his promise and Garrard stayed at Flat Rock until the 28th, waiting for Stoneman, and then marched to Covington. He there found that Stoneman had passed through Covington two days before and had gone south. Garrard then returned from whence he had come. Harassed, opposed and vigorously pursued by General Kelley, he accomplished no real service; he saved his forces and suffered but little loss, but he won no praise; he deserved none for anything he accomplished. He attempted to place the blame for his failure on General Stoneman. In his report to headquarters, he said: "On the 27th, the division was placed under General Stoneman, who ordered it to Flat Rock and abandoned it to its fate. After being surrounded by a superior force for over twelve hours, and contending against every disadvantage in hopes of benefiting General Stoneman in his attempt to destroy the railroad, it extricated itself from its perilous situation." Had he followed on after General Stoneman, in General Iverson's rear, he might have won for both a superb victory. Instead of being surrounded by a superior force, General Kelley, who opposed him, had less than one-third of the men General Garrard led. If General Sherman later read General Wheeler's reports, he would have wondered where the superior Confederate forces came from.

General Iverson, being thoroughly familiar with the territory where General Stoneman was to operate, was assigned to the pursuit of that officer. General Wheeler, who had so furiously chafed at being cooped up with infantry in the breastworks along Peach Tree Creek, decided to follow General McCook, who he seemed to fear most, and whose past was a sure indication that where he went, trouble would be raised for the Confederate outposts, railways and storehouses.

When General Wheeler got away from Hood's breastworks, at nine o'clock, in the night of the 27th, he needed no signal of the officers or scouts to tell him the purpose or design of the enemy. His military instincts told him that these skillful Federal generals would strike the railroad somewhere south of Atlanta, and at a point just sufficiently away to escape from the attacks of the Confederate infantry. In his breast most conflicting emotions arose. Released by General Hood, only when his pleading became well nigh irresistible, he was not only anxious to meet General Hood's expectations, but he was also well aware that his failure to stop the progress of the Federal cavalry meant the immediate evacuation of Atlanta, and with this, the crushing of the hopes of his countrymen for ultimate success in the war. It is also highly probable that, calm and self-possessed though he was, recent criticism had given a deep touch of sorrow to his heart. Envy had not been idle, and this had raised a horde of heartless slanderers, who were doing all they could to belittle his services to his country: to minimize the successes of his campaign and to destroy his reputation as a leader.

General Wheeler at this moment assumed a task at which any soldier might hesitate. Many Confederate cavalry leaders had faced Federal raiding forces; but generally the invaders had long lines to follow and could not set out three divisions, all numerically superior to those opposing, and all converging to a single point by different roads—all within ten hours' march of the place where it was proposed to strike the heaviest blow. Whatever was to be done must be done instantly and with fiercest determination. He could not count upon more than two-fifths as many men as those he was to fight. If he whipped one, the other two might unite, accomplish the purposes of the expedition, and then together might crush him; and this meant untold disaster to General Hood. There was no sleep for General Wheeler that trying night: its hours were long. His staff and the few troopers following behind might, by a cat-nap in the saddle, gain a momentary relief; but, for the leader, the man who was to checkmate the Federal plans, there could not be a single instant of unconsciousness. He weighed then less than a hundred and twenty-five pounds, but he was a great soldier all the same. In the mind and soul of this man, small of stature, was now centered the destiny of Hood's army.

Plan after plan suggested itself to the brave man, who, at a rapid trot, in the darkness, was leading his followers to the scene of danger. Those who rode behind him could not understand the conflicting emotions that passed through his mind. They knew but little of the dangers ahead— they did not fully comprehend what this forced march meant; but they all knew there was trouble somewhere to the front, and possibly before dawn, but surely at dawn they realized that a foe would be found and that a battle would be joined. It was yet too early for any well-defined plan to take shape in the mind of the Confederate leader. Of only one thing he was absolutely sure, and that was when he found his enemies, he would give them no rest or peace until they were driven back behind the Federal fortification. It is difficult for a cavalry commander to always conceal from his followers the purpose or plans of an expedition. Those riding behind General Wheeler disturbed him with no questionings or suggestions. They sympathized with him in the stress and turmoil that filled his soul in this period of anxious foreboding and planning. The hours now passing were fraught with ever-present dangers. The ninety days that preceded the experiences of this night had been the most eventful of any ninety days any cavalry commander had ever faced, but now was to come the hardest of all.

From May 8th to September 5th, 1864, covering the retreat from Dalton to Atlanta, there had been imposed upon the cavalry of the Army of the Tennessee, a service, which for length, sacrifice, constant exposure, varied experiences and extent of losses, was never experienced by the same number of horsemen who followed the Confederate colors in an equal number of days.

General Wheeler pressed onward with great rapidity, to overtake the fifteen hundred men who had been sent forward on the morning of the 27th, and by a rapid ride of thirty miles, he caught up with the troops that had gone before. Through prisoners and scouts, he there learned that the force which had crossed at Campbellton was commanded by General McCook. General Wheeler at this time fully realized the difficult task before him, and its responsibilities, to a less great man, would have been appalling. Had he been left alone to face General McCook, there would have been no disturbing element in his work, but from couriers and other means of communication, it became necessary for him to divide the men he could use in this crisis, so that no one of the three Federal divisions could, for any considerable period, march unmolested. It was of the greatest importance to leave neither Stoneman, Garrard nor McCook unopposed for even half a day. This also meant that in all three cases the men pursuing must be vastly inferior in numbers to the command they were to endeavor to defeat or drive away.

He could only give Iverson fourteen hundred men; Kelley six hundred men; while he himself took the brigades of Hume and Anderson—counting, all told, eight hundred riders. With this limited force, General Wheeler vigorously assaulted the Federals at Flat Shoals. In disposing his forces as the necessity of the moment suggested, he was extremely generous to his subordinates. He gave Iverson the most; Kelley the second largest command; while he himself, with fragments of two brigades, undertook the destruction of General McCook. To do this, he had in the beginning less than eight hundred men as against three times that number.

When General Wheeler arrived at Flat Shoals, it was not yet light; day was just breaking. It was bright enough to see the enemy and that was enough for General Wheeler. He instantly ordered an attack upon the flanks of the Federals. He had managed, during the night, to get a portion of his command in front of the enemy, and with the forces in front and Wheeler in the rear, the Federals soon realized that they had gone upon an expedition in which there would be more than marching and burning. General Wheeler dare not waste a single moment. The Federals had secured strong and favorable positions; but he had no time to reconnoiter for position. He knew where the enemy was, and that was all that he desired to know just then. He had come to defeat them, and defeat them he must. Although his forces were inadequate, he advanced boldly to the attack. The Federal forces withstood the assault for a brief while. These responses from the enemy only caused General Wheeler to renew the attack more viciously, and shortly the enemy began to retreat. Their rearguard was not disposed to run, and they fought over every inch of ground. In this first conflict, General Wheeler captured three supply wagons and a number of prisoners, and from these he discovered that Stoneman had gone to Covington, and that the men he was now fighting were McCook's division. He was fortunate enough to learn from the captured prisoners that Macon was the real point of attack, and that Stoneman, Garrard and McCook were supposed to unite at that point and destroy Macon with its precious stores and manufactories, which were so essential to the preservation of Hood's army; then march to Andersonville and release thirty thousand prisoners, and in Stoneman's wagons were guns to arm these prisoners.

General Hood was not disposed to let Wheeler get very far from him. He relied with absolute confidence upon his invincible courage and indomitable will. He felt stronger when Wheeler was near. In a little while, after Wheeler had left on his night ride, General Hood sent him a message, by a trusted courier, to say that if the enemy's course was not such as to require all his men, to detach some officer to continue the pursuit, and he himself should come back to the front. He wisely added, by way of parenthesis, that he would rely on General Wheeler's judgment as to what would be the wisest thing to do. General Hood had not caught the real import of this cavalry expedition. He did not know the thorough preparations General Sherman had made to render this movement a decisive one; he did not know the vast force engaged in the campaign, nor did he at once take in what its success meant to his beleaguered army in and around Atlanta. He had not yet fully comprehended what faced General Wheeler in the work assigned him, nor how much depended on his success.

Wheeler's one oft-reiterated command was, "Attack! Attack! Assault! Assault!" wherever an enemy could be found.

General Wheeler quickly discovered that General McCook's men, something over twenty-five hundred, had gotten in their work on the railroad, four miles below Jonesboro. He knew at once that he alone was in a position to discomfit McCook. He resolved to trust Iverson with Stoneman, while he would assault and crush McCook. General McCook had found it necessary to stop and rest at Fayetteville. The strain on man and beast became unbearable and General McCook submitted to nature's inevitable decree for rest. This halt did much towards his undoing.

General W. H. Jackson had done some skirmishing with McCook during the day, and he had informed General Wheeler that if he would take care of the enemy's rear, he would gain their front and secure their capture. General Wheeler could not rely much upon Jackson. He was now fifteen miles behind, and Hume's brigade of only five hundred men was the chief ground of General Wheeler's hope in the pursuit. When Line Creek was reached, the bridge was gone—the Federals had destroyed it and had barricaded the opposite bank. Fights had no terror for General Wheeler. He boldly marched up to the banks and managed to get a position that enfiladed the barricades on the opposite shore. The attack was furious. In a little while it caused the enemy to yield. Within an hour the bridge was rebuilt, and General Wheeler's troops had passed over. The night was intensely dark: objects could only be seen at a very limited distance. General Wheeler, taking the extreme advance, courageously and vigorously pushed forward. Almost every half hour the enemy had barricaded the road, and the first notice the Confederates had of their presence was a volley from their guns.

With the dawn of another day, General Wheeler became even more persistent and pressed the charge against the enemy with ever-increasing vigor. He knew that now he only had about seven hundred men. He sent one column around their flank, while he led the other upon the Federal center. Breaking through McCook's lines, he routed their horses and captured more than three hundred prisoners, with their arms and equipment. The Federals were diligent in taking advantage of the various positions which the country afforded, and met each charge with stout resistance; and during the running fight, hand-to-hand encounters were frequent—more than fifty Federals were killed in these face-to-face struggles. Nothing could stay the impetuous advance of Wheeler and his men. Barricades, hills and rail fortifications had apparently no terror for the pursuers. They were after the enemy, and as long as they saw the enemy, they followed him with unfailing vigor.

Human nature had nearly reached its limit with General Wheeler's troops when he was reinforced with Colonel Cook's two squadrons, of the 8th Texas; these hard-riding Texans had followed in the wake of the conflict—the dead soldiers, broken-down horses and wrecked wagons told them where they were needed. They could see that savage work had gone on a little while before, and General Wheeler's followers appeared to be calling, with earnest pleas, for them to hasten and help destroy the fleeing and vanquished foe. They were few in number, but they rushed on, for they well knew how much their presence was needed at the front.

General Ross also came on with two fragments of regiments, making General Wheeler's available command now seven hundred men.

Jackson and Anderson were still fifteen miles in the rear, and they could bring no help to Wheeler at this time, in the very throes of the combat that was to determine the mastery in this expedition.

Like Forrest in pursuit of Streight, Wheeler and his followers were absolutely relentless. They marched seventy miles in twenty-four hours. Hunger and fatigue seemed to have fled from the minds and bodies of the ragged pursuers, and a strength and endurance above human animated and encouraged them in the work war had at this hour put upon them. They were ready and willing to fight and harass the Federal forces so long as a single man was left. The beasts, many of them, were dropping by the roadside. They could not stand the intense strain that was being put upon them. The long marches, the incessant galloping and heavy burden in transporting the men and ammunition, had tremendously told upon the helpless horses; but a great issue was at stake, and horse flesh was not to be considered. Colonel Ashby, with two hundred men, was directed to gallop forward, and, if possible, to get in front of General McCook. He was further ordered, if an enemy was found, not to consider the disparity in numbers, but to go at them promptly and remorselessly. Scouts were sent in every direction to look for the enemy. Out on the LaGrange Road, about three miles away, the Federal cavalry was found, dismounted, in a dense wood. Colonel Ashby, who always put himself in front, informed General Wheeler that he had struck the head of the advancing Federals, and that they were then forming a line of battle. The only answer General Wheeler made to Ashby was to make the attack, and do the best he could with the means at hand.

General Wheeler now had less than four hundred men in the column. The long trail of killed and wounded that lay along the line of pursuit told what had depleted his following. The first advance upon McCook was checked, and for a moment Wheeler's forces were stayed; but, in an instant, General Wheeler directed all bugles to sound the charge, and the brave little Confederate general, at the head of the advance, bade his men to follow and he would lead. The rebel yell was the response to this heroic call. No man hesitated for an instant or desired to get away. Wheeler was leading them and in front was the enemy. General Wheeler drove his column through the Federal lines and crumpled them up into a confused mass. Up to that time, only two of General McCook's brigades had taken part. There was yet a reserve brigade some distance away.

In less than three-quarters of an hour General Wheeler had captured three hundred prisoners, two hundred men had been killed or wounded, and best of all, he captured six hundred fresh horses for the tired Confederates to mount.

In the fierceness of this struggle, General Wheeler had almost forgotten himself and his own safety. He was recalled to the real situation by the heavy firing in the rear, and there he beheld McCook's reserve brigade attacking the Confederate lines. General Wheeler turned about and quickly faced this new danger. By voice and example, he pleaded with his soldiers to stand firm and meet the coming shock. They responded as he asked; they boldly charged the new foes, broke their lines, captured over a hundred prisoners and sent this reserve brigade in search of General McCook, to seek safety.

General McCook had gotten his breath and was organizing his forces again for battle. Unexpectedly to Wheeler, he charged with fierceness on the Confederates, who were now beginning to yield. General Humes had been taken a prisoner, and it looked like the thin Confederate line would be swept away, and McCook would avenge the damage that had been inflicted upon him a few moments before.

At this critical period, while looking, listening and hoping, rapid riding was heard, and then in a little while, some riders clad in gray galloped to the front. General Anderson's men had come to relieve the plight into which General Wheeler's daring had brought him. General McCook, like all the McCooks, was dead game, and so he barricaded himself in an impassable ravine, against which General Wheeler at once realized it was useless to go. But the flank was the point where General Wheeler frequently struck home, and he instantly turned his men in that direction. Here General Wheeler was able to cut off two of McCook's regiments.

When these were separated, they became scattered, a majority of them surrendered, bringing to General Wheeler a battery, a wagon train, a pack mule train and much needed arms and ammunition.

Among the captured was something that was very pleasing to General Wheeler—that was three hundred and fifty Confederate officers, who had been picked up by McCook in convalescent camps along his route. Gratifying as was the recapture of these Confederate officers, General Wheeler had no time to waste and no season for congratulations. Turning about, he charged at McCook's troops, again cutting them in two, and drove both fragments before him in a rout. After fighting so bravely, the Federals, in this last conflict, did not measure up to the splendid standard they had set in the earlier fighting, and by a sort of common consent and agreement, every command began to look out for itself. General Roddy, with a few dismounted men, appeared upon the scene. This was counted as Confederate infantry, and this destroyed all hope of victory in the minds of the Federals.

Night now came on, and the darkness was so intense that it was impossible to keep trail of the fleeing enemy. They were traveling by stars or blindly following the roads. Confederate patrols were sent out in every direction, and before daylight four hundred prisoners were caught.

This campaign was one of the most skillful efforts on General Sherman's part in his fight for Atlanta. General Wheeler's courage, genius and indomitable will won success for the Confederates. And no general, with such inadequate means at his command, could accomplish more against such vast odds.

On the 26th of July, General Sherman telegraphed that he had sent around by his right, three thousand five hundred cavalry, under McCook; and by the left, five thousand, under Stoneman. He believed that McCook and Garrard would destroy the railroad to Macon and that they would be able to march to Andersonville, and release the Federal prisoners, but he had forgotten the manner of men who were across the Federal path.

Not for a single moment did General Kelley lose his grip on Garrard. Nor did Iverson ever hesitate in his pursuit of Stoneman.

Stoneman had caught the real greatness of this campaign, which General Sherman and General Grant believed would be fatal and final to the defense of Atlanta. Ambitious and enthusiastic, he suggested to General Sherman that after traveling ninety miles to Macon, and destroying the immense stores and the great manufactories there, he should then pursue his way to

Andersonville, forty miles southwest of Macon. Here were thirty thousand Federal prisoners. Stories of their sufferings and privations moved Stoneman to not only vigorous but patriotic effort. He was so hopeful of capturing not only Macon and all in it, according to General Sherman's instructions, but he felt equally sure of undisputed success and victory, and he took along with him guns to arm the prisoners at Andersonville, when they should be released. This numerous array of men, armed, and this great multitude of prisoners, turned loose, would have not only brought tremendous desolation, but would have terrorized the people of Georgia outside the armies of General Hood and the garrison at Macon and a few important points. It was a noble ambition. It was a splendid design, but in the end it turned out that Stoneman did not have the nerve, the dash and the grit necessary to consummate the splendid conception. He made a rapid and unmolested march through Covington, Monticello, Hillsboro and Clinton, down to the very gates of Macon. He got so close to the city that some of his artillery threw shells into its suburbs.

Macon, at that time, happened to have a sagacious and experienced soldier in its boundaries. General Joseph E. Johnston, after being relieved of command of the army of Tennessee, at Atlanta, had gone to Macon to rest and recuperate, and in dignified quiet to await another call from his country, to stand for the defense of its liberty. There were large numbers of prisoners at Macon as well as at Andersonville. When at Macon, the story of the approach of Stoneman and his associates became known, the prisoners were speedily moved to points further south. The garrison, and the convalescents and all, however old or young, that were able to bear arms, were hastily summoned and organized, to resist the coming of the invaders. Breastworks and fortifications were erected under the direction of General Johnston, and every possible effort was made to prepare for sternest defense, the city with its rich stores.

General Stoneman was to have had the co-operation of General Garrard, and incidentally of General McCook, but he had gone southward for ninety miles without opposition, and the march had been so easy and so little opposed, and he had been able to burn so many stores and trains, that he felt he had the world in a sling, and that there was nothing could stay his progress or interfere with his success. He was only a little more than twenty miles from Jonesboro when he passed Covington; Garrard could have reached him, by an easy march, in eight hours. Had he waited for McCook or Garrard, with whom he was directed to co-operate, he would have largely increased his chances for success and victory; but it looked so feasible, and he was able to move with such rapidity, that he cast prudence to the winds, and he rode forward without even the suggestion of doubt crossing his mind. He thought he surely saw the beckonings of greatness. He was certain he heard the voices of fame whisper in his ears: "Forward! Forward!" He did not know what was behind him, nor did he care. He knew as well as the Confederates themselves that the exigencies around Atlanta would permit of the removal of not more than four thousand cavalry, and he was certain all these would not dare follow him, and let Garrard and McCook roam at will around and south of Jonesboro and Lovejoy. Sherman had some reserve horsemen, and these must be guarded against.

No Confederate cavalryman ever faced graver responsibilities or greater difficulties than General Wheeler in this expedition. His mounts were thin, wearied and worn. His men were only fairly armed. Stoneman had fresh, well-fed mounts, and he could out-march and out-ride anything that Wheeler and his associates could put behind him. The men in gray were hardier and better seasoned, but their means of transportation were very much limited.

General Wheeler put into Iverson's mind all that the success of the Federals meant. Iverson knew it all, but the defiant and hopeful spirit of the brave Confederate leader helped him to greater effort and firmer resolves. He bade him pursue Stoneman, fight him wherever he found him, and hang on to his flanks and rear with a savage grip, and never give him a moment's rest until he had run him to bay.

Stoneman could ride faster than Iverson. He bade him do with Stoneman what he would do with McCook. Iverson had some Georgians and Kentuckians, all told, thirteen hundred men, but they were veterans. Many of these had been long trained in General Wheeler's school and some of them in Forrest's, and that meant that wherever they met an enemy there would be real, sure enough fighting. When Stoneman reached Macon he was surprised to find such intense opposition. He had expected to ride into the city with little ado, but when he saw the organized troops and temporary fortifications, and guns behind them, and men behind these, he appears to have lost his nerve. Between Stoneman and his subordinates there was not that sympathy and confidence that such an occasion as this demanded. Had Stoneman pushed on to Andersonville, he could have done the Confederacy tremendous and irreparable damage, but he hesitated and lost. He then realized that he had made a great mistake to ride away without McCook or Garrard. He had hoped and trusted that one or the other would follow him, and with forty-five hundred men, before the gates of Macon, there would have been little question of its capture. He understood now that his ambition had led him to disregard the plainest dictates of military prudence, and instead of going on and swinging around Macon to Andersonville, and then into Alabama, if necessary, on which line he could always keep ahead of the Confederates who were pursuing him, he resolved to retrace his steps and go back from whence he had come. The coming had been easy, but the going back was to be a far different and more difficult job. Iverson's men, although handicapped by the bad condition of their horses, had been enabled, during the time Stoneman had lost around Macon, to come up with a strong vanguard. General Iverson was experienced, brave, vigorous and enterprising. He had not hitherto had the opportunities and confidence that a separate command gives, but he realized his responsibilities now, and he knew that continuous and savage attack was the only method with which he could win. He had kept himself well in touch with Stoneman's movements. The people along the line were friendly to him, and there was no difficulty in his learning where Stoneman was and what Stoneman had.

When Stoneman turned about, he had only gone a few miles when he found the gray-coated men athwart his path. He had lost his head. He was brave, but he was not his greatest in disaster, which is a most important qualification in a cavalry general. He assaulted Iverson's forces with moderate vigor. He found them unyielding. They met assault with assault. They returned shot for shot. They had artillery, and they knew how to use it, and General Stoneman quickly realized that he was now to have the fight of his life, and not only the fight of his life, but a fight for life.

Through the morning of September 1st, the battle was kept up, but in the afternoon the Confederates became more aggressive, and they assaulted Stoneman's left flank, and drove it in, and from that moment Stoneman's troops seemed to have parted with their courage and their faith of ultimate victory.

Colonel Silas Adams, with a brigade, went one direction; and Colonel Capron, with another brigade, went another, both riding hard and striving furiously to get away from their pursuers. Stoneman gathered a portion of his advisers around him and communicated to them his judgment.

They unanimously agreed that he had lost. He made a heroic but very foolish resolve to fight with six hundred men, long enough to enable Adams and Capron to get the start of Iverson's troops, and through this to make their escape.

It would have been more soldier-like to have let Capron or Adams fight in the last ditch while the leader rode away. It looked and sounded heroic for the commander to make such a sacrifice, but Federal generals like Pleasanton, Sheridan, Wilson or Buford, nor Confederate, like Forrest, Wheeler, Shelby, Morgan, Marmaduke, Stuart or Hampton, would never have entertained such a proposition. They would have kept all their forces together and fought it out in the last ditch. When the Confederates cut Stoneman's command into two parts, they had won the victory, and turned his forces into scattered bands, whose chiefest aim was personal safety and escape.

Separated from Stoneman, Adams and Capron began a rapid retreat. They rode as fast as their horses could carry them, and only fought when there was no escape from battle.

It did not take long to arrange the details of General Stoneman's surrender. He made it with tears in his eyes, and he was oppressed and humiliated at this sad and untoward ending of a campaign, which at its commencement opened to him vistas of glory and renown. It required but a brief while to conclude negotiations for Stoneman's capitulation, and the ink was not dry upon the paper which set forth the terms, until General Iverson, with his powers quickened and the hopes of his men enhanced by the surrender of Stoneman, started Breckinridge and his Kentuckians in pursuit of the fleeing Federals, who, every moment, became less capable of resistance or battle. He marched his prisoners to Macon under escort. These had expected to enter the city as conqueror; instead, they came as dejected captives. Their dreams of glory turned into fixed visions of failure and despair.

Adams and Capron, in order to avoid those behind them, swung to the right, leaving the track which they had traveled from fifteen to twenty-five miles west of them, and through Eatonton and Madison and Athens they hurried with all possible haste to find safety. These raiders returned far more quickly than they had come. By their detours they increased the distance, but they increased their speed. Their tired horses were exchanged for the mules or horses of the people of Georgia, along the path, and they rode with exceeding haste. Familiar with the country and spurred to highest effort, with a desire to punish these invaders, Breckinridge, with the Kentucky brigade, rode hard after the fleeing Federals. A brief sleep here and there, and with cat naps on their horses, they pushed on with almost boundless energy, and the rearguard of the fleeing Federals, neither night nor day, was free from the assaults of the ragged Kentucky riders.

The bravest men, under such circumstances, become more or less demoralized. These Federal soldiers felt the depressing effect of the rout and defeat of Stoneman, and they dropped out, sometimes in companies and sometimes in squads, forgetting that their only safety lay in keeping together and presenting a bold and defiant rear to the advancing pursuers. So rapid was the march and so fierce the pursuit that the horses of the Confederates, even with the swapping they were able to do along the road for fresher mounts, either mules or horses, made their progress comparatively slow and tedious.

Adams made a shorter run and escaped with half his command. Capron veered more to the east. They united south of Athens. On the 31st day of August they rode with fiercest energy. Their tired steeds were spurred and belabored to the limits of mercy. The object was to get a few hours and some miles between them and the men who were following, so that they could lie down and take part of a night's rest, preparatory to their final spurt into Sherman's lines. At a little place called "Jug Tavern," fifteen miles out from Athens, they felt that their labors had been rewarded, and they had enough space between them and their pursuers to enable them to make it safe to enjoy brief repose.

Colonel W. C. P. Breckinridge, who was commanding General Williams' Kentucky brigade, and was foremost in pursuing Capron, realized his entire force could not ride with such speed as would enable him to overtake Adams and Capron. He had hung savagely upon their rear, and also kept the inner line to Atlanta, to drive the Federals as far east as possible; but his horses had limitations, and Colonel Breckinridge, with grief and apprehension, saw man after man drop out. He beheld steed after steed with the white frost upon its skin, which betokens the failure of its physical vigor, lie down upon the road and refuse to move further. Hastily assembling his entire brigade, now numbering less than five hundred men, for review, he had his inspector general ride down the line and order out from the several regiments and battalions the men who had the hardiest and freshest horses. When these were counted they numbered only eighty-five. He placed these under command of Lieutenant Robert Bowles, one of his trustiest officers, and bade him ride hard and follow the trail of Adams and Capron, and attack them wherever and whenever found. These eighty-five men caught the inspiration of a great opportunity, and so cheering and yelling and waving adieu to their comrades, whose going had been prevented by the weariness of their mounts, they rode away. Those left to come on by easier stages groaned in spirit as they saw their more fortunate comrades ride away. They cursed the fate that deprived them of the chance to win glory in this pursuit.

Colonel Breckinridge told Lieutenant Bowles that he would follow him with the remainder of the brigade, with all possible haste; thus the eighty-five men set out to run down their demoralized enemies.

Capron and Adams had finally gone to sleep on the bank of a small stream known as Mulberry River, which was crossed by a wooden bridge. Out in the woods and timber the animals were tethered, and the men laid down anywhere and everywhere, if they only might catch a few moments' rest. Five hundred and fifty Federals comprised all who were left of these two brigades. Many were dead and wounded. Scores had been captured, as wearied they fell from their horses, on the rapid marches they had made since leaving Macon. Just before daybreak, on the morning of the 3d of September, they heard the rebel yell and the sharp crack of the revolvers resounding through their camp. Around the outskirts of the camp a number of the negroes, who were riding the mules and horses they had taken from their masters, were asleep. At the first charge of the Confederates, the mules immediately stampeded, and with the terror-stricken negroes rushed through the camp of the sleeping Federal soldiers. The cries of the frightened negroes, combined with the shouts of the attacking forces, added to the confusion and discomfiture of the Federals. Thus rudely aroused from their slumbers, they mounted their tired steeds and started in a wild rush and dashed across the bridge, along the road they believed would lead to safety. The galloping of the steeds and the crowding of the animals onto the wooden bridge caused it to give way and dropped those who were passing over it into the river below, and cut off the escape of those who were behind. The eighty-five Confederates were busy everywhere. The Federals were completely demoralized. They gladly surrendered when called, and asked for protection. They had not realized in the darkness how small the force that had assailed and scattered them, but without arms they were helpless,

395

and they were so completely exhausted that their powers of resistance had vanished.

In his report Colonel Capron said, "Just before daylight, the morning of the 3d instant, a body of the enemy's cavalry came up in my rear, and, as near as I can ascertain, passed around the main body of the pickets on both flanks, striking the road where the negroes lay. The negroes became panic-stricken and rushed into the camp of my men, who were yet asleep (we having been in camp about one hour and a half), throwing them into confusion. The enemy now charged into my camp, driving and scattering everything before them. Every effort was made by the officers to rally the men and check the enemy's charge, but it was found impossible to keep them in line, as most of them were without arms and ammunition. Partial lines were formed, but, owing to the confusion which ensued in the darkness, they soon gave away. A stampede now took place, a portion of the men rushing for the woods and the balance running down the road and attempting to cross a bridge over the Mulberry River, in our front. The enemy still continued to charge my men, killing, wounding and capturing a large number. In their rush across the bridge it gave away, precipitating many of them into the river. The men now scattered in every direction. I became separated from my command, and made my escape through the woods, arriving at this place on the morning of the 7th instant."

This combat at Jug Tavern was always held by those who participated in it to be, considering numbers, one of the really great victories of the war.

There was no chance to pass Mulberry River, into which the bridge had fallen, and the early hours of the morning were spent in gathering the fugitives up and down the bank, and those hiding themselves out in the woods, hoping to escape imprisonment. Finally some three hundred were gathered together, and hardly had they been corralled, when General Breckinridge, with those who had been left behind, rode up to help their comrades who had been able to ride on before and achieve such a great victory. Their prisoners were marched to Athens. A great feast was prepared. The townsfolk and country folk gathered to thank the Kentuckians who had punished the Federal raiders. Congratulation and gratitude were the order of the hour. Capron, escaping on foot, found his way to the Federal lines, but a large proportion of his force were made prisoners, and there was hardly an organized squad from his command left to ride the thirty miles that intervened between them and safety, behind Sherman's fortifications around Atlanta.

Chapter XXIV

FORREST'S RAID INTO MEMPHIS, AUGUST 21, 1864

General Forrest, like most soldiers, had special animosities, and one of his was General Cadwallader Colden Washburn. It might be said that they were men of such disposition that they would certainly have instinctive dislike for each other. Both were brave and extremely loyal to the Cause they espoused, and neither saw much of good in those on the opposite side. As they came to face each other in Western Tennessee and Northern Mississippi, many things occurred to increase rather than lessen their antipathies.

General Washburn was born May 14th, 1818, at Livermore, Maine. Beginning life on his father's farm, he had a brief experience in a country retail store, then as schoolmaster, then emigrated west and studied law. In Milton, Wisconsin, in 1842, he began practice. The law was slow in that section at that period, and he became an agent for settlers desiring to enter public lands. He was in Congress from 1855 to 1861. Refusing re-election, he raised a regiment of cavalry in Wisconsin, and in October, 1861, entered active service. He was associated with Curtis in Arkansas, and was particularly valuable at the Battle of Grand Coteau. In 1862 he was made brigadier general. By November he was advanced to major general. He was prominent in the siege of Vicksburg, became commander of the Department of the Gulf, warred vigorously in Texas, and came to be commandant at Memphis in 1864.

He had been instructed by General Sherman as to the necessity of destroying Forrest. General Washburn organized the expedition under General S. D. Sturgis, which met such tremendous defeat at Bryce's Cross Roads on June 10th, 1864. He was cognizant of, and accessory before the fact, of Sherman's offer of promotion to General Mower if he would pursue and kill General Forrest. What is known as the assault of Fort Pillow had particularly aroused feeling on General Washburn's part. When charged by General Forrest with inciting the negro soldiers in his department to refuse quarter to Forrest's men, he parried but did

397

not explicitly deny what Forrest stated he had done. Reading between the lines, it is easy to discover that if General Washburn did not suggest or approve this declaration of his colored troops, he was not unwilling for them to go forth with a fixed purpose to kill without exception such of Forrest's cavalry as by the exigencies and fortunes of war fell into their hands.

The failure of General Forrest under General Lee, at Harrisburg in July, 1864, had rendered General Forrest anxious to avenge his losses, and apparent defeat there; and he resolved to give General Washburn and his troops a real lesson in the uncertainties of war. When A. J. Smith retreated after his victory at Harrisburg, Forrest pursued him with his usual persistence. General Sherman, who did a great deal of telegraphing and seemed to have had an accurate knowledge of the conditions in West Tennessee, on the 16th of June had wired E. M. Stanton, Secretary of War, in regard to General Forrest, "We must destroy him if possible." On the same day, he telegraphed, "We must make the people of Tennessee and Mississippi feel that although a bold, daring and successful leader, he will bring ruin and misery on any country where he may pass or tarry. If we do not punish Forrest now, the whole effect of our vast conquest will be lost."

In carrying out these instructions, a large part of the northern portion of Western Tennessee was laid waste, and, like the Shenandoah Valley, was reduced to the condition, over which it was boasted by Generals Grant and Sheridan, that if a crow flew, he must take his rations with him.

General Sherman also said, "I had previously written to General Washburn that he should employ A. J. Smith's troops and any others that he could reach, to pursue and if possible destroy all of Forrest's men." General Sherman seemed to think more of Forrest and his operations than he did of those who were opposing him in his march to Atlanta.

When, at this time, it was proposed to give Forrest command of all the cavalry, operating with Johnston's army, be it said to the credit of General Joseph Wheeler that he endorsed General Johnston's recommendation, and thereby showed himself to be a man of the highest patriotism, of transcendent nobility of character, and of almost unparalleled devotion to the Southern Cause. General Wheeler offered to serve under General Forrest in any capacity Forrest might suggest. No one who now studies General Wheeler's campaigns can doubt that he was one of the greatest soldiers the war produced, and this proposal to serve anywhere in any capacity under General Forrest demonstrated that his manhood and patriotism were of the same standard as his capacity for leadership. Ranking General Forrest, he waived all such considerations and cheerfully proposed to become Forrest's lieutenant in the contemplated assault on Sherman, and follow where Forrest would lead.

In the assault on General A. J. Smith's rear, Forrest received a severe and painful wound. He never thought of personal danger and was ever absolutely indifferent to fear. Previous to the Battle of Harrisburg, General Forrest had asked for a furlough and sought to be relieved of his command, but this was denied him by reason of the exigencies of the hour.

Harrisburg was a bitter memory to Forrest. In that battle, three of his brigade commanders were wounded and all the colonels were either killed or wounded. Four miles from Tupelo at Old Town Creek, in pursuing A. J. Smith, Forrest himself was struck by a ball in his right foot. It was reported that Forrest had been killed. This created intense consternation among his own soldiers, and inexpressible joy among his enemies. Forrest felt that in the Battle of Harrisburg his troops had acted with supreme courage, and on that battlefield that they did not have a fair chance. This deeply rankled in his heart. The successes of his previous campaigns had made him believe that with anything like an even show his troopers were invincible, and he dreamed of and sighed for an opportunity to blot out the sad and bitter memories of that dreadful day, when he saw his bravest and best go down in a conflict which was not fought according to his judgment, nor along the lines upon which he was accustomed to operate. After the battle, he issued a statement in which he said, "Future generations will never weary of hanging garlands on their graves." Who was responsible for Harrisburg has been the source and cause of acute and extended criticisms. Some have said that Forrest on that occasion failed to fight as he always fought before and that he hesitated where hesitation was bound to be fatal.

Forrest was a born leader. He had always done best where he was the head. Subordinate, he was restive, and he could only do his best and accomplish most when he was supreme.

General Washburn had sent these several forces after Forrest, and Forrest resolved to teach General Washburn a lesson he would not soon forget. The wound which General Forrest received at Old Town Creek was one from which he never recovered fully. After this casualty he was compelled to go in a buggy, a plank across the dashboard holding his leg in an elevated position, but his power as a leader lost none of its effect from the fact that he was riding in a dilapidated buggy rather than astride a breathing, moving, chafing war-horse.

On the 20th of July, General S. D. Lee, between whom and General Forrest there was, probably unconscious to both of these patriotic men, some feeling, was transferred to the army under General Hood at Atlanta, and with the departure of Lee came General Richard Taylor, lovingly called by his friends and his soldiers, "Dick" Taylor. He and Forrest were kindred spirits. They looked at war through the same lenses. They were alike brave and aggressive and restless spirits that enjoyed the dangers and excitement of campaigns and battles, and were not averse to strife as strife. They were warriors by nature, and the fury of battle and the storm of conflict had no terrors for their valiant hearts.

General Sherman had told his superiors that if Forrest could be taken care of, he could handle Johnston, and so on the 20th of July, he telegraphed General Halleck as follows: "A. J. Smith has orders to hang on to Forrest and prevent his coming to Tennessee." It was at this time that rumors came to the Federals of the death of General Forrest. On the 2d of August, 1864, Washburn telegraphed to Sherman: "I have a report that Forrest died some days ago of lockjaw." This news General Sherman reported to General Grant. It was then that he wired Washburn, "Is Forrest surely dead? If so, tell General Mower I am pledged to him for his promotion, and if 'Old Abe' don't make good my promise, then General Mower can have my place." (Official Records, Volume 39, Part 2, page 233.)

Though Mower had not killed Forrest, on the 12th of August, 1864, he received his commission as major general, and Sherman said to Stanton: "Please convey to the President my thanks for the commission for General Mower, whose task was to kill Forrest. He only crippled him; he is a young and game officer."

Early in August Generals Washburn, A. J. Smith, Mower and Grierson, by their joint effort, had concentrated a very large force at Memphis, consisting of ten thousand infantry, four thousand cavalry, three thousand colored troops, and three Minnesota regiments. The infantry of this contingent was moved as far as possible by rail, the cavalry was marched overland, and on the 9th of August had reached the Tallahatchie River between Holly Springs and Oxford, Mississippi. At that time Forrest had five thousand, three hundred and fifty-seven men, but the tremendous mortality among his officers had seriously impaired the efficiency of his force. Pathetically, General Chalmers informed General Forrest, "Both of my brigade commanders are wounded, also a brigade commander of General Buford's division, and most of the field officers of the command were either killed or wounded in the late engagement."

This advance looked formidable and sorely taxed the genius of General Forrest to face. He was opposed by nearly three to one. It was important to hold the prairie country of the Mississippi, for it was prolific of supplies. Forrest was given carte blanche by General Maury, who was then in immediate command of the territory to be invaded. Forrest was still unable to ride horseback, but nevertheless he resolved to meet his foes. General Chalmers was ordered to destroy all the bridges on the railroad leading south from Holly Springs. By the 14th of August, General Smith had reached a point nearly to Oxford, Mississippi. The force in front of Forrest was thirteen thousand infantry and four thousand cavalry. With his small force, now inadequately mounted, there was no hope for him successfully in the open to fight this great enemy. By the 18th of August Forrest had sufficiently recovered to take to the saddle. He could only use one foot in the stirrup. The other hung loose. The power of no commander in the war was taxed to a greater tension than Forrest at this moment. He dare not face and fight his foes on the field. No courage, no alignment with the past experiences of the Federal commanders and the caution and care engendered by their numerous failures could avail to halt this great army, now organized and sent out to rout and destroy Forrest. Numbers alone, in the field, could defeat this well-armed, well-disciplined corps, but, alas for Forrest, he did not have and could not get the numbers. With only one to three in the coming expedition, the task to most men would have appeared impossible. Had he taken counsel of fear and even of ordinary prudence, he would sullenly have retired before the advance and have been content with delaying his enemies and inflicting what loss he could by way of unexpected assault and quick reprisal. Strategy, skill, surprise, must now win, if winning were at all possible.

Forrest sat down to unravel the difficulties of the hour. Something must be done outside mere resistance. The hour for that expedient alone was gone. Forrest had something that oftentimes was better than legions. Nature had lavishly bestowed on this untutored soldier a something that could now and then defeat the greatest odds, and out of apparent overwhelming adversity win superbest victory. The thing Forrest had could not be bought. No education could supply it. It could only come as nature's gift and in this supreme hour it came to the rescue of the Confederate leader. The moment called for a transcendent military genius, and this gift nature had bestowed without stint upon the unlearned but born soldier.

There was no lack among Forrest's men of courage, and upon any dangerous or difficult expedition which he was to enter, it was not a question as to whether his men could fight, but a question as to whether their beasts could carry them to the point to which their great commander had decided to move. The selection of the best horses was now begun. All the men were good enough, but on the work Forrest had now mapped, a strong, dependable horse was as important as a hard, courageous rider. Each man did his best to put his steed upon his mettle. Every soldier was longing to go. None knew where, save the general, but that was all they asked, to be allowed to follow him. With sad hearts, hundreds of the brave troopers looked on intently while their horses were examined and condemned, and with ill-suppressed grief heard the depressing words, "Fall out." Danger surely, physical weariness certainly, mayhap death, was ahead, but every soldier was burning to go, and when the sorrow-bringing words came that shut out all but one in three of the corps, a wide disappointment spread abroad in every regiment.

Forrest left Chalmers with four thousand men in front of the enemy. He was ordered to persistently attack and oppose them in every way possible, to delay their march and to assail their flanks and communication. Incessant rains had fallen for some days. The roads were muddy, and the streams were full to the banks. Forrest's chance in the expedition which he now undertook was dependent upon the secrecy with which it should be consummated. If Smith knew that he was not in front, he and Grierson and Hurlbut would run over the small force commanded by Chalmers and march to Vicksburg. No sooner had the sun gone down on the 18th of August than Forrest left Oxford with his two thousand men, the best mounted that he could cull and select. The word to mount was anxiously awaited. These chosen men had gone with their leader before. It was raining furiously—had been raining almost constantly for forty-eight hours previously. With their soggy clothes hanging about their drenched limbs, they were impatient to try out another conflict, and see what glory had in stock for them in a new encounter. The darkness of night was approaching when, amid the thunder and downpour, these Forrest followers sprang into their saddles, gave rein to their steeds, and with a long drawn-out rebel yell, set forth, defying weather, to once again contest with their foes. Rain, floods, mud had no terror for them where their general and duty pointed the way they must go. Marching all night west and north, when the day dawned, notwithstanding the conditions which faced him, he had swung clear off the route of the Federal Army, and was miles away before any Federal officer or commander dreamed that Forrest was gone. Traveling all day on the 19th and part of the night, on the morning of the 20th he had reached Senatobia. This was a long ride for Forrest and his followers. One raging stream and insecure bridge were crossed, and by courier he told Chalmers that he would soon cross another, and, like Columbus, passing westward with only one command, westward, westward, he was going northward, northward.

Forrest directed Chalmers again to "Hold the enemy and press them so as to engage and hold their attention." Chalmers was faithful to his trust. He fought all day—all night—all hours, and no whisper came to the Federal commander that Forrest was gone away. The aggressiveness of Forrest's lieutenant hid the mystery of his departure within the Confederate lines.

General Forrest was too much of a leader not to know that this extraordinary task which he had undertaken could only be accomplished by rapid movement and by concealment of his plans. In the early part of August, in Mississippi, usually copious rains fall. The streams at that season are almost always full. This rendered them far more difficult to bridge and made fording impossible. Forrest could ferry his men and their accoutrements and ammunition and artillery, but the horses must swim. In a pinch he might, by rafting and swimming, get his men over the stream, but water was a deadly foe to powder, and without powder Forrest and his men would ride and swim in vain. This meant delay. Delay meant defeat. But above all, Forrest was a practical man. There was no emergency to which his resourceful mind could not rise. Fortunately for his plans on this occasion, the grapevine life of Mississippi is extremely exuberant. These vines run to the tops of the highest trees, sometimes one hundred and fifty feet. Larger than a man's arms, they would send out their tendrils to the very top of the highest trees and swinging over some limb would spread out their branches and cover the tree tops. These vines were flexible, almost like ropes, very strong. Forrest undertook, as an engineer, by sending forward his best and most intelligent troopers under brave and energetic commanders, to find those grape vines and use them as cables to span the river. Finding the trees convenient to the banks of the stream, the vines were cut down, twisted around the trees, tied as best they could be, carried across the river, and attached to trees on the other side. A ferry boat was placed in the middle of the stream and anchored. Cypress and other logs were cut into proper lengths, floated into the stream and attached at certain distances to these cables. At Hickahala Creek this novel bridge was first inaugurated. Forrest was kept in close touch with his engineers, who were constructing this strangely fashioned pontoon. Within four or five miles from the stream, all the cabins, houses, barns, stables and gin houses were stripped of the flooring and shedding. Each horseman carried on his shoulder one of these planks. Within an hour the planks were laid, the soldiers dismounted, each man led his horse on the boards and crossed the stream in double file. The cables began to stretch, and by the time all the command had passed over, the planks had become submerged, the water was two feet over the flooring and with difficulty the horses could be led across. Nature seemed at this point to be piling up insuperable obstacles in Forrest's path. He had truly gone seven miles when another stream, twice as broad and equally as deep stood out with its currents and floods to bid the Southern men stay their march. No long drawn out planning was necessary to figure out some way to outwit the defiance of Cold Water River. If a sixty-foot span could be made of grapevines, why not one of a hundred and twenty feet, and the answer was a sharp command to the pioneers to unsling their axes and build the required structure. One hundred and eighty minutes under the whip and spur of necessity saw the new bridge completed, and the men, houses, cannon and caissons speeding across the apparently unsafe length. The horses were led two abreast, the guns were unlimbered and willing hands and seasoned arms dragged them over to the side where Forrest was pointing the way, it may be to danger, but where glory they believed would crown their army and enterprise with a deserved and splendid success. This circumstance so delayed him that on the night of the 20th he was still at Hernando, Mississippi, twenty-five miles from Memphis. The condition of the roads was almost indescribable. The tramping of the horses made a foot of slush, and the wheels of the ammunition wagons and the cannon caissons cut deep ruts in the roads. The cavalry went at a slow walk, and ten horses were hitched to each piece of artillery.

Notwithstanding all of these precautions, half of Forrest's guns had to be left at Penola. It became apparent that they would not be carried along with sufficient rapidity to justify Forrest in running the risk their movement involved. Still twenty-five miles away from Memphis, Forrest knew he must travel all night. It was a task at which any leader might hesitate, but now hesitation meant disaster, and the lionhearted leader was undertaking amongst the greatest feats he had attempted to perform. Tremendous issues were involved. To save at this period Northern Mississippi Territory and to prevent the junction of General Smith's forces with those of General Sherman at Vicksburg was vital to the hopes of the Confederate authorities. Rain, storm, mud, floods, deep currents, accelerated by torrents, were the contingencies Forrest must face, but he never had stopped for these things before and through the darkness of the night there was only one command, "Forward," "Forward," "Forward." It was bad enough for those who rode. The beasts who bore the men, weakened by the already grievous burdens laid upon them, were spurred to speedier tramp, but hard as were these pressed with their human loads, the awfullest of the terrors of that terrorful night came to the dumb sufferers who pulled the swaying gun carriages and heavy caissons through the ruts and slush of the ever-lengthening pathway. No cry of mercy could avail for these speechless creations. Slashed with hickory or oak wythes, blood streamed from their mouths from the sawing of their bits to keep them straight in the sunken depths of the muddy way, they passed with indescribable suffering the horrible night. When the limits of physical resistance they reached and no longer left with strength or will to continue the impossible tasks that were being laid upon them, with sullen indifference some of these creatures, ready to die rather than proceed another step, with a determination born of despair, refused to make another effort and bade defiance to their pitiless riders and drivers, who were slashing, jerking and beating in their seemingly mad efforts to urge forward these faithful brutes who had done all they could to help in the effort to save the land of those who, with apparently merciless hearts, called for such terrible strain. Horses have wills as well as men, and defying their owners, some stood still in their tracks and no cruel blows could bring them to move a muscle or pull an ounce. The great crisis was ahead. If the one horse would go down another would be harnessed, and if the led horses had all been used, then a luckless trooper with a strong or powerful mount was bade strip his steed, stow his equipment on a gun carriage or caisson, and take his chances farther on to win from his enemies a something to ride, which the exigencies of the hour had taken away from him. The new team took up the burdens their predecessors had laid down, and the sullen horse was led out into the woods, or now and then, fearing that he might prove of value to the enemy, a shot was fired into his heart to end his sufferings or to destroy that which by some possibility might some day aid those who were fighting the cause for which he had met so violent a death.

Forrest had intended to strike Memphis on Sunday morning. One-fourth of all of his horses had broken down under the tremendous strain to which they had been subjected. There were no horses left in the country, the Federals and the Confederates had taken them all, and the dismounted men, dejected, sad and disappointed, were compelled on foot to retrace their steps along the paths which they had come.

There were three generals in Memphis that Forrest particularly desired to capture, Generals C. C. Washburn, Stephen A. Hurlbut and R. P. Buckland. They were scattered over different parts of the city. By three o'clock General Forrest had reached the limits of the city, called his troops around him, and gave to each commander accurate and definite instructions as to what would be done. Scout after scout returned to bring the details of the Federal positions, and even citizens, to whom had been secretly and silently conveyed the news of the coming, slipped by the Federal sentinels to tell Forrest all he needed to know of his enemies' whereabouts, in order to make surprise and capture sure. Above all, it was earnestly impressed on the squads who rode into the city that there was to be no shouting, no cheering, no battle cry, and that not a gun must be fired under any circumstances. The leaders were told that if they met any Federal troops they were to ignore them, to be extremely careful, bring on no battle and engage in no fighting, but to rush forward over all that opposed.

Forrest's brother, William H., had often rendered most valiant and efficient service to his brother. He had selected with great care forty scouts. These were as reckless and as brave as their captain. They were to advance, capture the pickets, and without waiting for the balance of the men to ride at full speed to the Gayoso hotel, surround it and prevent the escape of General Hurlbut. Forrest had learned accurately the position of the Illinois infantry. They were stationed at a place close to the road along which Forrest must pass.

Colonel Longwood was to follow Captain William Forrest. Upon reaching a prominent place in the city, he was to station a portion of his troops as a reserve, and the balance were to proceed to the wharf and capture any transports that might be there. To his younger brother, Colonel Jesse Forrest, General Forrest assigned one of the most important and difficult things to be accomplished. He was allowed to choose his own associates. The service would be furious, fierce, reckless, dangerous. He was to ride straight to the house of General Washburn on Union Street, which had been located carefully by General Forrest, who knew Memphis as well as he knew his plantation, and Jesse Forrest was to effect the capture of General C. C. Washburn. It makes one tremble almost half a century after this occurrence to realize the sensation of these men, however brave, as they engaged in this wonderful enterprise. Forrest decided with Colonel T. H. Bell and detachments of Newsom's, Russell's and Barteau's regiments, and the two pieces of artillery under Lieutenant Sale, to remain in the suburbs, believing that it would be necessary for these brave and adventuresome spirits who had gone to the city on this reckless mission to have support and backing when they returned. Forrest felt that it was hardly possible for all of the three parties he had sent into the city to successfully accomplish their respective missions and then come out without much loss or possible defeat. He hoped that the boldness of his movements and the recklessness of the execution would terrorize and paralyze his foes, but even he doubted if all could emerge without some failure.

The day was just beginning to break when the detachments all moved forward. The morning was foggy and a pall of darkness hung over the scene of operations. Captain William Forrest, with ten men well in advance, rode along the line designated for his approach, and, challenged by the Federal sentry, replied that he was a detachment of a Missouri regiment with rebel prisoners. He was ordered to dismount, but instead he rode up to the sentinel, who suspected nothing when Captain Forrest had cried out, "All right," and supposed that he had dismounted. As soon as Captain Forrest could discern the form of the picket, sticking his spurs into his horse's flanks, he caused him to spring forward, and then using his pistol as a bludgeon, he knocked the Federal trooper unconscious to the ground. Forrest directed his companions to follow him instantly, and charged upon the reserve pickets, but one of these was enabled to fire his gun before they were surrounded, and this one shot saved the Federals great loss and deprived the expedition of some of its results.

There was nothing now left but to ride recklessly and rapidly into the heart of the city. The Rubicon was crossed. The die was cast. The thrill and enthusiasm of the dangerous work in which they were engaged so stirred the hearts of the men that they forgot their orders and instead of obeying the directions of their commander as to complete silence, they began vociferously to give the rebel yell.

Near the Gayoso hotel, Captain Forrest came suddenly upon a Federal battery of six pieces. This he charged, and the artillerists, driven from their guns, sough refuge in buildings in proximity to the battery. The Confederates were in such a hurry that they failed to have done what would have afterwards been a very valuable thing—spike the guns.

It did not take Captain William Forrest long to reach the Gayoso hotel. He rode into the corridor, and his men were placed around the building so as to prevent the escape of General Hurlbut. Fortunately for General Hurlbut, that night he slept out and when Colonel Chalmers battered upon the door, it was opened by a beautiful young woman who pleaded for protection, but alas Hurlbut was gone.

Colonel Jesse Forrest rode with great celerity, but the unfortunate discharge of the gun of the picket had given warning, and a Federal cavalryman of the 6th Illinois regiment rode swiftly up to General Washburn's house, beat upon the door with his sabre, and cried out that Forrest's cavalry were in possession of the town and were in sight of the house, moving for Washburn's capture. General Washburn did not even take time to dress, but fled away in his night clothes through the alleys from the back door, across the garden, and running half a mile found safety in the fort. A Federal lieutenant, W. H. Thurston, in his official report, said, "The general ran away for a safe place in the fort, which was fully a half mile from his home, when he was but three squares away from the provost marshal's office; and all this without giving any orders or commands as to what should be done by the troops." All that Colonel Forrest got of the general's belongings was a uniform and some personal effects, which he brought to his brother, the general, and which the next day were returned with Forrest's compliments under a flag of truce. That war is not without its courtesies is shown by the fact that two or three weeks later, General Washburn returned these compliments by sending to General Forrest a full, complete, handsome uniform of a Confederate major general.

The detachments which had been assigned to the capture of General

Buckland also arrived too late. The unfortunate enthusiastic yells of the Confederates, and an occasional shot from rifles, alarmed the sentinel who watched Buckland's house, and the general, hastily and negligently dressed, sought safety at some other point.

Memphis at this time was garrisoned by about five thousand men, combining a mingling of cavalry, infantry and artillery. There was little left to do but to search in the stables and get all the horses and capture all the prisoners possible. The detachments which had been scattered in the city now found it wise and prudent to retreat. The battery which they had captured was again manned and turned loose upon them. Without questioning whether it was wise or unwise, the Confederates rode at the gunners and dispersed them, killing or wounding twenty of their number, and thus were enabled to avoid further trouble from this quarter. As there were no horses convenient, they could not carry the pieces away. By this time they were glad enough to get away themselves. Only when they came to retire did they realize the hazard and peril of the enterprise in which they had taken part. Its audacity appalled the participants when they fully took in the extent of the dangers through which they had passed and of the all nigh incalculable risks they had assumed.

General Forrest was now ready to retire. He felt sure his mission had been accomplished. Smith in Mississippi did not want Forrest in Memphis, one hundred miles in his rear. Sherman or no Sherman, the capture of Memphis would be an immeasurable calamity. No commander could safely forecast what Forrest would or could do. Rains, floods, mud-filled roads, seemed no barrier to this wonderful man of war, and to leave him alone in West Tennessee with two thousand daring followers filled the minds of the Federal commander with apprehension and his heart with dread. Twice he had an engagement to make a junction with Sherman's forces at Meridian, but when he made that agreement, he had not dreamed that Forrest would turn on Memphis, force the commanders there to flee in their night clothes into the forts, and his horsemen ride through its streets capturing, killing and destroying all that came in their paths from daybreak until nine in the morning.

In the depths of their souls they cried out against the conditions that made them face the ubiquitous and impossible Confederate leader. No man's reputation was safe who was sent against this redoubtable chief. He came when he was not expected, he fought against any sort of odds. Nature could pile up against him no obstacles that could thwart his will, and to them he went and came as he planned, and no human foresight could avail against his strategy or his onslaughts.

It was a humiliating thing for General Smith to do, but he was stirred by this strange happening. If he went on, Forrest might undo all a year's planning and garrisoning had done and West Tennessee again become Confederate territory. If he went back along the line he had come, he must march on roads, the very sight of which made cavalry wish they had never come to war. The Federal commander debated earnestly and long. He talked with his associates and then resolved to turn his face northward, forego the meeting at Meridian and save what Forrest had left in his trail to Memphis.

When Forrest learned definitely what General Smith had determined to do, he rejoiced with exceeding great joy. He felt that his work was not in vain. He had not destroyed the army that was capable of inflicting immeasurable injury upon his country, but he had caused it to withdraw and stayed for a while the impending blow which, had it fallen, would have brought down with it all hopes of maintaining any great Confederate force between Atlanta and the Mississippi River. The consciousness of having delayed the inevitable, if only for a few weeks or months, was a source of profound satisfaction to the man who in the past summer had done more constant, difficult fighting than any officer who wore the gray.

As they marched away, a portion of the 6th Illinois Cavalry under Colonel Starr viciously assaulted the Confederate rearguard. As Forrest was always at the post of danger, he was on hand there. They were so close together that in the charge Colonel Starr and General Forrest engaged in a hand-to-hand encounter, and the Federal commander was seriously wounded and rendered unfit for further battle. A short distance away from Memphis, General Forrest sent back a flag of truce, proposing the exchange of prisoners and telling General Washburn that a number of his officers had been captured and were without clothing, and informed General Washburn that he would wait at Nonoonah Creek for a reply. When General Forrest arrived there he found a note from General Washburn, stating that he had no authority to exchange prisoners, but that he would be very glad if General Forrest would allow his officers to have the clothing which he sent with his note. General Forrest was ready to be humane. The half-clad, bare-footed soldiers touched his sympathies. He had no reason to love General Washburn and those he commanded, but he had such profound satisfaction in the work of the night in Memphis that it softened his animosities and he cheerfully did all that he could to mitigate the woes of his unfortunate and dejected captives, who, now six hundred in number, were encountering woes and hardships that touched the hearts of even the foes, some of whom had urged negro soldiers to give no quarter to Forrest's men. Those least able to travel were paroled and turned loose, while the stronger and best clad were kept for yet another day of marching. It was during this march that General Forrest skillfully and craftily managed to get some supplies for his nearly famished men. In Memphis, the work was too fierce for food contemplation, and when some miles from the city, hunger began to assert its claims with no provisions to meet its outcry, General Forrest then despatched a flag of truce to say to General Washburn that if he would not accept Confederate parole, he would at least feed those he was forcing him to carry away as prisoners on a trying and debilitating march. Two wagon loads of supplies were sent by the Federal commander in response to this appeal, and it pleased General Forrest greatly to see that after giving his prisoners all the rations they could consume or carry, there was enough to shut out hunger in his command for at least thirty-six hours.

Here, eager marching was the order of the day. There was nothing now between Forrest and Smith. He had a wide country in which to operate. The streams were full and the roads were bad, but these same difficulties would face his enemies.

There was no telegraphic communication; Chalmers was anxiously waiting news from Forrest and so, to relieve his anxiety and distress, at Hernando he despatched a courier with a message stating, "I attacked Memphis at four o'clock this morning, driving the enemy to his fortifications. We killed and captured four hundred, taking their entire camp, with about three hundred horses and mules. Washburn and staff escaped in the darkness of the early morning, Washburn leaving his clothes behind."

The prisoners were cumbersome. Prisoners are not a good asset on a trip like this, and so Forrest paroled them and proceeded on his march to Panola, where he arrived on the 22d of August.

Forrest was not altogether without some apprehension as to what his enemy might do in case they heard that Forrest had gone, and so from Panola he sent the swiftest courier he could find with the following message to Chalmers: "If the enemy is falling back, pursue them hard. Send Buford to capture their foraging parties. Keep close to their camp.

Order Captain Henderson to scout well to their right to ascertain if there is any movement this way." Forrest told him in addition that he would rest for two or three days at Grenada, if possible.

By the 23d of August General Smith had paused in his advance into Mississippi. Smith had turned around. The strategy and genius of Forrest was too much for him and so he retreated north from Mississippi and left Forrest a clear way to his friends and comrades. Forrest was able to telegraph to General Maury on the 29th: "Enemy left Holly Springs at two o'clock yesterday, marching rapidly in the direction of Memphis and La Grange. They say they are ordered to reinforce Sherman."

EXPLANATORY NOTE

In the preparation of these sketches I have relied greatly upon Dr. John Allen Wyeth's "Life of General Forrest," one of the most entertaining war books ever published; General Basil W. Duke's "Morgan and His Men"; Major H. B. McClelland's "Life and Campaigns of Major General J. E. B. Stuart"; "Hampton and His Cavalry," by Colonel Edward L. Wells; "Shelby and His Men," by Major John N. Edwards; "Campaigns of Wheeler and His Cavalry," edited by W. C. Dodson, and published under the auspices of Wheeler's Confederate Cavalry Association; "Confederate Military History"; Captain John W. Morton's "Artillery of N. B. Forrest's Cavalry," and the compilations of official records of the Union and Confederate Armies, published by the United States Government.

This last work is one of the most remarkable of its kind ever issued by any government. It contains all despatches, letters and reports of every kind, bearing upon the conduct of the war. It tells, day by day, in the words of the actors, the events which were taking place in the four years' struggle. In these contemporary writings, those who were carrying on this mighty struggle speak for themselves, and they furnish the historian with the most truthful and accurate accounts of what those who were engaged in the bitter war were doing or thought they were doing each day.

Governor Joseph D. Sayers and General W. T. Hart, of Texas, have been most generous in giving me data concerning items dealing with Texas troops. Dr. John A. Lewis of the 9th Kentucky Cavalry and Major A. E. Richards, Second in Mosby's Command, and General Theodore S. Garnett of Virginia and Colonel J. Will Hall of Missouri have laboriously and thoroughly perused copy and made many valuable suggestions. Captain H. H. Mathews of Breathed's Battery, Stuart's Artillery, sent accounts of many things that were new concerning the campaigns of Stuart.

The principal agency used by General Hampton in securing information for the cattle raid of September, 1864, was Colonel George D. Shadburn. His courage, intelligence and energy secured the most important facts necessary for the movements of General Hampton's forces, and in the

413

pursuit his valor and intrepidity won the highest commendation of his commander. Colonel Shadburn still survives, and lives in San Francisco, California.

Captain O. F. Redd of Lexington, Kentucky, sent valuable data about the campaigns of Shelby and Marmaduke. I am particularly indebted to Rev. R. Excell Fry of Gadsden, Alabama, for investigations and report about Forrest's pursuit of Streight. Mr. W. P. Lay of Gadsden, Alabama, has rendered the South his debtor for investigating important matters concerning Forrest's pursuit and capture of Streight. He secured from John H. Wisdom the facts of his great ride from Gadsden to Rome, in his effort to head off Colonel Streight. Without his help, it would have been impossible to have secured the facts of the wonderful performance of this patriotic Alabamian. Colonel Henry George and General H. A. Tyler have furnished me much new matter in regard to the Battle of Bryce's Cross Roads.

In no case have I completed a chapter without referring it to one or more soldiers who participated in the events undertaken to be described. To General Basil W. Duke, Colonel William A. Milton and General John B. Castleman, and to Governor James B. McCreary I acknowledge my obligation, for not only facts but timely suggestions.

The preparation of this book has been a work of love. It has cost immense labor and much of ease and time. But for the industry and patience of my secretary, Miss Mary McNamara, I could not have prepared the manuscript or made the investigation necessary to write this book. I am deeply indebted to Mr. Logan N. Rock and Mr. S. G. Tate, my associates in the practice of law, and to George T. and Mrs. Settle for proofreading and correction.

Made in the USA
Las Vegas, NV
31 October 2023

79993630R10246